SOUTH ARABIAN NECROPOLIS

OBJECTS FROM THE SECOND CAMPAIGN (1951) IN THE TIMNAˁ CEMETERY

by RAY L. CLEVELAND

M.A., Ph.D. (Johns Hopkins)

Research Associate, Oriental Seminary, Johns Hopkins University, 1959–64
Honorary Associate, American School of Oriental Research in Jerusalem

with foreword by Wendell Phillips

Sc.D., Pd.D., Litt.D., J.D., L.H.D., D.C.S., H.H.D., D.C.L., LL.D.
President, American Foundation for the Study of Man

Published with grants from the
A. W. Mellon Educational and Charitable Trust
and the Sarah Mellon Scaife Foundation

THE DIRECTORS OF THE AMERICAN FOUNDATION
FOR THE STUDY OF MAN HAVE THE HONOR OF DEDICATING
THIS VOLUME WITH DEEPEST APPRECIATION TO

Samuel F. Pryor

FOREWORD

The volume prefaced by this Foreword presents to interested scholars—and to any persons who may find in it something worthy of their attention—the majority of objects, other than pottery, which were discovered in the early months of 1951 in the ancient necropolis known to South-Arabian archaeologists as the Timnaʻ Cemetery. The 1951 season of excavation at this site, located a mile and a half northeast of the ancient city of Timnaʻ itself, was actually the second of two campaigns conducted there by the American Foundation for the Study of Man under my leadership and under the general archaeological direction of Professor William Foxwell Albright, whose fame as an Orientalist and Palestinian archaeologist is too well known to require description here.

The first campaign in the Timnaʻ Cemetery, conducted during the spring of 1950, was under the supervision of Professor A. M. Honeyman of the University of St. Andrews; our expedition was at work in Wâdī Beihân for seven intensive weeks that spring, and the excavation in the cemetery was under way nearly all of that time. The more striking finds made during that season are touched on in my book, *Qataban and Sheba*. Professor Honeyman's study of the finds of that campaign has continued as time in his busy schedule has permitted, and we may hope that the publication of the materials assigned to him will appear soon.

The second campaign in the Timnaʻ Cemetery covered a longer period of time than did the first, lasting from February 19, 1951, until May 3, 1951. It is not surprising, therefore, that many more objects were discovered during that season, including numerous items of great interest either because of their inscriptions or from the point of view of art history. In his Louvain monograph, *Pièces épigraphiques de Heid Bin ʻAqîl,* published in 1952, Dr. A. Jamme, W. F., described part of the inscribed objects. It included a very limited number of photographs, which were made in the field and therefore not of the best quality. Some half a dozen imported pottery fragments were published by Professor Howard Comfort of Haverford College in his appendix to *Archaeological Discoveries in South Arabia.* No other objects, except for a few outstanding sculptured pieces published with detailed comparative data by Dr. Berta Segall in scholarly journals, have been made available in publications until the present time, apart from random photographs in *Qataban and Sheba.*

Groups of objects from the Timnaʻ Cemetery were displayed soon after being brought to this country in special exhibits in New York, Baltimore, and elsewhere. Later, for several months of 1961, a select group from the second campaign was on display at the Honolulu Academy of Arts with other South-Arabian artifacts and art objects belonging to the American Foundation for the Study of Man. More recently the same group was shown in Tokyo under the joint auspices of His Imperial Highness Prince Mikasa, the University of Tokyo, and Pan American World Airways.

The author of *An Ancient South Arabian Necropolis* did not participate in any of our earlier expeditions to Arabia. His graduate training in a program combining general Semitic linguistics and archaeology began just after the close of the 1950 and 1951 expeditions to Wâdī Beiḥân, and he first undertook part-time work on a descriptive catalogue of the objects from the second campaign in the Timnaʿ Cemetery as a research assistant on the Arabian Publication Project, as it is entitled at the Johns Hopkins University, in the autumn of 1957. The volume which has now resulted is exactly what was already envisioned at that time, though it has been found necessary to defer the study of the pottery (being prepared by Dr. Gus W. Van Beek of The Smithsonian Institution) to a subsequent publication. Exhaustive comparative study of the objects presented in this volume would delay its publication more than desirable, and we hope that the careful and minute descriptions, in connection with the large selection of photographs, will make this volume useful to all interested in the ancient Near East, especially the Arabian Peninsula.

Professor Albright, as general editor of the Publications of the American Foundation for the Study of Man, has been available to the writer of this volume for counsel and guidance. Even though other responsibilities demand his time, he has always shown the greatest interest in this publication, as well as in all other aspects of our research program for Arabian archaeology. The undersigned wishes once again to express his most sincere appreciation to Professor Albright. We also wish to thank Dr. Gus W. Van Beek of The Smithsonian Institution for devoting evenings to the reading of the manuscript and for offering numerous useful suggestions.

The Johns Hopkins University for more than ten years has provided space for our project in Baltimore, and the American Foundation for the Study of Man has always been most appreciative of the facilities thus extended by a great university which has been seriously cramped for space to house its faculty and other research projects. Professor Wilfred G. Lambert was most friendly and co-operative as chairman of the Oriental Seminary after 1959.

Once again, on behalf of the Directors of the American Foundation for the Study of Man, I wish to express grateful appreciation to the field staff of our Arabian expeditions and to the contributors—government and academic organizations, corporations, companies, and individuals—who made this research possible. In addition, I express my thanks to the A. W. Mellon Educational and Charitable Trust and the Sarah Mellon Scaife Foundation for their generous support of our publication program during the past decade. Finally, I wish to record again my deep gratitude to Mr. Samuel F. Pryor for his continuing interest and generous support of our work both in the field and at home. It is our pleasure and honor to dedicate this volume to him.

Honolulu, Hawaii   WENDELL PHILLIPS
December, 1964

CONTENTS

AN ANCIENT SOUTH ARABIAN NECROPOLIS

INTRODUCTION

In this descriptive catalogue, the objects from the second campaign (1951) of excavation in the cemetery of ancient Timna' have been divided into twenty-two main groups. This has been done on purely typological lines, since there is no basis for presenting the majority of the objects as burial groups or for grouping them according to strata. The division used should serve a practical purpose; those who use these descriptions and illustrations will frequently be pursuing the study of a single form or type of object, and the present arrangement will be found convenient in such cases. The descriptions of the objects have been made as standard in form as practicable. A brief identification of each object is usually followed by a full description. The material of the object is given near the end of the description, and after this come only the dimensions in most cases, arranged according to height, width, and thickness, except where these dimensions are not applicable.

Most of the users of this volume will ask one question most often, "When was this object made?" The descriptions of the objects, with rare exception, include no dates, though approximate dates could have been suggested in certain cases. In general, specific dating can be only tentative at the present time, and it has seemed advisable to leave the whole question open in the present publication. A *terminus ad quem* can be stated with certainty. The cemetery belonged to the city of Timna', ancient capital of Qataban, and there is no other site nearby which might have continued to use the cemetery after the destruction of that city about A.D. 10 or a little later.[1]

The development of ancient South-Arabian art and handicraft is rapidly becoming better known with the aid of comparative stylistic analysis, palaeography, and pottery chronology. Comparative study of our material has been begun by Berta Segall,[2] Jacqueline Pirenne,[3] and others. The question of palaeography is bound up with the diverging views held by various scholars in regard to the chronology of ancient South Arabia, and discussion of them would only complicate the task of the present writer. The only stratified site excavated in Wâdî Beiḥân was Hajar Bin Ḥumeid, which is located some nine miles south of Hajar Koḥlân (Timna'). The study of the pottery, as well as the other materials, from Hajar Bin Ḥumeid is being

[1] See W. F. Albright, "Zur Chronologie des vorislamischen Arabien," in *Akten des Vierundzwanzigsten Internationalen Orientalisten-Kongresses, München, 1957* (Wiesbaden, 1959), pp. 153–55.

[2] "Problems of Copy and Adaptation in the Second Quarter of the First Millennium, B.C.," *American Journal of Archaeology*, Vol. 60 (1956), pp. 165–70; "The Arts and King Nabonidus," *American Journal of Archaeology*, Vol. 59 (1955), pp. 315–18; "Sculpture from Arabia Felix: the Hellenistic Period," *American Journal of Archaeology*, Vol. 59 (1955), pp. 207–14; "Notes on the Iconography of Cosmic Kingship," *The Art Bulletin*, Vol. XXXVIII (1956), pp. 75–80; "Sculpture from Arabia Felix: the Earliest Phase," *Ars Orientalis*, Vol. II (1957), pp. 35–42; "The Lion-Riders from Timna'," in Richard LeBaron Bowen, Jr., and Frank P. Albright, *Archaeological Discoveries in South Arabia* (Baltimore, 1958), pp. 155–78.

[3] "Notes d'archéologie sud-arabe," *Syria*, Vol. XXXVII (1960), pp. 326–47; Vol. XXXVIII (1961), pp. 284–310; Vol. XXXIX (1962), pp. 257–62; *Le Royaume Sud-Arabe de Qataban et sa Datation* (Louvain, 1961); and other publications.

1

carried out by Gus W. Van Beek. His publication, which will in fact establish the first ceramic chronology for South Arabia, is now in the final stages of preparation, and after its completion he has consented to undertake the study of the sherds and miniature pottery vessels from the Timna' Cemetery. This study is expected to provide a scientific basis for postulating the span of time during which the cemetery was in use, and therefore the temporal limits of the objects found in it. To anticipate the publication of the pottery chronology in attempting to assign dates to all of the objects from the cemetery would be only informed guessing.

Appendix I has been added to the descriptive catalogue of objects in order to supply some idea of what the burials in the Timna' Cemetery looked like as they were excavated, and two plans are included to give the total lay-out of the areas excavated during the 1951 season. The type of structure and the general plan of the excavated areas will be found in Appendix I, the plans, and the selected photographs (Plates 108–20).

The registry of all objects recorded during the second campaign in the cemetery has been included as Appendix II. Owing to transportation difficulties and limitations, many of the finds had to be discarded at the site. Other objects were retained by the British officials in Aden for the museum there. A representative collection is also housed in Pittsburgh at the Carnegie Museum, which participated in the expedition. The balance of the collection, except for a very few pieces located elsewhere, remains together and was at The Johns Hopkins University from 1953 to 1964; it is now in The Smithsonian Institution on a long-term loan basis. The registry of objects comprising Appendix II gives a complete listing and indicates as far as possible the present location of every item not now in the main collection, as well as an indication of the nature of many objects which could not be included in the catalogue because of the lack of complete descriptions and photographs. The registry may also be used as an excavation number index, since page references are given for pieces described in the catalogue.

The author wishes to acknowledge a number of the photographs with thanks. The photograph in Plate 67 by Raymond M. Sato was supplied through the courtesy of the Honolulu Academy of Arts. The photographs made by William B. Terry which have been used are Plates 1, 3, 5, 7, 9, 11, 15, 17 (except lower left), 18, 19, 20 (above), 21, 22 (above), 23, 24, 25, 26 (except upper left), 28, 29, 31, 32, 33, 34, 35 (upper right and lower left), 38 (above), 41 (lower left), 42 (above), 43, 44, 45, 48 (above), 49, 50, 51, 52 (above), 54, 55, 61 (below), 62 (upper right), 63, 64, 65, 69 (right center and lower left), 89 (top center), 91 (upper left), and 93 (TC 2012). The photograph of TC 1310 on Plate 68 is a field photo, and Plates 108–20 are the work of the field photographers. Photographs of objects now in the Carnegie Museum and in the Aden Museum were supplied by those museums. The rest of the photographs were taken by the author. The line-cuts were drawn by G. Palamoudian, the field draftsman, except for the drawings of TC 711, TC 1129, TC 1581, and TC 2063, which were made by the author.

Excavation in a cemetery which was used over a long period of time, such as the one at Ḥeid Bin 'Aqîl (the modern name of the place where the necropolis of ancient Timna' is located), can provide large numbers of objects of artistic and typological value, as the catalogue demonstrates, but investigations of the remains of a burial area can never provide the kind of information derived from the excavation of a stratified site, employing the best contemporary archaeological techniques. The objects found in the Timna' Cemetery provide new data and raise many questions about chronology, as well as about life and death in ancient South Arabia. So while this collection supplies many new details about the past of South Arabia, it also urges us on to further controlled excavation.

System of Transliteration

ا	ʾ		ط	ṭ		غ	ġ
ب	b		ظ	ẓ		ف	f
ج	g		ى	y		ص	ṣ
د	d		ك	k		ض	ḍ
ذ	ḏ		ل	l		ق	q
ه	h		م	m		ر	r
و	w		ن	n		ش	š
ز	z		(س)	s		س	ś
ح	ḥ		ع	ʿ		ت	t
خ	ḵ					ث	ṯ

I

HUMAN HEADS SCULPTURED IN ALABASTER AND OTHER STONE

These sculptured human heads, mostly of alabaster, vary in size and in detail, but are a closely related group. They all have many stylistic characteristics in common, the most notable of which are listed in the following paragraphs.

a) All of the heads exhibit frontality and symmetry, apparently a result of the more or less mechanical way in which they were made. The bearded male, TC 1588, which far excels most of the other pieces in realistic plasticity, still has strict frontality—even though it is not so strikingly obvious.

b) Many of the heads have rather angular features (as TC 873). In most examples, the front has the aspect of a flat mask to which the background is joined by perpendicular walls.

c) Nearly all of the objects in this category were ornamented with inlay—the eyes, the eyebrows in many cases, the moustache and beard also in the case of some or all of the males (it is not certain in a few instances which sex is represented). The sockets designed to receive the inlaid eyes are shaped rather naturally in outline. Some of the sockets are rounded out in the bottom (as in TC 806), while others are flat with vertical sides (as in TC 873). Most of the eye inlays themselves have been lost, but the few found (TC 1884 and TC 3000) are of limestone and have circular depressions in the center—possibly to receive a second, colored inlay.

d) The noses, with rare exceptions, are long, narrow and high-ridged, meeting the face at a sharp angle rather than gently blending into the cheek.

e) Many of the foreheads protrude nearly as far as the high ridge of the nose, leaving the eyes and cheeks in a recessed plane.

f) The mouths are typically small, raised lozenges with a horizontal groove to separate the lips, although there are minor variations.

g) The tops of the heads are usually cut off flat just above the hair line and left roughly tooled. They seem to have been cut off thus in order to fit into niches or "house-shrines." See Wendell Phillips, *Qataban and Sheba* (New York, 1955), opp. p. 238, below, for large stelae with niches containing such heads as these.[1] (Examples of what were recognized as "house-shrines" were first found in the first campaign in the Timna' Cemetery, and these are scheduled to be published by A. M. Honeyman.)

h) The ears are often set too high on the head and often protrude outward unnaturally. They frequently blend into the background, which is not finished in detail.

A. SCULPTURED HEADS WITHOUT INSCRIPTIONS

TC 539 (Plates 1 and 2)

Sculptured human head, broken from a point immediately behind the left eye across to the back of the right ear. The neck is broken away, the tip of the nose is broken on the right, and the right side of the jaw is chipped. The top of the head is cut off flat at the hair line and left roughly tooled. The eyebrow grooves are slender and gracefully curved. The eyes are recessed between upper and lower lids, which protrude somewhat. A circular hole is bored into the center of each eye, the right one to a depth of 7 mm., the left one to less than half that depth. The

---

[1] Opp. p. 224, above, in the London edition.

nose has depressions to represent the nostrils and a horizontal depression on each side about 7 mm. above the lower end of the nose. A chiseled groove, flaring out in a dovetail at the ends, marks the mouth. The lower part of the face has a heavy appearance, being wide and flat. Alabaster. 11 cm. by 8.5 cm. by 7 cm. (Purchased at the site.)

TC 806 (Plates 2 and 3)

Sculptured head of a woman (compare with TC 1975). The mouth is small and has raised lips. The tip and lower ridge of the nose are broken. Parallel grooves indicate the nostrils. The eyes are hollowed out to receive inlays. The eyebrows are grooved, perhaps for inlays. Locks of hair appear below the ears. Simple incisions represent the ears. The top of the head is cut off flat just above the hair line. The neck is elongated and the lower 2.5 cm. of it was left unpolished, presumably because it was not exposed, being inserted in a base. The back of the piece has steps, or successive set-backs of *ca.* 6 mm. each, most likely indicating that the object was made from a fragment of a capital or other architectural member; cf. line-cuts in Carl Rathjens and Hermann von Wissmann, *Vorislamische Altertümer* (Hamburg, 1932), p. 45, Fig. 11. Alabaster. 23.5 cm. by 13.5 cm. by 9 cm.

TC 873 (Plate 4)

Sculptured head, apparently of a woman (as there is no beard). The rear sides are broken off. The mouth is small. There are sockets for eye inlays, grooves for eyebrows, and a vertical groove high on each cheek, apparently for inlays; the last mentioned seem to represent cautery marks. The high-ridged nose is chipped. The ears and locks of hair are broken away. Alabaster. 17.5 cm. by 12 cm. by 11.5 cm.

TC 914 (Plate 6)

Small human head. There are grooves for eyebrows, grooves as outlines of the eyes, and rounded depressions in the center of the eyes. The purpose of the small holes bored at each side of the mouth is unknown. The neck is long and cylindrical and has horizontal grooves running across the front. The nose is broken and the top of the head is battered.

This piece has many of the characteristics of the miniature heads described below in Section D. Alabaster. 15 cm. by 8.5 cm. by 7 cm. (dimensions from field catalogue). (Carnegie Museum.)

TC 1230 (Plates 5 and 6)

Sculptured head, probably of a woman. The sockets for inlaid eyes are relatively deep. The ears (roughly chiseled) are placed very high, at the level of the forehead. The top of the head is cut off flat at the hair line. The nose is much elongated. The locks of hair below the ears are damaged. The neck is broken off. The back of the head is left roughly tooled. Alabaster. 11.3 cm. by 9 cm. by 10 cm.

TC 1316 (Plate 7)

Sculptured head of a woman, somewhat battered. Around the sockets to receive eye inlays is a low ridge. The top of the head is cut off at the hair line. Locks of hair extend out below the ears. The nose (broken) is narrow. A vertical, angular ridge is seen in the middle of the chin. The ears protrude unnaturally. In general the face is less angular than most of those in this group. Alabaster. 16 cm. by 14 cm. by 13 cm.

TC 1329 (Plate 8)

Sculptured head, probably of a woman. The neck is broken off, and the upper right part of the face is broken away. The left cheek is chipped, as is the ear on that side. The long narrow nose is broken badly. The socket for an inlaid eye is preserved on the left, as is the eyebrow groove above it. A stepped hair line can be seen above and in front of the ear. Alabaster. 17 cm. by 13.5 cm. by 10 cm.

TC 1361 (Plates 8 and 9)

Sculptured head of a man. The upper part of the head is broken off, as is the nose. The sockets for inlaid eyes are large. The back of the head is rounded. The features are well proportioned. A row of holes were bored in the eyebrow grooves for the attachment of inlays. There are similar drillings for the beard and moustache, and also one centered below the lower lip; those belonging to the beard are on the edge of a ridge which runs from ear to ear down the sides of the face and under the chin. Alabaster. 12.5 cm. by 10.5 cm. by 12 cm.

TC 1381 (Plate 10)

Back part of sculptured head of a woman, including ears and side locks of hair, split from front part through dark-red banding in the stone. The back side is flat and roughly tooled. The ears are set very near the top of the head, and the lobes are pierced (on the left ear the holes drilled from top and bottom do not go completely through). Alabaster. 15 cm. by 12.5 cm. by 5 cm.

TC 1406 (Plate 12)

Sculptured head of a woman. There are five holes drilled in each eyebrow groove, apparently for attaching inlays. The nose is broken along its entire length, and the face and forehead are battered. There appear to have been locks of hair below the ears which are now broken away. The neck is long, flaring slightly at the bottom. Alabaster. 18 cm. by 10 cm. by 8 cm. (dimensions from field catalogue). (Carnegie Museum.)

TC 1543 (Plates 10 and 11)

Sculptured head of a woman. The back is nearly flat, but rough. The face slopes back toward the top. The neck is broken away. The left cheek is chipped. There are large sockets for inlaid eyes (the right socket is slightly lower than the left one) and eyebrow grooves. The high narrow nose has two grooves on the lower end to indicate the nostrils. There are long locks of hair below the ears. Gray alabaster. 13 cm. by 11 cm. by 10 cm. (Stolen in 1962 while in Baltimore for study.)

TC 1556 (Plate 12)

Sculptured head of a woman complete with both inlaid eyes. A row of holes has been drilled along each eyebrow groove. The nose is very long and slender. The ears and locks of hair are not symmetrical. The back is flat. Alabaster. 20 cm. by 10 cm. by 7.5 cm. (dimensions from field catalogue). (Aden Museum.)

TC 1588 (Plates 13 and 14)

Sculptured head of a man. The right cheek, chin and nose are chipped. The neck is almost entirely broken away. A large section of the top of the head is chipped. The eye sockets are about 1.5 cm. deep. There are eyebrow grooves, a groove for an inlaid moustache, and a triangular cutting below the lower lip (for a goatee?). A deep (8 mm.) groove runs from 1.6 cm. below the ears around under the chin for attaching of beard; behind this groove is an offset (maximum *ca.* 1.2 cm.) which was probably hidden by the beard. The short-cropped hair was completely done in stone; there are tool marks over the top, sides, and back. The back of the head is rounded naturalistically. The ears are finished in realistic detail. White alabaster with orange and brown veining. 20.5 cm. by 15 cm. by 15.5 cm.

TC 1589 (Plate 14)

Female head sculptured on flat background. Alabaster. 12.5 cm. by 10 cm. by 5.5 cm. (dimensions from field catalogue). (Aden Museum.)

TC 1603 (Plate 15)

Sculptured human head, probably from a statuette (or high relief with head in the round, as TC 1557); beginning of flaring high on the neck is evidence that this was not a detached head. The nose, chin, and left ear are chipped. The top of the head is cut off flat at the hair line. The back of the head is rounded and polished smooth. The eyebrows are slender, very long, and almost straight. Above and below the eyes are ridges representing lids. In the center of the eyes are circular depressions. The nose seems to have been well proportioned, although it is very badly damaged now. The mouth is small, with protruding lips. The lower part of the face is broad and full. Alabaster. 10 cm. by 7.2 cm. by 7.4 cm.

TC 1710

Rear part of a male head, consisting of left ear, back of head and rear part of the right ear. The sides of the head and the back of the neck are polished, but the back of the head is rough with tool marks. The top of the head is cut off flat. Gray calcite. 9 cm. by 8.5 cm. by 5 cm.

TC 1795 (Plate 17)

Fragment of sculptured head, consisting of the right side of the face and all of the nose and mouth. The tip of the nose and the chin are chipped. The eyebrow groove tapers toward the outer end. The upper and lower eyelids are rounded ridges from which the eye is separated by grooves; there is a circular depression in the center of the eye. The nose is rather large and angular; depressions represent the nostrils; a horizontal depression appears low on each side of the nose. The mouth is small, but protrudes sharply in the middle. Three grooves run horizontally under the chin, perhaps representing wrinkles. Alabaster. 8.5 cm. by 4.5 cm. by 4.2 cm.

TC 1882 (Plate 16)

Sculptured female head. The ears are very high and pierced. There are roughly tooled locks of hair below the ears. The long neck is entirely polished. The nose is broken. Alabaster. 26 cm. by 16 cm. by 14 cm. (dimensions from field catalogue). (Carnegie Museum.)

TC 1975 (Plate 18)

Sculptured head of a woman. The nose and left ear are broken. The upper front edge of the forehead is chipped on the right side. The eye sockets are horizontal ovals. The eyebrow grooves are narrow and shallow. There are locks of hair covered with tool marks below the protruding ears. The lips are very thin. The top of the head is cut off flat just above the hair line. The front of the neck is polished smooth from the chin down for about two-thirds of its length; below this point it was left rough with chisel and tool marks; the sides of the neck show rough tooling. A layer of plaster 6 cm. long and 5 cm. wide is preserved on the back of the head near the top. Alabaster. 23.5 cm. by 11.5 cm. by 13 cm.

TC 1982 (Plate 17)

Fragment consisting of lower part of the face from a sculptured human head. The top is broken away at eye level. The nose and the right part of the chin are chipped. The right part of the lower lip is missing. Above the mouth is a rounded, protruding moustache;

there is a vertical furrow reaching from the nose about two-thirds of the way down the center of it; the moustache is separated from the mouth by a narrow groove. The mouth has a deep groove and curves down toward the corners. Alabaster, highly polished. 11.5 cm. by 8 cm. by 4.2 cm.

TC 1999 (Plate 17)

Small sculptured head of a woman. Nearly all of the forehead is broken away. The eye sockets come to points at the ends. The end of the eyebrow groove on the right is preserved. A horizontal groove on the right temple at eye level was made when a hole was drilled into the front of the ear, apparently for pendants. Locks of hair are represented below the ears (broken off on the left). The angular nose with straight ridge contrasts with rounded cheeks and chin. Alabaster, gray with tan striations; the stone is somewhat friable. 10.7 cm. by 8.3 cm. by 7.5 cm.

TC 2013 (Plate 20)

Sculptured male head with tenon on back. The eyes are outlined by narrow ridges in a diamond shape with circles in the center. The hair above the forehead is indicated by staggered vertical incisions between horizontal incised lines. There is no neck. Alabaster, rather dark with prominent lighter streaks. 13 cm. by 11 cm. by 10.5 cm. (dimensions from field catalogue). (Aden Museum.)

TC 2041 (Plate 19)

Sculptured head of a woman. The tip of the right ear and the ridge of the nose are broken, while the face is generally battered. The eye sockets are nearly round. The top of the head is cut off flat. Locks of hair are represented below the ears, extending far down on the sides of the neck. The mouth is formed by a groove without raised lips. The nostrils are indicated by depressions on the lower end of the long, narrow nose. The lower face has a swollen appearance owing to the relative narrowness of the forehead. The back of the head is flat and very roughly tooled. The ears protrude almost straight out from the head. Alabaster, with prominent striations running vertically through the piece. 17.5 cm. by 11.5 cm. by 7.5 cm.

TC 2043 (Plate 21)

Sculptured head of a man. The piece is chipped in many places, and the nose is broken. Short chin whiskers run from ear to ear and are covered with tool marks. There is an indentation below the lower lip for a goatee and a groove for a moustache above the mouth. Long eyebrow grooves stand out above large, rounded eye sockets. Lug-like ears are set out from the head. The back of the head is irregular and slopes in toward the left side. Alabaster. 21 cm. by 12 cm. by 9.5 cm.

TC 2184 (Plate 22)

Sculptured head of a man. The lower part is broken off just below the mouth, and the upper tip of the right ear is chipped. The inlay of the right eye (made of limestone) is partly preserved; it appears to have had a circular cutting in the center for a secondary inlay. The eyebrow grooves are large and curve down at the outer ends. There is a groove for a moustache. The ears are formed in relief on flat protrusions. The whiskers, polished smooth, begin in front of the ears and run downward (presumably to the chin, which is missing). The back of the head appears to have been rounded, though a large area has been chipped away. The hair is indicated by tool marks. The cheeks are nicely rounded, but most of the other features of the piece are mechanical and angular. Alabaster. 13.5 cm. by 13 cm. by 13 cm.

TC 2259 (Plate 23)

Sculptured head of a woman. The neck is broken off, and the nose is badly chipped. There are sockets for eye inlays. The eyebrow grooves taper toward the ends. The forehead protrudes about 1 cm. beyond the eyes and cheeks. The mouth is small and has raised lips. The nose was very narrow. The ears stick out almost straight from the head. Locks of hair with tool marks appear below the ears. The back of the head is flat and roughly tooled. The top of the head is cut off flat *ca.* 1 cm. above the hair line. Alabaster with orange veining. 16.5 cm. by 15 cm. by 10 cm.

TC 2270 (Plate 20)

Small sculptured head, perhaps of a man without moustache or beard. The neck is broken off, and the forehead is chipped on the right. There are eye sockets and eyebrow grooves. The face and nose are much elongated. The mouth is faintly indicated by one straight incised line and a slightly raised lower lip. The ears are placed high on the head. Alabaster. 12 cm. by 9.5 cm. by 9 cm.

TC 2507

Sculptured head of a woman, similar in style to TC 806. The nose is broken. Alabaster. 28 cm. by 14 cm. by 12 cm. (dimensions from field catalogue). (Marietta College Museum.)

TC 3000

Eye inlay from sculptured human head. The end which would have been next to the nose is broken. The piece is shaped much like a section from a sphere, with the sides curved and the back cut off flat. A circular cutting 1.3 cm. in diameter in the front, a little off center, was apparently for a secondary inlay to represent the iris of the eye. Limestone. 2.3 cm. by 3.3 cm. by 1.5 cm. (This piece, lacking a field number, seems to belong to one of the heads described above, but exactly which one has not been determined.)

B. SCULPTURED HUMAN HEAD WITH INSCRIBED BASE

TC 1884 (Plates 24 and 25)

Small sculptured head on inscribed base.

Head. The absence of beard and moustache would indicate that this object represents a woman, although there are no locks of hair below the ears such as are found on the larger heads. The top of the head is rounded and covered with tool marks. The back of the head is roughly flattened, though at an angle, with the result that the right side of the head is not so deep as the left. The back of the neck is also somewhat flattened and at the same angle, but (unlike the head) it is polished smooth. The ears are placed very high on the head and both at the same distance from the rear of the head; as a result, the right ear is only 1.5 cm. back from the right eye, while the left ear is 2.8 cm. behind the left eye. There is a slight depression at the hair line, and the hair is raised above the surface of the forehead; the hair line dips lower on the right than on the left. The curved eyebrow grooves are wide, but shallow, and nearly meet in the center. The nose is long but otherwise approaches realistic proportions. The large eye sockets are bordered by incised margins; the right eye inlay (of limestone) is in place; a little below its center is a boring, probably designed to receive a colored inlay to represent the iris. The mouth is small, but the lips are thick; a vertical furrow appears above the upper lip. The long neck flares out wider toward the base. Alabaster. 14 cm. (height above top of base) by 6.5 cm. by 6.5 cm.

Base. There are two registers on the front of the base; the narrower, upper one is recessed about 4 mm.; one line of inscription appears on each; the upper reads *ṣbḥt,* the lower *ġrbm.* There is a raised horizontal band on either side of the base, the upper edges of which are even with the offset on the front; the band on the right is 3.5 cm. wide, the one on the left 2.5 cm. Traces of reddening appear on the front. The neck of the head is mortared into a roughly circular mortise centered in the top of the base. Limestone. 7 cm. by 10.5 cm. by 10 cm.

C. INSCRIBED BASES BELONGING TO HUMAN HEADS

TC 540 (Plate 26)

Inscribed base from which a sculptured human head has been broken. The head and base were made in one piece. The neck is an ellipse in section, 6.5 cm. wide and 5.5 cm. deep, with flattening on the ends and sides. It tapers slightly toward the top in the 3 cm. of height preserved. The inscribed front of the base is slightly convex; it reads (1) *ṣbḥt* (2) *ḏt/wrqn*; see Albert Jamme, W. F., *Pièces épigraphiques de Ḥeid bin ‘Aqîl* (Louvain, 1952), p. 144, §288, hereafter cited as *JaPEHA.* Horizontal tool marks appear on the sides of the base; the back and bottom are rough. Alabaster. Dimensions of base: 9.5 cm. by 9.2 cm. by 7.2 cm.; total height: 13 cm.

TC 1559 (Plate 26)

Long, cylindrical neck broken from sculptured human head. At the upper break there

is a faint trace of a ridge marking the beginning of the chin. The four-letter inscription on the front reads *trft.* Alabaster. 6.2 cm. by 4.8 cm.

D. MINIATURE HUMAN HEADS

TC 1582

Miniature head of a man. The left side of the face is obliterated; of the features, only the right ear and eye are distinguishable, and their details are not clear. The protrusion of the left ear is visible, but no details are discernible. The top of the head is flat; the back is somewhat flattened. The piece has a cylindrical form. This object is less than half the size of TC 914, which exhibits many of the same characteristics. Limestone. 4 cm. by 2.7 cm. by 2.5 cm.

TC 1998 (Plate 26)

Miniature head, less cylindrical than TC 1582. The upper rear part of the head is broken at an angle; part of the neck is broken away; and part of the right ear is broken off. The eyebrows are incised. There are ridges around the eyes and a depression in the center of each eye. The nose is narrow, and the bridge of the nose is high. A small hole is drilled in from each side of the mouth, which appears to be puckered up. The back of the head is flattened. There are traces of horizontal ridges immediately below the chin (cf. TC 2053). Limestone. 4.8 cm. by 3.2 cm. by 3.1 cm.

TC 2053 (Plate 26)

Miniature human head on a long cylindrical neck. The center of the nose is broken away, but the piece is otherwise undamaged. The top of the head is cut off flat at the hair line. The back of the head is rounded and displays rough tool marks. The ears are thick and heavy. The eyebrows are marked by clean incisions. The eyes are outlined by incisions and have circular depressions drilled into the centers. The nose is well proportioned and has a horizontal ridge on each side near the lower end. The mouth, with thick lips, has a depression at either end. Three broad grooves on front of the neck immediately below the jaw may represent neck bands or wrinkles. Limestone. 10 cm. by 3.6 cm. by 3.6 cm.

II

STATUETTES OF THE HUMAN FIGURE

The statuettes of men and women, except for one in Hellenistic style (TC 1777), exhibit the same frontality as the sculptured human heads. Alabaster is again the favorite (and almost exclusive) stone used. As far as can be determined, all of the statuettes except one or two were standing. The arms are at the sides with the forearms thrust forward and the hands doubled as though holding an offering in each fist. The majority of these sculptured pieces have the feet separated, and the figures are standing on rectangular bases, most of which are inscribed on the front with the name and tribe (or clan) of the person represented. Only fragments of most of the statuettes were found, often only the inscribed base with the feet. The only perfectly preserved example (TC 1518) is somewhat larger than average, although two bases with feet belong to much larger statues—almost half life size.

The largest published group of South Arabian statuettes offering comparative material belong to the Kaiki Muncherjee Collection now in the Aden Museum; see Carlo Conti Rossini, "Dalle Rovine di Ausàn," *Dedalo*, VII (1926–27), pp. 727–54. The statuettes in that case are nearly all standing figures of men, including representations of several kings of Ausan.

TC 563

Fragment of sculptured right hand and wrist from a large statuette. A hole with a maximum diameter of 2 cm. was drilled through the clenched fist, apparently to hold some offering or token; this is now fully exposed, as the longitudinal fracture of the piece runs through it. Only the back of the hand has been preserved; the ends of the grooves separating the fingers are visible. This frag-

ment belonged to a statuette similar to TC 1587, but much larger. Highly polished, gray alabaster. 6 cm. by 4 cm. by 10.5 cm.

TC 621

Fragment of statuette base with rear part of the left foot, which is 8 mm. from the left side of the base. The base is 2.5 cm. high. Alabaster. 3.7 cm. by 7 cm. by 5 cm.

TC 629 (Plate 27)

Torso of a statuette. The head and neck are broken away, but ridges on either side of the break indicate that the base of the neck was 7.2 cm. wide, with the shoulders only 3 cm. wider on each side. The right shoulder is chipped on the back, the left shoulder on the outside top. The rump is represented by such a pronounced and angular protrusion that a high *tournure* or bustle is suggested. The forearms are directed forward and broken off at the wrists. The left side of the torso is broken obliquely below the arm. Alabaster. 18 cm. by 13.5 cm. by 8 cm.

TC 631 (Plate 27)

Inscribed statuette base. Flat, rectilinear feet, with four notches to separate toes, stand on the slightly convex top of the base. The sides of the base are roughly chiseled even; the back is broken away; the front is chipped along the lower edge. An inscription on the front reads *s̲h̲tt*; see *JaPEHA*, pp. 17f., §125. White alabaster. 7 cm. by 10.3 cm. by 5.6 cm.

TC 679 (Plate 30)

Fragment of statuette (similar to TC 629), consisting of right arm and part of the side. The forearm is directed forward and broken off. White alabaster. 12.5 cm. by 7 cm. by 7 cm.

TC 715 (Plate 27)

Upper part of statuette torso. The neck is very thick (cf. TC 629). The collar bones are prominent and a flat groove runs down the center of the chest. The upper arms, with bulging biceps, are against the sides; the missing forearms were thrust forward (as indicated by ridges just above the break). The back is flat, except for a shallow groove to represent the spinal area. Alabaster of uneven tan color. 13.5 cm. by 13 cm. by 7 cm.

TC 738 (Plate 27)

Irregular fragment of an inscribed statuette base (including TC 739). The fragment consists of the right front corner, the left foot, and a bit of the back of the base behind the foot. The part of the one-line inscription preserved on the front of the base reads *kf*.[. The foot is wide, tapering toward the front; four grooves separate the toes; a notch crosses each of the four smaller toes in a straight line. The base was polished smooth on all sides, including the back, and only the bottom was left rough. The base is 4.4 cm. high and 6.2 cm. deep. Alabaster, blackened by burning except for a small part. 5.5 cm. by 5.5 cm. by 6.2 cm.

TC 744 (Plate 27)

Statuette base with feet and lower edge of ankle-length garment. The rear of the base is broken off. The front and sides of the base are divided into two horizontal bands, the lower of which is offset about 3 mm. on the front, less on the sides. The feet are rectilinear, with the ends of the toes running obliquely in a straight line; the tips of the big toes are flush with the front edge of the pedestal. The base is 2.1 cm. high. Alabaster. 3.5 cm. by 6.3 cm. by 4.7 cm.

TC 761 (Plate 30)

Fragment from a statuette of the type known as "daughters of god" (similar to the group from the Timna' Temple published by A. Jamme in the *Bulletin of the American Schools of Oriental Research*, No. 138 [April, 1955], pp. 39–47). This fragment consists of the center section of the torso with the left forearm, which is thrust forward and broken off above the wrist. Two partial lines of inscription are preserved, one on the chest be-

tween the arms and one below, running from the left side across the front and around on the right side (where it is illegible); the extant part of the inscription appears to be the name of the dedicator, but *bnt* at the beginning of the second line is the only complete word which can be read. As the fragment is smooth from weathering, it does not necessarily have any meaningful association with the place in the cemetery where it was found. Sandstone. 5.5 cm. by 7.5 cm. by 5.2 cm.

TC 765 (Plate 27)

Inscribed statuette base. Nothing remains of the statuette except the feet, which are placed well apart; incised lines separate the toes and indicate the nails. The top of the base is polished, but uneven; the sides of the base slope inward slightly toward the top. The one-line inscription across the front reads *ḥḍrm/sflyn*; cf. *JaPEHA*, pp. 158f., §311, Pl. v, below. The base is 5 cm. high. Alabaster. 6.3 cm. by 13.5 cm. by 10 cm.

TC 819

Fragment of a statuette base. The entire front and right side are missing. The outline of the left foot (except for the toes) and the heel of the right foot are preserved. The back of the base is squared, but unfinished. The preserved (left) side is crudely polished. The base is 5.2 cm. high. Alabaster. 6.5 cm. by 10 cm. by 11 cm.

TC 940 (Plate 27)

Human torso. The head and top of the shoulders are broken away. The forearms are thrust forward and broken off. None of the legs is preserved, as even the lower end of the long plain garment is missing. Alabaster. 11 cm. by 7 cm. by 6 cm. (dimensions from field catalogue). (Carnegie Museum.)

TC 944 (Plate 30)

Statuette base, battered (all the edges and corners are very badly chipped). Traces of the feet indicate that the toes were flush with the front. A one-line inscription reading [..]*ht/ srf*[.] fills the face of the base. Alabaster. 4.3 cm. by 9.5 cm. by 6.3 cm.

TC 1317 (Plate 30)

Wrist and hand from a statuette. The tip of the thumb is broken off. A hole with a diameter of about 7 mm. is bored 2.5 cm. down into the center of the doubled fist, but not completely through. A smaller hole comes in at a right angle beneath the thumb; this was drilled partly from either side, and it may have served to hold a pin which secured an object inserted in the larger hole. Alabaster (exposed surfaces tend to be slightly rust-colored). 4.6 cm. by 3.8 cm. by 6.3 cm.

TC 1518 (Plates 28 and 29)

Seated statuette of a woman. This large piece is perfectly preserved except for the chipped right thumb. The greatest effort was devoted to the head, which is quite large in comparison with the body, especially the stylized lower part of the body. The top of the head is cut off flat and left roughly tooled. The back of the head is rounded. The hair, indicated by tooling similar to that on top, ends in a straight line at the neck. Locks of hair just below the ears are visible from the front. The hair line makes one step at the temples between the forehead and the top of the ear. The ears protrude unnaturally and blend into the hair behind. A hole drilled in from the front of each ear lobe meets a hole drilled from the bottom; the connecting opening is somewhat smaller than the holes. A deep eyebrow groove runs above either eye. The eye sockets are in the shape of lozenges and are quite large. A vertical groove, apparently a cautery mark, appears about 1 cm. behind each eye. The nose is very straight, but tapers pleasingly toward the top. A sunken area surrounds the mouth, which is a raised oval with a horizontal groove (rounded in section) to separate the lips.

From the neck down, the figure is somewhat conical, except for the thick arms. The upper arms are at the sides, the forearms are directed forward, and the fists are closed with the thumbs upward. A rounded depression appears in the space surrounded by the thumb and forefinger. An irregularity in the top of the left wrist has been filled with plaster and evened off level with the surrounding surface. The breasts are small. A ridge encircles the lower part of the body; on the front it indicates the knees, while below each elbow it has a jog or step which seems to indicate the side or end of a chair or seat; the ridge continues across the rear as the back of the seat.

The toes are visible at the front corners of the body. The base, approximately 4 cm. high, protrudes about 1.5 cm. on the front and about 8 mm. on the sides. On the back the base is flush with the slightly convex back of the statuette. Chunks of plaster adhere to the bottom of the base near the center. The rear of the object, except for the neck and upper part of the back, displays tool marks which were not removed by the superficial polishing. The body is generally smoothed, but only the face is highly polished. Alabaster. 34.5 cm. by 15 cm. by 14.5 cm.

Dozens of seated statuettes, mostly very crude and of uncertain provenience, are published in Carl Rathjens, *Sabaeica II* (Hamburg, 1955), pp. 203–18. One of those shown on p. 216, Photo 219–20, has a stepped ridge on the sides similar to that on TC 1518; the object is there called a *Schemelsitzer*; the rectangular seats are clearly detailed in Photo 221–25. Other crude seated statuettes are shown by Carl Rathjens and Hermann von Wissmann in *Vorislamische Altertümer*, pp. 188ff., but they offer little of comparative value for our piece. A seated statuette of a male in the museum at Suweidā in Jebel ed-Durūz offers some comparisons, but it is of unknown provenience; see *Syria*, VII (1926), Pl. LXVI, above. This is dated by H. Bossert to early in the first century B.C.; *Altsyrien*, p. 34, #490. One statuette of this general type in the Muncherjee Collection (Aden) has been published; see *Dedalo*, VII (1926–27), p. 738, right.

TC 1542 (Plate 30)

Fragment of a statuette base with part of the right side, the front and the bottom, as well as most of the right side. The bottom is roughly tooled. The side is partly polished, but tool marks still show. The two-line inscription on the front reads (1) [ ]*bm*[ ] (2) [ ]*yṯ*[ ]. The base is 5 cm. high. Alabaster. 6.5 cm. by 6 cm. by 8.5 cm.

TC 1546

Fragment of a statuette, consisting of the right foot (broken from the pedestal), leg, and part of a garment. The leg is very thick. The foot is represented by an angular protrusion on the front of the leg with incisions to indicate toes. White alabaster. 4.8 cm. by 4 cm. by 3.2 cm.

TC 1566 (Plate 30)

Torso from statuette of a woman. The lower body is rectangular in section with rounded corners. There is a prominent curving ridge across the lower back to indicate the rump. The hands are held across the abdomen just below the breasts, with the fingers interlaced. A band or cuff around each wrist is indicated by incisions. White alabaster. 8 cm. by 7 cm. by 3.8 cm.

TC 1587 (Plates 30 and 31)

Statuette of woman on inscribed base. The head is broken off and missing. The top of the left shoulder is chipped. The arms are at the sides and the forearms thrust forward. Most of both hands are broken off, but wide grooves, tapering toward the back, which were stylistic representations of the fingers, are partly preserved. Shallow breasts are indicated between the forearms. The rump protrudes in a ridge across the lower part of the back. The legs are oval in section (*ca.* 4.5 cm. front to back, 2.7 cm. from side to side). The feet extend out more than 2 cm. in front of the legs, resulting in the appearance of extremely large feet. Grooves demark the toes. The fronts of the feet are almost square, with the smaller toes only slightly receding behind the line of the great toes. The sides and back of the rectangular base (3.6 cm. by 8.3 cm. by 7.8 cm.) are roughly tooled, while an attempt was made to polish the top between the feet. The front of the base, bearing a one-line inscription reading *fyšt*, is polished smooth. White alabaster. 21 cm. by 10.5 cm. by 9 cm. Cf. *Dedalo*, VII (1926–27), pp. 737, 739, above.

TC 1777 (Plates 32, 33, and 34)

Female torso (including TC 1803). Sculptured in Hellenistic style, this figure has been identified as the goddess Isis; see Berta Segall, "Sculpture from Arabia Felix," *American Journal of Archaeology*, Vol. 59 (1955), pp. 213f., Pl. 60, Fig. 14. It was probably made in the first century B.C. The larger fragment (TC 1777) is the lower part of the body and the upper thighs. The back is tooled to shape, but is not polished smooth. A cylindrical

stand fills in the space behind the legs. A large fold in the garment crosses the lower abdomen, dropping down from left to right. The pleats below this all run obliquely from left to right. Another large fold hangs down from the left hip; it is chipped most of its length. The smaller, upper fragment (TC 1803) forms the right shoulder and side. Two tresses fall on the top of the shoulder. A twisted fringe runs from the end of the shoulder to the center of the chest. On the two fragments together it can be seen that the folds of the garment radiate across the abdomen from the Isis knot between the breasts. White alabaster. 27 cm. by 11.5 cm. by 10 cm.

TC 1816 (Plate 35)

Fragment of a statuette of a standing figure (same type as TC 1587, but larger) with forearms directed forward. All of the front of the object is missing, along with the head, shoulders and all but bare traces of the arms. A vertical groove in the middle of the back ends at the sharply protruding (*ca.* 1.2 cm.) rump, which is formed by an offset at the waist line. Most of the thick left leg is intact (including traces on the front of what appears to be the strap of a sandal with raised object in the center), but the right leg is broken off square about 1 cm. below the lower end of the long garment. The body is roughly rectangular in section. Alabaster, slightly blackened about the lower part of the piece. 31 cm. by 14 cm. by 10 cm.

TC 1818 (Plate 35)

Badly pitted statuette with very squat body. The head is missing entirely. A one-line inscription on the face of the base (which is 4.5 cm. high) is illegible. Rectangular projections represent the feet. Traces of the arms suggest the typical votive position with the forearms directed forward. Porous limestone. 13.7 cm. by 9.6 cm. by 8.8 cm. Cf. *Sabaeica II*, p. 218, Photo 239–40; this piece has a much smaller base, but has the same general squat appearance.

TC 1885 (Plate 35)

Base from large statuette with feet intact. The right corner is chipped. The well proportioned feet (each 5 cm. by 12.2 cm.), about

2.5 cm. apart, cover most of the top. The toes and nails are demarked by incisions. The top of the base between the feet slopes up slightly toward the rear, then drops down at the heels. The bottom is covered with rough tool marks. A tenon 3 cm. deep and 7 cm. square is centered on the bottom. Two plain bands, the lower *ca.* 2 cm. wide, the upper *ca.* 1.8 cm., run around the front and sides of the base; the upper is recessed 3 to 4 mm. behind the lower. White alabaster. 10.5 cm. by 14.5 cm. by 16 cm.

TC 1890 (Plate 35)

Right wrist and hand from statuette. The fingers and most of the thumb are broken off, but it is rather clear that the fingers were extended straight out, rather than being doubled into a fist. The grooves which separated the fingers extend over the back of the hand. On both the index and middle fingers are traces of a pair of transverse grooves at the edge of the break; these may have indicated the knuckles. Traces also remain of the grooves separating the fingers on the inside of the hand. Alabaster, nearly white. 5.5 cm. by 4 cm. by 9 cm.

TC 1981 (Plate 35)

Right arm from statuette with small part of side attached. The outer part of the shoulder is chipped. The thumb and the fingers are broken off. The arm is bent at a right angle at the elbow, with the forearm thrust forward. The hand is similar to TC 1890, but about half the size, and no transverse grooves are preserved. The back, side, and front of the arm are flat; the edges are rounded. The inside of the forearm is rounded. The space between the arm and the side of the body is not cut out. Reddish-brown calcareous stone with black streaks. 12 cm. by 5.5 cm. by 11.2 cm.

TC 1990

Fragment of a statuette, consisting of the left shoulder and part of the chest (the break is diagonal, from the right shoulder across to the position of the left elbow). The head is missing. The base of the neck is circular. The arm is not indicated separately from the body. The flat, left breast is the only feature represented. Limestone. 6.5 cm. by 7 cm. by 3.3 cm.

TC 2064 (Plates 35 and 36)

Female statuette on inscribed base (including TC 2189), similar to TC 1587, but wider and flatter. The head is broken off and missing. The left shoulder is chipped. The arms are at the sides with the forearms directed forward and broken off. A ridge on the right arm indicates a sleeve ending just below the elbow. The breasts are small and flat. The plain garment reaches to the ankles. The space between the feet is not cut out. The fore part of each foot is very stubby. Short grooves delineate the toes. The base, 10 cm. wide and 5 cm. high, is polished on the rear in the same plane as the flat back of the figure. There are two unequal lines of inscription on the front of the base reading (1) *fr't/ḏt/ḏr* (2) *ḥn*; the upper line runs from edge to edge of the base, while the lower one is centered. Alabaster with rusty tint and striations. 21.5 cm. by 11 cm. by 5.7 cm. Cf. *Dedalo*, VII, pp. 732f., 737, 739, above.

TC 2531 (Plate 35)

Base from statuette with feet in place. Nearly all the edges are chipped, some extensively. Each foot rests on a sort of platform (*ca.* 8 mm. high), which is of the same shape as the outline of the foot, but larger; these are suggestive of thick soles of sandals, but there are no straps visible around the feet. A horizontal hole is drilled into the front of each of these platforms, approximately in the center and slightly cutting into the top of the base; the hole under the left foot is 1.6 cm. deep, the one under the right 2 cm., while both have diameters of *ca.* 5 mm. The feet are closer together at the toe than at the heel, owing to the fact that the outer edges of the feet are placed nearly parallel to the sides of the base. The feet (without platforms) are 11 cm. long. The toes, separated by shallow grooves, recede naturally toward the outside in a curve. The base, nearly 7 cm. high, is square and has a shallow offset near the bottom on the front. Alabaster, very light gray. 10.5 cm. by 15.5 cm. by 15.5 cm.

TC 2533 (Plate 35)

Right hand from statuette. The fingers and thumb are broken off. A bracelet (or cuff) encircles the wrist. Dark gray stone. 4.5 cm. by 4.2 cm. by 5 cm.

III

STYLIZED FACE PLAQUES

The objects from the Timna' Cemetery in this group lack any exact parallels among previously published artifacts from South Arabia.[1] Owing to the large number of ancient objects from the same period which are known, it is rather surprising that such face plaques have not appeared before, even though no other major cemetery has been excavated on a large scale. Although this particular type of memorial might have been peculiar to Qatabân, it is more probable that similar examples existed elsewhere. That none has been found and published must be regarded as accidental. The purpose of these plaques, as the presence in some instances of a personal name indicates, seems to have been to represent the deceased and preserve his memory.

Face plaques belonging to a related tradition from Petra are illustrated by Crystal M. Bennett in "The Nabataeans in Petra," *Archaeology,* Vol. 15, No. 4 (Winter, 1962), p. 239. These have square eyes, either raised or incised, and bar-shaped noses of varying relative sizes and so are comparable to one found at Madâ'in Ṣâliḥ (see J. A. Jaussen and R. Savignac, *Mission archéologique en Arabie,* Vol. I, p. 427, Fig. 217). None of the four examples pictured by Miss Bennett constitutes an exact parallel with our Timna' pieces, but the similarity in form and conception is striking and obvious. The Nabataean plaques known are uninscribed, and this fact has permitted Miss Bennett to speculate that they represent deities, describing them as "crude portable stone idols" ("The Naba-

taeans in Petra," p. 238) and referring also to what she calls " 'face idols' " from Hadhramaut and Yemen. Though the use of objects of this type could conceivably have been different in such distant regions, there is no reason for concluding that they were. One may cite as further evidence the grave stele with stylized face and Old Aramaic inscription from Teimā which was sketched by Charles Doughty (see Adolf Grohmann, *Kulturgeschichte des Alten Orients: Arabien* [in *Handbuch der Altertumswissenschaft*], p. 51, Fig. 8).

Another large group of crude faces on stone slabs, described as Thamudic, have been found by Diana Kirkbride in Wâdî edh-Dhaiqeh near Ramm in southern Jordan (see *Illustrated London News,* August 13, 1960, pp. 262–63; also *Revue Biblique,* Vol. 67 [1960], pp. 232–35, Pl. XII). Miss Kirkbride points out (in the first reference cited) that they may not have been idols, but rather memorials. In this judgment she seems certainly to be correct.

In the collection of face plaques from Timna' two fairly distinct types are found. Type A includes those plaques having the outline of the eyes represented by raised lozenges with circles in the center and having the nose represented by a long narrow raised bar. Plaques of this type generally have a raised border on all four sides. Two inscribed stelae in Vienna which display no features other than two incised eyes may have some relationship to our Type A, but they do not constitute parallels; see H. Bossert, *Altsyrien,* p. 382, #1313, #1314, description on p. 101. A stele in the University Museum, Philadelphia, has the eyes and mouth in raised lozenges, a bar-like nose, and raised brow; it is strikingly similar to Timna'

---

[1] G. Lankester Harding's *Archaeology in the Aden Protectorates* (London, 1964), which appeared as the present volume was going to press, contains photographs of four face plaques purchased from native treasure hunters at the Timna' Cemetery (p. 48, Pl. XLIII, 24–27).

plaques of Type A, but is on a large stele without raised borders; see G. Ryckmans, "Les religiones arabes préislamiques," *L'histoire génerale des religions,* p. 307, left (also in Bossert, *Altsyrien,* p. 382, #1311). A badly damaged plaque with incised eyes and eyebrows may be mentioned in passing, although the details are somewhat different; see A. Jamme, "Les antiquités sud-arabes du Museo Nazionale Romano," *Monumenti Antichi,* Vol. XLIII (1955), Pl. x:468, described on p. 82.

The plaques classified as Type B are much more highly stylized, and except for the presence of the intermediate stages some examples would not have been recognized for what they are. The one characteristic feature of the pieces comprising Type B is the presence of two U's (either raised or depressed) to represent the outlines of the eyes. Some examples have raised discs for the centers of the eyes, and some have a bar nose. In the most simplified examples, nothing more than the two U's are present. Raised borders are usual, often with a name inscribed on the upper or lower border.

An anomalous object, which does not specifically belong to the typical face plaques of this group, is added as Type C, for lack of a more appropriate place for listing it.

TYPE A

TC 504 (Plate 36)
Fragment from right (viewer's left) of face plaque broken on an angle from the upper center to within 5.5 cm. of the lower right corner so that very little of the nose is preserved, but all of the right eye. The cheek and eye are on a recessed (*ca.* 5 mm.) surface which is arched at the top above the lozenge-shaped eye (6 cm. wide by 4 cm. high); the margin on the side, the area above the eye (minimum width 5.5 cm.), and the nose are all on the same plane. The outline of the eye is a rounded ridge; inside of this is a raised disc, now damaged, with a diameter of *ca.* 1.8 cm. No certain evidence of a lower margin is preserved. White alabaster. 13.5 cm. by 10 cm. (preserved width) by 6.5 cm.

TC 1544
Face plaque, badly damaged. The left edge (viewer's right) and lower part are broken away, and a large chip is missing at the lower right corner. As a result, neither eye (both are *ca.* 6.5 cm. wide and 3.8 cm. high) is complete at the outer ends; the outlines are ridges converging in points at the nose and curving above and below circular discs (diameter *ca.* 2 cm.) which form the centers of the eyes. Above each eye, extending from the nose to the margins at the sides, are large eyebrow ridges. The nose is bar-shaped, but narrows near the top from a width of 2.5 cm. at the lower part to *ca.* 1.5 cm. at the point where it meets the upper margin (*ca.* 1.6 cm. wide with a pecked surface). Calcareous aggregate. 19 cm. by 12.5 cm. by 6.6 cm.

TC 1574 (Plate 36)
Face plaque on roughly squared block. The eyes (*ca.* 3 cm. high by 6.5 cm. wide with discs *ca.* 1.4 cm. in diameter) are similar to those of TC 1544. The nose is smaller, measuring only *ca.* 1.5 cm. by 5.5 cm. The inner points of the eye outlines intersect with the nose *ca.* 1 cm. below its top, while the eyebrow ridges spring from the very top of it. A faint incision, curving up at the ends, may represent the mouth or may be an accidental scratch. No borders are preserved. Calcareous aggregate. 15 cm. by 17 cm. by 6.5 cm.

TC 1668 (Plate 37)
Face plaque with same features as TC 1544. Slightly raised margins of varying widths appear at the top, bottom, and sides of the front surface. The nose is bar-shaped and runs up to meet the upper margin, on which is an inscription reading *fr't/ġrbm* in crudely incised letters (see *JaPEHA,* p. 92, §211). Chisel marks running in random directions are visible over most of the surfaces. Chalky limestone. 16.5 cm. by 12 cm. by 4 cm.

TC 1692 (Plate 38)
Block with incised face. The outline is a large V flattened at the point for the chin. At the upper sides of the V are ears represented by double-line incisions. Even with these are the outlines of eyes, which are

roughly lozenge-shaped. Between the eyes is a broad bar-shaped nose formed by incisions in the form of a square-cornered U. Below the nose, which is not centered exactly, is the mouth, formed by a lozenge bisected by a horizontal incised line. The surface is pitted. This piece may be only the upper part of a larger stele, the lower part of which has been broken off, but whether it is or not remains uncertain. Poor quality marble. 12 cm. by 10 cm. by 4 cm. Cf. *Sabaeica II,* p. 22, especially Photo 257; also Bossert, *Altsyrien,* p. 382, #1315; Jamme, *Les albums photographiques de la collection Kaiky Muncherjee* (Rome, 1955), Plate, bottom row, second from right.

TC 1822 (Plate 37)

Face plaque, broken obliquely on left (viewer's right) across both upper and lower corners so that only a trace of the raised margin on that side is preserved. The lower margin (mostly destroyed) is *ca.* 1 cm. in width, the right and upper ones *ca.* 3 cm. The badly damaged upper margin was occupied by an inscription, of which no letter is certain except for the final *t* of the first name (followed by a word divider). The nose is represented by a large bar 6.5 cm. long, *ca.* 2.3 cm. wide at the bottom and *ca.* 1.6 cm. wide at the top; the upper end intersects with the upper margin and is flush with it. Below the nose are traces of a small raised mouth. The eyes are horizontal lozenges with circles in the center; there are no eyebrows as on TC 1544. Oölitic limestone. 12 cm. by 15.5 cm. by 5.5 cm.

TC 2008 (Plate 37)

Face plaque, broken irregularly on left (viewer's right) and chipped on right. The outline of the eyes are represented by ridges in the form of horizontal lozenges, in the center of which are raised discs. Immediately above the eyes, the inner ends of which run together, is a ridge following the contours of the eyes and representing the brows. The nose, widening from top to bottom, intersects with the inner ends of the eye outlines, but does not extend above this point as does the nose on several of the plaques described above. A simple groove just below

the nose represents the mouth. The lower margin bears a line of inscription, upside down, reading (as preserved) [ ].'l/d̲t[/]. Limestone. 13.5 cm. by 16.3 cm. by 7 cm.

TYPE B

TC 675 (Plate 36)

Fragment from the (viewer's) right of face plaque. The finished edge on the right is preserved in a small area, the remainder being broken away along with part of the upper corner; the top and bottom are chipped; the vertical break at the left runs through the bar-shaped nose. There is a trace of a narrow, raised margin at the top of the face. Only the lower stroke and left upright of the U-shaped eye outline and the disc in the center are preserved. One line of inscription across the lower part of the face reads *ynds̆*[]. Oölitic limestone. 11 cm. by 12 cm. by 6.2 cm.

TC 831 (Plate 37)

Face plaque, blackened by fire over much of the front surface. Margins less than 1 cm. wide appear at the sides and the top of the face; the margin at the bottom is wider (*ca.* 2 cm.) and bears a crude inscription which cannot be read with certainty (the right end of it is completely chipped away, and the surface of the stone is elsewhere badly pitted). A long slender bar-like nose runs from the upper margin to the lower, diminishing in width toward the top. On either side of it are U-shaped eye outlines so large that they fill the spaces fully; in the center of these are discs nearly 2 cm. in diameter. The rear of the block is irregular. Porous calcareous stone. 11.5 cm. by 15.8 cm. by 6 cm.

TC 920 (Plate 38)

Face plaque, damaged at the corners and edges. On the front are raised margins *ca.* 2 cm. wide at the bottom and on the sides, 1.2 cm. wide at the top. The raised bar-shaped nose, 7.2 cm. long by *ca.* 1.7 cm. wide, meets the upper margin; a space of 5 cm. is left between it and the lower margin, and no mouth is found here. The eyes are represented by a large U on either side of the nose; these are not formed by ridges as on most of the face plaques, but by grooves. The one on the (viewer's) left is 5.5 cm. high, 6 cm. wide, the other 6 cm. by 6 cm.; both are about 1 cm. from the nose, 2.5 cm. from the upper margin, and against the margins on the sides. Poor quality alabaster. 15.4 cm. by 20.2 cm. by 5.3 cm.

TC 1074 (Plate 38)

Fragment from (viewer's) upper right of a face plaque. At least one-third is broken away at the bottom, possibly more, along with the extreme left part. Across the top of the front is a wide (*ca.* 3.3 cm.) margin bearing an inscription which reads '*lr'b/dmd.* [ ]; the *b* is slightly shorter than the neighboring letters, but while the upper left corner is damaged, there is little possibility that there was an oblique stroke indicating that the letter was *k*; the lower parts of the first two letters ('*l*) are chipped away. The U-shaped eye outline on the right, in the center of which is a raised disc, is intact except for the lower part; to the left of this is the upper part of the bar-shaped nose, then the right vertical stroke of the left eye outline. Chisel marks show up as white lines on the stone. Red coloring is present on the raised features of the face. Light brown, hard limestone. 14 cm. by 17.5 cm. by 7 cm.

TC 1366 (Plate 39)

Face plaque, most simplified of this group, consisting solely of two raised U-shaped eye outlines on a plain background which is surrounded by a raised border. Below the upper margin, which is very narrow, is a groove about 1 cm. wide. Oölitic limestone. 11.8 cm. by 20 cm. by 5.1 cm.

TC 1604 (Plate 39)

Face plaque, chipped at (viewer's) upper left and at various places around the raised margin. Although the eyes are U-shaped stylizations with a raised disc in the center of each, the nose and mouth are both completely represented, the nose as a bar 6.7 cm. long and 2.3 cm. wide at the lower end, diminishing to 1.3 cm. where it meets flush with the upper margin; the mouth is a rather shapeless ridge 2.9 cm. wide. Porous marble. 11.3 cm. by 13.2 cm. by 5.7 cm.

TC 1638 (Plate 39)

Fragment consisting of (viewer's) upper left corner of face plaque. The raised (*ca.* 4 mm.) margin across the top, 2.3 cm. wide, is filled with the last part of a crude one-line inscription which seems to read]*ydfgt*, though this is not a certain reading; the margin on the side is narrower, *ca.* 1 cm. The eye is composed of a U-shaped ridge and a small centered disc; they are in relief equal to the height of the raised margins. Porous limestone. 7.5 cm. by 6.5 cm. by 4.5 cm.

TC 1645 (Plate 39)

Fragment, upper central part of plaque with most of raised bar nose, part of U-shaped ridge forming outline of eye, raised disc in center of eye, and three (or four) letters of an inscription on the upper margin reading]*dkr*[. as far as preserved. Marble. 9.5 cm. by 10 cm. by 7 cm.

TC 1709 (Plate 40)

Face plaque, nearly square, with features similar to those of TC 1604. There are raised margins at the top, bottom, and sides. U-shaped ridges with raised discs in the center represent the eyes. A very long, narrow bar nose stands between these eyes, and below the nose is a raised mouth shaped roughly like a horizontal lozenge. Limestone. 15 cm. by 14 cm. dimensions from field catalogue). (Carnegie Museum.)

TC 1744 (Plate 40)

Face plaque with raised margins at the top, bottom and sides. Facial features, including bar nose, U-shaped eyes with centered discs, and the mouth, have been deliberately chiseled away, and the chisel marks are clearly visible in those places. The upper margin, *ca.* 2.2 cm. wide, bears a one-line inscription reading *yšrḥwddz.* . (the final two characters are damaged and illegible). The margins at the sides and bottom are 1 cm. wide or slightly more. Limestone. 12.5 cm. by 15.2 cm. by 4.5 cm.

TC 2039 (Plate 39)

Thick block with stylized face on front. Within narrow raised margins at top, bottom, and sides are two raised U's representing eyes and a bar nose between—all approximately equidistant from top and bottom. The background is covered with shallow chisel marks, all of which run horizontally. Limestone. 10 cm. by 8 cm. by 8.3 cm.

TYPE C

TC 1276 (Plate 40)

Upper part of a polished plaque which has been worked apparently to represent a human face. The plaque itself has many of the same characteristics as some of those found in Chapters VIII and IX; the front was essentially flat and polished, the upper corners, as viewed from the front, are rounded, and it tapers in width from top to bottom. As it now appears, the plaque has two shallow depressions on the front with ridges above and a broad ridge between indicating the principal features of a human face. Alabaster. *Ca.* 9 cm. by 8 cm. by 4 cm. (dimensions from field catalogue). (Carnegie Museum.)

IV

RELIEFS AND FRAGMENTS
BEARING HUMAN FIGURES

Almost as numerous as the human heads and statuettes of human beings are the reliefs and fragments of reliefs which bear the human figure. Most of the reliefs of this group exhibit the same general artistic characteristics as the other categories of sculpture from the Timna' Cemetery, viz., strict frontality, angular appearance, and stereotyped positions. One head in high relief (TC 1846) even has eye sockets for inlaying of the eyes in different material; this piece is not essentially different in execution from the treatment of the heads in the round, but only happens to be set on a background. Another object included in this group (TC 1557), while having a body set on a plaque, has the head cut free and finished in nearly every way as the larger heads discussed above, even having the top of the head cut off flat at the hairline, again probably to be fitted into a niche or recess. Other high reliefs (e.g., TC 1307 and 1852) are not essentially different in style from some of the standing statuettes except for the background plaque. One (TC 1847) has the arms directed forward as do the standing and seated statuettes.

On the other hand, even where the general treatment is essentially the same, there are notable differences between the free-standing sculptures and the reliefs. One of the principal variations between the reliefs and the statuettes is that while the latter most frequently have the forearms directed forward, the former usually have the hands held across the stomach, often with the tips of the fingers just touching. Of the reliefs, only one (TC 1847) has the forearms directed forward. Two examples (TC 1294 and 1851) have the arms out at the sides and bent at the elbow.

Almost as common as the position with both hands across the stomach is the position with the left hand holding an offering against the stomach and with the right hand raised in salutation (see TC 553, 709, 1662, 1776, and 2530).

There are several exceptions to the generalized statements made above. TC 648, with an elaborate treatment of the collar and necklace, may represent Hellenistic art. TC 1294 has the head facing right (as does also TC 870), the shoulders forward, the lower limbs right; this is of course suggestive of Egyptian positioning. The treatment of the hair, eye, and other features about the head is distinctly different from the usual forms seen in this group of reliefs. The representation of the hair in TC 1776, as well as the loose garment flung over the right shoulder, marks this piece off from the others. TC 1851, with a *himation* over the left shoulder and the arms held out to the sides, is likewise distinctive.

TC 506

Fragment of relief with front view of left foot of human in high relief, resting on deep lower margin or base of plaque. (Cf. 1619, which is of the same type, but larger.) Grooves separate the toes. The foot is 1.8 cm. wide. The right foot was slightly more than 3 cm. from the left, as shown by a shallow ridge at the break. The background is 1 cm. thick, the base is 1.3 cm. high and stands out 1.5 cm. from the background. Except for the bottom, all flat surfaces (including the back) were smoothed. White alabaster. 3.6 cm. by 9.8 cm. by 2.7 cm. (Possibly belongs to TC 2108, but intervening fragments are missing if this is so.)

TC 553 (Plate 41)

Two fragments of a relief of a woman in a position similar to that seen in TC 2530 The lower left fragment contains the left forearm across the stomach with hand clasping an offering (which seems to be cone shaped); two bracelets encircle the wrist. Folds of a garment circle down across the lower part of the body from the left side. The upper right fragment (catalogued as TC 1165) shows the right shoulder and arm; the forearm is raised as if in salutation (as in TC 1776), but the hand has been broken off. The sleeve of the garment ends in a hem above the elbow; a seam runs along the top of the shoulder, and pleats radiate from the neck. The flat back of the relief is roughly tooled. The background is about 2.8 cm. thick; maximum preserved height of the relief above the background is 3 cm. The width of the body was about 21.5 cm. Gray alabaster with brown streaks. Lower fragment: 17.5 cm. by 14 cm. by 5.5 cm. Upper fragment: 14 cm. by 15 cm. by 5.8 cm.

A comparable memorial stone bearing a high relief of a woman is in the British Museum; see R. D. Barnett and D. J. Wiseman, *Fifty Masterpieces of Ancient Near Eastern Art in the Department of Western Asiatic Antiquities, British Museum* (London, 1960), photograph on p. 74, description on p. 75. The date given, "about 2nd century A.D.," appears to be too late by some three centuries at least, and the object may well have come from the cemetery at ancient Timna'.

TC 648 (Plate 41)

Fragment from relief of a woman. Part of the left shoulder and upper chest are preserved. An elaborate necklace and a broad collar cross the preserved portion. The background is 2.5 cm. thick; the back is tooled even. White alabaster. *Ca.* 13 cm. by 14 cm. by 6.5 cm.

TC 709 (Plate 41)

Fragment consisting of upper left corner of a relief. The open right hand of a person raised in salutation is at the left edge (cf. TC 1776). A hole with a diameter of 5 mm. is drilled through the background between the thumb and probable location of the neck (comparable to that of TC 1307); the hole

was either for the purpose of attaching the relief to a wall by means of a copper fastener or for a separate necklace (as on TC 1664). The background averages *ca.* 2.6 cm. in thickness; the back is very roughly tooled. The left edge of the plaque is tooled even along the front edge. White alabaster with faint streaks of rusty brown. 9 cm. by 8.5 cm. by 3.6 cm.

TC 726 (Plate 41)

Fragment of high relief with upper arm, part of chest and section of collar intact. This relief apears to have been similar to TC 2108, but in the present case the background, 2.5 cm. thick, extends 3.8 cm. out from the left side of the figure; the edge of the background is squared off and polished smooth. Orange alabaster, gray toward the outer edge. 5.8 cm. by 9 cm. by 4.2 cm.

TC 870 (Plate 42)

Two joining fragments (including TC 1033) from the upper right corner of a plaque with the relief of a person. The figure, with head shown in profile (turned to right), is within a high margin *ca.* 1.5 cm. wide. The hair is marked by criss-cross incisions. A front view of the right shoulder is shown, but the part of the left shoulder preserved suggests that it was represented in a side view. The garment has a low-cut V-neck. The background is not of uniform thickness; in front of the head it is 1.9 cm., behind the head it is 1.5 cm., gradually increasing to 2 cm. in the corner of the panel. The back of the plaque is smoothly polished except at the left edge, where it is roughly tooled (perhaps the stone has been re-used). Alabaster. 8.3 cm. by 9.5 cm. by 2.9 cm.

TC 961 (Plate 53)

Upper left corner of a large relief panel with a border raised a full 3 cm. above the background. The only preserved feature of the original scene is the upper end of a hand raised in salutation, palm forward; the four fingers are preserved. At the right side of the fragment is a trace of an obliterated raised feature, certainly the head of a human figure. At the extreme left top of the fragment is a ridge indicating that there had been a second raised margin above the first. Alabaster, burned over the front surface. 11.5 cm. by 16 cm. by 8.2 cm.

TC 1117 (Plate 42)

Fragment of plaque with high relief of human figure. A broad, round face with strict frontality and traces of the shoulders is all that is preserved on the flat background (without raised margins). The top of the head is cut off even with the upper edge of the background. There are grooved eyebrows, incised outlines of eyes with circular holes for inlaid irises, and ears adjoining the background. The background is broken off rather straight near the left ear. Alabaster. 13 cm. by 16 cm. by 6 cm. (dimensions from field catalogue). (Carnegie Museum.)

TC 1294 (Plate 43)

Stele with human figure in relief. The upper corners and the lower left corner are broken. The head and lower part of the body face right, while a front view of the shoulders and arms is shown; curiously, there is a front view of the left eye. The open hands are held out to the sides of the shoulders. There is a tight collar or neck band, a large ear pendant, and a fairly narrow head band. The figure stands on a raised (3 mm.) band 1.5 cm. wide which runs across the lower edge of the face of the plaque. The stele tapers toward the bottom (estimated width at the top is 13.5 cm., at the bottom, 11 cm.). The top and sides are polished smooth, while the back and bottom are tooled even. The bottom has been cut in from the rear, apparently to form a tenon (2.8 cm. thick) for insertion into a base. The background is 4.2 cm. thick. White alabaster. 22.5 cm. by 13 cm. by 5 cm.

This piece is discussed by Berta Segall in "Some Problems of Copy and Adaptation," *American Journal of Archaeology*, Vol. 60 (1956), p. 169, Pl. 65, Fig. 13. Similar stance, but much different detail appears on a relief in the Muncherjee Collection, Aden; see *Dedalo*, VII, p. 741, left middle.

TC 1307 (Plate 44)

Stele with high relief of female (?) figure. The upper left corner is broken away, and the lower corners are chipped. This piece is similar in general to TC 2064 (Chapter II: Statuettes) except that a plaque background is

present and it is thus treated as high relief; furthermore, the hands are placed across the stomach rather than cut free and directed forward. The feet were apparently not represented; the bottom of the garment was cut off straight. *Ca.* 1.5 cm. back from the face of the garment is an offset of 1.3 cm., behind which is the tooled bottom of the piece. The hands are placed across the stomach, palms inward and fingers interlaced. Circular hollows are cut in the centers of the eyes. A bronze wire is inserted through the background above the shoulder. The background was approximately 14 cm. wide at the top and 13.2 cm. at the bottom; it has a thickness of about 2.8 cm. Alabaster. 23 cm. by 14.2 cm. by 7 cm. (Stolen in 1962 while in Baltimore for study.)

TC 1358 (Plate 41)

Triangular fragment from lower center of a plaque bearing a relief. The raised (*ca.* 1 cm.) lower margin (3 cm. wide) has a one-line inscription reading]n/mhs(n)[; the word divider is unusual in that it consists of two vertical lines rather than a single line; the ṣ does not have the central vertical line in the lower portion as is more frequently found. The curved border of a garment (similar to TC 553) touches the lower margin. The top corner of the fragment has a trace of some feature (probably an arm or hand across the stomach, as TC 2530 or TC 1557). White alabaster. 11 cm. by 10.3 cm. by 4.8 cm.

TC 1557 (Plate 45)

Stele bearing the figure of a woman in high relief. A one-line inscription on the base reads gb'm/hn'mt. The background ends at the shoulders, leaving the head free and completely sculptured around the sides and rear; the top of the head is cut off flat. There are pierced ear lobes, eyebrow grooves, grooves outlining the eyes, and circular depressions in the center of each eye. The lips, especially the upper one, protrude. A small circular depression appears on the front of the chin. Grooves on the front of the neck represent wrinkles or neck bands. The hands are held across the stomach, palms inward, with the tips of the fingers touching; a bracelet encircles each wrist. The garment has a wide plain neck and sleeves ending in hems at the middle of the upper arms. The back of the object is tooled even with long horizontal tool marks, except above the left shoulder, where there are oblique tool marks. Gray alabaster. 24.3 cm. by 16.5 cm. by 7 cm. The forms of the characters in the inscription suggest a date in the second half of the third century B.C. or later.

TC 1567 (Plate 48)

Sculptured human head on rectangular background plaque which is broken obliquely across the neck. A slight ridge at the break indicates the top of the left shoulder. The top of the head is rounded unevenly above the hair line. Rough protrusions indicate the ears. The eyebrows are marked by grooves; the eyeballs bulge out between ridges marking upper and lower eyelids; there are circular depressions in the centers of the eyes. The mouth looks puckered. The background plaque has a slight flange along the front of the (viewer's) right edge; the left edge of the plaque is chipped. Light gray alabaster, streaked with dark gray. 9.5 cm. by 10 cm. by 5 cm.

TC 1619 (Plate 46)

Four joining fragments (including TC 1661 and TC 1722) composing a stele with the figure of a woman in high relief. The head is missing. The hands are held across the stomach with the finger tips touching. The figure stands on a pedestal 2.4 cm. high and 3 cm. deep. The background plaque, 1.4 cm. thick, is polished smooth on the sides and back; a curious recess *ca.* 1.5 cm. deep at the bottom of the back suggests that the stone has been re-used (the recess extends 4 cm. from the bottom and from the right side to within 1.8 cm. of the left side; the back of the recess is roughly tooled, the sides chiseled even). Alabaster. 28 cm. by 13 cm. by 5.4 cm.

TC 1639 (Plate 46)

Plaque bearing human head in high relief. The body was most likely present originally, but only the top of the shoulders is now preserved. The ears are spread out on the background. Eyebrow grooves run across above the eyes, which are outlined by ridges. The nose is broken. The top of the head is cut off crudely at the hair line. A hole through

the background on either side of the face even with the mouth was apparently for the purpose of attaching the plaque to some other surface. Alabaster. 12.5 cm. by 10.5 cm. by 6 cm. (dimensions from field catalogue). (Aden Museum.)

TC 1662 (Plate 41)

Fragment of a high relief on a plaque. Only the right shoulder and raised arm of a human (cf. TC 2530) are preserved. The background, 2.4 cm. thick, extends only 3 mm. beyond the arm on the side. The back is flat with horizontal tool marks; a margin *ca.* 1 cm. wide has been chiseled along the edge. Light-colored alabaster. 9.5 cm. by 10.3 cm. by 5.4 cm.

TC 1663 (Plate 47)

Stele with high relief of human figure. The head and feet are missing from the body, which characteristically exhibits strict frontality. The hands are placed across the stomach with the finger tips touching. The background, *ca.* 1.3 cm. thick, extends about 8 mm. out from the right arm but undercuts the left arm slightly. Poor quality alabaster. 15.5 cm. by 10 cm. by 4.5 cm.

TC 1664 (Plate 52)

Fragment of stele bearing right shoulder of human figure in high relief. The head is broken off at the level of the shoulders, exposing a drilled hole, apparently for hanging a necklace in place, *ca.* 4 mm. in diameter and 5 cm. in length, running behind the neck even with the face of the background. A hole was drilled from either side, and the two met to the right of center; the one drilled from the (viewer's) right is a little lower at the juncture than the one from the left. The background is 2.8 cm. thick at the side of the arm, from which it extends out nearly 1.5 cm. The background above the shoulder increases to a thickness of 4 cm. at the neck; it is polished smooth on the sides and back, as many of the stelae are. Alabaster, gray on the front, white at the back and right side. 8.5 cm. by 13 cm. by 8 cm.

TC 1776 (Plate 49)

Two adjoining fragments forming the upper part of a plaque or stele bearing in relief the figure of a man with his right hand raised in salutation. A raised margin, 3.5 cm. wide along the top, 2.3 cm. at the right side, surrounds the figure; the left side of the plaque is completely broken away. A tunic-like garment is draped over the right shoulder. Part of a dagger handle with pommel is visible in the center of the chest just above the break. Tooled dots in regular rows represent the texture of the beard, while the hair is indicated by equally spaced vertical and horizontal grooves (marking off raised squares of about 3 mm.). The background is recessed 2 cm. behind the border and is *ca.* 1.7 cm. thick. Rusty-brown alabaster. 15.1 cm. by 18.5 cm. by 3.6 cm.

The treatment of the hair is reminiscent of that of the archaic bronze statue of Ma'adkarib from the temple of the moon god 'Ilmaqah ('Ilumquh) at Mârib, as is the dagger. See Frank P. Albright, "Catalogue of Objects Found in Marib," in *Archaeological Discoveries in South Arabia* by Richard Le-Baron Bowen, Jr., and Frank P. Albright, in *Publications of the American Foundation for the Study of Man,* Vol. II (Baltimore, 1958), pp. 269f., no. 11, and p. 283, Figs. 196–98; also W. F. Albright, "Notes on the Temple 'Awwâm and the Archaic Bronze Statue," *Bulletin of the American Schools of Oriental Research,* No. 128 (December, 1952), pp. 38f.

TC 1846 (Plate 50)

Narrow stele, broken obliquely at the neck of the human head in high relief which it bears. A ridge at the edge of the break shows the line of the top of the left shoulder, indicating that the entire body may have been represented; the side of the shoulder was flush with the edge of the background plaque (cf. TC 1847). The top of the head was cut off flat at the hair line, and the tool marks from this operation remain. There are narrow eyebrow grooves and deep eye sockets. Nearly all of the long nose has been broken off. There are two horizontal grooves below the nose; the upper one was apparently intended to differentiate the moustache from the mouth, while the lower one separates the lips. Almost immediately below the lower groove is a circular depression, presumably for an inlaid goatee. The sculptured beard protrudes to a maximum length of 7 mm.

from the chin, with the size decreasing towards the ears. The stele itself averages 3 cm. in thickness. The back, now extensively chipped, seems to have been covered with horizontal tool marks. The sides and top of the stele are tooled even, but only the front surface was polished smooth. White alabaster with light brown streaks. 20.5 cm. by 9.5 cm. by 7.5 cm.

TC 1847 (Plates 47 and 48)

Stele, in two pieces which have now been rejoined, with the relief of a human figure. The upper part is broken off somewhat below the top of the shoulders, so the head is entirely missing. Drilled in from the side of the right shoulder and exposed for nearly its full length by the break (*ca.* 3 cm.), was a hole (diameter *ca.* 6 mm.) which ran down slightly toward the interior; except for the inner tip, which curved toward the rear of the piece, the hole was scarcely 1 mm. from the front surface. The background is about 3 mm. wider on each side than are the shoulders. The upper arms are at the sides of the body with the forearms directed forward; the left arm is broken off at the elbow; the fingers and thumb on the right hand are missing. The figure is clothed in a plain dress-like garment reaching to below the knees. The front of the body is flat, and this surface meets the perpendicular sides in a slight rounding; the height of the relief of the body is *ca.* 1.4 cm. The legs, nearly square in section, are separated from each other by approximately the width of one leg (1.5 cm.), with the background between them standing out slightly above that to the sides. The stubby feet, which rest on a high (5.5 cm.) pedestal, have grooves to mark off the toes.

The pedestal or base extends 2.5 cm. (maximum) out from the background, a distance equal to the thickness of the background. The face of the base has been partly polished, but not completely, for many of the deeper tool marks are still visible; it may have remained unfinished and an intended inscription possibly not added. Except for the right side of the base, the sides and back of the stele are polished smooth; the bottom is roughly tooled with some effort made at smoothing. White alabaster with rusty tint on some surfaces. 19 cm. by 8.4 cm. by 6.3 cm.

TC 1851 (Plate 46)

Fragment of a plaque bearing a high relief, comprising chest, shoulders, and upper arms of a man. A *himation* is draped over the left shoulder; it runs across and around the right side of the body, while what is presumably a loose end hangs down; the right shoulder is left bare. The arms are held out to the sides and bent at the elbows (cf. TC 1294); the left arm is broken below the elbow, the right arm at the elbow. The top of the right shoulder is broken off along with the head. Although the front of the body (maximum thickness 3 cm.) is flat, the arms are rounded nicely. Very little of the background, averaging 1.8 cm. in thickness, is preserved. The back of the plaque is polished smooth. White alabaster. 11.5 cm. by 25 cm. by 4.8 cm.

TC 1852 (Plate 48)

Fragment of a stele with a human figure in high relief. The head and part of the upper torso are broken away obliquely from the end of the right shoulder to the left hip; the background on the (viewer's) left, the elbow of the (object's) right arm, and the bottom of the stele (including the feet and the base) are also broken away completely. The hands are held across the stomach, palms flat against the body with the tips of the fingers touching (all the fingers are shown as having equal length). The front of the body is flat (*ca.* 2.6 cm. higher than the background), while the sides are beveled outward and the edges broadly rounded. The small section of background between the legs is 4 mm. behind the surface of the background at the side of the leg. The back of the piece is tooled with very large, long tool marks over 2 cm. apart running obliquely. A margin 1.5 cm. wide is evenly chiseled at the left (i.e., the viewer's left when looking at the back) edge of the back; the background is 2.2 cm. thick at this edge. Slightly grayish alabaster. 20 cm. by 15 cm. by 6.8 cm.

TC 2108 (Plate 52)

Fragment of a stele with a human figure in high relief. The head and right part of the body are broken away in a curve from left of the neck to the right hip; from this point the lower break runs back obliquely down to the left, leaving neither the bottom of the gar-

ment nor the legs. The left hand (none of the right hand is preserved) is held across the stomach with the palm inward; the tips of the fingers probably met those of the right hand. The fairly prominent breast, as well as the bracelet, indicates that this is the representation of a woman. The garment has a wide neck with a raised hem around it; a raised seam runs from the neck across the shoulder and down the side of the arm to the raised hem of the short sleeve. There is a bracelet on the wrist. The background (1.3 cm. thick) is flush with the outer side of the arm and curves inward with the line of the shoulder; the head was undoubtedly cut free. The back of the stele is polished smooth, but the edge of the background (which is slightly beveled) is chiseled even and only incompletely polished. White alabaster. 13 cm. by 8 cm. by 3.4 cm. (May belong with TC 506, but if so the intervening fragments are missing.)

TC 2173 (Plate 52)

Sculptured head of a man on a rectangular plaque. The lower right corner of the plaque is broken off, and the nose is chipped. The hair is indicated by vertical and horizontal grooves forming raised pyramidal squares between. The eyebrow grooves curve down toward the center of the face; the eye sockets appear rather close together. The nose is well proportioned and has depressions to represent the nostrils. Below the nose is a groove for inlaying a moustache. The mouth is a V-shaped groove. A round cutting below the lower lip apparently received an inlaid goatee. A large groove running under the chin from ear to ear, behind which is a sort of broad flange, held the plaster (?) whiskers in place. Alabaster. 17 cm. by 12 cm. by 8 cm. (This piece was photographed in Baltimore in 1953, but could not be found in the collection after 1958.)

TC 2530 (Plate 51)

Damaged stele with relief of a corpulent woman. The face, right forearm and hand, and the lower part of the body are broken away. The left hand clutches a symbolic offering against the stomach; the right hand is raised in salutation. The wide neck of the garment is bordered by a single row of incised dots. The breasts are represented as distinctly circular and rounded; the nipples are each a dot outlined with an incised circle. Two rounded ridges representing bracelets (or the hem of the sleeve and one bracelet) encircle the left wrist. On either side of the body, beginning immediately below the elbows, are segments of the twisted fringe of the garment which originally seemed to have formed a continuous fringe circling across the front of the skirt (cf. TC 553 and 1358).

The lower edge of the background plaque is not preserved. The half of the rear of the plaque behind the left side of the body is very roughly tooled, while the half behind the right side is chiseled quite even. The slightly curved line dividing the two areas is almost parallel with the side of the plaque. The thickness of the background varies from 3.1 cm. beside the right hip (the back is here chiseled even) to 4.4 cm. at the left side of the neck. The background slopes away from the body at all points preserved. The (viewer's) right edge of the stele is beveled, slanting in toward the back, while the small section of the left edge preserved is approximately square with the face. Grayish alabaster. 21.5 cm. by 18.5 cm. by 6.4 cm.

A striking parallel with raised right hand and small bundle against the stomach is in the Muncherjee Collection; it also has two bracelets at the wrist, but seems to represent a man. See *Dedalo*, VII, p. 741, right middle.

$$\longrightarrow \quad V \quad \longrightarrow$$

FRAGMENTS OF MISCELLANEOUS RELIEFS

TC 695 (Plate 53)

Fragment from a relief. This seems to be a very small part of a rather large scene. There is a bit of raised (1.1 cm.) border with traces of perpendicular grooves (flat on the bottom with vertical sides in section; 6 mm. wide, 2 mm. deep) spaced 2.5 cm. apart. That this is a margin or border seems to be confirmed by a fragment from the Timna' Temple (TTI 98); comparison can also be made with the upper margin of TC 900 (in the following chapter). Running into the border or margin is a raised (7 mm.) feature with longitudinal V-shaped grooves (5 mm. center to center); what this is intended to represent, perhaps a garment, wing or palm frond, is not at all clear. The background is 2.3 cm. thick near the raised feature, 2.5 cm. toward the other end of the fragment. The back has been chiseled fairly even, though tool marks are still visible. Alabaster, blackened on the front. 10 cm. by 8 cm. by 3.2 cm.

TC 853 (Plate 52)

Fragment of a relief bearing a segment of the trunk of a stylized tree with two sheath-like appendages, one slightly higher than the other. Traces of a third, higher yet, on the (viewer's) left indicate that they are on alternating sides of the trunk at evenly spaced heights; each has a shallow groove in the center following the curve of the sheath. The relief stands out 6 mm. from the background on the left side, 8 mm. on the right. The whole fragment is somewhat smooth from exposure. The back is very roughly tooled. The surface of the front was blackened by fire before the piece was broken. The complete scene most likely consisted of a palm tree flanked by mythological animals, a motif which is attested in a fragmentary relief from

the large temple excavated in the city of Timna' itself;[1] fragments TC 933 and 2534 also seem to belong to scenes of this type. Alabaster. 6.5 cm. by 10 cm. by 5.3 cm.

TC 933 (Plate 52)

Fragment of relief which flaked off at surface of stone due to heat (may possibly belong to the same relief as TC 853, above, since it also comes from the upper terrace of Complex III). Preserved is the hind part of the body of a mythological animal, most likely a cherub, with upper parts of the hind legs and back edge of the lower part of the wing. The relief is raised 7 mm. above the background. Alabaster, blackened by fire. 7.5 cm. by 6.5 cm. by 1.3 cm.

TC 1032 (Plate 53)

Fragment of bas-relief with upper margin preserved. Part of a crescent encircling the solar disc in a three-quarter circle is preserved. Above the recessed panel containing the relief a single crenelation in the form of a truncated triangle (2.6 cm. high and 6.5 cm. wide at the base, 2.2 cm. at the top) is preserved. It is divided into four horizontal strips, the face of each of which slants inward toward the bottom, leaving a slight offset; the crenelation itself is set above a plain raised border 8 mm. wide. At the left side of the panel is a flat raised border with beveled edges (1.6 cm. wide at the base); to the left of this are short sections of three successively recessed vertical strips, the face of each of which slopes inward toward the cen-

---

[1] See Ray L. Cleveland, "Cherubs and the 'Tree of Life' in Ancient South Arabia," *Bulletin of the American Schools of Oriental Research*, No. 172 (December, 1963), pp. 55–60; see references there for comparative material and for discussion of the origin of the motif in the art of Syria and Mesopotamia.

tral panel. The first is 1 cm. wide at the top (it has a beveled edge), the second 8 mm., while the third is not intact to its full width. The relief and the primary border are raised 3 mm. above the background of the panel. Calcareous sandstone. 11.5 cm. by 13 cm. by 4.6 cm.

For a discussion on one use of the crescent and disc motif, see Berta Segall, "Notes on the Iconography of Cosmic Kingship," *The Art Bulletin*, Vol. XXXVIII (1956), pp. 77f.

TC 2534 (Plate 53)

Fragment of a relief on a thick slab of stone. None of the original edges are preserved. Only a bit of the feathered wing in low relief from a cherub or similar composite animal, along with some unidentified and damaged feature in higher relief beside it, is preserved. The identification as a feathered wing is suggested by comparison of this piece with an alabaster plaque from Yemen, now in Istanbul, which bears the complete figure of a composite creature with wings displaying exactly the same treatment of the details (see H. Bossert, *Altsyrien*, pp. 99, 375, #1286). The other feature, which is *ca.* 1.2 cm. wide and 3.7 cm. long, has a groove along the center of it; there are aparently no parallels for this feature. Light-colored alabaster with a few rusty-brown flaws, blackened on part of the face. 7.5 cm. by 8 cm. by 7.7 cm.

See also A. Jamme, "Les antiquités sud-arabes du Museo Nazionale Romano," *Monumenti Antichi*, Vol. XLIII (1955), p. 98, Pl. XII, #480, which offers possible parallels.

VI

REPRESENTATIONS OF IBEX

Second only to bulls, ibex were the animals most frequently represented in the art of ancient South Arabia. This animal was undoubtedly far more common in ancient times than at present and may possibly have had some special significance in the superstitions or religion of the people, although the majestic appearance of the ram may in itself have been sufficient to inspire sculptors to attempt to capture its beauty in stone. The representation of ibex was not limited either to elaborate art forms or to the region of South Arabia, for depictions of the species have been found in nearly all parts of Arabia, often among the graffiti of pre-Islamic nomads.

Most frequently it was the head of the ibex, with the long heavy recurving horns, which was in art, not singly but in long friezes of duplicates, often stylized.[1] The heads on these friezes were sometimes for use on the edge of a table or altar, though they were frequently quite large, for use as decoration on architectural members. On the other hand, the entire body of the ibex in profile, often with greatly exaggerated horns, is found in low relief, especially in decorated panels around an inscriptional monument (as TC 900).

TC 546 (Plate 53)

Fragment from a large ibex-head frieze (like TC 962, 1047, 1093, and 1095), consisting only of a bit from the top of the head and part of the horns. The transverse ridges

[1] This art form, like so many others, has ancestors in the oldest centers of higher culture. For instance, an architectural scene on a fragment of an alabaster vase found at Ugarit has a row of ibex heads represented in profile across the top of a temple; see Claude F.-A. Schaeffer, *et al.*, *Ugaritica III* (1956), p. 165, Fig. 118, and p. 180, Fig. 126. The scene is dated by Ch. Desroches-Noblecourt to the very end of the XVIII Dynasty; *ibid.*, p. 218.

across the front of the horns, a characteristic of the species of ibex found in Arabia, are represented by rather deep horizontal grooves (shaped somewhat like chevrons). The background between the horns has not been cut away as deeply as that beside the head; in fact, the vertical center ridge or carination in it is flush with the surface of the horns, while from there it slopes back to some 5 mm. behind the surface of the horns at the edges. On the left of the head is a trace of the main background, which recedes rapidly from a depth of 1.5 cm. near the top of the fragment to *ca.* 3.5 cm. near the bottom of the fragment. Limestone, somewhat smoothed by weathering. 11 cm. by 8.8 cm. by 3.5 cm.

TC 852 (Plate 53)

Fragment of an ibex-head frieze with two heads preserved. The horns of the one on the (viewer's) right are broken off. The heads have an elongated, cylindrical shape, with the smooth horns blending into the head itself. The round bulging eyes are the only features indicated. The background between the horns is in the form of a rounded ridge which protrudes to the same plane as the horns and which tapers to a point at the intersection of the horns with the head. The background is rounded back below the head. White alabaster. 7.4 cm. by 6.2 cm. by 3 cm.

TC 859 (Plate 53)

Fragment from the right edge of a multiple-paneled relief; cf. *Handbuch der altarabischen Altertumskunde* (Copenhagen, 1927), ed. Ditlef Nielsen, p. 168, Fig. 61. The fragment contains the upper part of one panel with the large striated horn of an ibex facing left and the lower right corner of a panel above with the hind knee of a crouching ibex and trace of the tail. Between the two panels is a raised margin 2 cm. wide; the vertical margin along the right of the panels has a maximum width of *ca.* 3.8 cm. The background is recessed 3 mm. behind the surface of the flat relief and the margins; the background, as well as the striae on the horns, is covered with a thin rough coating of lime. Light-colored alabaster with a tan tint; a brown banding is exposed over the back surface of the piece. 10 cm. by 10.3 cm. by 6.4 cm.

For previously published examples of exaggerated horns recurving back to the tail, see *Sabaeica II*, p. 257, Photo 454, and *Altsyrien*, pp. 99, 378, #1295; also cf. TC 900 and 1071.

TC 900 (Plate 54)

A large fragment from the upper left of a monumental inscription, bearing part of a relief panel with an ibex to the right of the central inscribed panel and part of the bucrania frieze which ran across the top of the inscription and extended over the ibex panel to the left edge of the slab. At the very top of the fragment is a row of raised tegular panels resembling dentils; the only one with its width fully preserved is 3.8 cm. wide. These panels are 7 mm. apart and raised 5 mm.; they were at least 3 cm. from top to bottom; their faces slant outward toward the bottom. Above the band of tegular panels there was most likely a margin or decorated band, possibly with one or more louvred panels; cf *Handbuch der altarabischen Altertumskunde*, p. 169, Fig. 63; also A. Caquot and A. J. Drewes, "Les monuments recueillis à Maqallé (Tigré)," *Annales d'Ethiopie*, Vol. I (1955), pp. 27–29, Pl. IX-XI; and more particularly W. L. Brown and A. F. L. Beeston, "Sculpture and Inscriptions from Shabwa," *Journal of the Royal Asiatic Society*, April, 1954, Pl. XXII, Fig. 1, left.

The bucrania frieze is separated from the band of tegular panels above by a fillet 8 mm. wide; this fillet is even with the surface of the reliefs and with the borders and margins preserved on the fragment. At the (viewer's) left side of the bucrania frieze is a flat margin *ca.* 1.5 cm. wide. The heads, of which two complete ones, most of a third and a bit of a fourth are preserved, have an overall height of 9.4 cm. The heads themselves

occupy slightly less than one-half of this space, while the long, slender horns, curving up like the upright members of a lyre, occupy the rest. Between the horns of each head, a plain flat oval object, tapering slightly toward the top, reaches from the crown of the head to the upper margin. No details are shown on the heads, only the outline. Similar heads appear on the monument fragment found at Shabwa cited above, although on those heads the features are shown.

The bucrania on a fragment in the Kaiki Muncherjee Collection are interesting parallels; see Carlo Conti Rossini, "Dalle rovine di Ausàn," *Dedalo,* Vol. VII (1926–27), p. 742, left. Long horns such as these may be representative of those which actually appeared on some breeds of cattle, as is suggested by the treatment of horns in Egyptian art; see Heinrich Schäfer, *Von ägyptischer Kunst* (Leipzig, 1930), Pl. 28: 2. The elongated object between the horns, however, calls for some explanation, and its possible connection with the sun-disc and dual feathers of the Hathor cow cannot be overlooked; cf. Hans Bonnet, *Reallexikon der ägyptischen Religionsgeschichte* (Berlin, 1952), p. 279, Fig. 72. It is quite possible that bucrania of this general type were copied from Egyptian art, since the Hathor cult continued through the entire period of Qatabanian history. The bucrania panels in the Muncherjee Collection mentioned above may be of special significance in this respect, as suggested by the curious hatching of the central object.

Below the frieze of bulls' heads is a raised border 2 cm. wide above the ibex panel on the left and 1.8 cm. wide above the central inscriptional panel at the lower right of the fragment; this border intersects a vertical one 1.9 cm. wide which separates the ibex panel from the inscription. Of the ibex, which faces the inscribed panel, the neck, head and part of the exaggerated horn are preserved. Prominent chin whiskers are a feature of the head; the ear blends into the thick tip of the horn; cf. TC 1071, on which the tip of the horn touches the ear, but does not combine with it. While the ibex figure in profile on this fragment faces toward the inscription, others do not; see Rathjens and von Wissmann, *Vorislamischen Altertümer*, p. 113, Photo 67, and A. Jamme in *Monumenti antichi*, Vol.

XLIII (1955), Pl. v, 431; these two are so strikingly similar that one is tempted to assume direct copying.

White alabaster with dark bands along the back surface of the fragment. *Ca.* 26 cm. by 17 cm. by 7 cm.

TC 918 (Plate 53)

Small block with three battered ibex heads on it; the one at the right is mostly broken away. Limestone. 9.5 cm. by 8.5 cm. by 4.5 cm. (dimensions from field catalogue). (Carnegie Museum.)

TC 962 (Plate 57)

Large block bearing four ibex heads from architectural frieze. The plain, stylized heads may be described as being nearly cylindrical with a low carination down the center. At the lower end of each head is a flat, square protrusion, 2 cm. high and the same width as the head, to represent the chin whiskers. The round, protruding (and almost pointed) eyes are at the very edge of the head some 9.5 cm. above the end of the chin whiskers. At eye level the heads begin to widen toward the transversely ridged horns, which are 9 cm. long, and to blend into them.

The treatment of the background between the horns is the same as that on fragment TC 546, i.e., it has not been cut away as deeply as the background beside the head, and a central vertical carination is flush with the surface of the horns. From about 1 cm. below eye level to the base margin (*ca.* 15 cm.), there is a raised band about 1.5 cm. wide on the background running down from either side of each head. These bands are the stylistic vestiges of the shoulders and forelegs of the animal; cf. *Qataban and Sheba,* opp. p. 238, above (opp. p. 224, below, in the London edition), where the hoofs are clearly visible on a frieze pictured there. Directly beneath the chin whiskers and between the legs is a stylized representation of the lower part of the body in the form of a raised semi-circular disc *ca.* 3.6 cm. wide and *ca.* 2.7 cm. high. The distance between the legs, within a pair, varies from 4.5 cm. to 5 cm., while the space between pairs is *ca.* 1.5 cm.

The raised margin along the bottom of the face of the block is nearly 4 cm. wide. The lower margin, the legs and the body are

raised *ca.* 4 mm. above the background, while the heads themselves protrude about 5 cm. from the background. The cutting of the block on the two sides varies somewhat, apparently to fit against neighboring blocks; both sides are even along the front, but somewhat irregular with large tool marks toward the rear. The right side has a straight vertical edge at the front, but is slightly concave vertically behind the front margin and is beveled (sloping in toward the rear). The left side is similar, but more sharply beveled, forming an angle of about 66° with the face. The top is fairly even and is cut square with the face; near the back it becomes more uneven and slopes down slightly. The bottom, even at the front and rougher toward the back, is somewhat concave; it is approximately square with the face. The back is quite irregular. Fossiliferous limestone. 31.5 cm. by 37.5 cm. by *ca.* 25 cm.

TC 1000 (Plate 56)

Large stone block containing frieze of one damaged and eight complete ibex heads of the same size and type as those on TC 962. The principal differences are that the heads of TC 1000 protrude only *ca.* 4 cm. from the background, the horns curve back farther over the top of the block (but are actually shorter), and the horns are more widely spread apart immediately above the head. The stylized representations of the bodies are more squarish, and the raised lower margin is only 3 cm. wide. Only the left horn of the first head on the (viewer's) left is preserved, owing to the extensive damage done this end of the block by exposure to the weather. The top of the block is even and is square with the face, but it is of uneven width owing to the irregularity of the back. On the top, just behind the right half of the central head, is a clearly incised circle (3 cm. in diameter) with a line through it, i.e., the Old South Arabian character *w*; no traces of other letters can be seen, but the indistinct lines of a small + appear a little to the rear and right.

The entire right end of the block is fairly even and approximately square with the face, though not exactly, as it slants in slightly toward the rear; the side is not exactly vertical, since it slants inward very slightly toward the bottom. The bottom is entirely even, and it is square with the face, except where it has been cut into at the left end. This stepped cutting begins along the inside of the left leg of the third ibex from the end; the cutting, at the face, comes up 6 cm., within 1 cm. of the body of the animal, and then runs horizontally for 6 cm. to the outside of the right leg of the same ibex. At this point it turns upward again for 3.8 cm., rising to the level of the lower edge of the chin whiskers of the second head from the end; the cutting then continues horizontally to the weathered end of the block (some 14 cm. as preserved). The cuttings diminish in size toward the rear, i.e., the surfaces are not square with the face of the block. The left end of the block does not retain any of its original surface, but there is nothing to suggest that the frieze was originally longer. The back is irregular and has not so much as been tooled even. Fossiliferous limestone. 30 cm. by 82.5 cm. by *ca.* 20 cm.

TC 1047 (Plate 57)

Large block with frieze of four ibex heads very similar to those of TC 1000 except that the heads protrude *ca.* 5 mm. more. This frieze is somewhat unusual in that the nose and whiskers of the second head from the right is about 5 mm. longer than on the others. The top of the block is slightly rough and somewhat rounded. The sides are fairly even and are square with the face. The bottom is rougher and slants up toward the back. The back is irregular. Fossiliferous limestone. 30 cm. by 36.5 cm. by 18.5 cm.

TC 1071 (Plate 55)

Pair of ibex carved from a single stone. From either side the profile of an animal is seen in low relief. On the front the heads appear in high relief with the chin whiskers detached from the background (the whiskers have been broken from the head of the left ibex). On top, two pairs of horns curve in low relief as far down the back as the tails. The back of the object follows the profile of the animals, but lacks details of the legs. The flat bottom is rough with some pecked tool marks. White alabaster with yellowish striations. 16.3 cm. by 8.4 cm. by 12.2 cm.

TC 1093 (Plates 58 and 59)

Large block bearing frieze of four ibex heads nearly identical with those of TC 962. The legs are less weathered, and the narrowing of the fetlock joint and the widening of the hoof is therefore clearly visible. The low relief varies from *ca.* 4 mm. to 6 mm. in height. The raised lower margin tapers in width from 5.3 cm. at the right to 4.1 cm. at the left; the block is actually *ca.* 2 cm. higher at the right end than at the left, and part of this difference was made up in the increased width of the margin. The top of the piece is even and somewhat rounded. The sides are even along the front but rougher toward the rear; the right side is approximately square with the face, while the left side slants inward toward the rear. Except along the front edge, the bottom is rather rough with a number of tool marks; it is approximately square with the face. The back is irregular and thickens considerably toward the bottom. Fossiliferous limestone. 34 cm. by 38.5 cm. by *ca.* 24 cm.

TC 1095 (Plate 59)

Large block which formed an outside corner of an ibex-head frieze. There are four heads on the front of the block and one on the left end; all are similar to those of TC 962, TC 1093, and others. The snouts of all those on the front except of the second from the left are broken away. Although the head of the corner ibex on the front is only a maximum of 1.8 cm. from the corner, the head on the end is 3.4 cm. from the corner. This corner between the lower parts of the heads is treated as the shoulder of both animals and is cut off square at the top at the same level as the tops of the shoulders shown in relief elsewhere. The sides of the upper parts of these two adjacent heads and of the horns continue straight back until they meet in a 90° inside corner. The corner head on the front has a maximum depth of *ca.* 6 cm. from this corner, that of the head on the end only *ca.* 4.5 cm., the same distance as the completely preserved head on the front protrudes above the background. Owing to the unequal arrangement, the end ibex, as viewed frontally, is lopsided, for the (animal's) right shoulder and leg are of normal width (*ca.* 1.6 cm.), but the left leg is approximately 2.5 cm. wide.

The average maximum spread of the horns (outside measurements) of the four heads on the front is about 8 cm., but the horns of the ibex on the end occupy some 9.2 cm. The raised lower margin, appearing on both front and left end, is 3.5 cm. wide. The face of the end panel is 9.6 cm. wide. The top of the block is slightly rough and somewhat rounded. The right end is rough, and it is approximately square with the face. The bottom is fairly even, though marked by minor irregularities; it also is approximately square with the face. The back is quite irregular except at the left end, where it is cut in at an angle to the width of the end ibex panel. The 10 cm. or 11 cm. band on the back along the end with the head is fairly even, and it forms an obtuse angle with the face of the end. Limestone. 32.5 cm. by 39 cm. by *ca.* 22 cm.

TC 1144 (Plate 53)

Fragment of an architectural member, polished on the underside, with three stylized ibex heads from a longer frieze preserved on the front edge. The heads are characterized by straight lines and flat surfaces, bulging eyes placed high on the heads, and very short, V-shaped horns spread wide apart, the end of each running into the horn of a neighboring head. Inside the V of each pair of horns the background is smoothly chiseled in a beveled plane between each horn and the top of the block, forming a chevron tapering in width from the center to the ends. The top of the fragment, which must not have been exposed to view except along the front, has been chiseled even in the triangular space between the horns of each head, but it is otherwise rough and displays several long tool marks. Light-brown alabaster, striated in such a way that it has the appearance of the grain in wood, and discolored gray on the front and upper part of the break on the left. 5.3 cm. by 9.5 cm. by 9.5 cm. Cf. *Sabaeica II*, p. 258, Photo 457.

TC 1145 (Plate 53)

Fragment from the edge of an alabaster table top with an ibex-head frieze along the front. One of the two preserved ibex heads is complete except for the chin whiskers; long curving horns, rather narrow, and raised circular eyes are the only features indicated. The

other head, to the left, is preserved only from the eyes up; a rectangular mortise has been cut out where the lower part of the head would be. The sculptor may have broken the nose, then inserted a new piece of stone (now lost) in its place to complete the head rather than discard the entire frieze. The table top, 4.4 cm. thick, is polished on the top, but left rough on the bottom. Alabaster with bands of red, brown, and gray. 5 cm. by 7 cm. by 8.5 cm.

TC 1188 (Plate 60)

Fragment constituting the lower part of an ibex-head frieze, badly broken. Traces and parts of the noses of seven heads appear above an inscription reading *d̲tm/tkrbs/bs̆h*. Each end of the piece bears the profile of a kneeling ibex in low relief. A rounded groove running horizontally along the bottom of each profile, *ca.* 2 cm. above the lower edge of the stone, continues around onto the front until it intersects the nearest letter of the inscription, for it represents the outline of the leg of the animal, which the artisan felt compelled to indicate as far as possible on the front, as well as on the side. The fragment corresponds to the protruding member found on the end of H I 28 (from the site of Hajar Bin Ḥumeid). The noses of the ibex were rounded as those of TC 1145, rather than angular as those of TC 1144. At the upper rear of the fragment is a section of the raised margin of the table top and the polished surface of the depressed central part of the top. The raised margin or border is raised *ca.* 1.2 cm. above the main surface of the top; the central part of the table top is 3.8 cm. thick. The bottom of the protruding member bearing the ibex frieze drops 3 cm. below the rough bottom of the table top, as though it was designed to overhang whatever object the table rested on. Numerous parallel chisel marks appear on the bottom of the protruding member. The fragment has been subjected to burning after being broken. Dark mottled alabaster. 8.5 cm. by 17.3 cm. by 11 cm.

TC 1215 (Plate 60)

Fragment of ibex frieze preserving parts of five heads on the front. Traces of two pairs of horns belonging to the third and fourth head from the left end are visible on the top, along with indications that, at the rear, the horns met a raised margin of some kind. The left end of the frieze is preserved in a small area which depicts the neck of the animal on the end in low relief. The heads are rounded; low bumps indicate the eyes. The space between the two horns of each pair appears as a rounded ridge indiscernible in shape at the ends from the horns. White alabaster. *Ca.* 5.5 cm. by 12.4 cm. by 5 cm.

TC 1296 (Plate 60)

Two joining fragments of an ibex-head relief (including TC 1313). Of the six heads making up the complete frieze, which must have belonged to a larger object, only the second from the right is fully preserved, and it is lacking the tips of the horns. The stylized heads are elongated and cylindrical, tapering slightly in width toward the bottom. The end of the nose is cut off square with the background. The bulging eyes, circular as viewed from the front, are located high on the head and so near the edges that they form ridges running horizontally to the background. The cylindrical head is split *ca.* 6 mm. above the eyes to form the horns, which blend into the lines of the head; a ridge with a slight carination between the horns widens as the horns spread farther apart toward the top and back.

A profile of a head and presumably the body of an ibex were shown in relief on each end of the frieze. The right end, which is more complete, shows part of the horn, the head, the ear, the neck and the shoulders. Since the surface of the flat relief was made flush with the outside edge of the horn, the head itself is withheld some 5 mm. (maximum) on the front from the head as shown in profile, producing a somewhat grotesque appearance (in *Sabaeica II*, p. 258, Photos 458, 459, is an even more exaggerated example of the same phenomenon). The profile on the left end preserves a bit of the tip of the horn as it recurves up past the ear and within 3 mm. of it. Three or four tool marks in a straight row across the break on the front of the left fragment indicate that the frieze was deliberately broken. White alabaster. 10 cm. by 19.5 cm. by 6.7 cm.

TC 1445 (Plate 60)

Fragment of ibex-frieze. Three heads with the fronts broken off are present, along with the tip of one horn belonging to a fourth head on the right. As the top was left rough behind a chiseled margin, this fragment appears not to represent the edge of a table top, but rather an architectural member which was probably polished smooth on the lower side (as TC 1144). The preserved evidence indicates that the eyes were bulging stylizations on the sides of the heads rather than on the fronts. The horns were relatively short, thick and spread wide in a V, with a rounded ridge filling the space between the horns of each pair. White alabaster, with a dark-reddish band near the bottom. 5.7 cm. by 10.5 cm. by 5 cm.

TC 1642 (Plate 60)

Battered fragment of an ibex-head frieze. Parts of four heads are preserved. The best preserved (second from the left) has bulging eyes and large horns with a rounded ridge between them. The stylized head tapers considerably in width from top to bottom. The top of the piece is rough, but whether or not the underside was finished cannot be determined. Dark reddish-brown calcareous stone. 7.2 cm. by 11.2 cm. by 8.5 cm.

TC 1745 (Plate 60)

Fragment of an ibex-head frieze on which the lower parts of four stylized heads (similar to those of TC 1144) are preserved. The front of each head is in two beveled planes meeting in an angular ridge running down the center; the sides of the heads are straight, and they taper in width toward the bottom. The head at the right end of the fragment is twisted slightly in a counterclockwise direction to make the side of the head parallel with the vertical edge (from which it is separated by *ca.* 5 mm.) of the stone; the other end of the frieze is missing. The bottom is polished smooth, as would be appropriate for an overhanging architectural member. Alabaster with bands of white and pinkish-tan. 5 cm. by 12 cm. by 10 cm.

VII

REPRESENTATIONS OF BULLS

Along with the ibex, the bull stands as one of the two animals most frequently represented in the sculpture from the Timna' Cemetery. The bull's head, usually single and mounted on a plaque, is most common, although fragments of a few statuettes of complete bovines were also found. The heads are mostly executed in remarkably realistic detail, and the finer examples constitute some of the most attractive sculptured objects from the site. In artistic merit these heads rival, and in some cases surpass, the majority of the sculptured human heads.

In the case of the bucrania, as in the representation of other forms in South-Arabian art, strict frontality is observed, and alabaster is again the usual material. The heads are all angular to some minor extent, i.e., the front of the head is rather flat, and the sides are more or less perpendicular to it. The features generally indicated are the nostrils, the outline of the muzzle, the eyes (usually shown as being on the side of the head), the wrinkles above and in front of the eyes, the horns, and the ears.

The presence of these representations of the bull in the cemetery at Timna' verifies the great significance of the bull in the religious thought of the ancient Qatabanians, although what the association was is not clearly understood. Turning to another ancient Semitic culture for comparative material, we find that the place of the bull in Canaanite mythology seems to be somewhat parallel; in both cases the bull was associated primarily with a particular deity, but was apparently not considered to be sacred in itself. The presence of bucrania and other representations of the bull at Timna' in such quantities and the realism of the representation indicates that the sculptors of the city were quite familiar with bovines, as they were also well acquainted with the appearance of ibex.

TC 633
Fragment of bull's head, consisting of eye and stylized lines above and in front of it. Alabaster, blackened on the front. 5.5 cm. by 6.5 cm. by 2.2 cm.

TC 696 (Plate 61)
Fragment of a relief, preserving upper right corner of a recessed panel and part of the borders. The frontal view of a bull's head with striated horns and an acanthus leaf between them appears in low relief. The ears point out to the sides from the base of the horns; the upper end of the eyes, represented by two circular ridges, are at the same height as the ears. The relief touches the borders of the panel at both top and side. The upper margin had at least three bands; the lowest is raised 8 mm. above the background of the panel and is *ca.* 3.6 cm. wide; the second was a row of tegular panels 3.3 cm. wide, *ca.* 1.6 cm. high, *ca.* 5 mm. deep (they slant out toward the bottom), and separated by slots 4 mm. wide. Only a broken ridge is preserved to indicate that a third raised margin surmounted the dentil-like panels. To the right of the relief, traces of only two bands of the border remain: the one nearer to the relief is a plain band 1.1 cm. wide intermediate in height between the background of the panel and the wide band forming the lower part of the upper border; the second band, of which only a bit is preserved, was flush with the wide band of the upper border. The back of the fragment displays long horizontal tool marks. White alabaster. 13 cm. by 8 cm. by 5.3 cm.

Cf. Adolf Grohmann, "Zur Archäologie Südarabiens," in *Handbuch der altarabischen*

Altertumskunde, p. 169, Fig. 62, which shows a relief with a frieze of bucrania displaying somewhat similar treatment, although the horns are not striated and a stylized plant is represented above the head in place of an acanthus leaf.

TC 725 (Plate 60)

Sculptured bull's head projecting from a broken plaque of an undetermined kind. The upper part of the head is damaged; the horns and the right eye are missing. The mouth is indicated by a simple, but poorly incised, groove across the lower end of the head; two oblique grooves on the nose represent the nostrils. There is a straight groove across the face just above the nostrils, apparently to mark a fold in the muzzle. There are four ridges in front of the right eye, which is itself not preserved, and they circle part way under the eye. The ears are angular and are quite far back; the right ear extends farther down the side of the neck than does the left. The right edge of the plaque is not parallel with the vertical center of the head, but slants in toward the top at an appreciable angle. The plaque is 4 cm. thick, and the head, which is 6.7 cm. high, extends out 7 cm. from the face of the plaque. Dark alabaster with reddish-brown bands. 7 cm. by 5.9 cm. by 11 cm.

TC 733

Horn from bull's head. It is fairly small, with a maximum diameter of 2 cm. White alabaster with a brown band on one side. 3 cm. by 1.7 cm. by 2 cm.

TC 872 (Plate 68)

Small bull's head, badly damaged. Details of the features are not preserved. Three parallel grooves encircle the neck forming two narrow bands. The part of the object behind the neck is in the form of a block rounded on the bottom. Whether this head belonged originally to a larger object from which it has been broken or whether it is nearly complete is not clear; if the latter is true, then it was more likely attached to some kind of plaque. Limestone, yellowish on the surface. 3.7 cm. by 2.5 cm. by 6.2 cm.

TC 900

Fragment of a plaque with a band of bucrania in low relief; see **Chapter VI.**

TC 1019 (Plate 60)

Fragment of a thick relief, preserving the fore part of a bullock on its knees, facing right, including the front of the head. The background of the relief is recessed 3 mm. behind the border in front of the animal and below it; the face of this margin, which is beveled on the edges, is 1.5 cm. wide on the right and at least that wide at the bottom (full width not preserved). To the right of the margin is a panel or second margin recessed 6 mm. behind the first margin. Yellowish-white alabaster with brown banding on the back of the fragment. 10.5 cm. by 10.5 cm. by 5.9 cm.

TC 1038

Fragment of a small bull's head, consisting of left eye and left part of the muzzle. Stylized lines run vertically in front of the eye; a horizontal groove just above the lower break marks the limit of the hair and beginning of hairless nose proper. White alabaster. 3.7 cm. by 1.3 cm. by 2.3 cm.

TC 1177 (Plate 68)

Fragment of a large bull's-head spout with a groove through the top center. The upper right part of the head is represented by this fragment, with part of the side of the groove; the horn has been broken off entirely. The bulging eye is placed on the rounded corner between the front and side of the head. This head was nearly three times the size of the usual "offering-table" spouts which came from the city of Timna' itself. The treatment of the eye is completely different, as is also the treatment of the ear, which points upward, flush with the edge of the head rather than out to the side. This piece is more like an example of uncertain provenience published in *Sabaeica II,* pp. 276f., than others from Wâdî Beiḥân. The groove was 5 cm. deep and is 6 cm. from the outer side of the head; supposing a width of about 4 cm. for the groove, the total width of the head would have been about 16 cm. The position of the eye suggests a height of about 17 cm. for the head, which dimension fits in satisfactorily with the estimated width. Limestone. 9.5 cm. by 7 cm. by 14 cm.

TC 1216

Bull's horn, broken obliquely. White alabaster. Maximum diameter, 2.8 cm.; length, 5.5 cm.

TC 1277 (Plate 60)

Fragment consisting of right half of bull's head, broken vertically through the center. The horn, which was at the very front, is broken off. The ear, mostly missing, was joined to the background. Enough of the background is preserved to show that it was a plaque 2.2 cm. thick, with a roughly even back. The raised eye, which is nearly circular, is surrounded by a ridge with pointed corners at top and bottom; three vertical ridges curve around the front of the eye. The mouth is indicated by a single groove. White alabaster. 7 cm. by 3.2 cm. by 5.8 cm.

TC 1301

Bull's head, lacking the graceful proportions of most of the examples in this collection. There is a square tenon on the back. 9.5 cm. by 10 cm. by 7.5 cm. (dimensions from field catalogue). (Aden Museum.)

TC 1302 (Plate 62)

Bull's head, similar in appearance to TC 1390. The right horn is broken; there is a thickened band around the base of the left horn. The eye sockets (for inlays) are pointed at top and bottom. Five stylized ridges in front of each eye fan out toward the top. A double ridge runs around the end of the muzzle. The grooves representing the nostrils are shaped like tear drops. Alabaster. 17 cm. by 15 cm. by 12 cm. (dimensions from field catalogue). (Aden Museum.)

TC 1309 (Plate 62)

Bull's head. The right horn was broken off, but has been rejoined; the tip of the left horn is broken, and the end of the muzzle is chipped on the left. This head has an unusual bump centered on the top, but is otherwise similar to most of the other examples in the collection. The stylized vertical lines in front of the eyes exhibit a somewhat distinctive treatment, and there are vertical ridges above the eyes also. A raised band encircles the base of each horn, as is quite common. The nostrils are widely spaced and horizontal rather

than oblique. The mouth is indicated by a long narrow groove. Alabaster. 17 cm. by 11 cm. by 12 cm. (dimensions from field catalogue). (Carnegie Museum.)

TC 1310 (Plate 68)

Bull's head, similar to TC 1312, but having a circular depression in the center of each eye to receive an inlay. The right horn is broken off. 12 cm. by 11.5 cm. by 10 cm. (dimensions from field catalogue). (Marietta College Museum.)

TC 1311 (Plate 63)

Bull's head. The horns and ears are broken off. The eyes are outlined with ridges which meet in a point at top and bottom. Three broad, vertical ridges appear in front of each eye, curving down and back to a point below the center of the eyes; the one nearest to the eye in each case curves across the top of the eye. The eyes are on the side of the head, at the front, while these ridges are mostly on the front. A broad ridge runs across the top of the nose and curves around to the end of the nose on either side; simple oblique grooves represent the nostrils. Unlike most of the heads, this one has a vertical hollow on either side of the nose separating the muzzle from what has the appearance of wide jowls. The head extended out 8 cm. from a plaque or background, of which only traces are preserved. Highly polished white alabaster. 14 cm. by 9.5 cm. by 9.7 cm.

TC 1312 (Plate 62)

Bull's head, broken at the upper left side, so the horn and eye are missing. In front of the right eye are four vertical ridges, and another short pointed one fills in the space above the eye. A double ridge, in form like a composite bow, runs across the end of the muzzle; two crescent-shaped glyphs indicate the nostrils. The groove representing the mouth is nearly semicircular and placed far back, with the ends touching the background. None of the background itself is preserved, but a slight ridge at the break along the left side and bottom of the head indicates its position. A wide shallow groove, apparently added crudely after the head was finished, runs around the sides and top of the head between 1.5 cm. and 2 cm. out from the background. Its purpose is obscure, unless it was a cut designed to remove the head from the background (at the top, the break follows this line). Grayish-white alabaster. 14.5 cm. by 12.5 cm. by 7 cm.

TC 1327

Ear from bull's head, somewhat similar to those on TC 1602, but larger and supplied with a vertical depression on the outside to represent the concave part of the ear. Since a thin ear would be too fragile in stone, all of the ears observed on the heads of bulls have a thick backing and are nearly as deep as they are long; even so, few of them have survived intact. White alabaster. 2.7 cm. by 2.6 cm. by 1.8 cm.

TC 1328

Large horn, with more pronounced curve than usual, from a sculptured bull's head. A raised band *ca.* 7 mm. wide encircles the base of the horn; the maximum diameter of the horn above this band is 3.7 cm., the horn being oval in section. The preserved length of the horn (only the extreme tip is missing) from above the band is 5.3 cm. on the inside of the curve. The head from which this horn has been broken was about the size of TC 1390, i.e., *ca.* 19 cm. long. White alabaster with a very slight grayish cast. 7.8 cm. by 4.5 cm.

TC 1380 (Plate 60)

Bull's head, similar in size and appearance to the smaller bull's-head spouts found at Timna', but this piece (though flat on top) lacks the grooved channel. The horns, ears, and end of the nose are broken off. The left eye is a grooved circle, while the right eye is less regular and more in the form of a lozenge. Above and below each eye is a short wedge-shaped glyph; the two of them at each eye would coincide if extended through the eye. Three grooves in front of each eye form two ridges curved along the front and top of each eye. In section, the neck is in the form of a somewhat rounded triangle with an acute corner at the bottom. White alabaster with gray and orange streaks. 6.5 cm. by 6.3 cm. by 7.5 cm.

TC 1390 (Plate 63)

Large bull's head. The horns, ears, and rear part of the head, including all indications of possible attachment to a background, are missing. Several dozen small surface fractures or pits scar the front of the head. The realistically rounded muzzle has two horizontal ridges running across it above the widely-spaced, wedge-shaped glyphs incised to represent the nostrils. The mouth, near the back and partly broken away, is indicated by a broad groove. Four wide ridges in front of each eye curve back above the eyes. Round eye sockets, placed within recesses pointed at the two ends, are designed to receive inlays. The top of the head and front of the head meet in a slightly rounded right angle. A hole 5 mm. in diameter is bored straight down in the center of the top of the head to a depth of 2.5 cm. at a point about 1 cm. back from the front edge. White alabaster. 18.8 cm. by 14.5 cm. by 8.5 cm.

TC 1394 (Plate 68)

Neck of large bull's head with part of the base. The head belonging to this neck was approximately the same size, and perhaps shape, as TC 1804. The neck tapers in height from 16 cm. at the base to 12.2 cm. at the break, which is about 10 cm. out from the base; the width of the neck is more constant, varying from *ca.* 12.5 cm. at the base to 10.5 cm. at the break. The base, as preserved, has a maximum thickness of 4 cm., but may have been much thicker; on the right of the neck the base extends out approximately 1 cm. in a sort of flange following the curvature of the neck. This extension continues around to the center of the top; from this point the upper edge of the base or background panel departs on a horizontal tangent to *ca.* 2 cm. beyond the right side of the neck at which point it is broken off. None of the base is preserved on the bottom or lower left side of the neck. White alabaster with rusty colored banding. **17 cm. by 16 cm. by 15.5 cm.**

TC 1401 (Plate 68)

Hoof and lower leg from high relief of fore part of bull in frontal view. A bit of the base or raised lower margin on which the hoof rested is preserved on the right side of the hoof, and very slight ridges at the break at the rear of the leg verify the former existence of a background plaque. The cleft between the two parts of the hoof is represented by a vertical groove, V-shaped in section. Just above the hoof the fetlock joint is encircled by a rounded ridge. The lower part of the leg has a maximum width of 2.6 cm. Dark gray alabaster. 6.5 cm. by 3.8 cm. by 2.2 cm.

TC 1519 (Plate 64)

Complete stele with an inscribed panel at the bottom and a bucranium toward the top of a polished plaque. As viewed from the front, the top of the stele is bowed, i.e., it curves up toward the corners. The face of the plaque, which is of uniform width, is recessed 6 mm. behind the face of the inscribed panel, which may be considered to be a base in form. The bull's head is approximately two-thirds of the way up on the 22 cm.-high plaque. The upper right of the bull's head is missing and the left horn is broken off; the back of the ears are not separated from the background. Three stylized ridges run vertically in front of each eye; a double horizontal ridge, curving down slightly at the ends, runs across the front of the nose. The glyphs representing the nostrils are very short and are quite far apart; a curved groove indicates the mouth. The "base," 6.9 cm. high, bears a two-line inscription reading (1) *t̲wb'l* (2) *d̲yn'm*; see *JaPEHA*, p. 211, §369. All sides of the stele, including the back, are polished smooth except the right side, on which tool marks show through rough chiseling; the head is only 1.6 cm. from this edge, although it is 2.2 cm. from the left edge. The "base" is 4.5 cm. thick, while the plaque is 3.9 cm. thick. White alabaster with an orange streak near the bottom of the plaque. 29 cm. by 10.2 cm. by 7.9 cm.

TC 1602 (Plate 69)

Bull's head, little damaged except that the horns are broken off. A rectangular tenon on the back (5 cm. by 4.3 cm.; 3 cm. deep) was designed for attaching the bucranium to a background (perhaps a wall); the tenon is superficially chiseled even, but tool marks and other irregularities are still visible. The back of the head is chiseled even around the outer edge so the head would fit tightly against the background. The eyes are formed by slight recesses, pointed at top and bottom; in the center of each eye is a circular hole *ca.* 8 mm. in diameter to receive an inlaid iris.

In front of each eye are four stylized, vertical ridges which curve around the front of the eye. A slight ridge across the nose marks the top of the muzzle, while the nostrils are represented by small grooves which are placed rather far apart. The ears are thick projections cut off flat on the outside, rounded elsewhere. White alabaster. 10.3 cm. by 10.5 cm. by 10.8 cm.

TC 1605 (Plate 61)

Stele with a stepped base and polished plaque which carried the fore part of a bull in frontal view. The bull's head, which was sculptured in the round, has been broken off and lost; the legs, with the dewlap between them, have been preserved in relief. The figure, 9.5 cm. high from hoof to shoulder, stands about 2 cm. above the top of the base of the stele and is centered horizontally on the face of the plaque. The plaque itself, 19.3 cm. high, tapers in width from 12.8 cm. at the top to 9.1 cm. at the bottom and varies in thickness from 5 cm. at the top to *ca.* 4 cm. at the bottom (the face of the plaque slants inward toward the bottom to produce an offset at the juncture with the base).

As viewed from the front, the top of the plaque is bowed, i.e., it curves up toward the corners. On the front, the top of the base is about 9 mm. deeper than the lower end of the plaque, though the two parts are flush on the back; on the (viewer's) left the base is 1 cm. wider and on the right 1.4 cm. The base, 5 cm. high, is divided into two steps of equal height; the upper step is 11.8 cm. wide and has an average thickness of *ca.* 4.8 cm. It meets the lower step in an offset of *ca.* 3 mm. on the front and 7 mm. on either side; the lower step is approximately the same width as the top of the plaque (actually some 4 mm. wider, partly accounted for by the extreme corners of the plaque being broken off). The bottom of the base is chiseled even along the front, but is otherwise roughly tooled. The sides and top of the stele are polished smooth, while the back is rough, covered with short vertical tool marks. Light-colored alabaster with a rusty tint. 24.8 cm. by 13.2 cm. by *ca.* 5 cm.

TC 1637 (Plate 69)

Rear part of a small pedestal for a statuette of a bull, with back hoofs in place at the rear corners. The size of the base and the hoofs suggests a bull some 12 cm. long. The pedestal, which is preserved to a maximum length of 6.4 cm., appears to have been about 10 cm. long; it is 6.2 cm. wide and 1.2 cm. high. The hoofs have vertical grooves down the center marking the cleft. In the interval since the object was made, expansion of the stone has produced a longitudinal split near each side of the pedestal, in both cases going through one of the hoofs. All three preserved edges carry an incised decoration consisting of two bands (formed by three incised lines) with trios of vertical incisions spaced alternately in the two bands. Limestone. 2 cm. by 6.2 cm. by 6.4 cm.

TC 1686 (Plate 65)

Polished plaque with intact bucranium in upper center. The bull's head is 9.8 cm. high from the nose to the top of the forehead, and it extends out 5 cm. from the background. The ears are not cut free from the background, and each has a shallow groove in the outside to indicate the concave part of the ear. The horns are 3.5 cm. long (measured on the inside of the slight curve), and the base of each horn is encircled by a raised band. The angle formed by the top and front of the head is rather sharp, as is usual with the Timna' bucrania. The vertical eyes each have four stylized ridges curving around the front of them. The front of the muzzle is marked by a double horizontal ridge, the ends of which turn down. The nostrils, indicated by curved grooves, are close together. A curved groove represents the mouth.

The background plaque lacks any kind of margins or borders; it is about 5 mm. narrower at the bottom than at the top. The sides have been chiseled even and are square with the face. The bottom is beveled up toward the back at an angle of approximately 45° and exhibits two parallel, horizontal tool marks nearly as long as the width of the plaque. The top has been chiseled square with the face along the front edge; ca. 1.5 cm. back it slants downward and bears two horizontal tool marks which together extend nearly the entire width of the plaque. The back displays long oblique tool marks except near the left, where the marks are short and horizontal.

The background is ca. 4.8 cm. thick. White alabaster. 27.5 cm. by 21.5 cm. by 10 cm.

TC 1804 (Plate 68)

Large sculptured bull's head. The front of the head is broken off just in front of the ears, while the neck is broken ca. 5.5 cm. behind the ears, leaving no indication of the background to which it was joined. The left ear, which is undamaged, extends 3.3 cm. out from the head; the outer side of it has a vertical depression to represent the hollow of the ear shell. Radial incisions in the depression indicate the veining of the ear; the tip and upper side of the right ear are broken, but it is otherwise the same as the left. A groove curving in the form of a tall U represents the mouth. White alabaster with rose and rusty colored streaks. 15.8 cm. by 14 cm. by 10 cm.

TC 1805 (Plate 60)

Bull's head, of the smaller size belonging to a plaque. The piece is broken obliquely from behind the right eye to the front edge of the left ear (of which a trace remains). The left horn is entirely missing, while the right ear is partly broken off. Three stylized, raised bands appear in front of each eye. The muzzle is shown by a pronounced thickening, especially at the sides. Two curved grooves, rather widely spaced, indicate the nostrils. Light-colored alabaster with rusty-brown streaks. 6.4 cm. by 6.3 cm. by 4.2 cm.

TC 1880 (Plate 66)

Stele with bull's head centered horizontally on the face near the top. Both horns are broken off, but the ears, although detached from the background by a space of 9 mm., have survived intact. The outside of each ear has a rounded depression to represent the concave part of the shell. The eyes are nearly circular, but pointed on top and bottom. Four stylized, raised bands appear in front of each eye, running vertically from a line even with the lower end of the eye up to the base of the horn. An additional oblique band appears above each eye, tapering to a point near the front center of the eye. The sides of the muzzle are thickened and have a puffy appearance. A single flat ridge runs across the front of the nose. The grooves representing the nostrils are a little longer than usual; they stand nearly parallel to each other, curving inward at the bottom. The head protrudes a maximum of 4.4 cm. from the background.

The background itself, broken on both the upper and lower corners on the (viewer's) left, is 4.5 cm. thick. It tapers from an estimated original width of 20.5 cm. at the top to an estimated original 16.3 cm. at the bottom. The sides and top of the stele are polished smooth, while the bottom, which slants up somewhat toward the back, is chiseled even. The back is rough, displaying large horizontal tool marks, except at the sides, where margins have been chiseled even. White alabaster with rose and rusty colored streaks (as the stone of TC 1804). 27.1 cm. by 19 cm. by 9 cm.

TC 1889 (Plate 68)

Fragment of a stele bearing a bucranium. The fragment consists of the upper right corner of a polished plaque preserving the outline of most of the bull's head, which has been broken off except for the left ear. The left edge of the plaque is broken off almost vertically through the extreme tip of the ear on that side; the lower break runs slightly upward across the nose toward the right edge of the plaque. The head, excluding the ears, was 6.5 cm. wide and an estimated 5.5 cm. long. A hole about 7 mm. in diameter was bored 2.2 cm. into the background immediately above the center of the head. The plaque, 4.5 cm. thick, tapered sharply in width toward the bottom; it had an estimated width of 12 cm. at the top, which is bowed (i.e., curved up toward the corners), and an estimated width of 9 cm. at the lower break. The right side and top are polished; the back exhibits many short oblique tool marks, except along the edges, where margins have been chiseled. Grayish alabaster with a red streak at the lower break, blackened by fire at the right, over the back, and on part of the front and top. 9 cm. by 9.2 cm. by 6 cm.

TC 2018

Bull's hoof and lower leg, apparently from a statuette slightly smaller than TC 2079. A groove on the front of the hoof represents the cleft between the two parts. A horizontal groove running around the front and sides

above the hoof marks the lower limit of the fetlock joint. The leg above this point is smaller than the joint. White alabaster with a slight rusty-gray tint. 2.5 cm. by 1.4 cm. by 1.9 cm.

TC 2076 (Plate 66)

Stele, broken across the lower part into two pieces, with a bull's head centered on the face near the top. The horns are broken off, while the ears (which are not detached from the background) are preserved. There are four stylized ridges in front of each eye and a curved band across the nose above the nostrils. The plaque, 3 cm. thick, has nearly vertical sides. Alabaster. *Ca.* 29 cm. by 14 cm. by 7 cm. (dimensions from field catalogue). (Aden Museum.)

TC 2079 (Plates 68 and 69)

Pedestal or base for the statuette of a bull. Of the statuette itself, only three of the hoofs are preserved (the left hind hoof is broken off, leaving a hollow in the surface). Four horizontal bands extend around the sides and front, each of the upper three recessed slightly behind the one below; the rear of the pedestal is plain, though polished smooth. The top of the pedestal measures 6.1 cm. wide and 13.2 cm. long, while the bottom is 7.1 cm. by 14.1 cm. The three offsets between the bands average only about 1 mm. each, but the faces of the upper bands slant inward toward the top, thus producing increased diminution in width and length. The heights of the bands (from top to bottom) are *ca.* 1.3 cm., 1.4 cm., 1.9 cm., and 2.6 cm.; there is a slight bevel on each offset which is not included in these measurements. The total height of the pedestal is 7.3 cm. Each of the upper two bands on the front bears one line of inscription: (1) [y]ḥm'[l/] (2) [ḥ]d[r]n. The first letter of line 1 is entirely restored, and the upper parts of the last two characters in that line are missing; only the lower tip of the first letter of line 2 is preserved, and of the third letter there seems to be the lower tip of an *r; cf. JaPEHA,* p. 107, §235. White alabaster with yellowish tint. 8.2 cm. by 7.1 cm. by 14.1 cm.

TC 2182 (Plate 67)

Plaque with a bull's head filling much of the face, broken off obliquely at the lower edge of the head, which is intact except for the tips of the horns. The head does not extend out from the background as far as most of the examples do. The nose is not undercut at all, and the horns (which are cut free) are so near to the background that the ears had to be placed in relief below rather than behind the horns. The horns are very short (estimated length 4 cm.) and broad (4.2 cm. in diameter at the base); the base of the horns is marked by a groove. Each eye is formed by a circular groove *ca.* 1.4 cm. in diameter, which has a short vertical groove above and below. Three stylized ridges run vertically in front of each eye. Two parallel grooves mark a band in the form of a composite bow across the muzzle just above the nostrils. The nostrils are depicted by almost circular depressions coming to a point at the lower end; these are on the front rather than the bottom of the nose. There is a long narrow groove across the bottom of the nose to mark the mouth. The background plaque, 3 cm. thick, is polished on all sides, including the back. Grayish alabaster with brown streaks. 19.8 cm. by 25.7 cm. by 7.8 cm.

TC 2218 (Plate 68)

Small conical object with flat bottom and bull's head at apex. The sloping sides are straight to within 2.5 cm. of the small end; there is a small offset at this point, where the narrower neck begins. The neck is *ca.* 1.5 cm. long, while the head takes up only about 1 cm. The head is quite crudely made with very angular features. The body of the object is *ca.* 4 cm. high from bottom to the beginning of the neck; in this distance it tapers in diameter from 3.1 cm. to 2 cm. The object seems to have been a gaming piece or possibly a

weight (it weighs approximately 85 gm.). White alabaster with brown striations at the top. 6.5 cm. by 3 cm.

TC 2244

Spout in the form of a bull's head, badly weathered. Ridges at the break indicate that the fragment was broken at the point where the neck joined the body of some larger object, very likely some kind of offering table. Details of the features are obscured by the weathering. A groove about 5 mm. wide runs vertically down the front, centered between the bulging eyes and large nostrils. The larger longitudinal groove on the top is 2.4 cm. wide and 1.5 cm. deep. Sandstone. 5.5 cm. by 6.2 cm. by 8.8 cm.

Cf. Rathjens and von Wissmann, *Vorislamische Altertümer*, pp. 54ff., where objects of a similar type are interpreted as roof spouts which functioned like the lion-headed spouts **of Greek cornices.**

TC 2505 (Plate 69)

Broken bull's head. The muzzle and part of the left eye are preserved. A rounded ridge outlines the eye, which is pointed at top and bottom. Four stylized vertical ridges appear in front of the eye. A narrow raised band, which turns down at either end, runs across the nose about 1 cm. above the nostrils. The nostrils, which are in the form of triangular glyphs, are on the front of the nose rather than on the bottom. A groove curving back in a semicircle indicates the mouth. A trace of the background on either side of the nose shows that the head protruded 5.3 cm. from a polished plaque. Light-colored alabaster, blackened on the front of the head by fire. 15.5 cm. by 12.6 cm. by 9.5 cm.

VIII

MEMORIAL STELAE WITH UNDECORATED PLAQUES AND INTEGRAL INSCRIBED BASES

During the second campaign of excavation in the necropolis of ancient Timna' several dozen memorial stones were found which are characterized by their stark simplicity and austere beauty, thirty-four of which were available to the writer for study. Each of these memorials, mostly rather small, are made of a single piece of stone (exclusively alabaster), but nevertheless have two distinct formal parts, a highly polished flat plaque without any decoration above and an inscribed base below. The base is usually wider than the plaque and sometimes deeper as well. Several of the bases are stepped, i.e., have two or more horizontal bands successively recessed (TC 714, 1523, 2009, 2082, and 2183). The inscriptions consist only of the name of the individual and the name of his (or her) clan or tribe. The greater part of each piece is generally the upper plaque, always highly polished in an even plane without any suggestion of decoration. Many of them flare out slightly toward the top and have a concave frontal view at the top vaguely suggestive of the inside of a crescent (see TC 1522, 1616, 1736), while other examples are straight across the top and have rounded corners (as TC 1621, 2078). What significance the bowed shape of the top may have had can only be conjectured.

The stelae with integral bases are to be regarded as a variation of the stelae with polished plaques and separate bases, generally of limestone, which far out-number them (see Chapter IX: Memorial Stelae with Separate Bases). The inscribing of the name on both varieties calls for no special explanation, but what meaning the ancient South Arabians may have attached to the undecorated polished plaques remains rather in the realm of

speculation. It may well be, however, that they bear some relationship to the *maṣṣēbôt* of Canaan and the *'anṣâb* of central and northern Arabia.

The inscriptions on the majority—but by no means all—of the objects in this group and the groups immediately following were published by Albert Jamme, W.F., in his *Pièces épigraphiques de Ḥeid bin 'Aqîl*. These objects are being republished in the present catalogue with additional photographs and, in some cases, more detailed descriptions. Having as much of the collection as possible together in one publication should render it more conviently accessible.

TC 685 (Plate 70)

Fragment of a stele broken off just above the top of the base, so scarcely any of the polished plaque is preserved, though the base is complete. The piece is polished on the front and bottom, roughly tooled on the sides and back. The base extends *ca.* 1.2 cm. out from the edge of the plaque on either side. The upper corners of the base, which is 2.6 cm. high at the ends, are beveled and slightly rounded. The one-line inscription which nearly fills the face of the base reads *ddnmr/ḥdrm*; see *JaPEHA*, pp. 145f., §291 and photograph on Pl. ii, center. The plaque is 6.7 cm. wide. Alabaster. 4.7 cm. by 9.7 cm. by 2.7 cm.

TC 714 (Plate 70)

Stepped base with traces of a plaque along the break at the top. The plaque was *ca.* 10 cm. wide at the face (*ca.* 9.7 cm. at the back) and 3.8 cm. deep. The base consists of three successively recessed bands, or steps, on the front and sides. Each of the bands slants inward slightly toward the bottom on both front and sides, and at each band the base (like the plaque) is slightly narrower at the back than at the face. The upper band is offset 1.5 cm. from the plaque on the front, 5 mm. on the left side (and presumably the same on the right side, where the outline of the plaque is not preserved). At this band, the base is thus 11 cm. wide at the face (*ca.* 10.7 cm. at the back) and 5.4 cm. deep; this upper band has a height of 2.5 cm. The central and lower bands are each offset *ca.* 5 mm. on the front and *ca.* 4 mm. on the sides from the step above.

At the central band the base is 11.6 cm. wide at the face (11.2 cm. at the back), and 5.5 cm. deep; this band is 2.8 cm. high. At the lower band the base is 12.4 cm. wide at the face (12 cm. at the back), and 5.9 cm. deep; this band is 3.2 cm. high. The face, sides, and top of each step is highly polished (though now chipped in many places), the corners are all rounded, and the offsets are slightly beveled. On the face of both the upper and the center band appears one line of inscription reading (1) *yšrḥ'tt* (2) *ṣmt*; the second line is very widely spaced in order to fill the entire line; cf. *JaPEHA*, pp. 163f., §320 and photograph on Pl. IV, above. The back of the piece is flat and rough with large horizontal tool marks. The bottom of the base slants upward toward the back. White alabaster with rusty tint. *Ca.* 9.6 cm. (maximum preserved height) by 12.4 cm. by 5.9 cm.

TC 741 (Plate 70)

Fragment of a stele, consisting of the base and the lower part of an undecorated plaque. The base is offset *ca.* 1 cm. from the plaque on both the front and the sides, but the back is flush. The plaque is 14.3 cm. wide and 2.8 cm. thick; broken obliquely, it is preserved to a maximum height of 5.2 cm. above the top of the base at the left side. Near the center of the plaque, which is polished smooth only on the face, is an oblong hole (3 cm. long) passing through the stone and representing a flaw; four smaller holes of the same kind appear in the base, but these do not go through. The face of the base, 6 cm. high, bears a one-line inscription near the top reading *bḥrm/mhṣn'm*; see *JaPEHA*, pp. 152f., §302. The bottom of the stele is irregular, as are the sides to a lesser degree. The back is rough

with long, wide, oblique tool marks. White alabaster. 11.5 cm. by 16.8 cm. by 4.3 cm.

TC 990 (Plate 70)

Base of a stele, with the outline of a plaque at the break on the top. The face of the base was flush with the face of the plaque, but the sides of the base extend beyond the edge of the plaque (1 cm. on the left, 1.2 cm. on the right). The plaque is 6.8 cm. wide near the face, 6.5 cm. at the back. A two-line inscription on the base reads (1) *rzḥn* (2) *drḥn*; cf. *JaPEHA*, p. 60, §165. The face of the base was chipped at the lower edge near the right before the lettering was incised, and the first letter of the lower line is crowded to the left. The face of the stele is polished, but the sides and bottom are only chiseled even; the back was left rough with tool marks. The angle formed by the face and the bottom of the base is slightly acute. White alabaster. 5.3 cm. by 8.9 cm. by 4 cm.

TC 1107 (Plate 70)

Base of a relatively thick stele, less finely finished than most of the examples in alabaster. Traces of the plaque remain at the break along the top. The sides, back, and bottom are roughly tooled. A beveled offset of 2 mm. separates the base from the plaque; this offset continued around to the rough sides, but appears as scarcely more than a shallow groove there. The polished front bears a two line inscription reading (1) *twbn* (2) *wqš*; see *JaPEHA*, pp. 143f., §287. White alabaster with rusty-brown imperfections. 6 cm. by 7.2 cm. by 4.9 cm.

TC 1213 (Plate 70)

Complete stele with polished plaque and integral base. As seen from the front, the plaque is straight across the top, has rounded upper corners, and tapers in width toward the bottom, where it meets the base in an offset. The width of the base is equal to the greatest width of the plaque (near the top). The one-line inscription on the face of the base reads *n'mt/dr't*; see *JaPEHA*, pp. 135f., §278. Alabaster. 16 cm. by 10 cm. by 5 cm. (dimensions from field catalogue). (Carnegie Museum.)

TC 1333 (Plate 70)

Fragment of a stele, consisting of the base and the lower end of the polished plaque. The base was deliberately chipped at the bottom with a tool which left a mark. The plaque, broken off horizontally, is 11 cm. wide at the face (10.8 cm. at the back), *ca.* 3.3 cm. thick, and it is preserved to a maximum height of 1.5 cm. above the top of the base. It meets the base in a beveled offset of 5 mm. on the front, 6 mm. on the left side, and 8 mm. on the right side. The faces of both the plaque and the base are polished smooth. The sides of the piece are chiseled even, but the back and bottom are very rough and exhibit large tool marks. The face of the base is 6.3 cm. high and bears a one-line inscription near the top reading *m'dkrb/mhṣ[n'm]*; see *JaPEHA*, pp. 153f., §303. The upper left face of the base has been chiseled off flush with the face of the plaque in an irregular area; this was done after the inscription was completed and obliterates all of the last three letters and the upper parts of the preceding four (including the word divider), but they are virtually certain nonetheless. White alabaster. 8.3 cm. by 13.2 cm. by 4.5 cm.

TC 1364 *(Plate 70)*

Base of a stele with the outline of a plaque at the break on the top. The plaque was 13.1 cm. wide at the face (*ca.* 13.3 cm. at the back, as the right edge is not square with the face) and *ca.* 3.4 cm. in maximum thickness; it is set back *ca.* 6 mm. from the face of the base. The base is *ca.* 1.8 cm. wider than the plaque on both sides. A one-line inscription, in large letters placed toward the top of the face of the base, reads *r'b'm/ḏḏrḥn*; see *JaPEHA*, p. 59, §163. The back of the base is extremely irregular. An even margin *ca.* 2 cm. wide was chiseled on the edges of the sides and bottom bordering on the face. White alabaster. 9 cm. by 16.8 cm. by 7.4 cm. (average thickness, *ca.* 6 cm.).

TC 1378 *(Plate 70)*

Small stele, badly battered and chipped, consisting of undecorated plaque and integral base. The base is 3.2 cm. high, the plaque 7.7 cm. The plaque is the same width at the top as the base (6 cm.), but since it tapers to 5.2 cm. at the point where it meets the base, there is an offset of 4 mm. on each side, and these offsets are beveled. The lower 1.5 cm. of the face of the plaque is slanted inward to

form a beveled offset of *ca.* 2 mm. with the base. A one-line inscription on the front of the base reads *[w]hbm/rḥb[n]*; see *JaPEHA*, pp. 166f., §325. The back of the stele is somewhat rounded, but remains uneven. White alabaster. 10.9 cm. by 6 cm. by 4 cm.

TC 1522 *(Plate 71)*

Stele with an undecorated plaque and an integral inscribed base. The top of the plaque is bowed, i.e., it curves up toward the corners. The plaque tapers from a width of 11.3 cm. at the top to 8 cm. at the bottom and is *ca.* 10.5 cm. high. The base, which is 4.5 cm. high and 9 cm. wide, is *ca.* 5 mm. wider on both sides than the bottom of the plaque, which it joins in a beveled offset. The lower 8 mm. of the face of the plaque slants in toward the bottom, leaving a shallow beveled offset where it meets the base. The one-line inscription on the upper half of the face of the base reads *s'd'l/m'hr*; see *JaPEHA*, p. 120, §254. The back of the stele is extremely rough, with several large vertical tool marks visible, and it is vaguely rounded. The edges at the top and sides adjacent to the face are chiseled even. The back of the base is cut off obliquely at the bottom. White alabaster. 15 cm. by 11.3 cm. by 5 cm.

TC 1523 *(Plate 71)*

Stele with a small, undecorated plaque and an inscribed, stepped base. The plain upper part, or plaque, chipped at both upper corners on the face, tapers slightly in width toward the bottom (6.6 cm. to 6.1 cm.); the upper corners are rounded, and the top, which slants down somewhat toward the rear, is rounded down onto the back. The flat, polished face is 8.8 cm. in height; the polished sides, especially the left one, slant in toward the back, with the result that the back of the upper part of the stele is on the average 1 cm. narrower than the front. The stele is relatively quite thick in proportion to its height and width, having a maximum thickness (near the top) of 4.8 cm. The upper part of the stele meets the base in a concavely beveled offset on the front and sides (averaging *ca.* 3 mm. offset).

The base has two horizontal bands around the front and sides, the upper recessed behind the lower, and these give the impression of two steps. The upper step is 6.8 cm. wide at the face (6.3 cm. at the back) and 2.5 cm. high. It meets the lower step in a concavely beveled offset of *ca.* 2 mm. on the front, 3 mm. on the right side and 4 mm. on the left side. The lower step was 7.9 cm. wide at the face (it is now chipped on the right; 7.6 cm. at the back) and 3.5 cm. high. On the face of each step appears one line of inscription reading (1) *ḏrmt* (2) *ġrbm*; see *JaPEHA*, p. 84, §198. The back of the stele is slightly convex and is covered with closely spaced horizontal tool marks. The bottom of the stele, which forms a slightly acute angle with the face, is roughly tooled. The top is partly smoothed, but irregular. Light-gray alabaster. 14.8 cm. by 7.9 cm. by 4.8 cm.

TC 1541 (Plate 70)

Inscribed base from a broken stele. The break at the top slants down toward the rear; not enough evidence is preserved to indicate for certain that this was an integral stele and not a separate base. Most of the lower half of the face has been chipped away, leaving only the upper tip of the first and last letters in the second line of the two-line inscription, which reads (1) *n'mm* (2) [. .]*m*. The spacing suggests that there were only three letters in the second line, but this depends on whether the first letter was *d*, *n*, *s*, or *q*. The sides, back, and bottom of the base are somewhat irregular, but tool marks have been worn away. Rusty-brown alabaster with light striations. 6.5 cm. by 8.1 cm. by 4.8 cm.

TC 1573 (Plate 70)

Lower part of a relatively large stele, broken diagonally from near the lower left corner up to the right side of the undecorated, polished plaque. The face of the base and the plaque above it are flush, divided only by a shallow groove at the level of the offset of 1 cm. on the side (preserved only on the right) which indicates the top of the base. The preserved height of the stele above the top of the base is *ca.* 7.5 cm. The edge of the plaque slants inward slightly toward the bottom, indicating that the width of the plaque tapered from top to bottom. Toward the top of the polished face of the base, which is 7.2 cm. high, is a one-line inscription, with guidelines at top and bottom, reading *lḥym/yl'[b]*. Only

the lower end of the last letter is preserved; see *JaPEHA*, p. 111, §241. The sides and bottom of the piece are smoothed for *ca.* 1.5 cm. along the edges adjacent to the face, but the rest of the sides and bottom is rough. The bottom forms an acute angle with the face, and the rear part slants up toward the back. The back is rough, with long horizontal tool marks 2 to 3 cm. apart. Light rusty colored alabaster with a few red bands. 15 cm. by 16.5 cm. by 6.5 cm.

TC 1615 (Plate 71)

Stele consisting of an undecorated plaque and an integral inscribed base. As seen from the front, the upper corners of the plaque are broadly rounded; it is 11.5 cm. high and tapers in width from 10 cm. near the top (below the curve of the rounded corners) to 9.5 cm. near the bottom. The base is distinguished from the plaque by a shallow offset on the front and sides. The base is 5 cm. high, 10.4 cm. wide at the face, and *ca.* 8.7 cm. wide at the back; the bottom of the base is chiseled even and is approximately square with the face. The one-line inscription which nearly covers the face of the base reads *kbrm/ḏrḫn*; see *JaPEHA*, pp. 47f., §149 and photograph on Pl. xv, below. The back of the stele, quite rough, is rounded in horizontal cross section, and it diminishes in thickness near the top. Light-colored alabaster without luster. 16.3 cm. by 10.4 cm. by 4.7 cm.

TC 1616 (Plate 71)

Stele with a polished plaque and an integral inscribed base. The plaque, averaging *ca.* 3.5 cm. in thickness, tapers in width from top to bottom (from 6.8 cm. to 5.4 cm); in frontal view, the top is bowed, i.e., curved up toward the corners. The base, in contrast with the plaque, increases in width from *ca.* 6.4 cm. at the top to 7.5 cm. at the bottom. It meets the plaque in a beveled offset of *ca.* 5 mm. on the front and approximately the same on the cruder sides. The two-line inscription on the face of the base reads (1) *r'b'm* (2) *qḥlwm*; see *JaPEHA*, pp. 126f., §264 and photograph on Pl. xvi, above. The bottom of the base is square with the face and, like the top and sides, chiseled even. The back of the stele is irregular. White alabaster. 15 cm. by 7.5 cm. by 4.3 cm.

TC 1621 (Plate 71)

Stele with a polished plaque and an integral inscribed base. The top of the plaque is flat, and the upper corners are rounded (as viewed from the front). The plaque tapers in width from 9.5 cm. at the top to 8.3 cm. at the bottom. The face of the plaque is flush with that of the base, from which it is separated by a rounded groove (*ca.* 7 mm. wide), which is partly smoothed, but with tool marks still visible. The height of the plaque, measured from the center of the groove, is 14 cm., and it averages 5.5 cm. in thickness. The face of the base, measuring 6 cm. by 9.9 cm., bears two lines of inscription reading (1) *skynt* (2) *ḏrḥn*; see *JaPEHA*, pp. 51f., §154. Tool marks are visible on the top, sides (where they are horizontal), and bottom of the stele. The front edges of the sides and bottom have been partly chiseled even and superficially polished. There is a curved offset on either side of the stele where the wider base meets the plaque. The right side of the stele slants inward toward the rear. Large horizontal tool marks appear on the back. Light-colored alabaster with yellow cast. 20.4 cm. by 9.9 cm. by 6.6 cm.

TC 1641 (Plate 72)

Stele, consisting only of a polished plaque with an inscription rather crudely incised on the lower part of the face. The upper left corner and top are chipped. The top is slightly bowed, i.e., it curves up toward the corners as viewed from the front. The piece tapers in width from an estimated 9.8 cm. at the top to 7.2 cm. at the bottom. The two lines of inscription on the lower part of the polished face read (1) *yḥrm/m* (2) *ḥḍrm*; see *JaPEHA*, p. 154, §304. The bottom of the stele was chiseled even and is approximately square with the face. The sides were chiseled even along the face, but are now somewhat battered. The back is irregular and displays several large tool marks. Mottled alabaster with striations roughly parallel to the face. 14.5 cm. by 9.3 cm. by 6.4 cm.

TC 1678 (Plate 72)

Stele with a polished plaque and an integral inscribed base. The plaque is rounded at the top, as viewed from the front, and tapers in width from 9.6 cm. near the top to 8.6 cm.

just above the point where it meets the base. The face of the plaque is flush with that of the base, from which it is separated by an irregular, shallow cutting. The base is *ca.* 5 mm. wider than the bottom of the plaque on the right side, *ca.* 4 mm. on the left. The face of the base, measuring *ca.* 9.5 cm. by *ca.* 3.5 cm., has on the upper half a one-line inscription reading ʿqrb/ḏrḥn; see *JaPEHA*, p. 54, §158 and the photograph on Pl. xvii, below. The top, sides and bottom of the stele have been worked with a chisel, but are still somewhat irregular. The back is very rough, with a few tool marks visible. Alabaster, mottled gray and red. 13.4 cm. by 9.7 cm. by 4.4 cm.

TC 1691 (Plate 70)

Stele with an undecorated polished plaque and an integral inscribed base. The maximum preserved height of the plaque above the top of the base is 5.9 cm., at which point it is broken off obliquely. The polished face of the plaque, except the bottom (which slants inward to form a shallow offset at the upper limit of the base), is on the same plane as the face of the base. The plaque tapers in width toward the bottom and meets the base in a beveled offset of *ca.* 5 mm. on both sides. A one-line inscription on the upper part of the face of the base reads [*w*]*hbʾl/ḍmrn*; see *JaPEHA*, p. 164, §321 and the photograph on Pl. xviii, above. There seems to be a trace of the first letter at the edge of the chipped area, while only the right fork of the *h* is missing. The back of the stele is irregular. The average thickness of the piece is *ca.* 4.7 cm. White alabaster with a brownish tint and dark striations. 10.4 cm. by 8.1 cm. by 5.5 cm.

TC 1728 (Plate 72)

Fragment of a stele, consisting of most of an inscribed base, broken on the bottom and right side, and the lower part of an undecorated plaque. The preserved face of the plaque, apparently once highly polished, is badly battered; it is 12.1 cm. wide at the face and is preserved only to a maximum height of *ca.* 3 cm. The face of the plaque is recessed 5 mm. behind the face of the base. On the left side, the base extends *ca.* 8 mm. beyond the edge of the plaque. The end of the base and the edge of the plaque on this side both slant in toward the rear. The right edge of the plaque is approximately square with the face; the right end of the base is not preserved. There is a one-line inscription on the face of the base (near the top) reading [. *b*]*m/dṛḥn*; the second letter, approximately the upper half of which is preserved, could possibly be *d* rather than *b*, but there is no trace of a cross bar. Light-colored alabaster with brown bands. 8.5 cm. by 14 cm. by 5 cm.

TC 1736 (Plate 72)

Large stele with a broad polished plaque and an integral inscribed base. As viewed from the front, the upper edge of the plaque is bowed, i.e., it curves up toward the corners. The plaque tapers in width from 23.2 cm. at the top to 20.2 cm. at the bottom. The polished face is not exactly flat, having a bulge of several centimeters near the center; it is recessed nearly 3 mm. behind the face of the base. On either side the base extends some 7 mm. or 8 mm. beyond the edge of the plaque. The base, which is 7.7 cm. high, tapers in width from an estimated 23.2 cm. at the bottom (the lower left corner is chipped) to 22 cm. at the top. The one-line inscription on the face of the base reads *'nmrm/dygr*; see *JaPEHA*, pp. 65f., §172. The top and sides of the stele have been chiseled even, but are only superficially polished. The bottom has not been polished at all. The back is rough and somewhat concave in horizontal cross section, i.e., it is thinner along the vertical center than at the sides. White alabaster, with brown banding exposed over the entire back surface. 33 cm. by 23.2 cm. by 5.6 cm.

TC 1768 (Plate 73)

Stele with an undecorated, polished plaque and an integral inscribed base. The upper corners of the plaque are rounded as viewed from the front. The plaque tapers in width from 9.8 cm. near the top to 8.6 cm. just above the base. The face of the plaque is not perfectly flat. The upper part is in the same plane as the face of the base, but the lower part slants inward slightly so as to produce a shallow offset at the top of the base. The offset is *ca.* 2 mm. deep and is beveled at an angle of about 45°. At the left side the plaque meets

the base in a crude offset of 7 mm., at the right side in an offset of 5 mm.

The face of the base, 5.1 cm. by 9.5 cm., bears an inscription in two lines reading (1) *dyrt* (2) *ḥdrm*; the first letter of line 2 is chipped off except for the three upper prongs. The top and sides of the piece are chiseled roughly even along the front edges, but are otherwise rough with large tool marks. The back of the plaque displays large tool marks, vertical at the top and horizontal at the sides, and it is rounded into the sides and top. The back part of the base has not been rounded thus, so is larger and also less regular. The bottom of the base is irregular, except along the front where it has been evened square with the face. Alabaster, dark gray toward the bottom and front from exposure to heat, light brown toward the top and back. 21.5 cm. by 9.7 cm. by 6.4 cm.

TC 1773 (Plate 72)

Stele with an undecorated polished plaque and an integral inscribed base. As viewed from the front, the top of the plaque is bowed, i.e., it curves up toward the corners. The plaque tapers in width from *ca.* 7.9 cm. at the top to 6.2 cm. at the bottom (at the face; 6.8 cm. near the back, as the sides slant in toward the front). The polished face slants inward near the bottom to form a shallow offset at the top of the base. The sides of the base are almost entirely chipped away; on the right the offset is beveled at about a 45° angle (the offset is preserved *ca.* 7 mm. beyond the side of the plaque). On the left the offset is *ca.* 8 mm. and is virtually square with the edge of the stele. The base, about 2.5 cm. high, bears a one-line inscription on its face reading *mškmm*. The sides of the plaque were chiseled even. The back of the stele is irregular and displays several large tool marks. White alabaster. 11.5 cm. by 7.9 cm. by 4.5 cm.

TC 1787 (Plate 72)

Stele with a polished plaque and an integral inscribed base. The top of the plaque, as seen from the front, is somewhat rounded, and the upper corners are rounded into the sides. The plaque tapers in width from 12.2 cm. at the top to 10.7 cm. at the bottom and meets the base in a slightly beveled offset on the front and sides. The one-line inscription, which nearly fills the polished face of the base, reads ṣdqm/ġrbm; see *JaPEHA*, p. 94, §214. The base is *ca.* 4.5 cm. high. White alabaster. 18.5 cm. by 13.4 cm. by 3.8 cm. (dimensions from *JaPEHA* and field catalogue). (Carnegie Museum.)

TC 1835 (Plate 73)

Stele, chipped along the left side (especially at the corners), with an undecorated polished plaque and an integral inscribed base. In frontal view, the upper corners of the plaque are rounded, while the top is flat. The plaque tapers in width from 8.4 cm. (maximum) near the top to 6.6 cm. at the lower end where it meets the base. The face of the plaque is flush with the base, from which it is separated by a shallow groove. On the right the base extends 1.1 cm. beyond the edge of the plaque in a square offset; the left end of the base is broken away. Only part of the two lines of relatively crude inscription is preserved, since much of the face of the base has been chipped off at the left: (1) ʾhn[gr.] (2) ġr[bm]. The last two letters are completely missing, but supplied to form the name which is extremely common in the Timnaʿ Cemetery. The bottom of the base, which slants up toward the rear, is roughly tooled. The sides and top of the stele were chiseled even and slightly polished along the front edges. Light-colored alabaster with rusty streaks. 11.6 cm. by 8.4 cm. by 4.5 cm.

TC 1842 (Plate 73)

Stele with an undecorated polished plaque and an integral inscribed base. The top of the plaque is gently rounded, but the corners are virtually square. The plaque tapers in width from 10.7 cm. at the top to 8.8 cm. at the bottom and meets the base in a sloping offset on the front and sides. The one-line inscription fairly high up on the face of the base reads nʿm/ġrbm; see *JaPEHA*, p. 88, §204 and photograph on Pl. XVIII, below. The maximum height of the base is *ca.* 4.5 cm. White alabaster. 19 cm. by 10.7 cm. by 5.3 cm. (all dimensions from *JaPEHA* and the field catalogue). (Aden Museum.)

TC 1871 (Plate 73)

Stele, chipped on upper left corner and in a small area on the face at the right side, with a plain polished plaque and an integral inscribed base. The upper corners of the flat-topped plaque are rounded. It tapers in width from the top (which is slightly wider than the base) to the lower end, where it meets the base in a square offset on front and sides. Except for a band at the bottom, the face of the base is filled with a one-line inscription which reads tnʿmm/hnʿmt. White alabaster. 27.5 cm. by 15 cm. by 6 cm. (dimensions from field catalogue). (Carnegie Museum.)

TC 1872 (Plate 75)

Stele with an undecorated plaque and an integral inscribed base. In frontal view, the top of the plaque is bowed, i.e., it curves up toward the corners; the plaque tapers in width from 10.2 cm. at the top to 8.6 cm. at the bottom. The face of the plaque slants inward at the very bottom to produce an offset at the top of the base; the right edge of the plaque meets the end of the base in an offset of *ca.* 5 mm. (the left end of the base is broken away).

The face of the base, which was 4.5 cm. by 9.9 cm., is chipped at the lower right corner; it bears a one-line inscription reading [. .]ʿn/ḏṣwʿ[n]. The first two letters are completely missing, while the final letter is broken off obliquely, leaving the lower half of *n* (this could be part of another letter, but the name ṣwʿn is known from TC 1651 and TC 1879; see Chapter IX, section B, and Chapter X, section B. The top, sides, and bottom of the stele are chiseled even. The back is irregular and displays some large tool marks. White alabaster, with a brown band exposed over much of the back. 19.5 cm. by 10.2 cm. by 4.3 cm.

TC 1873 (Plate 70)

Fragment of a stele, consisting of the right part of an integral inscribed base and a bit of the undecorated plaque. The break runs obliquely from the right edge of the plaque (*ca.* 3 cm. above the top of the base) down to the bottom of the base, apparently a little to the left of the original center of the piece. The face of the plaque slants inward to meet the base in a beveled offset of *ca.* 3 mm.; the edge of the plaque, which has been smoothed in its entire width, meets the end of the base in an offset of 1.2 cm. The face of the base,

5.5 cm. high, bear a one-line inscription on the upper part reading *ṯwbn'*[*m*/ . . .]. Only the lower tip of the *m* is preserved, none of a word divider; the length of the line remains unknown. Light-colored alabaster. 9 cm. by 9.8 cm. by 4 cm.

TC 1919 (Plate 73)

Small, crudely shaped stele with flat, polished face. The top of the stele, which has been partly smoothed, is bowed, i.e., it is concave as seen from the front. The right edge has been chiseled somewhat even for 5.6 cm. from the top. Below this is a beveled offset of *ca.* 5 mm. which forms the only indication of a formal base; the left side displays the same treatment, but here the offset was apparently chiseled off accidentally. The stele tapers in width from 5.8 cm. at the top to 5.2 cm. just above the offset (at the face; the stele widens toward the rear). The crude two-line inscription at the lower end of the face reads (1) *'bdḵr* (2) *yn'm*; see *JaPEHA*, p. 112, §242. The bottom and back of the stele are rough and display tool marks. White alabaster. 8.8 cm. by 6.3 cm. by 2.7 cm.

TC 1925 (Plate 73)

Fragment of a stele, consisting of the lower part of an undecorated plaque and an integral inscribed base, the lower left corner of which is broken off. The break across the plaque is irregular, but nearly horizontal; the face of the plaque is preserved to a maximum height of 6 cm. The plaque is 10 cm. wide where it meets the base, and it increases in width toward the top (at 6 cm. its estimated width is *ca.* 11 cm.). The plaque meets the base in an offset of *ca.* 4 mm. on the front and 1 cm. on either side. The base, 6.5 cm. high, increased in width from 12 cm. at the top to an estimated 13 cm. at the bottom; a one-line inscription completely fills a recessed trapezoidal panel on the face of the base near the top. The panel, with the surface tinted by reddish or pale orange coloring, is 1.6 cm. high, 10.8 cm. long at the top, and 11.1 cm. long at the bottom; the inscription reads *mrṯdm*/*ygr*; see *JaPEHA*, pp. 72f., §182. The bottom and sides of the stele are chiseled even and partly smoothed. The back displays a number of large tool marks, mostly vertical.

White alabaster. 13 cm. by 12.7 cm. by 3.9 cm.

TC 1948 (Plate 75)

Fragment of a stele, consisting of the left part of an integral inscribed base and traces of the upper plaque. The left end of the base extends 1.2 cm. beyond the edge of the plaque; on the front the plaque meets the base in a beveled offset of 3 mm. The base is 5.8 cm. high and (assuming that the word divider in the one line of inscription was approximately in the center) was about 12 cm. wide before it was broken. The preserved part of the inscription reads [. . .]*m*/*yn'm*; there may be either more or possibly fewer than three letters entirely missing. The bottom of the base is rough; the side has been chiseled somewhat even. Several large tool marks, nearly vertical, appear on the back. Light tan alabaster. 6.5 cm. by 8.7 cm. by 4 cm.

TC 2009 (Plate 73)

Fragment of an elaborate stele, consisting of the lower end of a polished upright member or plaque and an integral base with three horizontal bands on the front and sides bearing an inscription on the upper two bands on the front. The upright plaque has been broken off obliquely from just above the top of the base on the left up toward the right side, where the maximum preserved height is 4 cm. The face of the base is chipped at the lower right corner and along the left side. The left rear of the base is broken obliquely from the center of the back to the left end near the chipped area of the face, leaving the polished surface of the upper band on the left side intact only in one tiny area (none of the other steps is preserved on this side of the base). The upright member, which is 4 cm. thick and 7 cm. wide at the bottom, meets the top of the base in an offset of 1.7 cm. on the front, 2.2 cm. on the right side (the offset at the left side was the same) and 1.6 cm. on the back. The top of the base measured 11.3 cm. in width and 7.5 cm. in depth.

The upper two of the three horizontal bands on the front and preserved side of the base are each recessed behind the one below in stair-step fashion; the offset between the upper and center band, as also between the center band and the lower, is *ca.* 6 mm. on the front and slightly less than 5 mm. on the right side (there are no offsets on the back). The upper band is *ca.* 2.8 cm. high on the front, the second *ca.* 2.6 cm. and the lower *ca.* 3.3 cm. (the heights vary slightly on the side). The faces of the bands are vertical, except for those of the center and lower bands on the side, which slant out slightly toward the bottom. One line of inscription appears on each of the upper two bands on the front, reading (1) *ḏ'yb[n]* (2) *ḏ̣grb[m]*. Only a tip of the lower right of the final letter of each line is preserved, but the readings are fairly certain; see *JaPEHA*, pp. 82f., §196. The bottom of the stele is polished smooth, while the back of both the base and the plaque displays tool marks. White alabaster, with darker striations. 13 cm. by 12.3 cm. by 8.7 cm.

TC 2010

Fragment from the face of an integral inscribed stele base. The presence of a word divider followed by *ḏt* indicates that the fragment comes from near the center of the base, and the size of the characters suggests that the base was approximately 13 cm. wide; traces of *m* precede the word divider. Both the lower edge of the base and the beveled offset between the base and the upper plaque are preserved; the height of the base was 3.3 cm. White alabaster. 3.8 cm. by 4.2 cm. by 1.2 cm.

TC 2078 (Plate 74)

Large, narrow stele with an undecorated plaque and an integral inscribed base. The face of the plaque is flush with that of the base, from which it is separated by a somewhat irregular groove; the base is further indicated by a crude offset on either side. The face of the plaque was about 10.2 cm. wide near the top (just below the unevenly rounded top) and tapers to 8.5 cm. at the point where it meets the base. The thickness of the stele at the middle is *ca.* 6.7 cm. The back has been tooled (with horizontal strokes) roughly round for two-thirds of the way down from the top; below this point is an irregular protrusion. The sides have been chiseled even along the face. The face of the base is 8.5 cm. high and 9.2 cm. wide; two lines of inscription, with heavy guidelines, read (1)

n'mm (2) *yn'm*; see *JaPEHA*, p. 114, §245. There is no space between the lines, for the lower guideline of line one serves also as the upper guideline of line two. Whitish-gray alabaster, containing mica. 30 cm. by 10.2 cm. by *ca.* 9.7 cm.

TC 2082 (Plate 73)

Fragment of a stele, consisting of a base with three horizontal, successively recessed bands on the front and sides and the lower part of an upright member or plaque. This piece is similar to TC 2009, but lacks an inscription. At the point where the plaque meets the base it is 8.8 cm. wide, 4.9 cm. deep, and preserved to a maximum height of 4.8 cm. (on the left side; on the right side it is preserved to a height of only *ca.* 2 cm.). The back of the plaque is flush with the back of the base, and all of the back is covered with closely placed horizontal tool marks. On the front and sides the plaque is withheld *ca.* 1.8 cm. from the edges of the top of the base. The top of the base is 6.7 cm. deep and 11.9 cm. wide at the face (*ca.* 12.6 cm. at the back, as the upper part of the base widens out on the right side). The total height of the base is 10 cm., of which the lower band takes 4 cm. and each of the upper two bands *ca.* 3 cm.; the upper two bands meet in an offset of *ca.* 4 mm., as do the lower two. White alabaster with light brown bandings. 15 cm. by 13.7 cm. by 7.5 cm.

TC 2090 (Plate 73)

Fragment of a stele, consisting of an integral inscribed base and the lower part of a polished plaque. The plaque, preserved to a maximum height of 3.8 cm. at the right side (1.5 cm. on the left side), is 3.8 cm. thick and 11.7 cm. wide at the face. It meets the base in a beveled offset of *ca.* 1 cm. on the right side, 7 mm. on the left side, and 3 mm. on the front. The chipped face of the base, *ca.* 4.6 cm. high, increases in width from 11.3 cm. at the top to 15.3 cm. at the bottom. The one-line inscription, nearer to the upper edge of the face than to the lower, reads *s'dm/bn/qḥlwm*; see *JaPEHA*, pp. 125f., §263 and photograph on Pl. XXIII, above. The sides and bottom have been chiseled, but are not completely even; the bottom is rough toward the rear and is slightly concave as viewed from the front.

The back is irregular and displays several very long horizontal tool marks. White alabaster. 9 cm. by 15.3 cm. by 5.2 cm.

TC 2183 (Plate 74)

Complete stele with an integral inscribed base divided into two horizontal bands on the front and sides. The upright member or plaque, which is polished on the front and sides, tapers in width from 8.8 cm. at the bottom to 7 cm. at the point 4 cm. below the top where the rounding of the top (as viewed from the front) begins. The plaque is 17 cm. high and 4.4 cm. thick; it meets the top of the base in an offset of *ca.* 6 mm. on the front and sides. The upper of the two bands on the base is recessed *ca.* 3 mm. behind the face of the lower on the front, *ca.* 5 mm. on the sides. The face of the upper band is 4.8 cm. high, and it increases from a width of 10.2 cm. at the top to 11.1 cm. at the bottom. The face of the lower band is 5 cm. high, 12.4 cm. wide at the top, and *ca.* 13.5 cm. wide at the bottom. One line of inscription, composed of large letters with heavy grooves, appears on the face of each band, and these read (1) *skynt* (2) *ġrbm*; see *JaPEHA*, p. 89, §206. The bottom of the base is squared for a maximum of 2.5 cm. from the face; farther back it is cut off obliquely and unevenly. The back of the plaque and of the upper part of the base has been chiseled even, but tool marks are still visible. White alabaster with light brown bandings. 27.5 cm. by 13.5 cm. by 6 cm.

TC 2240 (Plate 75)

Fragment of a stele, consisting of an integral inscribed base, broken on the top at the right front, with traces of a plaque on the left part of the top. The estimated width of the plaque is 15 cm., while its thickness as preserved at the left is 6.3 cm. It met the top of the base in an offset of 7 mm. on the front, 1.3 cm. on the side, and 2.5 cm. on the back. The top of the base is 9.5 cm. from front to back on the left (5 mm. less on the right by estimate) and 17.8 cm. wide at the rear; the front was about 8 mm. less in width, but cannot be measured exactly due to damage. The front and sides of the base are divided into three horizontal bands, successively recessed from bottom to top in stair-step fashion. The upper band on the front is 2.5 cm. high and 17.2 cm. wide; its face is very slightly concave from one end to the other (*ca.* 2 mm.). It meets the central band in an offset of *ca.* 4 mm. on the front, slightly less on the sides. The face of the center band is 2.6 cm. high and 17.7 cm. wide.

It bears a recessed panel, 1.7 cm. by 15.5 cm., containing a one-line, raised inscription reading *ṣbḥkrb/nʿmn*; see *JaPEHA*, pp. 156f., §307. The faces of the characters are flush with the face of the band, and the upper and lower ends of the letters blend into the face of the band. The central band is also concave, as is the lower one; it meets the lower band in an offset of *ca.* 4 mm. on the front and sides. The lower band is 4 cm. high and 18.8 cm. wide. The bottom of the base is rough and has a chiseled margin (*ca.* 2 cm.) along the front. The back of the base, which has no offsets, displays tool marks, as does the top of the base behind the plaque. White alabaster, rusty colored on the face and right side. 10.3 cm. by 19.1 cm. by 10.5 cm.

IX

MEMORIAL STELAE WITH SEPARATE BASES

Of all the objects found in the Timnaʿ Cemetery during the second campaign (1951), the type which boasts by far the largest single group of examples is the array of bases designed to hold upright polished plaques, all apparently without decoration or embellishment of any kind. Bases of this group and their accompanying plaques together formed units comparable to the monolithic or integral stelae included in Chapter VIII. Although some 180 bases of this type were recovered (including a limited number which may actually belong to other types of memorials), only a score or so of the plaques can be accounted for. Half a dozen plaques recorded in the field catalogue were discarded at the site, so now all or part of only some fifteen are in the collection (including some which are still in place in their bases). This situation may be explained in two ways: many of the nicely polished plaques may have been gathered and re-used, either while the cemetery was still in use or after it had passed out of use; or, as many of the plaques were quite thin, a high percentage of them might also have been so broken that no significance was attached to them by workmen or recorders.

The greater number of the bases are made of limestone of varying characteristics, although examples of alabaster (marble) are not uncommon. Some of the pieces, especially those of alabaster, are quite skillfully made and smoothly polished, but a large number of the limestone bases are rough and irregular, with only the face finished. Most of the bases are a little wider than they are high and perhaps half as deep as their width. A few exceptions are those which are rather flat and square, while there are also a number of other variations in form.

All of the bases are inscribed on the face with the name of the individual whose burial was being commemorated, followed by the name of the clan or tribe. In the majority of cases the inscription is in two lines, with the individual's name above the clan name, although on some bases the two are written in a single line. The demonstrative element $\underline{d}$ (m.) or $\underline{dt}$ (f.) frequently precedes the clan name. The latter is separated from the clan name by a word divider (a straight vertical line) if occuring in the same line; the former is not. The word divider is almost always used to separate the name of the individual from any letter or letters which follow it on the same line, but almost never employed after the name if it stands alone in a line.

The fifteen bases in this chapter with all or part of the plaque preserved are described first, followed by the much larger number of bases without any of the plaque preserved. The dimensions at the end of each description are given in the order height by width by depth (face to back).

A. DETACHED BASES WITH ALL OR PART OF THE PLAQUE PRESERVED

TC 1521 (Plate 76)
Stele base, bearing a two-line, raised inscription on the front reading (1) *nmrm* (2) *ḏdḥsm*; see *JaPEHA*, pp. 98f., §220. The long narrow plaque belonging to the base (TC 1521A) is undamaged, but the base itself is broken at the lower left and on the left rear. This base, which has a total height of 10 cm. and a reconstructed maximum width (at the bottom rear) of *ca.* 13.8 cm., is decorated in two horizontal bands on the front and sides. The lower band, 6.2 cm.

wide at the front, slants in somewhat toward the top; it is polished smoothly on the sides without decoration, while the upper part of this band on the front bears the second line of the inscription in raised letters 3.1 cm. high, the highest planes of which are flush with the raised lower part of the band with which they are connected. The upper band of the base, 4 cm. wide and bearing the first line of the inscription in raised characters 3.1 cm. high, is vertical and is set in about 8 mm. from the face of the lower band on the front, about 5 mm. on the sides. The polished offset between the two bands is slightly beveled and rounded.

The rectangular mortise in the top of the base measures 3.2 cm. from front to back, 8.3 cm. from side to side, and 2.7 cm. in depth; it varies in distance from the face between 4.2 cm. at the right end to 4.5 cm. at the left, while it comes within 1.8 cm. of either side of the base. The interior is tooled, the walls in vertical strokes, with chiseling near the top. The upright stele or plaque is somewhat narrower at the lower end than the longer dimension of the mortise; this member was held in place by white lime mortar, which is preserved in place except at the left end of the mortise. At the sides of the plaque, between it and the ends of the mortise, a gap averaging 1 cm. in width was filled with mortar, while there was a smaller gap (*ca.* 3 mm.) behind the upright member. The face of the plaque came into direct contact with the front wall of the mortise; the lower end of the plaque rested on a layer of mortar about 1 cm. thick. The top of the base, as the face and sides, is polished smooth; it measures 11 cm. from front to back, while the width increases from 11.5 cm. at the front to 12.7 cm. at the back. This refinement seems to have been intentional, designed to harmonize with the tapering plaque rising from it. The under side of the base is fairly even, exhibiting long, closely placed tool marks over part of the surface; the back, where preserved, is roughly tooled even.

The upright member, or plaque, is 32.2 cm. long, 1.7 cm. of which was sunk into the mortise. The top of the plaque, which curves up toward the corners, is 8.8 cm. wide, while the plaque tapers to a width of 5.6

cm. at the bottom face (the right side slants out at the bottom toward the back, where the width is 6 cm.). The face of the plaque is perfectly smooth, although it has a slight concavity in the central part amounting to some 3 mm. The uniform thickness of the plaque is about 3.3 cm. The edges, at the top, are polished smooth, but they exhibit some irregularities, especially on the left side; the back of the plaque is covered with long, closely spaced, horizontal tool marks, and the bottom displays a half dozen parallel tool marks running across the shorter dimension. The plaque is almost pure white alabaster with only traces of rusty color in a few spots, but the alabaster of the base has numerous brown and rusty-orange streaks. 42 cm. (total height of the two pieces with the plaque in place) by 13.5 cm. by 11.9 cm.

TC 1524 (Plate 75)

Fragment of a stele. This piece is the lower part, apparently, of a plaque attached to a base (as indicated by traces of plaster on the back), although as far as shape is concerned it could have been the base of an integral stele of the type in Chapter VIII. The sides are rough; the irregular bottom slants up toward the rear; only the face is polished, and it bears vertical scratches. White alabaster. 4.3 cm. by 8.5 cm. by 3.7 cm.

TC 1525 (Plate 75)

Upright plaque, broken at the extreme lower end. The plaque tapers in width from 8.8 cm. at the top to 6.4 cm. at the bottom, which fitted into a mortise *ca.* 6 cm. by *ca.* 2 cm. (as shown by the impressions in the adhering plaster). The top of the plaque curves up toward the sides in crescent form. The face, sides, and top are polished; the somewhat irregular back is rough, exhibiting a few tool marks near the top. The piece diminishes in thickness near the bottom, which also has a notch of *ca.* 1 cm. at the back and a smaller one on the left, forming a tenon. Plaster or mortar, which served to brace the plaque upright as well as to hold it solid in the mortise, clings to the lower back. Light-colored alabaster. 13.8 cm. by 8.8 cm. by 3.8 cm .

TC 1535 (Plate 75)

Stele base, with fragment of upright plaque in place in mortise, bearing a two-line inscription on the face reading (1) [.]*wf'm/yhn'm* (2) *bn/'ndm*; the shaft of the first letter of the upper line indicates either the letter *l* or *g*. The base is chipped on the right top and on the lower left corner and face. An upper band 4.3 cm. wide, running around the face and sides, is recessed *ca.* 3 mm. behind the band below; the lower band is 6 cm. wide on the sides. On the front a 2-cm. raised band underlines the second band, which is 4 cm. wide; the two principal bands on the face each bear one line of the inscription. In the right side of the base is a horizontal, rectangular cutting 2.2 cm. by 1.7 cm. approximately centered across the beveled offset between the two bands; as it is nearly filled with plaster and mortar, its depth cannot be determined. In the polished top of the base is a rectangular mortise withheld 3.1 cm. from the face; it is 3 cm. from front to back and 9.8 cm. long. A fragment representing the lower end of a black slate plaque remains in place with the plaster mortar filling the space around it. On the back of the base oblique chiseling partly obliterates the vertical tool marks; it is evident that the piece has been re-used because a mortise 2.4 cm. wide, 2 cm. deep, and preserved to a length of 6 cm. runs off the left side; it is parallel to the present top of the base and 4.5 cm. below it. A quantity of mortar remains in place in the disused mortise. The bottom of the base exhibits tool marks parallel with the sides. Base: light-colored alabaster with rusty-orange streaks; plaque: black slate. 10.7 cm. by 16. cm. by 9.9 cm.

TC 1536 (Plate 77)

Stele base with fragment of slate plaque in place in the mortise, bearing a one-line inscription across the top of the face in letters 3.5 cm. high: *bklm/ġrb*; see *JaPEHA*, pp. 161f., §316, Pl. XIII, above. The lower two-thirds of the face is plain, roughly smoothed, and displaying reddening. The base tapers slightly in width from 14.5 cm. at the bottom to 13.8 cm. at the top. The mortise in the top of the base, set back 1.7 cm. from the face, is 2.5 cm. from front to back and 10.5 cm. wide. The lower end of a black, slate plaque, 1.5 cm. thick, 10.3 cm. wide, is imbedded in very strong mortar. In the wide gap behind the plaque, chips of stone were placed in the mortar. The sides of the base, square with the face, are chiseled roughly even; the bottom is roughly tooled. The back, which has been broken on the top and sides, exhibits long vertical tool marks. Limestone. 10.5 cm. by 14.5 cm. by 6.5 cm.

TC 1568 (Plate 75)

Stele base with lower part of broken plaque in place. There is no inscription on this base. On the front and sides of the base are three steps or horizontal bands. The upper two are each recessed *ca.* 3 mm. behind the one below, which each meets in a beveled offset; the faces of the upper two bands are each *ca.* 1.8 cm. wide, while the lower has a maximum width of 2.3 cm. At a point even with the top of the base, the upright plaque, set in a mortise in the top, is 8 cm. wide at the face (slightly more at the back) and has a maximum thickness of 3.5 cm. (in the center). The plaque fits into the mortise with only narrow gaps at the front and sides filled with mortar; a rounded mass of mortar behind the plaque, designed to brace it, rises to *ca.* 4 cm. above the top of the base.

The back of the base has short tool marks (mostly vertical) except for a margin along the top, which has been chiseled even. The bottom is fairly rough, especially the rear half, while the front half has tool marks parallel to the sides of the base at intervals of about 8 mm.; the front edge was evened by chiseling. The bottom slopes up toward the rear so that the base tilts back considerably when placed on a level surface; a large patch of thin plaster (5 cm. by 8 cm.) preserved on the bottom bears the impression of a flat tooled stone, indicating that the stele base had been mortared in place. The top, face, and sides of the base are polished, as are the face and sides of the plaque. Light-colored alabaster with brown and gray areas. 10.5 cm. by 14.4 cm. by 9.5 cm.

TC 1569 (Plate 75)

Low stele base, with fragment of plaque in place in the mortise, bearing a one-line inscription on the face reading *yṣr'm/dḥsm*; see

JaPEHA, pp. 97f., §219. The mortise in the top, set back 2.2 cm. from the face, measures 6.3 cm. by 2.2 cm.; it is 2.5 cm. from the right side of the base, 2.1 cm. from the left. The fragment of the plaque is 5.2 cm. wide and has a maximum thickness of 1.9 cm.; it is held firmly in place with mortar. The face, top, and sides of the base are polished, although not to a high degree of perfection. The back, which slants in toward the right side, exhibits tool marks, as does the bottom (which is more even). The piece tapers in height from 5.5 cm. at the back to 4.7 cm. at the front. White alabaster. 5.5 cm. by 11 cm. by 10 cm.

TC 1572 (Plate 77)

Memorial stele, complete with inscribed base (somewhat crude) and small upright plaque in place. The two-line inscription on the face of the base reads (1) *yšrḥm* (2) *mᶜhr*; see *JaPEHA,* pp. 119f., §253. Traces of reddening appear on the face. The base tapers in width from 9.2 cm. at the bottom to 8 cm. at the top; it is slightly irregular, being 8.4 cm. high on the right, 8.6 cm. high on the left. The sides meet the back in widely rounded corners. The bottom is nearly square with the face. The mortise in the top, set back 1.2 cm. from the face, is *ca.* 5.8 cm. wide; its front-to-back dimension cannot be determined because of the mass of plaster covering the back of the base. This plaster originally covered nearly all of the back of both parts of the stele.

The upright plaque, which has a plain, polished face, is of uniform width (5.3 cm.); it extends 9.2 cm. above the top of the base and has a maximum thickness of 3.2 cm. The top, which curves up toward the sides, has been chiseled along the front, as have the sides (the right side has also been partly polished). The back of the plaque is irregular and exhibits a few long horizontal tool marks on the upper part where not covered by the plaster. Plaque: white alabaster; base: very porous limestone. 17.7 cm. (total height) by 9.2 cm. by 6.3 cm. (including thickness of plaster).

TC 1617 (Plate 75)

Complete upright plaque with undecorated, polished face. The base belonging to it was not found, or at least not identified. The width tapers very slightly, from 8.3 cm. near the top to 7.8 cm. at the bottom. As viewed from the front, the top is gently convex, and the corners are rounded. The top meets the face in an angle of about 70°. The sides are roughly square with the face; the left side is polished, while the right is roughly tooled with chisel marks along the front. The plaque thickens considerably from 2 cm. at the bottom to 6.2 cm. near the top. An evenly chiseled notch on the back at the bottom forms a sort of wedge-shaped tenon to fit into the mortise of a base; the back above the notch is irregular. Rusty-gray alabaster with brown stains. 16.7 cm. by 8.3 cm. by 6.2 cm.

TC 1640 (Plate 75)

Small upright plaque, complete. The width tapers from 6.5 cm. immediately below the rounded upper corners to 5.7 cm. at the bottom. The sides, which slant in slightly toward the back, have been smoothed, as has the face. The top, which bears several large tool marks and numerous small ones, slants down slightly toward the back. The back is irregular and is beveled at the lower end for insertion into the mortise of a base (the bottom itself is *ca.* 2 cm. thick). Light rusty alabaster with fine striations. 9.5 cm. by 6.5 cm. by 3.6 cm.

TC 1654 (Plate 77)

Complete stele, consisting of inscribed base with narrow upright plaque mortared in place in the mortise in the top. On the front of the base are three horizontal bands, successively recessed from bottom to top in stair-step fashion; one line of inscription fills each of the upper two bands. These read (1) *ᶜmwtn* (2) *rḥḥn*; see *JaPEHA*, p. 167, §326. As viewed from the front, the top of the plaque is well-rounded on the corners; it tapers in width slightly from top to bottom. The plaque is of alabaster, the base of limestone. 21 cm. by 8 cm. by 6 cm. (dimensions from field catalogue). (Carnegie Museum.)

TC 1667 (Plate 77)

Upper part of broken plaque from memorial stele. The two-line inscription on the face (near the top) reads (1) *mqf/ᵓsn* (2) *ḏmḥḏrm*; see *JaPEHA*, p. 207, §364. This fragment may have come from either an integral or a two-piece stele; in either case, the inscription on the polished plaque is most unusual. The polished top of the plaque curves up toward the corners; the width tapers from a reconstructed 12.3 cm. at the top to 10.5 cm. at the horizontal break. The edges are polished; the evened back exhibits long horizontal tool marks and has narrow chiseled margins at all three original edges. The plaque is somewhat thicker at the top than farther down. Grayish alabaster with rusty-brown streaks. 10.5 cm. by 12.1 cm. by 3.2 cm.

TC 1868 (Plate 77)

Stele base with fragment of plaque in place in the mortise. The front is divided into two horizontal bands of approximately equal width. The upper band, set back *ca.* 5 mm., bears a one-line inscription reading [.]*dyntġrbm* (without word divider). All but the lower part (two vertical strokes) of the first letter on the right is chipped; the letters are 3.5 cm. high. The mortise in the rough top of the base, set back 1.5 cm. from the face, measures 7 cm. by 2.6 cm. The plaque fragment in it, with a maximum width of 6.7 cm. and thickness of 2 cm., is surrounded with mortar. The sides of the base have been tooled even and have a chiseled margin along the face; the irregular back exhibits half a dozen fairly large tool marks. The roughly even bottom slants up toward the back. Limestone. 9 cm. by 12.2 cm. by 6.8 cm.

TC 1907 (Plate 77)

Complete plaque from two-piece memorial stele. The plain face is smoothed, but not polished, as are also the top and edges (sides). The top curves up toward the corners in a crescent form; the top and sides are beveled, forming an angle of approximately 110° with the face. The plaque tapers in width from 7.7 cm. at the top (at the face) to 6.1 cm. near the bottom. The bottom, which was inserted into a mortise, is irregular. The back is somewhat uneven, and short tool marks are visible over much of it. The left part of the piece is thicker than the right. Dull white alabaster, with chalky appearance. 18.2 cm. by 8.2 cm. by 2.5 cm.

TC 1917 (Plate 77)

Inscribed base with lower end of slate plaque in place in the mortise. The two-line inscription, occupying the upper two-thirds of the smoothed face, reads (1) *ḏmrm* (2) *ġrbm*; see *JaPEHA*, pp. 83f., §197, Pl. xx, center. Red coloring is visible over most of the face. Due to expansion of the slate plaque, the upper part of the base in front of the mortise was split off. The fragment, however, bearing the upper line of the inscription and part of the second, was recovered. The mortise in the top of the base, set back 1.6 cm. from the face, measures 7.7 cm. by 2.3 cm., while the plaque is 7.3 cm. by 2 cm. (it must originally have been about 2 mm. thinner), with the gaps filled with mortar. The sides of the base are even and smooth, but the bottom and back are completely irregular. Chunks of mortar adhering to the bottom show that the base was attached to an uneven surface. Limestone. 11.4 cm. by 11.2 cm. by 7.2 cm.

TC 2170 (Plate 77)

Inscribed stele base with lower end of plaque in place in the mortise. A one-line inscription with letters 3 cm. high across the upper part of the face reads ʿ*smm*/*dḫsm*; see *JaPEHA*, p. 99, §221. Owing to irregularity at the right of the face, the inscription is off center to the left. The face of the base is covered with long vertical chisel marks; the top forms an angle of about 100° with the face and exhibits chisel marks perpendicular to the face. The mortise in the top, set back some 3 cm. from the face, measures 3.2 cm. from front to back and is 8.5 cm. wide. The preserved fragment of the plaque, broken off just above the top of the base, is separated from the front of the mortise by *ca.* 7 mm.; this gap, like the much narrower ones at the sides and back, is filled with mortar (which spreads over the top of the base slightly in several places). The sides and back of the base are very rough and irregular, while the bottom, which has a patch of plaster adhering to it near the left end (showing that it was affixed to another surface), slants up irregularly toward the right rear corner. Grayish alabaster of poor quality. 9 cm. by 17.5 cm. by 9.8 cm.

B. DETACHED BASES WITH NONE OF THE PLAQUE PRESERVED

TC 503 (Plate 77)

Stele base with two-line inscription on the face reading (1) *ġlmt* (2) *'tbm*. The base tapers in width from an estimated 11 cm. at the bottom (the left corner is broken) to 8.3 cm. at the top. The crude mortise in the top, set back 1.1 cm. from the face, has a maximum depth of 1.5 cm. (near the front). The pores in the stone on the front, top, and left side are filled with fine ash. Porous limestone. 9 cm. by 10.5 cm. by 6.5 cm.

TC 535 (Plate 78)

Small, battered stele base with a one-line inscription on the face reading *nky'tdtgr*. The mortise in the top, set back 1.8 cm. from the face, lacks a back wall; it is *ca.* 6.5 cm. long and 1 cm. deep. The bottom of the base is uneven, while the back is completely irregular. The ends (sides) were superficially evened. White alabaster of poor quality. 5.6 cm. by 10.3 cm. by 5.5 cm.

TC 556 (Plate 78)

Stele base, badly damaged, with a crude two-line inscription on the face of somewhat uncertain reading: (1) *yšrḥ'm* (2) *dwṭ*[.]; see *JaPEHA*, pp. 141f., §285 for variant reading. A shallow, irregular mortise in the top, set back 1.2 cm. from the face, is *ca.* 1 cm. deep. The sides and back of the base are irregular, but the bottom has been chiseled even. Calcareous sandstone. 8 cm. by 13 cm. by 6.3 cm.

TC 653 (Plate 78)

Stele base with a two-line inscription on the face reading (1) [*h*]*wf'm* (2) *ylġb*; see *JaPEHA*, pp. 147f., §294. The front and sides of the base are divided into two horizontal bands, with the upper band, *ca.* 3 cm. wide, recessed *ca.* 2 mm. behind the lower band, which is 4.5 cm. wide. Both bands slant in slightly toward the top; one line of the inscription is incised on each of the two bands. The crude mortise in the top, set back 1.7 cm. from the face, is roughly oval, flattened along the front; it measures 1.2 cm. deep, 3.5 cm. from front to back, and 5 cm. in width. The back, which displays horizontal tool marks except along the right edge where it

is chiseled, is not square with the sides. Large tool marks appear on the bottom, which is chipped along the edges (the entire piece is somewhat battered). Light-colored alabaster with rusty tint. 8 cm. by 8.2 cm. by 7.4 cm.

TC 674 (Plate 78)

Stele base with a two-line inscription on the face reading (1) *m'd'l* (2) *ddnm*; see *JaPEHA*, pp. 100f., §224, Pl. II, top. The base is considerably wider at the bottom (13.8 cm.) than at the top (11.8 cm.). The rectangular mortise in the top, *ca.* 6 mm. deep, comes within roughly 1 cm. of the face and the sides; it has no rear wall. *Ca.* 9 cm. by 13.8 cm. by 4.5 cm. (dimensions from *JaPEHA* and field catalogue). (Carnegie Museum.)

TC 677

Stele base, broken at the top front and right, with a two-line inscription on the smoothed face partly preserved: (1) [. . .]*t* (2) *ršm*. Only the lower tips of the first three (or possibly four) letters of the upper line are preserved. The rough, oval mortise in the top measures about 3.5 cm. from front to rear, 4.5 cm. wide, and 2 cm. deep. The sides of the bases are partly chiseled even, as is the front half of the bottom. The back part of the bottom is cut off obliquely and irregularly; the back itself is irregular. Limestone. 6.3 cm. by 8.9 cm. by 6.5 cm.

TC 697 (Plate 78)

Stele base with a two-line inscription on the weathered face reading (1) *rd'm* (2) *y*[.]'[.]; see *JaPEHA*, pp. 149f., §297. The second letter in the lower line has the upper circle and shaft of either *ṣ*, *ẓ* or *ṭ*. The mortise in the top of the base, set back 2 cm. from the face, measures 2.5 cm. from front to rear, 6 cm. in width, and 2 cm. deep; most of the interior is covered with mortar bearing the impression of the lower end of a plaque beveled at the rear. The face and sides of the base are divided into two horizontal bands; the upper one, recessed *ca.* 3 mm., is 3.7 cm. wide, the lower 4 cm. Each bears one line of the inscription. The bottom of the base is evened at the front; the lower back is cut off obliquely and is irregular. Porous limestone. 7.7 cm. by 10.3 cm. by 6.4 cm.

TC 716 (Plate 78)

Left part of uninscribed stele base, broken obliquely from front center to right rear of mortise. The mortise, set back 2.8 cm. from the face and coming within 3 cm. of the left side of the base, is 2.5 cm. deep and measures 3.5 cm. from front to rear by 6.2 cm. wide; it contains mortar 1 cm. thick in the bottom at the left end. The face is divided into two horizontal bands; the upper, 2 cm. wide, is recessed slightly behind the lower. The face, sides, and top of the base are polished, while the back and bottom are rough, though even. White alabaster with brown banding exposed across bottom. 5.5 cm. by 10.3 cm. (original width *ca.* 12.5 cm.) by 9.2 cm.

TC 724 (Plate 78)

Stele base with a two-line inscription on the face reading (1) *ʾky[y]t* (2) *rṣ̌[m]*; see *JaPEHA*, p. 127, §265. The base is damaged at the top left and the lower left of the face so the last letter of the second line is entirely missing. The face, top, and sides of the base are smoothed, while the back and bottom are rough. The base tapers slightly in width from bottom to top. The mortise in the top, *ca.* 2.5 cm. from front to back and 5.5 cm. wide, is crudely shaped. Sandstone. 8 cm. by 9.5 cm. by 4.7 cm.

TC 727 (Plate 78)

Stele base with a two-line inscription on the face reading (1) *ʾbḥqb* (2) *ġrbm*; see *JaPEHA*, pp. 79f., §191 and Pl. IV, below. The large, somewhat crude mortise in the top lacks a rear wall. The right side of the base is approximately vertical, but the left side slants in toward the top; as a result the base is nearly 1 cm. narrower at the top than at the bottom. The bottom of the base, which forms an acute angle with the face, has been chiseled even along the front; the back of the base is irregular. Sandstone. 7.5 cm. by 9.5 cm. by 5.4 cm.

TC 766 (Plate 78)

Stele base with a two-line inscription on the smoothed face reading (1) *ḥgrm* (2) *ḏrʾt*; see *JaPEHA*, pp. 136ff., §279, where the first line is read *ḥlrm*. The mortise in the top, set back 1.7 cm. from the face, measures 3.2 cm. from front to rear by 9.5 cm. in width and is *ca.*

1.2 cm. deep; a layer of mortar covers most of the bottom. The sides of the base are smooth; the bottom has been superficially chiseled even. The back is irregular, exhibiting vertical tool marks along the top. Limestone, yellowish at the front and top, pink at the lower rear. 10.6 cm. by 12.5 cm. by 7.2 cm.

TC 784 (Plate 78)

Stele base with a two-line inscription on the face reading (1) *kfym* (2) *ḏlyśn*; see *JaPEHA*, pp. 151f., §300, Pl. VI, above. The base tapers in width from 10.3 cm. at the bottom to 9.2 cm. at the top. The mortise in the top, set back 1.4 cm. from the face, and placed slightly nearer to the left side of the base than the right, measures 2 cm. from front to back by 4.1 cm. in width and has a depth of 1.8 cm. The sides are smooth, but like the face quite porous. The bottom is even and the back is uneven. Porous limestone. 8.7 cm. by 10.3 cm. by 4.8 cm.

TC 785 (Plate 78)

Stele base, broken around upper edges, with a two-line inscription on the smoothed face: (1) [. . .] *ʿm* (2) *ḏnhr*. The original top of the base is not preserved at any point, and the upper part of the first line is missing; the first three letters all have single long shafts. The vertical sides of the base, square with the face, are smooth. The mortise in the top of the base, set back 1.8 cm. from the face and from the sides, has a flat, tooled bottom; it measures 3.7 cm. from front to rear by 6.7 cm. in width. The back of the base is even but not smoothed; the bottom has been chiseled even. The lower part of the base has been blackened by fire. Limestone. 9.8 cm. by 10.3 cm. by 8 cm.

TC 786 (Plate 78)

Stele base with a somewhat crude two-line inscription on the polished face reading (1) *ṯwbn* (2) *mḥḍrm*; see *JaPEHA*, pp. 154f., §305. The very shallow mortise (5 mm. maximum depth) in the polished top, set back 1 cm. from the face, measures *ca.* 2 cm by *ca.* 5.4 cm. The bottom of the mortise, on which a small patch of mortar is preserved, slopes up toward the rear to meet the top. The polished sides of the base (especially the right one) slant in toward the back. The back and bottom of the base are irregular and somewhat rounded; the bottom slants up towards the rear. Grayish-white alabaster with brown banding exposed on the back. 6.7 cm. by 8 cm. by 5.4 cm.

TC 788 (Plate 78)

Stele base with a one-line inscription high up on the face. The left side of the base is broken off. The inscription reads *whb'l/d'k*[ ]; see *JaPEHA*, pp. 131f., §271, Pl. vi, below. The preserved right side of the base shows that it tapered in width from bottom to top. The mortise in the top, held back 1.5 cm. from the face of the base, has a depth of 1.6 cm. It varies between 2.6 cm. and 3.1 cm. in distance from front to back; its preserved length is 10.8 cm., and it comes within 1 cm. of the right side. Alabaster. 8 cm. by 12 cm. by 7 cm. (dimensions from *JaPEHA* and field catalogue). (Carnegie Museum.)

TC 812 (Plate 78)

Stele base with a one-line inscription along the top of the face in characters 3.4 cm. high reading *rd*[']*wm/š*[*hr*]. The proposed *r* at the end would admittedly have been crowded (no part of it is preserved); *šhr* occurs on TC 673 (Chapter XI, below). The base tapers in width from a reconstructed 13.7 cm. at the bottom to a reconstructed 12.2 cm. at the top. The mortise in the top, set back 1.6 cm. from the face, was 2.5 cm. deep; such thin walls were left around the ends and back of the mortise that they have broken away. The left side of the base is cut even; the right side is irregular except at the front edge. The bottom is rough with tool marks, and the back is irregular and rounded. Pinkish limestone. 8.5 cm. by 13.5 cm. by 7.5 cm.

TC 818 (Plate 78)

Stele base, broken vertically at right, with a two-line inscription on the upper part of the face reading (1) [.]*frm* (2) *drhn*; see *JaPEHA*, pp. 54ff., §159. Since in every case the letters of line 1 are almost directly above a letter of line 2, the first letter of line 1 must have been a letter without a shaft at the lower left. Centered between the lines of the present text, between the first two letters of line 2, is a *n*, slightly smaller than the *n* of the

present text, which apparently belongs to an earlier text. The base tapers from a reconstructed width of *ca.* 15.5 cm. at the bottom to *ca.* 13 cm. at the top. The mortise in the top, set back 1.5 cm. from the face and coming within 1.7 cm. of the left end, has a depth of 1.3 cm.; there is no rear wall, and none of the right wall is preserved. The left side of the base is roughly evened, but the back and bottom are irregular. Limestone. 13.5 cm. by 13.4 cm. by 7.2 cm.

TC 857 (Plate 78)

Stele base with a two-line inscription near the top of the face reading (1) [*t*]*wy*[*b*] (2) *m'dm*; see *JaPEHA*, p. 117, §250, Pl. vii, below. The initial *t* is virtually certain, while only the lower ends of the vertical members of the proposed *b* are preserved. The mortise in the top is 1.8 cm. deep; the walls at the rear and sides are broken away. Only the front wall (1.1 cm. thick) is preserved. The face of the base is smoothed; the sides and bottom are chiseled roughly even, while the back is irregular. Limestone. 9.3 cm. by 8.9 cm. by 5.5 cm.

TC 893 (Plate 78)

Stele base with a two-line inscription on the face reading (1) *z'ydm* (2) *m'hr*; see *JaPEHA*, pp. 118f., §252, Pl. viii, above. Guidelines appear at the top and center of each line of the inscription. The face and top of the base were smoothed, but are now marred. The mortise in the top, set back 2.1 cm. from the face, measures 6.4 cm. by *ca.* 2.3 cm.; it is 1.4 cm. deep. Tool marks cover most of the interior of the mortise. The sides of the base, chiseled even, are square with the face and top. The back of the base is even but rough; the bottom is chiseled even. Limestone. 8.6 cm. by 11.2 cm. by 6.6 cm.

TC 927 (Plate 78)

Stele base, broken along upper right edge, with a two-line inscription on the upper part of the face reading (1) *šhrm* (2) *dršm*; see *JaPEHA*, p. 128, §267. The mortise in the top, set back 1.3 cm. from the face, measures 4.7 cm. from front to rear by 9.4 cm. wide (reconstructed); it has a maximum depth of only 1.1 cm. The left rear corner of the mortise is angled off, although the right rear corner was square. The bottom of the mortise and the inside of the rear wall are covered with tool marks, while the inside of the front and side walls are chiseled even. The top, face, and sides of the base are polished smooth; the back exhibits long vertical tool marks except at the lower corners, while the bottom is covered with short tool marks. Light-colored alabaster with gray cast and vertical, rusty-tan striations. 9.8 cm. by 13.6 cm. by 7.7 cm.

TC 928 (Plate 78)

Stele base, damaged at the left face, with a one-line inscription along the top of the face reading *msykt/d̲r[ḥn]*; see *JaPEHA*, p. 35, §131. The spacing of an upper tip of the second letter from the end indicates *ḥ* rather than *'*; the last letter is established as *n* by the same criterion. Guidelines appear at the top and bottom of the line of inscription and also (the same distance, 2.4 cm., apart) in the unused space below the inscription. The mortise in the top, set back 1.5 cm. from the face, measures 2.2 cm. from front to rear by 9.5 cm. in width; it is nearly filled with dark-colored mortar. The top of the base has been polished in front of the mortise, but only chiseled behind it. The sides of the base are rough except for chiseled margins 1.5 cm. wide along the face; the bottom, bearing a few large tool marks, is roughly even, and the back is completely irregular. Dark, gray alabaster with deep-red and rusty-brown streaks. 8 cm. by 14 cm. by 6.7 cm.

TC 942

Fragment of a stele base, consisting of upper right of face and part of the mortise, bearing an inscription across the top of the face reading *lb'm/[ ]*. The mortise was 1.7 cm. deep. The side of the base slanted in toward the top. Limestone. 3.9 cm. by 7.2 cm. by 3.8 cm.

TC 958 (Plate 78)

Fragment of stele base, consisting of lower right part, with parts of two lines of inscription preserved: (1) *m['[m[r]* (2) *ḥdrm/[d̲]*. There is a choice between *'* and *w* for the second letter of the upper line; the lower stroke of the fourth strongly suggests *r*, although it is slanting slightly more than the lower part of the *r* in the following line. The

upper (horizontal) break runs through a line of inscription just below center, while the left break runs obliquely from the fourth letter down toward the left, cutting through the fifth letter of the second line. Traces of red coloring remain on the face. The side of the base is smoothed; the bottom is chiseled even at the front, rough toward the rear. The back is very rough and exhibits a few large tool marks. Limestone. 6.8 cm. by 11 cm. by 4.8 cm.

TC 964 (Plate 78)

Stele base with a one-line inscription along the top of the face reading *[t]b't/d̲r'n*; see *JaPEHA*, pp. 39f., §137. The large mortise in the top, set back 1.2 cm. from the face and an equal distance from the sides, is *ca.* 1 cm. deep and 9.8 cm. wide; it lacks a rear wall. The interior is covered with tool marks. The left side of the base is approximately vertical, but the right side slants in toward the top, with the result that the base is *ca.* 1.5 cm. narrower at the top than at the bottom; both sides have been superficially smoothed, but are still rough. The bottom, covered with very large tool marks, is even; the back is completely irregular. White alabaster with rusty-brown bands. 10 cm. by 13.5 cm. by 7.7 cm.

TC 1030 (Plate 78)

Stele base, broken at right and at left corners, with part of a one-line inscription preserved along the top of the face reading *[ ]m/d̲t/yḥm'[l]*. Only the shaft of the last letter is preserved, but there can be little doubt about the reading (on this tribe name, cf. TC 2079, in Chapter VII, above). The mortise in the top of the base, set back 1.6 cm. from the face and 1.4 cm. from the left end (side), measures nearly 3 cm. from front to rear and has a maximum depth of 1.7 cm. The bottom is covered with tool marks, while the inside of the front wall is chiseled even; a small amount of mortar adheres to the bottom at the left end. The left side of the base was chiseled even, but not smoothed. The back is rough, with a chiseled margin at the top; the bottom is very roughly tooled. The original width of the base, judging from the inscription, was *ca.* 19 cm. White alabaster. 7.5 cm. by 15.5 cm. by 7.5 cm.

TC 1031 (Plate 78)

Stele base, blackened by fire, with a two-line inscription on the face reading (1) *ḥrmt* (2) *ygr*, see *JaPEHA*, pp. 68f., §176. The face is divided into two horizontal bands. The upper, 4 cm. wide, is slightly recessed behind the lower, 4.8 cm. wide; one line of inscription appears on each. The mortise in the top of the base, set back 1.8 cm. from the face, measures 3 cm. from front to rear by 7.6 cm. in width and is 2.2 cm. deep. The base tapers in width from 11 cm. at the bottom to 10.5 cm. at the top. The sides of the base are evened and superficially smoothed; the bottom is squared off at the front and irregular toward the rear. The back is mostly irregular. Limestone. 9 cm. by 11 cm. by 6.7 cm.

TC 1039 (Plate 79)

Fragment of inscribed stele base, consisting of upper part of face and front wall of the mortise, with one line of inscription reading *yšrḥʿtt*; see *JaPEHA*, p. 17, §124. The mortise was set back 1.8 cm. from the face and was *ca.* 2 cm. deep; mortar adheres to the inside of the front wall. The sides of the base were polished. White alabaster. 3.2 cm. by 10.8 cm. by 2 cm.

TC 1052 (Plate 79)

Stele base bearing a one-line inscription across the top of the polished face reading *frʿm/ḏrʿn*. On the face of the base below the inscription, somewhat to the right of center, is a semicircular, smoothed depression with a diameter of about 4 cm. This seems to have been made by the craftsman in an attempt to remove a deep curved tool mark which is still partly visible. The mortise in the polished top of the base, set back 1.6 cm. from the face, is 6.5 cm. wide and 1.8 cm. deep; it lacks a rear wall. The interior is covered with tool marks. The sides of the base exhibit both tool and chisel marks; the bottom, which slants up slightly toward the back, is rough, as is the irregular back. Light tan alabaster. 8.2 cm. by 10.6 cm. by 5.5 cm.

TC 1087 (Plate 79)

Stele base with a two-line inscription on the face reading (1) *mlḥt/ḏ* (2) *t/ḏrḥn*. The base tapers in width from 15.3 cm. at the bottom to 13.2 cm. at the top; the face and the smoothed sides slant in toward the top at an angle of about 82°. The broad top (9.6 cm., front to rear) contains a mortise, set back 2.2 cm. from the face; this measures a maximum of 3.5 cm. from front to back (at the right; it narrows to 2.5 cm. at the left) by 9 cm. in width. It is about 2.5 cm. deep; the bottom is covered with mortar. The tooled back is vertical and was superficially chiseled along the top; the flat bottom has large tool marks parallel to the sides, over which is superficial chiseling. White alabaster. 8.2 cm. by 15.3 cm. by 11 cm.

TC 1135 (Plate 79)

Stele base, broken at the top, with a one-line raised inscription on the face reading *ʿmšl/ġrbm*; see *JaPEHA*, p. 92, §210. The two parts of the inscription are each set within a recessed panel. The raised letters come 2 or 3 mm. short of touching the margins at the top and bottom, but the word divider is treated as a central margin. The panels are 3.9 cm. high; the right margin is 4 mm. wide and the lower margin 1.3 cm. There is no margin at the left. The upper margin is preserved to a height of *ca.* 1 cm., though it originally must have been more (with the result that the recessed panels were nearer the bottom of the face than the top). The top of the base is broken off approximately even with the tooled bottom of the mortise in the top. The surface of the fracture at the right end has been crudely incised with a criss-cross pattern, and two holes *ca.* 6 mm. in diameter have been drilled down into the base, 1 cm. back from the face and 3.7 cm. from the right side, the other 1.3 cm. from the back of the base and 1 cm. from the side. The mortise measured about 8 cm. by 3 cm. The polished sides and back of the base are squared; the bottom is covered with short tool marks, bordered by roughly chiseled margins. Light-colored alabaster. 6.2 cm. by 13 cm. by 7.8 cm.

TC 1137 (Plate 79)

Crude stele base with a two-line inscription on the face reading (1) [*ḏ*]*bḥ*[*kr*] (2) *b/ḏtbw*; see *JaPEHA*, pp. 168f., §328. The left side of the base is damaged. The right side slants in toward the top, and the uneven top contains a mortise 2.5 cm. deep and measuring 7.2 cm.

by 2 cm. The back of the base is completely irregular and has a large protrusion at the lower center. The bottom has been roughly evened. Limestone. 9.5 cm. by 15 cm. by 7.8 cm.

TC 1184 (Plate 79)

Crude stele base with a two-line inscription on the face reading (1) *b'lt* (2) *rḥbm*; see *JaPEHA*, p. 166, §324. The face, which tapers in width from 10 cm. at the bottom to 9.2 cm. at the top, is fairly even, but has a porous appearance. The shallow mortise or depression in the top comes within 1 cm. or less of the face and sides of the base; it is not clearly defined at the back. The sides of the base have been chiseled, as has the front part of the somewhat irregular bottom. The back is completely irregular and slants in toward the bottom. Limestone. 6.5 cm. by 10 cm. by 7.5 cm.

TC 1186 (Plate 79)

Low stele base with a two-line inscription on the face reading (1) *'kbt/y* (2) *gr*; see *JaPEHA*, pp. 76f., §187, Pl. XI, top. The base is somewhat damaged, especially at the upper right corner. The mortise in the top, set back 2.4 cm. from the face, measures 6.5 cm. by 2 cm.; the bottom and front of it are covered with mortar. It had a depth of slightly more than 1 cm. The flat, square top of the base was polished smooth, as were the face and sides. The left side slants in toward the bottom, and the back of the base, which slants in sharply toward the bottom, exhibits a number of large tool marks. The bottom is roughly even, but shows few signs of tooling. Rusty-tan alabaster. 4.7 cm. by 8.7 cm. by 8.5 cm.

TC 1191 (Plate 79)

Stele base with a two-line inscription on the face reading (1) *hwšm* (2) *[y]gr*; see *JaPEHA*, pp. 66f., §173. The thickness of the base (front to back) varies from 6.4 cm. at the top to *ca.* 3.8 cm. at the bottom. The mortise in the top, set back 1.7 cm. from the face, measures 3.5 cm. from front to back and is 7.3 cm. in width. It has a depth of 3.2 cm. near the left end, but slopes up to the surface at the right end. Mortar adheres to the bottom and left end of the mortise. The sides, back, and bottom of the base have been partly chiseled

even. Limestone. 9.5 cm. by 11.5 cm. by 6.4 cm.

TC 1193

Battered right part of stele base with a two-line inscription on the face. The upper line reads *'šbm*[/ ; the only letter visible in the second line is *m*, which stands slightly to the left of the *m* in the upper line. The mortise in the top, set back 2 cm. from the face and 1.5 cm. from the right end, is 1.5 cm. deep; it measures 4.5 cm. from front to back, though lacking a rear wall entirely. The bottom of the mortise is covered with short tool marks. The right end of the base, square with the face and bottom, was polished; the left end is not preserved. The back and bottom have been roughly tooled even. White alabaster with horizontal striations. 7.8 cm. by 15 cm. by 7.2 cm.

TC 1211 (Plate 79)

Stele base with a one-line inscription along the top of the face reading *[']b'ns/dnm*; see *JaPEHA*, pp. 99f., §222. The face, chipped at several places at the top, is polished smooth, as are the top and sides. The mortise in the top, set back 1.2 cm. from the face and 2.3 cm. from the sides, measures 9.2 cm. by 3.5 cm., and is 1.5 cm. deep; the interior is covered with closely spaced tool marks. The right side of the base slants inward toward the top, while the left side is nearly vertical. The very rough back exhibits several very large diagonal tool marks; the bottom is rough, but more even. Light-colored alabaster with several dark streaks. 9 cm. by 14.6 cm. by 8.3 cm.

TC 1237 (Plate 79)

Stele base with a one-line inscription across the top of the face reading *'lyt/drḥn*; see *JaPEHA*, p. 53, §156. The large mortise in the top, set back *ca.* 1.5 cm. from the face and sides, has a maximum depth of 1.5 cm. The bottom of it is roughly tooled. The sides of the base have been chiseled even; the back and bottom are irregular. 10.8 cm. by 16.1 cm. by 8.7 cm.

TC 1273 (Plate 79)

Damaged stele base with a one-line inscription reading *[. r]km/hrn* or perhaps *[t]*

<u>km</u>/hrn. The inscription covers the upper two-thirds of the polished face. The mortise in the top of the base, set back 1.1 cm. from the face and 1.3 cm. from the right side, measures 4.3 cm. from front to back and is 1 cm. deep. The bottom of it is covered with small tool marks. The vertical sides of the base are polished, as is the face; the back and bottom are evened roughly. Gray alabaster. 5.8 cm. by 9 cm. by 6 cm.

TC 1300 (Plate 79)

Stele base, chipped, especially at lower corners, with a two-line inscription on the polished face reading (1) 'mt/<u>d</u>t (2) rḥbm; see *JaPEHA*, pp. 165f., §323. The base tapers in width from a reconstructed 15.6 cm. at the bottom to 14.3 cm. at the top. The mortise in the top, set back 1.8 cm. from the face, is 11.6 cm. long and *ca.* 1.3 cm. deep. The bottom, mostly covered with plaster, bears tool marks, while the walls at the front and sides are chiseled; there is no rear wall. The top of the base is polished; the sides are superficially smoothed. The back is split irregularly across a banding; the bottom displays tool marks perpendicular to the face. White alabaster. 8.5 cm. by 15.6 cm. by 5.9 cm.

TC 1304 (Plate 79)

Right part of stele base with a one-line inscription across the upper part of the face reading rdmyt[/. The mortise in the top, set back 2.4 cm. from the face and 5.4 cm. from the right end, is 1.5 cm. deep. It has no rear wall, and the left end is not preserved. The vertical side of the base is polished, as are the top and the face (though all are now marred); the back exhibits unusually regular, horizontal tool marks running the entire width of the fragment. Gray alabaster. 6.2 cm. by 12.5 cm. (originally *ca.* 23 cm.) by 5 cm.

TC 1305 (Plate 79)

Stele base with a two-line inscription on the polished face reading (1) <u>d</u>b'/<u>d</u>t (2) m'hr; see *JaPEHA*, p. 121, §256. The base tapers very slightly toward the top in both width and thickness. The mortise in the top, set back 2.1 cm. from the face, measures 11.6 cm. by 3.2 cm. and is somewhat more than 2 cm. deep (the bottom is covered with mortar, so

that exact depth cannot be determined). The sides and top of the base are highly polished. The back exhibits long, parallel, nearly horizontal tool marks in one large area, smaller vertical tool marks elsewhere. The bottom is rough, but fairly even. White alabaster with one narrow rust-colored band running horizontally through the middle. 10.5 cm. by 15.6 cm. by 8.4 cm.

TC 1306 (Plate 79)

Lower part of inscribed stele base, broken along the top of the one-line inscription on the face which reads 'qrbm/<u>dd</u>r'n. The characters, *ca.* 2.8 cm. in height, are 3 cm. above the lower edge of the face. The sides of the base slant in rather sharply toward the rear behind the chiseled margins about 1 cm. wide which run along the front edge. Most of the bottom is chiseled even, but the back bears very large, rough tool marks. Gray alabaster with rusty colored streaks. 8.3 cm. by 15.3 cm. by 6 cm.

TC 1315 (Plate 79)

Stele base with a one-line inscription across the top of the face reading 'bdm/<u>d</u>rḥbm. The upper half of the face exhibits reddening. The base tapers in width from a reconstructed 16.4 cm. at the bottom to 15.6 cm. at the top. The mortise in the top, set back 1.5 cm. from the face, is 13 cm. wide and lacks a rear wall. A thick layer of mortar on the bottom extended down over the back of the base and apparently up behind the plaque. Part of the mortar has been dislodged from the back. The bottom and back of the base are rough and irregular. Limestone. 11.5 cm. by 16.2 cm. by 6.5 cm.

TC 1341 (Plate 79)

Stele base with a two-line inscription on the polished face reading (1) sknm/<u>d</u> (2) t/ḥḍrn; see *JaPEHA*, p. 108, §236. The base tapers in width from 14.5 cm. at the bottom to 12.3 cm. at the top. The sides, square with the face, are smoothed, but are not as highly polished as the face. The mortise in the top, set back 1.6 cm. from the face, measures 3.5 cm. from front to rear by 9.8 cm. in width and is at least 1.5 cm. deep. The bottom is covered with mortar. The back of the base is rough with long, deep, nearly vertical tool marks; the bottom has been chiseled even in the front section, but is otherwise rough. Light-colored alabaster with pink streaks exposed on the lower part of the face. 11.6 cm. by 14.5 cm. by 7.5 cm.

TC 1354

Very crude stele base with a two-line inscription on the very porous face reading (1) *n'm* (2) *bwkn*; see *JaPEHA*, p. 134, §276. A shallow depression (mortise) in the top is indicated by a ridge at the front. The sides (now broken) were roughly evened, and the bottom was chiseled even. The back is broken obliquely. Limestone. 8.2 cm. by 9.4 cm. by 6.2 cm.

TC 1355

Stele base, broken at the top front, with a two-line inscription on the face reading (1) *fr['']t* (2) *'gln*. Each line of inscription occupies one of the two horizontal bands running around the front and sides (the upper one, *ca.* 3.5 cm. wide, is recessed *ca.* 4 cm. behind the lower). The lower third of the *f* and *r* of line one is preserved, but only the lower tips of the *t*, while none of the proposed *'* is preserved. The mortise in the top of the base measured about 7.2 cm. by 3.4 cm. and was 2.2 cm. deep; the interior is covered with tool marks. The back of the base bears deep, straight tool marks running from top to bottom; the bottom was roughly evened. Porous limestone. 7.1 cm. by 10.3 cm. by 7.5 cm.

TC 1359 (Plate 79)

Stele base with a two-line inscription on the face reading (1) *ḏb'n* (2) *ḏr'n*; see *Ja-PEHA*, p. 39, §136. There are two horizontal bands on the face, each bearing one line of the inscription. The upper band, *ca.* 5.2 cm. wide, is recessed some 4 mm. behind the lower, which is 6.1 cm. wide. These bands, which meet in a beveled offset, run around the sides of the base also. The sides, which slant in toward the rear, have been partly smoothed, but tool marks are still visible. The mortise in the top of the base, set back 1.5 cm. from the face, measures 1.8 cm. from front to back by 9 cm. in width and is *ca.* 2 cm. deep. Its rough, V-shaped bottom is mostly covered with mortar. The bottom of the base has been chiseled roughly even along the front,

but the rest of it is cut off obliquely and bears very large tool marks; the back is irregularly split. Gray alabaster with rust colored streaks. 11.6 cm. by 14.9 cm. by 7.6 cm.

TC 1360 (Plate 79)

Stele base with a one-line inscription across the top of the polished face in letters 3.3 cm. high reading *slml/mmn*. The base tapers in width from a reconstructed 16.5 cm. at the bottom (the lower right corner is broken) to 14.6 cm. at the top. The sides have been roughly chiseled and smoothed. A mortise in the top, lacking a rear wall, is set back 1.7 cm. from the face; it measures 11.6 cm. in width and is 1.1 cm. deep. The bottom is covered with small, closely placed tool marks; the walls are chiseled even. The bottom of the base has been tooled even. The back is filled out with a mass of crude plaster 2.7 cm. in maximum thickness. Mottled alabaster. 10 cm. by 16.2 cm. by 7.1 cm.

TC 1365 (Plate 79)

Damaged stele base with a two-line inscription on the face reading (1) *šrḥm* (2) *ršm*. The sides and top, now mostly chipped away, were squared and smoothed. The mortise in the top of the base, set back 1.4 cm. from the face and 2.3 cm. from the right side, measures 3.6 cm. (side to side) by 2.2 cm. (front to back) and is of an unusual shape. While the right wall is vertical, the left wall is oblique, running inward to meet the right side at the bottom of the mortise. The imprint of the plaque in the mortar indicates that it had a corresponding triangular shape. Limestone. 7.7 cm. by 9.2 cm. by 5.2 cm.

TC 1374

Lower part of a stele base, broken obliquely from near the upper left corner down to just above the lower right corner, with a two-line inscription reading (1) [.../b] (2) *n/'mrt*. The last two characters of the upper line are partly preserved. The lower corner of the mortise in the top of the base is visible *ca.* 1.5 cm. from the left side and face of the base. It was *ca.* 2.2 cm. from front to back. The sides and bottom of the base are roughly chiseled, while the back is irregular. Limestone. 7.4 cm. by 9.8 cm. by 7.5 cm.

TC 1376

Weathered and damaged stele base with a two-line inscription on the face reading (1) *nḥym* (2) *ḏkwn*; see *JaPEHA*, p. 151, §299. The last two characters of the lower line are separated by an unusually wide space. The base tapers in width from a reconstructed 13.1 cm. at the bottom to 10.8 cm. at the top. The rectangular mortise in the top, set back 1.2 cm. from the face, measures 8.1 cm. by 2.2 cm. and is 1.7 cm. deep. The face, sides and top of the base were nicely evened, but are now pitted. The bottom, which slants up slightly toward the back, is chiseled even along the front. The back is irregular. Limestone. 9 cm. by 12.7 cm. by 6.2 cm.

TC 1377 (Plate 79)

Broad stele base with an upper recessed band on the face and sides bearing an inscription. The upper band is 4 cm. high and has an average width of 20.5 cm. It is completely filled by the one-line inscription, which reads *šhrm/ḏhḏrn*; see *JaPEHA*, pp. 108f., §237. Alabaster. 11 cm. by 20.7 cm. by 5 cm. (dimensions from *JaPEHA* and field catalogue). (Carnegie Museum.)

TC 1387

Badly weathered stele base with a one-line inscription along the top of the face reading *'lyn/ḏrḥn*. The mortise in the top, set back 1 cm. from the face, measures 9 cm. in width and is 1.1 cm. deep; it lacks a rear wall. The back of the base is irregular. Porous limestone. 8.3 cm. by 13.2 cm. by 5 cm.

TC 1415 (Plate 79)

Stele base with a two-line inscription on the face reading (1) *ḥfnm* (2) *y'd*; see *JaPEHA*, p. 149, §296. The face and top, which bear traces of reddening, are chiseled even, but not polished. The mortise in the top, set back 9 mm. from the face, measures 2.4 cm. from front to rear by 6.8 cm. in width. The bottom of it is covered with mortar. The sides of the base are chiseled even along the front edges; the rear parts slant in toward the back and are irregular. The back of the base is irregular. Very hard calcareous stone. 9.2 cm. by 10 cm. by 5.2 cm.

TC 1446 (Plate 79)

Stele base with a one-line inscription near the top of the polished face reading *'mwšl/zbdm*; see *JaPEHA*, pp. 144f., §289. The base tapers in width from 12.8 cm. at the bottom to 11.6 cm. at the top. The mortise in the polished top, set back 1.6 cm. from the face and lacking a rear wall, is 9.5 cm. in width and *ca.* 1.3 cm. deep. The bottom of it is rough with tool marks, while the interior of the front wall has been chiseled even. The right side of the base is polished smooth; the left side is partly smoothed, but deep tool marks remain visible. The lower margin of the face is uneven, owing to the roughness of the bottom of the base. The back of the base, bearing several very large horizontal tool marks, is irregular. Light-colored alabaster with rusty-brown streaks. 7.4 cm. by 12.8 cm. by 7.7 cm.

TC 1448 (Plate 79)

Stele base with a two-line inscription on the face reading (1) *ḏry'm* (2) *h'ḏbwd*; see *JaPEHA*, p. 139, §281. The mortise in the top is set back 1.5 cm. from the face. It has no rear wall, the walls on the sides have been broken off, and the bottom of the mortise is roughly tooled. It has a depth of *ca.* 1 cm. The bottom of the base is rough; the back is irregular. Limestone. 6.5 cm. by 8.6 cm. by 5.3 cm.

TC 1502 (Plate 79)

Stele base with a two-line inscription on the face reading (1) *ḥmy/h* (2) *n'mt*; see *JaPEHA*, p. 103, §227. The base tapers in width from 10.1 cm. at the bottom to 8.7 cm. at the top. The face, top, and sides are smoothed; the face displays reddening. The mortise in the top, set back 1.3 cm. from the face, measures 5.2 cm. by 2.5 cm. and is filled with mortar. The back of the base displays vertical tool marks 1 cm. to 1.5 cm. apart; the front part of the bottom has been chiseled even, but the projecting back part is rough. Limestone. 6.5 cm. by 10.1 cm. by 5.2 cm.

TC 1503 (Plate 79)

Stele base with a two-line inscription on the face reading (1) *'byn* (2) *m/ygr*; see *JaPEHA*, pp. 62f., §168. The base tapers in width from *ca.* 12 cm. at the bottom to 9.3 cm. at the top.

All surfaces are badly pitted; the face bears faint traces of reddening. The mortise in the top, set back 1.3 cm. from the face, measures 2.5 cm. from front to rear by 4.9 cm. in width and is 1.7 cm. deep. The back of the base is irregular. Limestone. 8.8 cm. by 12 cm. by 5 cm.

TC 1504

Crude, low stele base, broken at the left end, with a one-line inscription on the front reading *rz'*[.]. Guidelines appear at the top and bottom of the widely spaced letters. A shallow (*ca.* 5 mm.) depression covers the entire top of the base except for a 1-cm. margin at front and sides. The bottom of it bears tool marks perpendicular to the face of the base. The back and bottom of the base are irregular. Limestone. 5 cm. by 15.5 cm. by 6 cm.

TC 1505 (Plate 79)

Stele base with a two-line inscription on the face reading (1) *ḥmy'* (2) *l/ḏrḥn*; see *JaPEHA*, p. 43, §142. A heavy rusty-red coloring was applied to the face before the inscription (as well as the guidelines at top and bottom of each line) was incised. The mortise in the top, set back 1.9 cm. from the face, measures 2.8 cm. from front to back by 6 cm. in width and is 1.2 cm. deep. A small amount of mortar is preserved in the left end. The surfaces of the piece are porous and crumbly. Limestone. 9.4 cm. by 10.3 cm. by 6.2 cm.

TC 1506 (Plate 79)

Stele base, broken at lower left, with a two-line inscription on the face reading (1) *mqf/r'b* (2) *'m/ḏr'n*; see *JaPEHA*, p. 206, §362. The base tapers in width from a reconstructed 9.9 cm. at the bottom to 8.9 cm. at the top. The sides and face are roughly smoothed, but not highly polished; the top bears tool and chisel marks, although it has been partly smoothed. The mortise in the top, set back 2 cm. from the face and located a little nearer the right side of the base than the left, measures 2.5 cm. from front to back by 5.6 cm. in width and is 2.1 cm. deep. The interior is covered with small tool marks. The back and bottom of the base are irregular. Alabaster, light grayish with rusty-brown areas. 7.6 cm. by 9.7 cm. by 9 cm.

TC 1520 (Plate 80)

Large stele base with three horizontal bands across the front, the center one bearing a one-line inscription reading *mwhbm/dḥsm*; see *JaPEHA*, p. 210, §368. The lower and central bands each has a width of *ca.* 3.5 cm., while the upper one is narrower, with a width of *ca.* 3 cm. Each of the upper two bands is recessed 3 mm. to 4 mm. behind the band below. The offsets are beveled and rounded, and the face of each band is polished. The top of the base, 7.3 cm. from front to back and polished smooth, contains a mortise set back 2.4 cm. from the face. It measures 3.3 cm. from front to rear by 9.5 cm. in width. The mortar in it, nearly all preserved, retains the shape of the plaque, rough on the bottom and smooth on the sides, which was inserted to a depth of 2.6 cm. The sides and bottom of the base were tooled roughly even and were chiseled along the front edge; the back, more uneven, displays larger tool marks, generally vertical. White alabaster with rusty-tan bandings. 11 cm. by 21.3 cm. by 8.7 cm.

TC 1527 (Plate 80)

Stele base with a one-line inscription across the polished face reading *klbm/yn'm*; see *JaPEHA*, p. 113, §244. The base tapers in width from 18.7 cm. at the bottom to 17.6 cm. at the top. The mortise in the top, set back 1.3 cm. from the face, is 12.8 cm. in width and 9 mm. deep. The bottom exhibits both tool and chisel marks, while the interior on front and sides is chiseled even; there is no rear wall. The sides and top of the base have been smoothed, although some chisel marks are still visible. The bottom of the base has one long, deep tool mark, near the rear, nearly parallel to the back, running almost from one side of the base to the other, while shorter tool marks perpendicular to the face appear on the front part of the bottom. Some chiseling was done at the front edge to even it.

The distinctive features on the back of the base indicate how the stone was separated from a neighboring block: a horizontal boss, *ca.* 2 cm. wide, runs from one side of the base to the other. Both above and below this boss are rows of parallel oblique tool marks; these two tooled areas are, in each case, one side of a narrow cutting or groove made from opposite sides of the block. After the cuttings were made, it was an easy matter to split the remaining stone, leaving a boss on either piece. White alabaster with rusty-tan bandings. 8.4 cm. by 18.7 cm. by 5.7 cm.

TC 1528 (Plate 80)

Fragment from right of stele base with a two-line inscription on the polished face reading (1) *ṣ[b .]* (2) *d̲t/hn[ʿmt]*; see *JaPEHA*, p. 105, §231. The second letter of the upper line is probably *b*, although the top of it is not preserved; no part of any of the letters supplied in the lower line is preserved. The small section of the top of the base preserved indicates that it was polished and that it contained a mortise, set back 2.2 cm. from the face and 2.8 cm. from the right side. The right side of the base is chiseled even along the front and top edges, but it is elsewhere rough with tool marks. The bottom displays tool marks perpendicular to the face, but has a chiseled margin along the front; the back of the base has been split away. Light-colored alabaster with rusty bands nearly parallel to the face. 12.4 cm. by 10.3 cm. by 4.8 cm.

TC 1533 (Plate 80)

Large stele base with a horizontal band (5 cm. wide) at the top of the polished front and sides, recessed *ca.* 5 mm. and bearing a one-line inscription on the face reading *ẓrb/d̲hnʿmt*; see *JaPEHA*, pp. 103f., §228, Pl. XII, below. The mortise in the top, set back 2 cm. from the face, measures 2.6 cm. from front to rear by 13 cm. in width and is at least 1.2 cm. deep; most of the interior is covered with mortar. The top of the base is polished in front of the mortise and to the sides of it, but the area behind the mortise is rough with tool marks. Mortar placed behind the plaque to brace it would have covered this area. The back of the base bears very large tool marks, approximately vertical, extending from near the top to the bottom. The bottom of the base has been chiseled even in the front section, while the rear part is somewhat irregular. Light grayish alabaster with rust-colored bands. 13 cm. by 17.7 cm. by 7.8 cm.

TC 1538 (Plate 80)

Stele base, in poor condition, with a two-line inscription on the face: (1) *s̲knn* (2)

ynʿm; see *JaPEHA*, p. 115, §247. Guidelines mark the top, center, and bottom of each line. A shallow depression in the top comes within 1 cm. of the face and *ca.* 1.8 cm. of the sides; the depression bears long tool marks. The bottom of the base is fairly even, but rough; the back is irregular. Limestone. 7 cm. by 15.2 cm. by 7.8 cm.

TC 1539 (Plate 80)

Stele base with a two-line inscription on the face: (1) *ytʿm* (2) *ġrbm*; see *JaPEHA*, pp. 86f., §202, Pl. XIII, below. The mortise in the top, set back 1.1 cm. from the face, lacks a rear wall; it is *ca.* 1.4 cm. deep and has mortar along the front and on the right side (where it forms a wall). Most of the bottom of the base is chiseled even, as are the sides; the back is irregular. Poor quality alabaster (marble). 6.6 cm. by 9.7 cm. by 4.9 cm.

TC 1540 (Plate 80)

Low stele base, battered, with the right side broken away. A two-line inscription on the face reads (1) *[hw]fʿm* (2) *[ʾ]ymn*. The edge of proposed *w* in the upper line is preserved, but none of the other supplied letters is. A ridge on the bottom of the mortise at the fracture indicates that about 2 cm. of the base is missing on the right, and presumably one complete letter at the beginning of each line. On the front, an upper band 2.6 cm. wide is recessed some 5 mm.; this band and the one below it both bear one line of the inscription. The mortise in the top, set back 2.4 cm. from the face, measures 4 cm. from front to rear and is 2 cm. deep. The bottom of it is covered with mortar *ca.* 5 mm. thick; it was 6.2 cm. wide. The top, face, and side of the base were smoothed; the back and bottom bear large tool marks. Gray alabaster. 6.4 cm. by 8.3 cm. by 10.3 cm.

TC 1590 (Plate 80)

Stele base with a two-line inscription placed high on the face: (1) *yṣrʿm* (2) *qḥlwm*; see *JaPEHA*, p. 125, §262, Pl. XIV, above. The face is the only surface polished; the sides have been chiseled even, as has the top in front of the mortise. The base tapers in width from 18.7 cm. at the bottom to 14.7 cm. at the top. The mortise in the top, set back 1.3 cm. from the face, has a maximum depth of *ca.*

1.6 cm.; the inner sides of the walls are chiseled on a bevel. There is no rear wall. The left end is damaged; the bottom of the mortise exhibits tool marks. On the back of the base are about half a dozen extremely large tool marks, nearly vertical. The bottom, somewhat rough (although it has been superficially chiseled along the front), slants up slightly toward the rear. Alabaster, mottled with gray, brown, and rusty-orange. 11.3 cm. by 18.7 cm. by 7.8 cm.

TC 1599 (Plate 80)

Large stele base with a one-line inscription across the top of the polished face reading d̲r'krb/d̲r'n; see *JaPEHA*, p. 33, §128, Pl. xiv, below. The face has a large chip at the left side. The mortise in the top, set back 3 cm. from the face, measures 3.3 cm. from front to back by 20.6 cm. in width and has a maximum depth of 1.6 cm. (at the left end; it is 1.1 cm. deep at the right end). The interior is covered with tool marks, although the inside of the front and ends has been chiseled superficially. The top is polished in front of the mortise and to the sides of it, but the area behind the mortise has been left roughly tooled; the rear left corner is broken off. The rough sides of the base have been partly chiseled at the top. The uneven back of the base bears extremely large tool marks, approximately vertical, while it was roughly chiseled along the top; the bottom of the base is chiseled fairly even, especially at the front. Alabaster, mottled gray, brown, and rusty-tan. 12.4 cm. by 24.6 cm. by 8.3 cm.

TC 1610 (Plate 80)

Stele base with a crude two-line inscription on the face reading (1) gn'm (2) 'ndm; see *JaPEHA*, p. 143, §286. The upper 3 cm. of the base is recessed on the front and sides and slants in toward the top. This band bears the upper line of inscription, while the lower line runs beneath the slightly sloping offset separating this band from the face below. The mortise in the top of the base, set back 1.4 cm. from the face, measures 2.5 cm. from front to rear by 6 cm. in width and is 2.4 cm. deep. The inner side of the rear wall of the mortise slants in so that the bottom of the mortise is only *ca.* 1 cm. from front to back. The interior is covered with tool marks, and

some mortar adheres to the bottom. The face, top, and sides of the base are smoothed. The upper part of the back is even, with chiseling at the top and long vertical tool marks below. The lower rear corner of the piece is cut off obliquely, leaving the chiseled bottom of the base only *ca.* 2 cm. from front to back. Light grayish alabaster. 8.5 cm. by 10.4 cm. by 6 cm.

TC 1611 (Plate 80)

Stele base with a two-line inscription on the face reading (1) ḥywt (2) ygr; see *JaPEHA*, pp. 67f., §174. About 1.5 cm. from the top on the face and the same distance from the bottom are horizontal depressions in the form of shallow rounded grooves. The base tapers in width from 12.6 cm. at the bottom to 9.7 cm. at the top. A mortise in the top, set back 1.4 cm. from the face, measures 6 cm. in width and is 1.5 cm. deep; it has no rear wall. The inside of the front wall has been smoothed, and the rest of the interior is covered with tool marks. The top, side, and face of the base have all been smoothed, but the stone does not take a polish. The back is irregular, while the bottom is partly rough and partly smoothed. Grayish-white alabaster of poor quality. 7.7 cm. by 12.6 cm. by 5 cm.

TC 1612 (Plate 80)

Stele base with a two-line inscription high on the face reading (1) [l]ḥy'm/bn/ (2) z̲rb/ d̲ygr/; see *JaPEHA*, p. 148, §295, Pl. xv, above. The base tapers in width from 13.5 cm. at the bottom to a reconstructed 11.1 cm. at the top (the upper right corner is damaged). The mortise in the top, set back 1 cm. from the face and 1.3 cm. from the left side, is 1 cm. deep. It has no rear wall and the right wall is broken away. The sides of the base are rough, although they have been partly chiseled. The back is irregular, but the bottom is chiseled even. Limestone. 11.5 cm. by 13.5 cm. by 5.7 cm.

TC 1618 (Plate 80)

Stele base, rather crude, with a two-line inscription on the smoothed face reading (1) z̲bym (2) d̲rḥn; see *JaPEHA*, pp. 46f., §147. The mortise in the top, set back 1.2 cm. from the face, measures 2 cm. from front to rear by 6 cm. in width and is *ca.* 7 mm.

deep. Traces of orange-red coloring appear on the face and top of the base. The top, sides, and bottom are partly chiseled; the back is irregular. 7 cm. by 10.3 cm. by 5.5 cm.

TC 1622 (Plate 80)

Small stele base with a crude one-line inscription along the top of the smoothed face reading *lt'm/srfm/*; see *JaPEHA*, p. 159, §312. The letters are only about 1 cm. high. A crude mortise, *ca.* 1 cm. deep, occupies nearly all of the top of the base. The front section of the sides and bottom of the base are smoothed evenly, while the rear sections are rough, as is the back of the base. Limestone. 5 cm. by 7.3 cm. by 3.7 cm.

TC 1624 (Plate 80)

Stele base with a two-line inscription on the face reading (1) *'wyfm/* (2) *ġrbm*; see *Ja-PEHA*, pp. 90f., §208. The relatively small mortise, placed toward the rear of the top (3.4 cm. from the face), measures 3.3 cm. from front to rear by 6.5 cm. in width and is 2.9 cm. deep. The interior bears tool marks. All the surfaces of the base are chiseled, but badly weathered and pitted. Limestone. 8.5 cm. by 14.5 cm. by 8.5 cm.

TC 1650 (Plate 80)

Low stele base with a one-line inscription on the face reading *n[b]t'l/ygr*; see *JaPEHA*, pp. 73f., §183. The large mortise in the top, set back 3.8 cm. from the face, measures 4 cm. from front to rear by 16 cm. in width and is *ca.* 3 cm. deep. The impression left in the mortar adhering to the bottom indicates that the plaque had a notch near the center running from face to back; the interior of the mortise is covered with large tool marks. The top of the base has a pecked surface, except for the margins (1 cm. wide) along the sides and a band (1.5 cm. wide) running from front to back across the center. Tool marks and oblique chisel marks are visible on the right side of the base. On the evened left side, which slants in toward the bottom, the letter *s* is found near the front with two short parallel vertical marks (reaching only as high as the shoulders of the *s*) to the right. This piece appears to be part of a re-used building block with a mason's mark on the beveled edge. The back and bottom of the base are irregular. Limestone. 7 cm. by 20 cm. by 12.7 cm.

TC 1651 (Plate 80)

Stele base with a one-line inscription across the top of the polished face reading *ẓrm/ dṣw'n*; see *JaPEHA*, p. 163, §318. The base, when found, was broken vertically through the center into two pieces, but has now been restored with only small fragments missing. The base tapers in width from 11.4 cm. at the bottom to 10.4 cm. at the top. The mortise in the top, set back 2 cm. from the face, measures 2.1 cm. from front to back by 7.5 cm. in width and is 1.9 cm. deep. The interior surfaces exhibit tool marks; some mortar adheres in the left end. The sides and top of the base are smoothed. The back is chiseled even, but numerous tool marks remain visible. The bottom bears large tool marks perpendicular to the face and has chiseled margins around the edges. White alabaster. 9 cm. by 11.4 cm. by 5.5 cm.

TC 1652 (Plate 80)

Stele base with a two-line inscription on the face reading (1) *mdtm* (2) *ygr*; see *JaPEHA*, p. 71, §180. The base tapers in width from 12 cm. at the bottom to 9.6 cm. at the top. The mortise in the top, set back 1.6 cm. from the face and coming within 1.2 cm. of the left side, 1.8 cm. of the right side, measures *ca.* 3 cm. from front to rear by 6.5 cm. in width and is 2.2 cm. deep. The interior is covered with tool marks. The bottom of the base is roughly evened, while the back is irregular. Limestone, with porous surfaces. 8.5 cm. by 9.6 cm. by 5.5 cm.

TC 1665 (Plate 80)

Stele base with a one-line inscription across the top of the face reading *qmlm/y[g]r*; see *JaPEHA*, pp. 77f., §189. Only the vertical shaft of the *g* is preserved; traces of reddening appear on the surface around the inscription. The base is damaged at the lower left corner and elsewhere. The face, top, and sides of the base have been partly smoothed. The mortise in the top, set back 1.7 cm. from the face, is 1.5 cm. deep. It has no rear wall and the narrow walls on the sides slant down toward the rear. The bottom of the mortise is rough, and mortar adheres in places. The bottom of the base has been chiseled at the front, but is elsewhere rough. The back is irregular. Limestone. 11.8 cm. by 15.3 cm. by 8.6 cm.

TC 1666 (Plate 80)

Stele base with a two-line inscription on the face reading (1) *'bḥq[b]* (2) *ḏt/ḏrḥn*; see *JaPEHA*, pp. 40f., §138. Deep guidelines appear at the top, center, and bottom of each line of the inscription. The corners of the base are damaged. The mortise in the top, set back 1.5 cm. from the face, measures *ca.* 2.8 cm. from front to rear by 6.2 cm. in width and is 2 cm. deep. The interior is covered with tool marks. The top and face of the base are superficially smoothed. The sides and bottom are roughly chiseled in part, and the back is irregular. Limestone. 11.2 cm. by 13.5 cm. by 6.2 cm.

TC 1690

Fragment from upper right face of stele base, bearing part of a line of inscription: *yšrḥ'm[/*. There was a mortise in the top of the stele base set back 1.4 cm. from the face and 2.1 cm. from the right side; it was about 2 cm. deep. Alabaster, mottled with light gray and brown. 3.3 cm. by 9.3 cm. by 2.4 cm.

TC 1702 (Plate 80)

Crude stele base with a two-line inscription on the face reading (1) *'mwśl* (2) *ḏrḥn*; see *JaPEHA*, pp. 53f., §157. The inscription is damaged at the upper right and lower left, but the reading is certain. The upper line is on a band 2.5 cm. wide, recessed slightly behind the lower band, 3.5 cm. in width. The face of the base exhibits vertical chisel marks, as do the sides; the chisel marks on the top are parallel to the sides of the base. A mortise in the top, set back 1.5 cm. from the face, measures 3.5 cm. from front to rear by 5 cm. in width and is *ca.* 1.3 cm. deep; the interior is covered with mortar. The back of the base is rough; the bottom is covered with a coat of plaster *ca.* 5 mm. thick, which rested on a flat surface. Limestone. 6.5 cm. by 8.6 cm. by 6.7 cm.

TC 1711 (Plate 80)

Stele base with a two-line inscription on the face reading (1) *ḥmym* (2) *ḏrḥn*; see *JaPEHA*,

p. 43f., §143. The letters of the lower line are not evenly spaced, for a wide gap was left between the first two letters. The face and sides of the base, which have been partly smoothed, slant in toward the top, while the top slopes down toward the rear. The crude mortise in the top, set back 1.3 cm. from the face, measures *ca.* 3 cm. from front to back by ca. 6.5 cm. in width and is 1.4 cm. deep. The interior is covered with tool marks. The back of the base is irregular; the bottom is rough with large tool marks, now somewhat weathered. Limestone. 6.5 cm. by 10.8 cm. by 5.1 cm.

TC 1716 (Plate 81)

Stele base with a two-line inscription reading (1) *ḥrbm* (2) *ḏrḥn*; see *JaPEHA*, p. 45, §145. The face, top, and sides are squared and smoothed. The mortise in the top, set back 1.4 cm. from the face, measures 2.5 cm. from front to back (at the top) by 5.5 cm. in width and is 1.8 cm. deep. Its walls slant in toward the bottom, where it measures 1 cm. by 4.5 cm.; the interior is covered with tool marks. The back of the base is irregular and slants sharply in toward the bottom, which was tooled and chiseled even. Limestone. 6.2 cm. by 8.6 cm. by 6.5 cm.

TC 1725 (Plate 80)

Stele base with a two-line inscription on the polished face reading (1) *'lym* (2) *ḏrḥn*; see *JaPEHA*, pp. 52f., §155. The right rear corner of the base is broken. The width of the base tapers from 13.1 cm. at the bottom to 10.8 cm. at the top. The sides, somewhat rough, were partly chiseled and superficially smoothed. The smooth top, chipped at the front center, contains a mortise measuring 2.1 cm. from front to rear by 8 cm. in width and *ca.* 1.5 cm. in depth. It is set back 1 cm. from the face; the interior is covered with tool marks. The back of the base is rough with long vertical tool marks; the bottom, chipped at the left rear, has tool marks perpendicular to the face. Alabaster, rusty-tan in color. 6.5 cm. by 13.1 cm. by 5.1 cm.

TC 1726 (Plate 80)

Stele base with a one-line inscription across the top of the face reading *rḍt/ḏt/ḏr(ḥn)*; see *JaPEHA*, pp. 61f., §167. The base tapers in width from 12.6 cm. at the bottom to 11.1 cm. at the top. The mortise in the top, set back 2.3 cm. from the face, measures 3.3 cm. from front to rear by 7.5 cm. in width and is 2.3 cm. deep. The interior walls have been chiseled, but tool marks are still visible. The top, face, and sides of the base have been superficially smoothed, but the surfaces are pitted and porous. The back displays large horizontal chisel marks, except for a low, irregular boss in the center. The front part of the bottom is chiseled roughly even, but the back part is irregular. Limestone. 7.8 cm. by 12.6 cm. by 9.5 cm.

TC 1727 (Plate 80)

Stele base with a damaged one-line inscription across the top of the face reading [.]šdm/ d̲rḥn/; see *JaPEHA*, p. 46, §146. Reddening appears at the upper center of the smoothed face. The sides of the base are crudely finished. The top is almost entirely occupied by an irregular mortise bearing long tool marks on the interior. The front wall of the mortise is *ca.* 1.8 cm. high at the right, *ca.* 1 cm. at the left, and it is broken in the center. The back of the base is irregular; the bottom, chiseled even, is square with the face at the right, but slants up toward the rear at the left. Limestone. 7.1 cm. by 16 cm. by 5.2 cm.

TC 1729 (Plate 81)

Stele base with a relatively faint one-line inscription across the top of the smoothed face reading ḥgrm/ylʿb; see *JaPEHA*, p. 110, §239. The left side of the base was mostly chiseled even, but the right side is rough. On the top, there is a step-down of 2 cm. about 1.4 cm. behind the face, leaving a wall, smoothed on top and chiseled on the back, standing in front of a lower level with large tool marks. A stele plaque would have been placed behind the wall, and the base of it plastered to give an appearance similar to that of a plaque inserted into a mortise. The back of the base is irregular; the bottom is roughly chiseled even. Very poor quality alabaster, somewhat porous. 12.8 cm. by 17.3 cm. by 7 cm.

TC 1742 (Plate 80)

Small stele base with a two-line inscription on the smoothed face reading (1) hnʿm (2)

[d̲]rḥn; see *JaPEHA*, pp. 42f., §141. The lower right corner of the face is chipped away, and the first letter of the second line is therefore entirely missing. The top of the h in the first line is also damaged. Conspicuous guidelines indicate the top, center, and bottom of each line. The sides of the base have been smoothed in part. The top, including the interior of the mortise (which lacks a rear wall), and the bottom have been chiseled. The mortise, set back 1 cm. from the face, is *ca.* 5.8 cm. in width and 1.2 cm. deep. The back of the base is irregular. Limestone. 6.3 cm. by 8.1 cm. by 4.1 cm.

TC 1743 (Plate 81)

Small stele base with a two-line inscription on the face reading (1) whbʾl (2) nbryn. The letters of the upper line are *ca.* 2.5 cm. in height, those of the lower *ca.* 2 cm. The face of the base, as the sides, has been smoothed A mortise measuring 2 cm. from front to back by 4.2 cm. in width and 1.4 cm. deep is set in the partly chiseled top of the base *ca.* 1 cm. behind the face; the interior is chiseled. The back of the base is irregular and the lower part of it slants in to meet the chiseled bottom. Limestone. 6.2 cm. by 8.1 cm. by 5.2 cm.

TC 1749 (Plate 80)

Stele base with a one-line inscription across the polished face reading [y]dʿm/g̲rbm; see *JaPEHA*, p. 86, §201. The first letter is entirely missing, because a large area is chipped. The left end of the base was broken off but has been rejoined. The mortise in the top (without rear wall), set back 2.3 cm. from the face, measures 12.7 cm. in width and is 1.2 cm. deep. The interior is covered with tool marks. The top of the base is mostly polished, as are the vertical sides; the back exhibits very large tool marks, while the bottom is rather rough, slanting up toward the rear. Grayish alabaster with light-colored striations. 7 cm. by 15.5 cm. by 5.5 cm.

TC 1750 (Plate 81)

Stele base with a two-line inscription across the face reading (1) q[y]nm (2) g̲rbm; see *JaPEHA*, pp. 94f., §215. A break along the top center of the face destroyed the top of the letter supposed to be y and the certain n.

Each line is on one of the two bands running around the front and sides of the base (the upper band, 3.6 cm. wide, is slightly recessed behind the lower, which is 4.5 cm. wide). The face is polished, as are the top and sides. The mortise in the top, set back 2.5 cm. from the face, measures 2.5 cm. from front to back by 11.4 cm. in width and is 2.7 cm. deep. The interior is covered with tool marks. The back and bottom of the base are rather rough, with a few large tool marks; the bottom slants up toward the rear. Alabaster, with rusty-gray and red streaks. 8 cm. by 17.2 cm. by 9.6 cm.

TC 1752 (Plate 81)

Stele base with a two-line inscription on the face reading (1) *bdrm* (2) *ġrbm*; see *JaPEHA*, pp. 81f., §194. The corners at the sides of the face are beveled. The face, sides, and top have been fairly well smoothed, although the right side is badly chipped. The mortise in the top, set back 1.5 cm. from the face, measures 2.7 cm. from front to rear by 6 cm. in width and is 1.3 cm. deep. Some mortar adheres to the interior, which has been partly chiseled. The back of the base is irregular, while the bottom has been roughly evened. Limestone. 7.8 cm. by 8.9 cm. by 6.2 cm.

TC 1757

Small, crude stele base with a one-line inscription across the top of the face reading *rgnm*; see *JaPEHA*, p. 18, §126. A crude mortise has been chiseled in the top; only the front wall, *ca.* 1 cm. thick, is intact. The sides and bottom of the base are roughly even along the front edge; the back is irregular. Calcite. 7.3 cm. by 8.6 cm. by 4.9 cm.

TC 1758 (Plate 80)

Right part of stele base with a one-line inscription across the face reading *'bkh*/[.. The mortise in the top, set back 1.5 cm. from the face, measures 2.4 cm. from front to rear and is 1.5 cm. deep (its width cannot be determined, as the left end is not preserved). The interior is covered with tool marks. The top, face, and right side of the base are smoothed; the back and bottom are irregular. The original width of the base was at least 14 cm., probably more. Limestone. 7.3 cm. by 10.1 cm. by 5.8 cm.

TC 1759 (Plate 81)

Stele base with a two-line inscription on the face reading (1) *'mt*/*dt* (2) *'zrdn*; see *JaPEHA*, p. 160, §313. Red coloring appears over the surface of the face. The mortise in the top, set back 1.3 cm. from the face, measures *ca.* 3 cm. from front to rear by 6.8 cm. in width and is 2 cm. deep; some mortar adheres to the bottom. The sides and bottom of the base are square with the face; the back is somewhat irregular. Limestone, extremely porous. 11 cm. by 11.9 cm. by 6.4 cm.

TC 1764

Badly damaged, tall stele base with a two-line inscription high up on the face reading (1) *ḥ*[....] (2) *dr*[*ḥn*]. The lower end of *ḥ* in the second line is preserved. The mortise in the top, now mostly missing, was 2.7 cm. deep and was set back 1.6 cm. from the face. The interior is covered with tool marks. The right side of the base slants in toward the top; the left side is entirely gone. The face has been smoothed, while the side which is preserved and the bottom were very roughly chiseled; the back is irregular. The base was originally *ca.* 15 or 16 cm. wide at the bottom. Limestone. 14.4 cm. by 10.5 cm. by 6.1 cm.

TC 1765 (Plate 81)

Badly weathered stele base with two horizontal bands running around the front and sides. The upper band (*ca.* 3.7 cm. wide) is recessed 5 mm. behind the lower band (*ca.* 4 cm. wide). A one-line inscription appears on each band on the front, reading (1) *ḥwtr't* (2) *t*/*dyṯ'n*; see *JaPEHA*, pp. 150f., §298. The mortise in the top, set back 2.5 cm. from the face of the upper band, measures 3.7 cm. from front to rear by 6.1 cm. in width and is 2.3 cm. deep. The bottom and inside of the rear wall are rough with tool marks, while the other walls have been chiseled even. The back of the base has several very large tool marks. The bottom is somewhat irregular and slants up toward the rear. Limestone. 9 cm. by 12.5 cm. by 10.1 cm.

TC 1766 (Plate 81)

Stele base with a one-line inscription across the face reading *'zm*/*ygr*; see *JaPEHA*, pp. 75f., §186. The face is the only surface which has been smoothed; the lower right corner is chipped. The base tapers in width from 12.2 cm. at the bottom to 11.4 cm. at the top. The top of the base is in poor condition, but indications of a mortise, measuring *ca.* 7 cm. in width, are preserved. The back and bottom of the piece are irregular. Poor quality alabaster. 9.5 cm. by 12.2 cm. by 5.5 cm.

TC 1767 (Plate 81)

Crude stele base with a two-line inscription on the face reading (1) *ṣmytt* (2) *d̲rḫn*; see *JaPEHA*, p. 58, §162. On the top is a step-down of 2 cm., about 2 cm. behind the face (compare TC 1729 above). The front edges of the top, sides, and bottom of the base have been chiseled; the back is irregular. Porous calcite. 12 cm. by 13.4 cm. by 5.8 cm.

TC 1779 (Plate 81)

Stele base with a one-line inscription across the top of the polished face reading 'l*š̌rḫ*/ *yn'm*; see *JaPEHA*, p. 113, §243. The face is damaged along the bottom. The mortise in the polished top, set back 1.8 cm. from the face, measures 12.7 cm. in width and is 1.4 cm. deep. It has no rear wall, and most of the left wall is missing; the inside of the front wall has been chiseled even, while the bottom of the mortise exhibits tool marks. The sides of the base have been chiseled even and partly smoothed along the front edges. The bottom has been roughly chiseled even, but the back is irregular and has several very large oblique tool marks. White alabaster with thick brown band at rear. 7.6 cm. by 16.9 cm. by 7.7 cm.

TC 1781 (Plate 81)

Right part of a very large stele base with a two-line inscription on the polished face reading (1) *mqf*/*nb*[. . . .] (2) *d̲ġr*[*bm*]. The minimum lengths of the lines are derived from the position of the mortise; the characters in the second line are much more widely spaced than those in the first line. The mortise in the polished top is set back 4.4 cm. from the face, 7.5 cm. from the back, and 10 cm. from the right side. It measures 3.2 cm. from front to rear and is 2.6 cm. deep; it was at least some 9 cm. in width. The interior is rough with tool marks. The right side of the base has been tooled roughly even. The back, slanting in toward the right, was split along

a brown banding. The bottom was chiseled along the front edge but is rough elsewhere, though fairly even. The original width of the base must have been approximately 29 cm. Alabaster, mottled grayish and light brown, with horizontal striations. 13.2 cm. by 16 cm. by 15.3 cm.

TC 1782

Small stele base, chipped at the upper left corner of the face, with a two-line inscription on the polished face reading (1) *ṣbḥ*[*t*/*d̲t*] (2) *ġrbm*; see *JaPEHA*, pp. 93f., §213. On the top, behind a ridge at the front, is an area depressed *ca.* 5 mm. and covered with tool marks. The sides have been smoothed, although the left one is badly damaged; the back and bottom are covered with tool marks. Alabaster, mottled tan and light brown, with narrow brown striations. 5.3 cm. by 7.2 cm. by 5 cm.

TC 1783

Stele base, damaged on left, with a two-line inscription on the face reading (1) *skn*[*m*] (2) *ġrb*[*m*]; see *JaPEHA*, pp. 89f., §207. Deep guidelines appear at the top and bottom of each line, lighter ones in the center. The mortise in the top, set back 1.2 cm. from the face, measures 2.7 cm. from front to rear by 4.6 cm. in width and is 1.2 cm. deep. The interior is covered with tool marks. The top, face, and sides of the base are smoothed; the back and bottom are irregular. Limestone. 7.1 cm. by 9.4 cm. by 5.2 cm.

TC 1789 (Plate 81)

Stele base with a two-line inscription across the face reading (1) *mskm* (2) *d̲rḫn*; see *JaPEHA*, pp. 49f., §151. The base tapers in width from 13 cm. at the bottom to 11.6 cm. at the top. The mortise in the top, set back 2 cm. from the face, measures 2.4 cm. from front to rear by 8.3 cm. in width and is 2.3 cm. deep at the right end, sloping up to a depth of 1 cm. at the left end. The rear wall is mostly broken away; the inside surfaces of the other walls have been chiseled even, but tool marks are visible on the bottom. The right half of the bottom is covered with mortar. The top, face, and sides of the base have been smoothed; the back is very rough, with large tool marks. The bottom has been mostly chiseled even. Limestone. 9 cm. by 13 cm. by 5.8 cm.

TC 1790

Stele base with a two-line inscription on the face reading (1) '*mynt* (2) *ḏt/'lm*; see *Ja-PEHA*, pp. 132f., §273. Red coloring appears on the face. The base tapers in width from 10 cm. at the bottom to 9.1 cm. at the top. The mortise in the top, set back 1.1 cm. from the face, measures *ca.* 1.6 cm. from front to back by 4 cm. in width. It is nearly filled with mortar, which bears the impression of the irregularly shaped lower end of the upright member. The sides and bottom of the base are roughly evened; the back is irregular. Porous, crystalline stone. 8.2 cm. by 10 cm. by 4.8 cm.

TC 1815

Left end of stele base with a two-line inscription on the polished face: (1) [..]*rm* (2) [..]*bm*. The top (similar to TC 1729) has a wall along the front 1.2 cm. thick and 1.8 cm. high, behind which is a roughly tooled area on which the lower end of the upright plaque rested. The left side and back of the base are tooled even, and the horizontal tool marks on the back are very long. The bottom, which slants up toward the rear, is roughly tooled even, except along the front where it has been chiseled. Dark, mottled alabaster. 11.3 cm. by 9.7 cm. by 6.6 cm.

TC 1817 (Plate 81)

Wide stele base with a one-line inscription extending the full width near the top of the polished face: *nb't/ḏt/ġrbm*. The mortise in the top, set back 3.2 cm. from the face, measures 3.5 cm. from front to rear by 11.9 cm. in width and is 2 cm. deep. The interior is covered with tool marks. The top of the base is polished smooth in front of the mortise and chiseled even to the sides, but the area behind the mortise has only been roughly tooled. The sides were polished smooth; the back is irregular, exhibiting several large vertical tool marks near the center. The bottom is partly irregular (toward the back) and partly evened with long tool marks perpendicular to the face, while a margin with oblique chisel marks runs along the front edge. Mottled alabaster,

light grayish and brown. 10.1 cm. by 22.2 cm. by 9.5 cm.

TC 1821 (Plate 81)

Stele base with a one-line inscription across the top of the polished face: *lḥy'm/dġrbm*; see *JaPEHA*, pp. 87f., §203. The base tapers in width from 15.8 cm. at the bottom to 14.8 cm. at the top. There is a raised band across the bottom of the face 3.3 cm. wide at the left and narrowing to 2.8 cm. at the right. The mortise in the top, set back 1.5 cm. from the face, measures 2 cm. from front to rear (although there is very little of the rear wall intact) by 11.2 cm. in width and is 1 cm. deep. The interior, mostly covered with mortar, was tooled on the bottom, while the inside of the front wall was chiseled and smoothed. The sides of the base have been smoothed. The back is somewhat irregular; the bottom, which slants up toward the back, bears large tool marks perpendicular to the face, except for a margin along the front edge with oblique chisel marks. Alabaster, light grayish in color, with horizontal light brown striations through the center. 10 cm. by 15.8 cm. by 7.5 cm.

TC 1843 (Plate 81)

Stele base with a two-line inscription on the face reading (1) *rkymt* (2) *ḏt/mlkn*; see *Ja-PEHA*, pp. 155f., §306. The face has been superficially polished. In the top, which was completely evened and polished, is a shallow mortise set back 1 cm. from the face. It measures 3 cm. from front to rear by 9.5 cm. in width and has a maximum depth of 9 mm. The interior is covered with tool marks; the bottom slopes up toward the rear. The left side of the base is squared and polished, as is also the bottom. The right side, which slants out slightly toward the rear, is mostly chiseled even, but not smoothed. The left part of the back is set in *ca.* 1.8 cm. from the right part. The latter part has been evened and bears vertical chisel marks, while the offset and the recessed left part bear tool marks and only a chiseled margin along the top. The piece has been re-used; the top, bottom, and left side, representing the original surfaces, display the highest quality of workmanship. Grayish, mottled alabaster. 7.5 cm. by 12.6 cm. by 7 cm.

TC 1845 (Plate 81)

Large stele base, right part badly damaged, with a two-line inscription on the face reading (1) [*lḥy*]'*m* (2) [*d̲y*]*gr* (only *y* of line two is completely missing); see *JaPEHA*, pp. 70f., §179. The face, sides, and top are polished. The mortise in the top, set back 2.6 cm. from the face, measures 3.8 cm. from front to rear and is 2 cm. deep; its estimated width is 17 cm. The bottom is covered with mortar at the left. The base tapered in width from an estimated 24.5 cm. at the bottom to 22.7 cm. at the top. The back of the base is entirely rough, while the bottom was chiseled even. Light-colored alabaster with dark-red streaks, blackened at right by fire. 10.5 cm. by 24 cm. by 10 cm.

TC 1853 (Plate 81)

Wide stele base with a two-line inscription on the face reading (1) '*lqdm* (2) *d̲ygr*; see *JaPEHA*, pp. 63f., §169. The edges of the piece are chipped at numerous points. The face, sides, and top of the base are polished. The mortise in the top, set back 1.9 cm. from the face, measures *ca.* 4 cm. from front to rear by *ca.* 16.5 cm. in width and is 1.5 cm. deep. The rear wall has been broken away; the interior is covered with tool marks, while bits of mortar adhere along the front. The back of the base is rough; the bottom is chiseled even except for a small area in the rear center which was left rough with tool marks. Light-colored alabaster, mottled. 8 cm. by 19.5 cm. by 7.5 cm.

TC 1859 (Plate 81)

Stele base with a two-line inscription on the face reading (1) '*byt*' (2) *ġrbm*; see *JaPEHA*, p. 80, §192. Guidelines appear at the top and bottom of each line, fainter ones at the center of each line; a trace of reddening is seen on the face in the lower center. The piece tapers in width from 14.5 cm. at the bottom to 12.3 cm. at the top. The mortise in the top, set back 2 cm. from the face, measures 3.4 cm. from front to rear by 9.3 cm. in width and is 2.5 cm. deep. Most of the interior is covered with mortar. The face, top, and sides of the base are smoothed; the back is rough. The bottom has been tooled and partly chiseled even. Limestone. 11 cm. by 14.5 cm. by 8.5 cm.

TC 1869 (Plate 81)

Small stele base with a two-line inscription on the face reading (1) *yt̲*'*m* (2) *ygr*; see *JaPEHA*, p. 70, §178. The base tapers in width (at the face) from 8.8 cm. at the bottom to 7.5 cm. at the top. The mortise in the top, set back 8 mm. from the face, measures 2.4 cm. from front to rear by 5.2 cm. in width; the bottom of it is filled with mortar. The face, top, and sides of the base are smoothed; the bottom is chiseled even. The back is roughly tooled and chiseled. Limestone. 6.2 cm. by 9 cm. (at the rear) by 5.3 cm.

TC 1876 (Plate 81)

Stele base with a two-line inscription on the face reading (1) '*mm* (2) *ġrbm*; see *JaPEHA*, p. 91, §209, Pl. xix, above. The polished face bears traces of reddening. The sides, chiseled even and partly smoothed, slant in toward the rear. The superficially polished top slants down toward the rear. The mortise in the top, set back 1.8 cm. from the face, lacks a rear wall; it is 12 cm. wide and 2.5 cm. deep. The inside of the front wall and part of the bottom are covered with mortar bearing the imprint of the lost stele. The back of the base is tooled; the bottom is chiseled even. White alabaster. 8.5 cm. by 16.3 cm. by 6 cm.

TC 1877 (Plate 81)

Stele base with a one-line inscription across the top of the polished face reading '*mm*/ *d̲tm*'*dm*; see *JaPEHA*, pp. 117f., §251. The mortise (lacking a rear wall) is set far back in the polished top (3 cm. behind the face); it is 13 cm. wide, and the interior is covered with small tool marks. The right side of the base is polished, but the left side is uneven and bears tool marks except where evenly chiseled along the front and top. The back of the base is tooled somewhat even; the bottom is tooled and partly chiseled along the front. Alabaster with striations of a light rusty hue paralleling the face. 7.7 cm. by 16.6 cm. by 5 cm.

TC 1878 (Plate 81)

Stele base with a two-line inscription on the face reading (1) *skynt* (2) *ġrbm*; see *JaPEHA*, pp. 88f., §205, Pl. xix, below. The upper left corner of the face has been lost since excavation. Guidelines appear at the top, center, and bottom of each line. This piece has apparently been re-used, for a crude, shallow mortise is found on the left side, set back *ca.* 1.5 cm. from the face. Some mortar is preserved in this depression, which measures 7 cm. by *ca.* 1.8 cm. The mortise in the top, set back 1.9 cm. from the face, measures 2.4 cm. from front to rear by 7.8 cm. in width; the bottom of it is covered with mortar. The face, sides, top, and bottom of the base are smoothed, though now scarred; the back is irregular. Limestone. 10.2 cm. by 10.8 cm. by 6.2 cm.

TC 1886

Low, crude stele base with a two-line inscription on the face: (1) *hl[q.]* (2) *ḏ[bġ]m.* The letters are neither carefully made nor clear, so the reading is not certain. The upper left front corner of the base was broken in excavation. The mortise in the top, set back 3 cm. from the face, measures 2.7 cm. from front to rear by 5.5 cm. in width and is 2 cm. deep. The piece is irregular except for the evened face, top, and right side. Limestone. 4.8 cm. by 10.2 cm. by 8.7 cm.

TC 1887 (Plate 81)

Stele base with a one-line inscription across upper part of the polished face: *lḥyʿm/ḏḏrḥn;* see *JaPEHA*, pp. 48f., §150. The base tapers in width from 17.6 cm. at the bottom to 16.2 cm. at the top. The mortise in the superficially polished top, set back 1.5 cm. from the face, measures *ca.* 4 cm. from front to rear by 13.8 cm. from the face, measures 2.7 cm. from front sloping up at the rear to meet the surface. Bits of mortar cling in some of the tool marks. The sides of the base are chiseled even and partly smoothed; the back has large tool marks, mostly vertical. The bottom is chiseled fairly even. Alabaster, light-colored, mottled with reddish-brown. 11.5 cm. by 17.6 cm. by 6.8 cm.

TC 1888 (Plate 81)

Unusually wide stele base with a one-line inscription across the top of the polished face: *lḥyʿm/mʾdm;* see *JaPEHA*, pp. 116f., §249 (where the *ḏ* is to be deleted). The mortise in the polished top, set back 2.6 cm. from the face, measures 2.2 cm. from front to

rear by 24.5 cm. in width and is 2 cm. deep. The bottom is covered with mortar. The right side of the base is mostly chiseled and smoothed, but more irregular near the bottom. The left side is chiseled even along the front, but irregular elsewhere. The back is rough with extremely large tool marks; the bottom is chiseled even. Light-colored alabaster with several dark streaks. 11 cm. by 28.7 cm. by 7.4 cm.

TC 1900 (Plate 81)

Stele base with a one-line inscription across the top of the polished face: *hw[kn/]ḏygr.* Owing to a large chipped area at the top center, only the lower parts of the proposed *k, n* and the word divider are preserved. These letters are suggested by the spacing and by the first element of the name *hwknʿm* occurring on stele base TC 4 (see *JaPEHA*, pp. 122f., §258). The width of the base tapers from 18 cm. at the bottom to 15.2 cm. at the top. The mortise in the polished top, set back 1.6 cm. from the face, is 12.2 cm. wide and 1.5 cm. deep; the rear wall is broken away along with much of the back of the base. The sides of the base are mostly even and smoothed; the bottom is tooled and chiseled fairly even. Light-colored alabaster with thick brown band across the back. 9.8 cm. by 18 cm. by 7.5 cm.

TC 1902 (Plate 81)

Badly weathered stele base with a two-line inscription on the face reading (1) *nbṭm* (2) *drʾm;* see *JaPEHA*, pp. 35f., §132. The last letter of line 2 is clearly *m*, so the drawing on p. 243 of *JaPEHA* is curious. The mortise in the top measures 2.1 cm. from front to rear by 7.4 cm. in width and is 2.5 cm. deep. Only the back of the base was left irregular, although the other faces are now damaged, especially at the edges and corners. Very porous, dark limestone. 10 cm. by 10.8 cm. by 6 cm.

TC 1903 (Plate 81)

Stele base with a one-line inscription across the top of the face: *]grm/ḥḏrn;* see *JaPEHA*, pp. 106f., §234. The shaft of the initial letter is clear and belongs to a *y, ḥ,* or more probably *ḥ* in view of *ḥgrm* of TC 1729 (above in this section). The mortise in the top, lacking a rear wall, is set back 2 cm. from the face, measures 13.7 cm. in width, and is 2 cm. deep (maximum). The bottom of it is irregular and bears several long tool marks. The inside of the three walls is chiseled even, slanting outward toward the top. The face and top of the base are even; the sides are partly evened. The back and bottom are irregular. Sandstone. 9.3 cm. by 17.7 cm. by 7.5 cm.

TC 1926 (Plate 81)

Stele base with a two-line inscription on the face: (1) *mlḥm* (2) *ygr*; see *JaPEHA*, pp. 71f., §181, Pl. xx, bottom. Guidelines appear at the top, center, and bottom of each line. The face, top, and sides are covered with reddening. The left center of the face and left top are chipped. The width of the base tapers from 13.2 cm. at the bottom to 12.4 cm. at the top. The mortise in the top, lacking a rear wall, is set back 2 cm. from the face; it is 7.6 cm. wide and 1.3 cm. deep. The bottom is roughly tooled, while the inner sides of the walls are chiseled even. The face, top, and sides of the piece are smoothed; the bottom is partly chiseled even. The back is completely irregular. Limestone. 8.8 cm. by 13.2 cm. by 6.7 cm.

TC 1927 (Plate 82)

Stele base with a two-line inscription on the face: (1) *blm* (2) *drḥn*; see *JaPEHA*, pp. 41f., §139. Guidelines appear at the top and bottom of each line. The mortise in the top, set back 2 cm. from the face, measures 3 cm. from front to rear by 7 cm. in width and is *ca.* 1.7 cm. deep. Some mortar adheres to the rough interior. Only the face of the base is smoothed; the top and sides are crudely chiseled. The bottom is tooled roughly even; but the back is irregular. Limestone. 9.4 cm. by 12.8 cm. by 8.2 cm.

TC 1928

Badly weathered stele base with a two-line inscription on the face reading (1) *ḥfnm* (2) *ygr*; see *JaPEHA*, p. 68, §175. Traces of reddening are visible on the face. The width of the base tapers from 15 cm. at the bottom to 11.8 cm. at the top. The mortise in the top, set back 2.5 cm. from the face, measures 2.8 cm. from front to rear (the rear wall is mostly missing) by 7.8 cm. in width and is 2 cm. deep.

Very porous limestone. 11.2 cm. by 15 cm. by 6.5 cm.

TC 1950 (Plate 81)

Stele base with a one-line inscription across the upper part of the polished face reading *ṣbḥkrb/dg̣rbm*; see *JaPEHA*, pp. 92f., §212. The mortise in the polished top, set back 1.3 cm. from the face, is 16.1 cm. wide and 1.6 cm. deep (there is no rear wall). The walls are chiseled even, while the bottom is covered with tool marks running from front to back; a patch of mortar remains in the right front corner. The sides of the base are chiseled and superficially smoothed at front and top, but rough elsewhere; the back, bearing some tool marks, is rather irregular. The bottom is tooled even (with long marks running from front to back). White alabaster, with a brown band at right rear corner. 6.7 cm. by 19.8 cm. by 5.8 cm.

TC 1994 (Plate 82)

Stele base with a one-line inscription across the top of the polished face reading *mʿdʾl/dhnʿmt*; see *JaPEHA*, p. 104, §229. The crude mortise in the top, set back *ca.* 1.2 cm. from the face, is *ca.* 10 cm. wide and 1.3 cm. deep (it has no rear wall). The walls are partly chiseled even on a bevel; the bottom is roughly tooled. The top of the base is chiseled even. The sides and bottom are roughly chiseled; the back is irregular. Grayish alabaster with rusty-brown streaks. 7.2 cm. by 14.5 cm. by 7.5 cm.

TC 1995 (Plate 82)

Stele base with a two-line inscription on the face: (1) *ḥqbm* (2) *ṭdʾm*; see *JaPEHA*, p. 147, §293, Pl. xxi, above. Deep guidelines appear at the top and bottom of each line; another was made in error *ca.* 3 mm. above the lower guide of line 2. The lower corners of the base are damaged and the face is chipped in several places. The width tapers from a reconstructed 17.5 cm. at the bottom to 12 cm. at the top. The carefully squared (chiseled) mortise in the top, set back 1.6 cm. from the face, measures 3 cm. from front to rear by 8 cm. in width and is *ca.* 9 mm. deep. The sides of the base are chiseled roughly even; the bottom and back are less regular. Sandstone. 12.2 cm. by 16.5 cm. by 6.6 cm.

TC 1996 (Plate 82)

Stele base with a one-line inscription filling the upper band across the top of the face: *ṯṯ[ymms]fʿn*. The proposed reading (within the brackets) is uncertain, as the upper half of the line is missing and the lower parts of some of the letters are damaged. The upper band, recessed slightly, was originally at least 5 cm. wide; the lower band is 5.5 cm. No part of the top of the base is preserved; the mortise measures 3.5 cm. from front to rear by 9.7 cm. in width and had an estimated depth of 3.5 cm. or more. The right side of the base, chiseled even, slants in toward the rear; the left side, as the back, is irregular. The bottom is chiseled even, slanting up toward the rear. Limestone. 10.3 cm. by 14.3 cm. by 7 cm.

TC 1997 (Plate 82)

Low stele base with a one-line inscription across the polished face: *tbʿkrb/ġrbm*; see *JaPEHA*, p. 96, §217. The mortise in the polished top, set back 2.8 cm. from the face, measures 2.2 cm. from front to rear by 8.6 cm. in width and is at least 1.8 cm. deep (the bottom is covered with mortar). The roughly chiseled and tooled sides of the base are vertical at the front, but slant in toward the bottom elsewhere. The back and bottom are rough, the latter displaying rather large tool marks. Alabaster, mostly blackened by fire. 3.8 cm. by 12.4 cm. by 9 cm.

TC 2014

Badly damaged stele base with a two-line inscription on the face reading (1) *ʾbnm* (2) *ylʿb*; see *JaPEHA*, pp. 109f., §238, Pl. xxi, below. There is a trace of the mortise preserved, but owing to damage no details are clear. The sides and bottom of the base are rough, the back completely irregular. Poor quality alabaster. 7.5 cm. by 9.8 cm. by 5.6 cm.

TC 2044 (Plate 82)

Stele base with a two-line inscription on the face reading (1) *shytm* (2) *ḏrḥn*; see *JaPEHA*, pp. 50f., §153. The mortise in the top, set back 8 mm. from the face, has no rear wall. At the right end the tooled bottom slopes up to meet the top surface; the inside of the front wall is chiseled even on a bevel. The left side of the base, slanting in toward the rear, is partly smoothed, as is the face. The

back is irregular, so that the piece is much thicker at the left than at the right. The bottom is rough. Conglomerate. 6 cm. by 11 cm. by 5.3 cm.

TC 2046

Weathered stele base with a two-line inscription on the face reading (1) *nʿmt* (2) *ynʿm*; see *JaPEHA*, pp. 114f., §246. Traces of reddening appear on the face and the top. The width of the base tapers from 11.2 cm. at the bottom to 9 cm. at the top. The mortise in the top, set back 1 cm. from the face, lacks a rear wall. It is *ca.* 6.3 cm. wide and 2 cm. deep; the front corners of it are rounded. The sides of the base are chiseled even along the front, left rough elsewhere. The back and bottom have been partly chiseled, but are not entirely regular. Very porous limestone. 8 cm. by 11.2 cm. by 5 cm.

TC 2047 (Plate 82)

Stele base with a two-line inscription on the face reading (1) *btʿ* (2) *hnʿmt*; see *JaPEHA*, pp. 101f., §225. The mortise in the top, set back 1.4 cm. from the face, measures 2.6 cm. from front to rear by 5.3 cm. in width and is *ca.* 1.5 cm. deep; it narrows toward the bottom. The face of the base is mostly smoothed. The top in front of the mortise is chiseled even; the sides, not square with the face, are rough. The back is irregularly convex; the bottom is roughly tooled even. Limestone. 6.5 cm, by 10 cm. by 7 cm.

TC 2048 (Plate 82)

Stele base with a two-line inscription on the face: (1) *klbt* (2) *ylʿb*; see *JaPEHA*, pp. 110f., §240. The upper line fills a band 3 cm. wide and recessed 4 mm.; the lower line, with slightly shorter letters, is on a band 4.5 cm. wide. The mortise in the top, set back 1.3 cm. from the face, measures 3.5 cm. from front to rear by 5.9 cm. in width at the front (5.1 cm. at the rear); it is 2 cm. deep. The interior, partly covered with mortar, exhibits irregular tool marks. The top and sides of the base are chiseled even; the back and bottom are rough but even. Vertical tool marks appear on the upper part of the back. At the right rear corner, *ca.* 2 cm. from the bottom, is a deep horizontal cut; the maker had apparently started to cut the piece off at this point by drilling numerous small holes in the same plane. Limestone. 8 cm. by 8.5 cm. by 6.8 cm.

TC 2052 (Plate 82)

Stele base with a two-line inscription on the face reading (1) *ḫfnm* (2) *ḏrḥn*; see *JaPEHA*, pp. 44f., §144. Guidelines appear at the top, center, and bottom of each line. The mortise in the top, set back 1.2 cm., measures 2.3 cm. from front to rear by 5 cm. in width and is 1.4 cm. deep. It is set slightly nearer to the right side than to the left. The sides of the base are chiseled roughly even, as is the bottom. The back, which exhibits several very large tool marks, curves in toward the bottom, so that the bottom of the base is only 1.5 to 2 cm. thick. Limestone. 7.8 cm. by 9.5 cm. by 4.7 cm.

TC 2066 (Plate 82)

Stele base with a two-line inscription on the polished face reading (1) *td'[. .'l]* (2) *qḥlwm*. There is a large damaged area on the upper left of the face. The lower end of a vertical shaft indicates that the fourth character is *g*, *l*, or *y*; the fifth is lacking entirely. The last two, with lower extremities preserved, are almost certainly *'l*, especially as a name of this length would be a compound. The tribal name of the second line appears on TC 18, 1590, 1616, 2090, and 2109. The base tapers in width from 18.6 cm. at the bottom to 17.2 cm. at the top. The mortise in the top, lacking a rear wall, is set back 1.5 cm. from the face; it is 14.5 cm. wide and 1 cm. deep. The inside of the front wall is chiseled even, and the bottom is tooled even. The top of the base has been partly polished, though chisel marks toward the rear have not been entirely removed; the back is irregular. The bottom is tooled fairly even and chiseled along the front; the bottom rear of the base is beveled, with two extremely long horizontal tool marks visible. White alabaster. 8.2 cm. by 18.6 cm. by 5.6 cm.

TC 2084 (Plate 82)

Stele base with a one-line inscription across the top of the smoothed face reading *'mt/ zknn*; see *JaPEHA*, p. 145, §290. The mortise in the top, lacking a rear wall, is set back 1.5 cm. from the face; it is 14.3 cm. wide and 1.5 cm. deep. The top, sides, and bottom of the

base are rough; the back is irregular. Hard, light brown stone, which has flaked when subjected to a hard blow. 11.2 cm. by 14.5 cm. by 6.3 cm.

TC 2085 (Plate 82)

Stele base with a two-line inscription on the smoothed face reading (1) *yšrḥ'm/* (2) *ḏygr*; see *JaPEHA*, p. 69, §177. Guidelines appear at the top, center, and bottom of each line. Reddening, now faint, was applied to the surface. The base tapers in width from 14.5 cm. at the bottom to 12.2 cm. at the top. The mortise in the top, set back 1.5 cm. from the face, measures 4.8 cm. from front to rear by 9.4 cm. in width and is 2.2 cm. deep; the right wall is mostly broken away. The interior is covered with tool marks, and mortar covers most of the bottom. The top around the mortise is chiseled even, with a narrow smoothed margin along the front. The sides of the base are chiseled even, with long horizontal chisel marks visible. The bottom is rough, the back completely irregular. Limestone. 12.1 cm. by 14.5 cm. by 8.5 cm.

TC 2088 (Plate 82)

Stele base with a two-line inscription on the face reading (1) *yṣr'm* (2) *ḏ'bm*; *JaPEHA*, p. 135, §277. Guidelines appear at the top of line one and at the bottom of line two, while a common guideline runs between the two lines. In addition, an incised line runs 2 mm. above the upper guideline, i.e., within 3 mm. of the top of the base. The mortise in the top, set back 1.4 cm. from the face, measures 2.6 cm. from front to rear by 5.9 cm. in width and is 2.1 cm. deep. The face and top of the base are smoothed. The sides are superficially smoothed; the left side slants in slightly toward the rear. The back and bottom are irregular, though some chiseling was done on the bottom. Limestone. 7.3 cm. by 8.7 cm. by 7 cm.

TC 2089 (Plate 82)

Stele base with two horizontal bands on the face, each bearing one line of inscription: (1) *yt't* (2) *ḏrḥn*; *JaPEHA*, p. 47, §148. Guidelines appear at the top and bottom of each line, at the center of the lower line, and somewhat below the center of the upper line. The upper band, recessed slightly, is 3.5 cm. wide, while the lower is 4.7 cm. The base tapers in width from 10.3 cm. at the bottom to 9.4 cm. at the top. The mortise in the top, set back 1.7 cm. from the face, measures 2.5 cm. from front to rear by 7 cm. in width; at the left end, it is *ca.* 3 cm. deep, less at the right. The impression in the mortar which fills much of the interior indicates a stele plaque which was irregular on the lower end with a pointed protrusion at the left. The top of the base, broken at rear and right of the mortise, was smoothed, as was the face. The sides are superficially smoothed; the bottom is rough but even. The back is more irregular with several large tool marks near the top. Limestone. 8.3 cm. by 10.3 cm. by 6.4 cm.

TC 2091 (Plate 82)

Right part of a broken stele base with a two-line inscription on the face: (1) *lbʾm [/bn/]* (2) *nʿ[m]*. If it is assumed that characters were equally spaced, four are needed to complete line one, more if line two was longer than reconstructed. The mortise in the top, set back 2 cm. from the face, measures *ca.* 4 cm. from front to back and is 1.8 cm. deep; the interior is covered with tool marks, vertical on the inside of the front wall. The face, top, right side, and bottom of the base are polished; the back is tooled roughly even. Light-colored alabaster with a rusty tint. 8 cm. by 13.3 cm. (estimated original width, 24.5 cm.) by 10 cm.

TC 2109 (Plate 82)

Stele base with a two-line inscription on the polished face reading (1) *drmm/* (2) *qhlwm*; see *JaPEHA*, p. 124, §260, Pl. xxiii, below (photograph retouched to block out irregular rear portions of piece). On the top, 1.3 cm. behind the face, is a cut running from one side of the base to the other. This cut leaves a wall *ca.* 1.6 cm. high with a smoothed top and a slanting back (increasing the width of the wall to *ca.* 1.9 cm. at the bottom), chiseled even. The surface of the rest of the top of the base, covered with large tool marks, rises irregularly toward the back, where it is *ca.* 1 cm. higher than the top of the wall at the face. Mortar adheres to part of this area. The sides of the base are roughly chiseled even and superficially smoothed; the right side slants out toward the back. The back is irregular and bears four extremely large tool marks, approximately vertical. The bottom is

rough. White alabaster. 10.8 cm. by 13.5 cm. by 9.5 cm.

TC 2116 (Plate 82)

Stele base with a two-line inscription on the face reading (1) *sknm* (2) *drʾn*; see *JaPEHA*, pp. 36f., §133, Pl. xxiv, below. The base tapers in width from 11.2 cm. at the bottom to 10 cm. at the top. The mortise in the top, set back 2.1 cm. from the face, measures 2.6 cm. from front to rear (narrowing toward the left end) by 6.8 cm. in width and is 1.5 cm. deep. The face and top of the base are smoothed; the left side is rough, though partly chiseled; the right side is even; the bottom is very rough; the back is irregular. Limestone. 8.5 cm. by 11.2 cm. by 7.2 cm.

TC 2159 (Plate 82)

Stele base with two horizontal bands on the face, each bearing one line of inscription: (1) *dʾyn* (2) *dʾlm*. The *d* is crowded in at the beginning of the lower line before the *ʾlm*, which is centered (it also occurs on TC 1790). The upper band, set in *ca.* 4 mm. behind the lower, is 3 cm. wide, corresponding to the height of the letters on it. The lower band is 3.5 cm. wide, with characters of equally greater dimensions on it. The mortise in the top, set back 5.1 cm. from the face, is 11.3 cm. wide and 1.3 cm. deep. Only the front of it is preserved, owing to an oblique fracture which removed the whole upper rear of the base. The face and top of the base are polished; the sides are even and smoothed. The bottom is rough with large tool marks (some plaster adheres in them). White alabaster with brownish band. 7.3 cm. by 14.8 cm. by 11 cm.

TC 2161

Weathered stele base with a two-line inscription on the face reading (1) *dkrt* (2) *hnʿmt*; see *JaPEHA*, pp. 102f., §226. The base tapers in width from 8 cm. at the bottom to 7 cm. at the top. The mortise in the top, set back 1.3 cm. from the face, measures *ca.* 1.6 cm. from front to rear by 4.4 cm. in width and is nearly filled with mortar. The sides of the base are even; the bottom is chiseled roughly even. The back is irregular. Very porous stone. 6.8 cm. by 8 cm. by 5.2 cm.

TC 2162 (Plate 82)

Damaged stele base with a two-line inscription on the face reading (1) *ynʿm* (2) *dt/*

hn'mt. The upper left and center of the face is chipped, so that the upper parts of the *n*, ' and *m* of line one are missing, but there is no doubt about the reading. Traces of reddening appear on the chiseled surface of the face. The base tapers in width from 11 cm. at the bottom to 9.8 cm. at the top. The mortise in the top, set back *ca.* 1 cm. from the face, measures *ca.* 2.3 cm. from front to rear by 6.5 cm. in width and is about 1 cm. deep. The bottom is filled with mortar. The top of the base behind the mortise slopes up irregularly toward the rear. The sides of the base are chiseled even; the bottom is tooled and partly chiseled even. The back is less regular and has mortar adhering to it at the upper left. Limestone. 8.8 cm. by 11 cm. by 6.6 cm.

TC 2163 (Plate 82)

Stele base with a two-line inscription on the face reading (1) *nbt'm* (2) *ygr*; see *JaPEHA*, pp. 74f., §184. Reddening stains the partly smoothed face. The mortise in the top, set back 2.7 cm. from the face, measures *ca.* 7.5 cm. in width and is 2.4 cm. deep. This depth is maintained back about 1.5 cm. from the front wall, at which point the bottom begins to slope upward until it reaches the surface of the top of the base some 6 cm. behind the front wall. The top in front of the mortise is smoothed; farther back it is rough and irregular. The sides of the base are superficially smoothed; the back is very roughly tooled even. The bottom is rather irregular. White limestone. 9.5 cm. by 11.5 cm. by 10.5 cm.

TC 2167 (Plate 82)

Large stele base with a one-line inscription across the top of the polished face reading '*mdkr/bn/m'hr*; see *JaPEHA*, pp. 120f., §255. The base tapers in width from 23.9 cm. at the bottom to 20.5 cm. at the top. The mortise in the top, set back 1.5 cm. from the face, measures *ca.* 5 cm. from front to rear (the rear wall is somewhat rough and indefinite) by 16.1 cm. in width and is 1.3 cm. deep (maximum). The interiors of the front wall and of the walls at the sides are chiseled even; the bottom and rear wall are roughly tooled. Mortar covers most of the bottom. The top of the base in front and to the sides of the mortise are polished; the area behind the mortise is irregular (partly chiseled and bearing

a large tool mark running from side to side of the base). The sides of the base are partly chiseled even and superficially polished along the front; the bottom is roughly even toward the front, irregular elsewhere. The back displays a half dozen very large oblique tool marks and is very rough. White alabaster. 11.7 cm. by 23.9 cm. by 11.4 cm.

TC 2168 (Plate 82)

Stele base with a one-line inscription on the polished face: *drmt*; see *JaPEHA*, p. 16, §123. Guidelines are at the top and bottom of the line. The base tapers in width from 14 cm. at the bottom to 12 cm. at the top. The mortise in the polished top, set back 1.7 cm. from the face, lacks a rear wall. It is 8 cm. wide and 1.3 cm. deep; mortar adheres along the front of it. The sides of the base are tooled roughly even; the bottom is roughly chiseled even. The back is irregular with very large oblique tool marks. White alabaster with rusty colored streak running obliquely across the face. 10 cm. by 14 cm. by 5.4 cm.

TC 2171

Small stele base with a two-line inscription on the weathered face reading (1) '*smm* (2) '*lrbn*; see *JaPEHA*, p. 133, §274. The mortise in the top, set back 1.2 cm. from the face, measures 2.7 cm. from front to rear by 4.7 cm. in width and is 1.6 cm. deep; mortar covers most of the bottom. The evened left side of the base is approximately square with the face, while the irregular right side slants sharply in toward the rear. The bottom of the base is chiseled even; the back is irregular. Limestone. 7 cm. by 8.4 cm. by 5.9 cm.

TC 2211 (Plate 82)

Stele base with a two-line inscription on the face: (1) *rdmt* (2) *drhn*; see *JaPEHA*, pp. 59f., §164, Pl. xxv, above. The base tapers in width from 15 cm. at the bottom to 12 cm. at the top. The mortise in the top, set back 1.5 cm. from the face, measures 2.7 cm. front to rear by 8.3 cm. in width. The entire bottom is filled with mortar (bearing the impression of a flat-bottomed plaque) to within 6 mm. of the top. The face, top, and sides of the base are evened, and the bottom is chiseled fairly even. The back, exhibiting a few large (but short) tool marks, is very rough. Limestone. 11.5 cm. by 15 cm. by 8.5 cm.

TC 2212 (Plate 82)

Stele base with a two-line inscription on the upper part of the smoothed face reading (1) *mrtdm* (2) *hn'mt*; see *JaPEHA*, pp. 104f., §230, Pl. xxv, below. The surface of the face had been reddened before the inscription was incised; guidelines appear at the top, bottom, and approximate center of each line. The base tapers in width from 10.6 cm. at the bottom to 9.3 cm. at the top. Except for the face, all of the base is irregular. Mortar and chips of stone were used to build up the upper rear of the base to hold the plaque in place; part of the impression of the lower end of the plaque is visible in the mortar. White alabaster of poor quality. 9.5 cm. by 10.6 cm. by 5.5 cm.

TC 2242

Crude stele base with a two-line inscription on the weathered face reading (1) *ḥmdmd* (2) *ġrbm*; see *JaPEHA*, pp. 85f., §200. The base tapers in width from 11.2 cm. at the bottom to 8.6 cm. at the top; the left side slants inward more than the right. The mortise in the top, set back 8 mm. from the face, lacks a rear wall. It is 6.1 cm. wide, 1.6 cm. deep, and 1.5 cm. from the left side but only 1 cm. from the right side. The sides and the bottom have been chiseled roughly even; the back is less regular. Porous limestone. 8 cm. by 11.2 cm. by 4.2 cm.

TC 2274 (Plate 82)

Poorly made stele base with a crude, two-line inscription on the irregular face reading (1) *śydm* (2) *d[ġ]rbm*; see *JaPEHA*, pp. 95f., §216. The mortise in the top, set back 1.1 cm. from the face, measures 2 cm. from front to rear by *ca.* 7 cm. in width and has a depth of 1 cm. The top of the base bears rough, parallel chisel marks, as do the sides; the bottom is roughly even. The back is irregular. Limestone. 10 cm. by 12.5 cm. by 5.6 cm.

TC 2277 (Plate 82)

Stele base with a one-line inscription across the top of the polished face; *'brdwdrḥn*. The mortise in the top, set back 1.8 cm. from the face, lacks a rear wall; it is 7.1 cm. wide and 1.1 cm. deep. The top is polished, and the sides are smoothed. The bottom (with closely spaced tool marks perpendicular to the face) is partly even, partly irregular. The back,

which has several large vertical tool marks, is also irregular. At the bottom rear is one very long horizontal tool mark. On the face, slightly less than 1 cm. from the bottom, is a rough cutting, below which the face is rough. This cutting (as well as the bottom of the base) slants up toward the left, leaving the base shorter at that end than at the right. Alabaster, light grayish with rusty tint. 7.1 cm. by 11.7 cm. by 4.9 cm.

TC 2278 (Plate 82)

Stele base, damaged at upper right face, with a two-line inscription on the face reading (1) [']*zm* (2) *ġrbm*; see *JaPEHA*, pp. 80f., §193. The *z* (not *t*) in line 1 is complete and clear; ' has been supplied as the letter completely missing, on the basis of the appearance of '*zm* on TC 1766. The base tapers in width from 9.7 cm. at the bottom to 8.7 cm. at the top. The mortise in the top, set back 1.6 cm. from the face, measures *ca.* 2.3 cm. from front to rear by 5.2 cm. in width and is 2 cm. deep. The top and sides of the base are smoothed. The bottom is tooled even (slanting up toward the rear) and chiseled along the front; the back is irregular. Sandstone. 9.7 cm. by 9.7 cm. by 5.8 cm.

TC 2536 (Plate 82)

Stele base with a one-line inscription across the top of the face reading *twbt/sbḥ*; see *JaPEHA*, p. 157, §308 (note that the correct reading is *s*, not *ṣ*). The mortise in the top, set back 1.5 cm. from the face, lacks a rear wall, and the right wall has been broken away. The mortise has a depth of 1.4 cm. The sides of the base are even near the front, and the bottom is partly even. The back is completely irregular. Oölitic limestone. 9.5 cm. by 13.8 cm. by 7 cm.

TC 2537 (Plate 82)

Crude stele base with a two-line inscription on the face reading (1) *ḥḍr* (2) *hrn*; see *JaPEHA*, pp. 140f., §283. The *r* of line two is faint but certain. Except for the evened and smoothed face, the base is mostly irregular. The mortise in the top, set back 1.5 cm. from the face, measures *ca.* 2 cm. from front to rear by *ca.* 3.5 cm. in width. The bottom of the base has been chiseled roughly even at the front. Poor quality alabaster. 9.5 cm. by 12.8 cm. by 5.6 cm.

ADDENDUM

The following detached stele bases were found among stored objects from Wâdī Beiḥân; although their numbers have disappeared, it is most likely that they are from the Timna' Cemetery. They have been assigned new numbers, arbitrarily beginning with 3001.

TC 3001 (Plate 82)

Stele base with a two-line inscription on the face reading (1) 'ḥrm (2) hn'mt. Guidelines appear at the top, center, and bottom of each line; in addition an incised line parallels the center guideline of line two at a distance of 5 mm. above it. Traces of reddening appear on the surface of the face. The base tapers in width from 11.8 cm. at the bottom to 9.5 cm. at the top. The mortise in the top, set back 1.4 cm. from the face, measures *ca.* 2.5 cm. from front to rear by 5.6 cm. in width. The bottom is filled with mortar bearing the impression of a plaque with jagged bottom. The sides of the base are superficially smoothed; the back is irregular. The bottom, slanting up toward the right, is irregular except for small chiseled areas at the front. Limestone. 7.5 cm. (at left) by 11.8 cm. by 6.3 cm.

TC 3002 (Plate 82)

Stele base with a one-line inscription across the top of the smoothed face: 'kbt/ḏt/'rgn. The top of the third letter is missing, but *b* must be read, as the only alternative is *ġ* which would not occur in the same root with '; 'kbt occurs also on TC 1186. The next to the last letter has only the shaft preserved; *g* must be read rather than the alternative *l*, as *r* and *l* do not occur in adjacent positions in Arabic roots. The front wall of the mortise in the top is broken away (accounting for the damage to the inscription). The mortise, set back *ca.* 1.7 cm. from the face, measured *ca.* 3.5 cm. from front to rear by 9.8 cm. in width and was slightly over 1 cm. deep. The sides of the base are roughly evened. The bottom is somewhat irregular, and the back is completely irregular. Sandstone. 10.5 cm. by 12.7 cm. by 8 cm.

TC 3003 (Plate 82)

Battered stele base with a crude two-line inscription on the polished face reading (1) qylm[/ḏ] (2) s'fm. The crude shallow mortise in the top lacks a rear wall. The bottom of the base is very roughly evened; the sides and back are irregular. Poor quality alabaster. 8.7 cm. by 11.8 cm. by 4.1 cm.

TC 3004 (Plate 83)

Low, well-made stele base with a one-line inscription on the upper register of the face reading r'bm/mwhbm. The upper register, a band 3.3 cm. wide, is set in 6 mm. behind the lower band, which is 3.5 cm. wide. The broad top of the base, like the face, is smoothly polished. The mortise in the top, set back 3 cm. from the face, measures 3 cm. from front to rear by 6.8 cm. in width. It holds the lower end of an alabaster plaque, broken off below the top of the mortise. The sides of the base are chiseled even and partly smoothed. The back is tooled roughly even, as is the bottom, which is chiseled along the front. Light-colored alabaster with slightly rusty tint. 7.4 cm. by 16.5 cm. by 10.4 cm.

TC 3005 (Plate 83)

Stele base with a two-line inscription on the face: (1) ṯwb'l (2) š'ṯmm. One line of the inscription is on each of the two polished horizontal bands which run around the face and sides. The upper band, 3 cm. wide, slants in slightly toward the bottom, giving the appearance of being recessed; the lower band is 3.5 cm. wide. The mortise in the smoothed top, set back 1.5 cm. from the face, is 10.5 cm. wide (from side to side) and has an irregular shape. From front to rear it measures *ca.* 3 cm. at the ends, widening out in the rear center to 5.3 cm. Except for the ends, which are more shallow, the bottom is filled with mortar to within 2.8 cm. of the top (the base may originally have had an almost square mortise, 6 cm. by 5 cm. and rather deep, which was later altered to accept a flat plaque). The bottom of the base is evened and bears closely spaced tool marks and chiseled margins along the front and sides. The back is somewhat irregular, exhibiting several very large, oblique tool marks. Light-colored alabaster with rusty tint. 7 cm. by 13.5 cm. by 9 cm.

X

BASES FOR DECORATED MEMORIAL STELAE

Related to those bases with a mortise in the top designed to hold a polished, undecorated, upright stele is the group of bases, often of similar appearance, which have a mortise shaped to receive an upright stele with a relief on the front or to receive some other type of stele. As only one of the bases in this group has any part of the upper member in place in the mortise, it is impossible to determine in many cases exactly what type of stele was used; in some case there may even have been the head or bust of a person.

The mortises in the tops of the bases in this group have a great variety of shapes. Some are square (TC 828) or nearly square (TC 1609); many are circular (TC 1774); some are straight along the back, rounded on the ends and front (TC 1623). Many are basically rectangular with a rounded bulge on the front to match a stele with a human relief on the face (e.g., TC 1737). A few of the bases included in this grouping could possibly have held stelae of the plain polished type, especially those few with rectangular mortises.

tise in the top, set back 1.9 cm. from the face, measures 2.6 cm. from front to rear by 15.1 cm. in width and has a depth of *ca.* 1.5 cm. The lower end of the plaque measured 2.2 cm. by 14.4 cm.; the gaps around it are filled with very hard, fine mortar, which also covers the bottom of the mortise to a depth of *ca.* 2 mm. Only the lower right corner of the plaque is preserved; it is polished on the face, back and side. On the face along the diagonal break is a low, curving ridge, almost certainly the hem of a garment such as found on TC 553 and TC 1358 (Chapter IV), suggesting that the plaque bore a human figure in low relief. The sides of the base are approximately square with the face and are polished smooth. The bottom, which slants up toward the back at about the same angle that the top slants down, is covered with small tool marks bordered on the front and right side by a chiseled margin. The back exhibits a score of very large vertical tool marks. White alabaster with a brown band exposed on the back of the base. 12.8 cm. by 18 cm. by 6 cm.

A. BASE WITH PART OF PLAQUE IN PLACE

TC 2037 (Plate 83)

Stele base with fragment of a plaque in place in the mortise. A one-line inscription across the top of the polished face reads '*bnt* [...]. The upper left of the base is broken, and three (or possibly four) letters are missing; the letters of the inscription are 2.3 cm. high and widely spaced. The base, which is 9.5 cm. high, tapers very slightly in width from bottom to top. The polished top of the base slants down toward the rear, meeting the face at an angle of 85°. The rectangular mor-

B. BASES WITH NONE OF THE UPPER MEMBER IN PLACE

TC 505

Somewhat battered stone object which appears to be a rectangular base for a thick, upright member. The one line of inscription preserved on the face reads *ḥdn*; there is a guideline at the top and bottom of the line and also in the middle. Some 3 mm. above the top of the upper guideline on the left are traces of another, presumably the lower guideline of the first line of the inscription, now missing. The sides, like the face, are vertical and smooth, while the back is chiseled even.

There was a mortise in the top, but the walls of it are entirely missing, and nothing of it remains except part of the bottom, which bears tool marks. There are ridges at the front left corner to show that the mortise was rectangular, about 6.5 cm. wide and 6 cm. from front to rear (where there was no wall). The bottom of the base is chiseled even in a few high spots, otherwise rough. Limestone. 5 cm. (originally *ca.* 7 cm. high by conjecture) by 9.3 cm. by 7.9 cm.

TC 828 (Plate 83)

Base with two horizontal bands on the front, each bearing one line of inscription: (1) ṣbḫt/ḏt (2) ḏrḥn; see *JaPEHA*, pp. 57f., §161, Pl. VII, above. The upper band (3 cm. wide) is set back 3 mm. from the lower (3.5 cm. wide), with a beveled offset of about 5 mm. width between them. The nearly square (7.2 cm. from front to rear by 8.8 cm. in width) mortise in the polished top, set back 1.8 cm. from the face, is nearly 2 cm. deep; the interior is covered with tool marks. A strip of the bottom, about 1.5 cm. wide along the front, slants up toward the front wall; the right wall has been broken away. The sides of the base, now chipped, were tooled and superficially chiseled even. The bottom is covered with tool marks except for the right front quarter, which is polished smooth; the piece is probably re-used, as the tooled areas indicate where a relief or raised margin has been removed. The back of the base, roughly tooled, meets the bottom in an irregular curve. White alabaster. 7.3 cm. by 12.5 cm. by 11 cm.

TC 845 (Plate 83)

Left half of a low base bearing a one-line inscription across the face reading [. . . ṭ]rṭbt[.]. Only traces of the ṭ are preserved, but it is almost certain; four or possibly five characters seem to have preceded this letter. Because the corner of the base is broken off vertically, it remains uncertain whether the final character is a word divider, the letter g, or the letter l. The oval mortise in the top, of which only the left half is preserved, appears to have been designed to receive the neck of an (alabaster?) human head. It is set back 2.2 cm. from the face, comes within 6.5 cm. of the left side, measures 4.9 cm. from front to rear, and

is 1.4 cm. deep. The interior is covered with small tool marks. The face, top, and left side are smoothly polished and square with one another. The bottom is tooled roughly even and has a chiseled margin along the front. The back is irregular. White alabaster with a few rusty streaks. 4.8 cm. by 9 cm. by 10 cm.

TC 965 (Plate 83)

Right half of base with two horizontal bands on the face, each bearing one line of inscription: (1) ḥywm[. . .] (2) ḏr[ḥn] or ḏr['n]. The upper band (2.3 cm. wide) is stepped back 5 mm. behind the face of the lower (*ca.* 3.5 cm. wide); they meet in a beveled offset. The bands extend around the right side of the base. The letters of the upper band are close together, those of the lower band widely spaced and somewhat larger. The circular mortise in the top, coming within 1.2 cm. of the face, 1 cm. of the back, and 2.1 cm. of the right side, has a depth (in the center) of 2.5 cm. and a maximum diameter of *ca.* 7.5 cm. The interior is rough with tool marks except for a chiseled margin around the top. The top of the base, the face, and side are polished smooth. The back is uneven; the bottom has several long tool marks (parallel to the side) near the center and flake marks near the side. Light-colored alabaster with fine yellowish-tan striations (horizontal). 6 cm. by 7.2 cm. by 10.7 cm.

TC 1115

Low base with a one-line inscription across the polished face reading ḏrḥn. Only the upper extremities of ḏ are preserved, as the lower right corner of the face is broken away. The right side of the base is also missing, with an oblique fracture running from the front corner to the rear center. The mortise in the top of the base, set back 1.7 cm. from the face, is 5.2 cm. wide (withheld 1.6 cm from the left side) and has a maximum depth of 1.3 cm., although the bottom is irregular. There was apparently no rear wall, with the mortise measuring 4 cm. from the front wall to the rear of the base. The interior is covered with tool marks except the front wall, which is chiseled even. The left side of the base, now badly chipped, was squared with the face and top; it was polished, as were the face and top. The back and bottom of the base are rough.

Light-colored alabaster with tan and brown streaks. 4.8 cm. by 8.5 cm. by 6.2 cm.

TC 1116 (Plate 83)

Fragment from the right of a stepped stele base with a two-line inscription on the face reading (1) *sm*[...] (2) *ġr*[*bm*]. The bottom of the piece split away across a banding, a little below the center of the lower line of inscription. Another fracture at the middle of the face and mortise ran vertically up from the bottom part way and then obliquely toward the right, removing the third letter of the upper line. The upper line is on a horizontal band 3.3 cm. wide set back 9 mm. behind the face of the lower band, which is preserved to a maximum width of 3.6 cm. The characters of line two were taller than those of line one. The bands continue around the right side with a reduced offset (*ca.* 6 mm.). The face, top, and most of the side are polished. The mortise in the top, set back 1.8 cm. from the face, measured approximately 5 cm. from front to rear and was 5.7 cm. deep; the interior displays rough tooling. No part of the bottom, back, or left side of the base is preserved. The original width of the base was probably *ca.* 17 cm. Light-colored alabaster mottled with brown. 7 cm. by 8.7 cm. by 9.8 cm.

TC 1136 (Plate 83)

Base with a circular mortise in the top and a two-line inscription on the face reading (1) *n'mm* (2) *drḥn*; see *JaPEHA*, p. 50, §152. The *n* is damaged but certain. The base tapers in width from 9.3 cm. at the bottom to 8.4 cm. at the top. The sides, square with the face, are polished smooth, as are the top and face. The mortise in the top, designed presumably to receive the neck of a human head (cf. TC 1884), has a maximum diameter of 5.3 cm. Its greatest depth (at the left) is 1.5 cm., while the central and right parts are only *ca.* 8 mm. deep. The mortise is set back 1.6 cm. from the face and 1.5 cm. from the sides. Only about two-thirds of the circumference exists, as the back of the base interrupts the circle. The back and bottom of the base are irregular; the bottom slants up toward the back. Light-colored alabaster with orangish-tan and brown streaks. 8 cm. by 9.3 cm. by 6.5 cm.

TC 1212 (Plate 83)

Fragment from left half of a base with a two-line inscription on the polished face reading (1) .*b*]*yt*/['] *or* .*ġ*]*yt*/[*s*] (2)]*fm*. The upper part of the last letter of the first line is missing, as also in the case of the letter, in the same line, which can be read either *b* or *ġ*. A shallow mortise was cut in the top, set back 1.6 cm. from the face. It was in the shape of a rectangle with the front corners (only the left is preserved) broadly rounded. It is *ca.* 6 mm. deep at the front, gradually less toward the rear (which is not preserved). The left side of the base, squared with the front and top, is roughly chiseled even. The bottom, preserved only at the front left-hand corner, was chiseled even along the front; the back of the base is entirely broken away. White alabaster (with a tendency to split along the grain). 7 cm. by 10.3 cm. (original width *ca.* 18 cm.) by 9 cm.

TC 1342 (Plate 83)

Low base with a shallow mortise or depression in the top. The upper left corner is broken, the upper right corner is chipped, and the back is broken away. The two-line inscription on the face reads (1) [']*myd'*[/.*y*]*t* or *myd'*[.*y*]*t* (2) *ddr'n*. The gap represents three vertical shafts of letters whose distinguishing characteristics at the top are broken off. The square depression in the top is set back 1.8 cm. from the face and 1 cm. from either side. It measures *ca.* 9.2 cm. in width (from side to side) and has a maximum depth of *ca.* 1.2 cm. The bottom is covered with small tool marks; the smooth walls of the depression slant outward toward the top. The sides of the base, like the face, are polished smooth. The bottom is even, exhibiting numerous tool marks. Light-colored alabaster with tan streaks. 6.2 cm. by 11.2 cm. by 10 cm.

TC 1507 (Plate 83)

Front part of a flat base with a circular mortise in the top and a one-line inscription across the front reading '*kbt*/*ġrbm*. A break runs from front to back, approximately in the center; the two fragments (1507 and 1949) were found separately on different days. The mortise, set back 2.9 cm. from the face, has a diameter of *ca.* 9.5 cm. and is 2.1 cm. deep; it comes within 2.5 cm. of the right side and

4 cm. of the left. The interior is covered with long, narrow tool marks. Mortar *ca.* 7 mm. thick is preserved on the bottom of the right part of the mortise, running slightly up on the walls. The face, top, and sides of the base are polished smooth; long, crisscrossed tool marks appear on the bottom, except for chiseled margins. Gray alabaster with rusty-brown streaks. 4.3 cm. (3.8 cm. at right) by 15.9 cm. by 9.7 cm. (6.7 cm. at right side).

TC 1608 (Plate 83)

Left part of a large crude base with a roughly circular mortise in the top and a one-line inscription across the front reading]*ḥl/rmḫn*. There may have been four or five letters more at the beginning of the line. The surface of the face is stained with red coloring. The mortise, set back 3.6 cm. from the face, is *ca.* 6.7 cm. from front to rear and its width is reconstructed as being *ca.* 8.5 cm.; the maximum depth is *ca.* 4.3 cm. The interior displays very large tool marks. The rough left side of the base is cut off square, but the back and bottom are irregular. Very porous limestone. 7.2 cm. by 19.5 cm. (originally about 30 cm.) by 14 cm.

TC 1609 (Plate 83)

Stele base with a one-line inscription on the polished face reading *šyḫt/ygr*; see *JaPEHA*, p. 78, §190. The rectangular mortise in the top, set back 2 cm. from the face, measures *ca.* 4.5 cm. from front to rear by 6.2 cm. in width and is 1.5 cm. deep; the interior bears small tool marks. The top of the base, broken at the back, is uneven, though superficially smoothed; the sides are squared and polished smooth. The bottom is very roughly tooled even, and the back is mostly irregular. Light tannish alabaster. 6.4 cm. by 15 cm. by 8.2 cm.

TC 1623 (Plate 83)

Left half of a base with a one-line inscription near the top of the face reading]/*'gln*. The shape of the mortise in the top—straight across the back, rounded at the end, and bulging at the front—suggests that it was designed to receive a decorated plaque rather than the usual rectilinear sort. It is *ca.* 1 cm. deep and measures *ca.* 5 cm. from front to back at the center. It comes within 1.2 cm. of the face

and 1.4 cm. of the left side. The interior is covered with tool marks, though there are traces of superficial chiseling. The left side of the base is chiseled even and superficially polished, with chisel marks visible in some places. The back is very roughly tooled even, as is the bottom, which also is chiseled around the edges. The fracture at the right end of the preserved fragment runs through a large cavity in the stone which was filled with mortar and stone chips. White alabaster with grayish and rusty colored streaks. 8.5 cm. by 12.5 cm. by 7.8 cm.

TC 1700 (Plate 83)

Stele base with a two-line inscription on the face reading (1) *fyšt/dt* (2) *drḫn*; see *JaPEHA*, pp. 56f., §160. Guidelines appear at the top, center, and bottom of each line. The mortise in the top was designed to receive a flat stele with a high relief on the front. In plan, the mortise is rectangular (*ca.* 2.7 cm. by 15 cm.) with a rounded protrusion on the front reaching within about 2 cm. of either end. The maximum measurement of the mortise from front to back at the center of the protrusion is 5.3 cm., and it is 1.6 cm. deep. The interior is covered with tool marks, though the tops of the walls have been chiseled more even; a small amount of mortar adheres at the left end. The base is chipped at the upper right and elsewhere. The squared sides, like the top and face, are highly polished. The upper part of the back exhibits long, parallel, vertical tool marks (*ca.* 6 mm. apart), with a chiseled margin of varying width across the top. The lower part of the back is rougher, tooled at the right and chiseled at the left. The bottom is irregular at the left rear corner, roughly tooled elsewhere, and roughly chiseled even at the front .White alabaster with grayish tint and rusty-orange streaks. 9.3 cm. by 18.5 cm. by 9 cm.

TC 1701

Left part of a stele base with a mortise similar to that of TC 1700, bearing a two-line inscription on the polished face reading (1) [.]*dn/dt* (2) [*šh*]*yrm*. In line two the *h* is almost certain, while the *š* is supplied to give the diminutive of the rather frequent name *šhrm* (cf. *JaPEHA*, p. 109). The top of the base, which was polished, is badly damaged.

The mortise was set back *ca.* 1.2 cm. from the face and came within 1 cm. of the left end; the interior is covered with tool marks. The left side of the base is evened and superficially smoothed, and the bottom is tooled and chiseled fairly even. The back, exhibiting a few horizontal tool marks, is rough. White alabaster. 10 cm. by 9 cm. (originally about 12 cm. wide) by 5.1 cm.

TC 1737 (Plate 83)

Large stele base with a one-line inscription across the top of the polished face reading *br'm/dt/ġrb[m]*; see *JaPEHA*, p. 82, §195. The upper left corner of the face is chipped, completely obliterating the final letter, restored as *m*. The mortise in the top, of the same general shape as that of TC 1700, was designed to receive a plaque approximately 17.5 cm. wide and 2.3 cm. thick, with a raised relief on the front an additional 2.1 cm. thick. The mortise is 1.5 cm. deep and comes within 1.3 cm. of the face at the center of the protrusion. The interior is covered with tool marks, those on the front wall being oblique and parallel. The sides of the base have been chiseled even and superficially smoothed, although tool marks are still visible. The back, which slants in slightly toward the bottom, displays very long, nearly vertical tool marks, except for the lower left where there is a natural depressed irregularity in the stone. The bottom is chiseled even. Light-colored alabaster with a rusty-gray cast and brown streaks. 11.4 cm. by 21.3 cm. by 7.4 cm.

TC 1774 (Plate 83)

Circular base, broken, with two horizontal bands of approximately equal width (4.3 cm.). The upper band, recessed *ca.* 6 mm. behind the face of the lower, bears a one-line inscription reading as far as preserved *]t/'h[y]rm*. Only slightly more than half of this unusual piece is actually preserved, as a nearly vertical break runs across it near the center. A circular mortise in the top has a diameter of 5.3 cm. and is 1 cm. deep; the wall surrounding it averages nearly 2 cm. in thickness. The bottom of the base was chiseled fairly even, though it is now chipped somewhat. Porous limestone. 8.7 cm. by 10.6 cm. by 7.8 cm.

TC 1788 (Plate 83)

Damaged stele base with a one-line inscription across the upper part of the polished face reading *[l]b'm/dt/y'[d]*. The name *lb'm* occurs on TC 1414, *y'd* on TC 1415. Below the ' of the tribal name is a vertical shaft lightly incised, as though the scribe had begun to make the wrong letter and then, realizing his mistake, abandoned the undesired shaft. The space above this letter is chipped, so it is not possible to determine what the upper part of the erroneous letter was. Of the *d* only the lower tip of the shaft is preserved, as with the initial *l*. The mortise in the polished top of the base (now badly chipped), set back 1.3 cm. from the face, has the same general shape as that of TC 1700. Its maximum dimension from front to back is *ca.* 4.5 cm., from side to side *ca.* 14 cm.; the greatest depth is near 2 cm. All the walls, especially the front one, slope in toward the center of the mortise; the interior is roughly tooled. The sides of the base were mostly smoothed. A brown banding is exposed on the back. The bottom is roughly tooled and chiseled. Light-colored alabaster with gray tint and dark streaks. 9.3 cm. by 17.6 cm. by 7.5 cm.

TC 1820 (Plate 84)

Small base with a circular mortise in the top and a two-line inscription on the polished face reading (1) *drmm* (2) *drhn*; see *JaPEHA*, p. 42, §140. The lower left corner of the face is damaged, but the inscription is not affected. The mortise, roughly oval in shape, *ca.* 4 cm. from front to back (although the rear wall is not complete), is 4.8 cm. from side to side and 2 cm. deep. The interior is covered with tool marks, which are vertical on the walls. The mortise is set back 1.2 cm. from the face and the sides. The polished sides of the base are square with the top and face. The irregular back of the base has five vertical tool marks. The bottom is roughly tooled even and chiseled along the front. Light-colored alabaster with grayish areas and rusty-tan streaks. 6.9 cm. by 7.2 cm. by 6.7 cm.

TC 1836 (Plate 83)

Large base with a one-line inscription across the top of the polished face reading *'bnt/dt/ dr'n*; see *JaPEHA*, p. 32, §127. Guidelines appear at the top, center, and bottom of the line of inscription. The mortise in the top, designed (as TC 1700) to receive a flat plaque with high relief on the front, is set back 2.5 cm. from the face. Its maximum measurement from front to back is 5 cm., while the right end (receiving the plaque itself without the relief) measures *ca.* 3 cm. from front to back. The interior is mostly covered with mortar, but it can be determined that the mortise is at least 3.2 cm. deep. The impression in the mortar shows that the bottom of the plaque slanted up toward the left, actually rising above the top of the base some 5 cm. from the left side. In anticipation of this anomaly, a boss was left on the top of the base to fill the gap. The inner walls of the mortise bear rather large tool marks. The top of the base is polished in front of the mortise, tooled and partly chiseled behind it. The left side of the base is roughly tooled and chiseled even; the right side is chiseled along the front, while the rest is irregularly concave. The back exhibits extremely large, long, oblique tool marks. The bottom has roughly chiseled margins (3 cm. wide) along the front and back, with a raised, irregular strip through the center. Light-colored alabaster with slight grayish tint and rusty streaks through it. 14.5 cm. by 26.2 cm. by 10.5 cm.

TC 1860 (Plate 83)

Base with a two-line inscription on the face reading (1) *ḥsynt* (2) *dr'n*; see *JaPEHA*, p. 34, §130. One line of the inscription is on each of the two horizontal bands which run across the face. The upper band (3.6 cm. wide) is recessed *ca.* 4 mm. behind the lower (4.5 cm. wide). The mortise in the top, set back 2.7 cm. from the face, measures 6 cm. from front to rear by 8.8 cm. in width and is 2 cm. deep; irregular tool marks appear on the interior. The face, top, and sides of the base are polished; the back is irregular. The bottom is somewhat irregular with only a few chisel marks along the front. The edges of the base have been chipped at many points. Light rusty colored alabaster. 8.2 cm. by 12.8 cm. by 13.5 cm.

TC 1879 (Plate 84)

Low base with an irregular mortise (somewhat rounded) in the center of the top, bearing a one-line inscription across the lower part

of the face reading *drmt/dtṣw'n*; see *JaPEHA*, p. 163, §319. The top of the base is broken off to a depth averaging about 1 cm., except for an area along the right side. The face is divided into two horizontal bands, the upper of which (2.4 cm. wide) is recessed some 2 mm. behind the lower (3.3 cm. wide). The inscription fills the lower band, which is damaged at the lower right corner. The mortise, set back 4 cm. from the face, was *ca.* 2.8 cm. deep; from front to back it measures 6.7 cm., from side to side a maximum of 9 cm. The mortar, covering the bottom to a depth of nearly 1 cm., bears the impression of the lower end of an object *ca.* 6.5 cm. wide and 5.7 cm. from front to back. This use of the mortise appears to have been secondary, as the original mortise was apparently 9 cm. by 2.8 cm., while the secondary mortise was superimposed, extending mostly out to the back. The top of the base and the face of it are polished smooth. The sides are chiseled even at the front and top, though they are irregular elsewhere. The bottom is even, covered with short, but fairly broad, tool marks, running generally from front to back. The back of the base is entirely irregular below the straight upper edge. White alabaster of somewhat dull appearance. 6.2 cm. by 19.7 cm. by 15.8 cm.

TC 1901 (Plate 83)

Small stele base with two unequal lines of inscription on the polished (but weathered) face reading (1) *'mnt/dt/y* (2) *gr*; see *JaPEHA*, p. 64, §170, Pl. xx, top. The letters of the upper line are *ca.* 2.4 cm. high, while those of the lower line are only 1.1 cm. The mortise in the top, set back 1.4 cm. from the face, measures 4.5 cm. from front to back (there is no rear wall) by 5.5 cm. in width (from side to side) and is *ca.* 1 cm. deep. The interior is irregularly tooled. The back of the base is somewhat irregular, and it slants in toward the bottom somewhat. The bottom is tooled and crudely chiseled in places. Rusty-mottled alabaster. 5.4 cm. by 9.4 cm. by 6 cm.

TC 2040 (Plate 84)

Stele base with a one-line inscription across the top of the polished face reading *dt/grbm*; see *JaPEHA*, pp. 84f., §199, Pl. xxii, above. The mortise in the top, set back 1.5 cm. from

92

the face, has the general shape of that in TC 1700. From front to back it measures 2.6 cm. at the left end, 3 cm. at the right end, and *ca.* 4 cm. at the center (owing to the protrusion). It is 19 cm. wide and has a maximum depth of 2.7 cm., though the right end is more shallow. Tool marks cover most of the interior, with some chiseling in evidence along the top of the rear wall. The top of the base, now badly chipped, was well smoothed; the sides were chiseled even and superficially smoothed. The bottom is mostly tooled roughly even (and broken at the right end); the back is irregular. Light-colored alabaster with rusty tint. 10.6 cm. by 22.8 cm. by 8.5 cm.

XI

BASES FOR STATUETTES OF BRONZE

Twenty-nine objects of the collection are grouped under one heading as statuette bases. A few of these bases have the outline of the feet cut around the small mortises for attaching the statuettes by means of doweling. The others only have mortises of varying sizes and shapes, usually in pairs, for the same purpose. While a small percentage of these bases have only the name of the deceased inscribed on the front, most of them have longer inscriptions, sometimes with a brief dedication to a deity. The inscriptions of at least eleven of the twenty-nine bases (possibly more, as some of the inscriptions are far from complete) contain the word *m'mr*. Although this word clearly refers to the statuette (in TC 1173, it occurs in parallel with *ṣlm*, "image"), its precise meaning is not certain. As A. Jamme points out, however, it must have some religious significance (see *JaPEHA*, p. 195). The word is found also on fragmentary inscriptions in this collection which may or may not have formed parts of statuette bases, viz., TC 969 (now in the Aden Museum), TC 699, 876, 929, 943, 1073, 1078, 1152, 1314, 1334, 1338, and possibly others.

Most or all of the statuettes themselves must have been made of bronze, as the statue of Ma'adkarib found at Mârib (*Archaeological Discoveries in South Arabia*, p. 283). As bronze was a rather valuable material which could be re-used, none of them was found with its base. Fragments, such as TC 1196, however, show us that the feet had dowels protruding from the soles as a means of attachment to the base.

TC 654 (Plate 84)

Right part of a base for a statuette. There is a possible trace of one of the mortises at the break. The three-line inscription reads (1) *ṭwb'*[*l*/... (2) *w*/'*nby*/*ṣl*[*m* ... (3) ./"*d̲n*[*s*...; cf. *JaPEHA*, pp. 173f., §333. The right side, the top, and the bottom of the base are square with the face and were polished smooth, though the edges are now badly battered. The back is tooled even. Alabaster. 10.6 cm. by 10.8 cm. by 5.3 cm.

TC 673 (Plate 84)

Large base for a statuette, damaged at the top, with a two-line inscription across the upper part of the face reading (1) *m'mr*/*m*-[*'dkrb*] (2) *d̲šhr*/*brṣfm*. Most of the upper line is broken (all of the proposed letters '*dk* are missing), but the first word is certain; see *JaPEHA*, p. 200, §352, Pl. ɪ, below. Traces of two mortises are visible in the top; one is 6.5 cm. from the right side of the base, the other *ca.* 2.5 cm. from the left side. Both seem to have been about 4 cm. from front to rear, but their shape cannot be determined with certainty. The top of the base is preserved only in a small area at the right side, and it seems to have been chiseled even, though it is now weathered. The face was superficially rubbed even, but has many pits and chips. The right side is finished similarly to the face, but slightly rougher; the left side was chiseled even and possibly rubbed very superficially. The back and bottom are tooled roughly even and exhibit some chisel marks. Limestone. 15 cm. by 19.7 cm. by 12.5 cm.

TC 921 (Plate 84)

Fragment of a base with two mortises in top and part of a two-line inscription preserved on the face: (1) [. . . .]*mn*/*bn*/'*myt*' (2) [*d̲r*]'*n*/*brṣfm*; see *JaPEHA*, pp. 179f., §338. The *y* given by Jamme in *ymn* does not appear at all on the fragment as now preserved. The piece is the re-used left front corner of a stone tabletop with raised margins at the side and front. The margin along the side is 3.7 cm. wide and *ca.* 7 mm. high; the one along the front was removed, but the area beneath it not completely smoothed. The break across the back runs through the two mortises, which which are of the type used to receive the dowels on the feet of bronze statuettes. The left mortise, set back 5.8 cm. from the face and 7 cm. from the left side of the piece, has its longer dimension (preserved to 3 cm.) running from front to back. From side to side it measures 1.7 cm., and it is 3.5 cm. deep.

The right mortise, less completely preserved, is separated from the left one by a space of 4 cm. and is also 5.8 cm. from the face; it was slightly deeper. The break at the right runs through the right mortise. From the position of the mortises in the top (presumably centered) the number of missing letters at the beginning of the upper line of the inscription has been estimated at four, those in the lower line at two. Light-colored alabaster with brown horizontal band just below the center. 8.2 cm. by 14 cm. by 9 cm.

TC 923

Base with a large section at upper right front broken off, removing all but lower left of the face, which bears a small part of a two-line inscription. Of the first line, only the lower tip of the final letter is preserved, while more than half of the lower line is legible:]/*dt*/*tbw*. On the top of the base, the break runs through a mortise located in the approximate center; it measured *ca.* 1.5 cm. from front to back, 3 cm. from side to side, and 2.5 cm. deep. It was apparently designed to accept a dowel (or dowels) on the bottom of a statuette. The sides of the base, squared with the top and face, are evened and partly smoothed. The back is chiseled even, as is the bottom. Limestone. 9.5 cm. by 11.4 cm. by 7.6 cm.

TC 957 (Plate 84)

Left part of a broken statuette base with a two-line inscription on the face: (1)]*ŝ*[. .] (2) *b*]*rsfm*. There is little basis for estimating the number of letters missing at the beginning of each line. A small mortise in the top, through which the break runs obliquely toward the

left rear corner of the fragment, is 2.8 cm. from the face and 6 cm. from the left side; it is roughly round and is 1.8 cm. deep. In front and behind are slightly depressed areas which would have matched the outline of the foot of the statuette, while the dowel in the bottom of the foot would have been fixed in the mortise. The statuette thus stood very near the front edge of the base (the toe would have been only about 1 cm. from the edge). There is no indication how far the missing mortise for the other foot was from the one preserved. The left side of the base was polished, as were the face and top, but all are now chipped and marred. The bottom is superficially chiseled even, but large tool marks are still visible. The fragment narrows to *ca.* 4 cm. at the rear, and no part of the original back surface seems to be preserved. White alabaster with a few, faint, rusty streaks. 8.5 cm. by 9.5 cm. (originally perhaps about 20 cm. wide) by 18 cm.

TC 973 (Plate 84)

Base with most of the left side broken away, bearing a two-line inscription on the face reading (1) *m'mr*/*dr'm*[(2) *m*/*wbn*/*qf'n*/*z*[. The number of letters missing at the end of each line is estimated at four and two. The letters of the upper line are shorter than those of the lower (2.8 cm. against 3.2 cm.). There are two small mortises in the pecked top; the right one, which is nearer the front (3 cm.) than the other, is rectangular (1.7 cm. by 1.1 cm.), but is set askew; it is 1.4 cm. from the right side. The break runs through the left mortise, which is 5.8 cm. from the face and 6.9 cm. from the right side; both mortises are *ca.* 1.7 cm. deep. These mortises were apparently designed for attaching to the base a statuette with the left foot advanced (as the bronze statue of Ma'adkarib from Mârib). The right side of the base is chiseled even and partly smoothed; the left side is preserved in only a tiny area at the lower rear. The bottom and back are tooled and partly chiseled even. Limestone. 8 cm. by 11.7 cm. by 11.1 cm.

TC 996 (Plate 84)

Broken base, consisting of a large part of a left front corner, including a large section of a polished face, which bears a two-line inscription: (1)]*rm*/*b'yṣm*/*ddrḥn* (2)]/*m'mrs*/*brṣfm*. The number of missing letters at the beginning of the two lines cannot be determined. Part of a mortise in the polished top of the base is preserved at the edge of the break; it is set back 4 cm. from the face and the same distance from the left side. It is 2 cm. deep and *ca.* 2.8 cm. wide, being roughly rectangular and placed askew. A second mortise presumably once existed to the right (at an undetermined distance) to receive the dowel of the left foot of a statuette. The left side of the base is chiseled even and roughly smoothed; the bottom is highly polished. Light-colored alabaster with undulating horizontal striations. 8 cm. by 14.4 cm. by 8.3 cm.

TC 997 (Plate 84)

Two joining fragments of base (TC 997 is the left end and TC 998 is the center part) with a two-line inscription on the upper part of the polished face: (1)]/*drḥn*[...] *rms* (2) *d*]*b*/ *brṣ*[*fm*]. It is estimated that some nine letters are missing at the beginning of line one, some three at the beginning of line two (assuming that the second line, which ends *ca.* 5 cm. from the left edge of the face, was symmetrical). Of the two mortises in the polished top, the left one is the better preserved. It is 3.2 cm. from the face and 3.5 cm. from the left side of the base. Roughly rectangular in shape, it measures 2.4 cm. from front to back and 4 cm. from side to side, with a depth of 2.4 cm.; only a lower corner of the right mortise is preserved. It had about the same depth as the other, from which it is separated by 7 cm. The left side of the base is tooled and very superficially chiseled. The back is polished smooth and the bottom is roughly tooled, though smoothed along the front and rear. White alabaster with vertical brown band running from side to side through the center. 12.3 cm. by 18.5 cm. (originally *ca.* 22 cm. wide) by 8.7 cm.

TC 1012 (Plate 84)

Fragment from the upper right side of a statuette base bearing an inscription on the face. The first parts of three lines are preserved, and these read (1) *m'mr*/*kl*[*y* (2) *brṣfm*[(3) *wn*/..[. The characters are *ca.* 2.3 cm. high. While the face of the piece is flat, the right side and back are rounded, as though

the object had been a drum or cylinder sliced off flat on the front. The side and back exhibit long, vertical chisel marks. The top is somewhat rough, though some of the higher spots have been chiseled off even. At the break is a foot-shaped mortise with a deeper cutting in the middle of it (maximum depth, 1.5 cm.). This mortise, some 5 cm. long and perpendicular to the face, is 7 cm. from the right side and 3 cm. from the face. Limestone. 11.5 cm. by *ca.* 10 cm. by 14 cm.

TC 1023 (Plate 84)

Two joining fragments of a low base or perhaps a tabletop (TC 1023 is the left corner and TC 1024 joins it on the right) with a one-line inscription on the face reading [ ]'*m*/*dt*/ *ḥdrn*/*wdr'n*/*brṣfm*. A third fragment, inadvertently discarded in the field, joined these on the right and added the letters [*m*]'*mr*/*yd* to the beginning of the line; see *JaPEHA*, pp. 201f., §354, where the *b* before *rṣfm* was omitted by error (also in the drawing on p. 248). A narrow mortise in the top of the base, the perimeter of which is chipped most of the way around, runs from front to back. It is set back 4 cm. from the face and is 8.7 cm. from the left side of the base. Its length is 5.8 cm., its width is *ca.* 1.5 cm. maximum, and its depth is 1.4 cm. The top of the base is coarsely polished; the left side is chiseled even and partly smoothed. A margin along the front of the bottom *ca.* 6 cm. wide is chiseled roughly even, while the rest is very rough with large tool marks. None of the back of the piece is preserved. Mottled alabaster with a brown banding exposed at the lower left of the face. 6.2 cm. (5.1 cm. at the face) by 21 cm. by 12.5 cm.

TC 1072 (Plate 84)

Base with a two-line inscription on the face reading (1) *m'mr*/'*m* (2) *ydm*/'*grm*; see *JaPEHA*, p. 202, §355, Pl. ix, below. Centered in the top of the piece is a small rectangular mortise (2.5 cm. front to back by 1.9 cm.) diminishing in size toward the bottom (it is 2 cm. deep); the interior is mostly chiseled. The top of the base is chiseled fairly even. The squared sides are roughly smoothed and the back is evened. In the bottom is a crude cross-shaped cut with maximum depth of *ca.* 1.8 cm.; the presence of this cut suggests that the piece was re-used. Limestone. 7.6 cm. by 9.4 cm. by 7.5 cm.

TC 1170 (Plate 84)

Statuette base, broken at the left side, with a two-line inscription on the polished face reading (1) *m'mr/rṭd'l/ḏt/h[rn]* (2) *brṣfm*; see *JaPEHA*, p. 203, §357. A fragment bearing the last two letters of line one appears to have been lost since the original study of this piece. The two small oval mortises in the top, set back 2.5 cm. from the face, are 6.5 cm. apart. The one on the right is 4 cm. from the right side of the base. Each mortise measures *ca.* 2 cm. from front to back by 1.2 cm., with a depth of 1.5 cm. Around the right mortise is a slightly depressed area roughly in the shape of a foot; a similar area is visible around the left mortise, but it is not depressed. The left mortise is about half filled with oxidized lead. The top of the base is smoothed, and the right side, squared with the face and top, is coarsely smoothed. The back is very rough with large tool marks. The bottom is tooled roughly even and exhibits small, short marks; the top and back part of the base seem to have been subjected to intense heat. White alabaster. 10.3 cm. by 14.5 cm. (originally *ca.* 16.5 cm.) by 10.5 cm.

TC 1172 (Plates 84 and 85)

Large statuette base with a two-line inscription on the face: (1) *m'mr/šmnr/bn/'bḥḍ/brṣf* (2) *m/z̧fryn/(m)*; see *JaPEHA*, pp. 203f., §358. The letters of the upper line are 4.3 cm. high and those of the lower line 2.5 cm. to 2.8 cm. Line two is not centered, but starts at the right edge of the face and runs only to the middle. The isolated *m* at the end of line two has been partly obliterated and is certainly a mistake. That the *m* of *rṣfm* was carried over to the lower line indicates that the inscription was not well planned. In the top of the base, which is evened and coarsely smoothed, are two carefully designed cuttings for attaching the feet of a statue. The right one (for the left foot) is 11 cm. long, while the other (for the right foot, which turned out more than the left) is 12 cm. long. In both cases there is a depression (*ca.* 3 mm. deep) corresponding to the outline of the statue feet. At the front, which is *ca.* 5 cm. wide, the corners are nearly square; the width

diminishes to *ca.* 3 cm. at the rear, where the heel is rounded. Two deeper (*ca.* 1.8 cm.) transverse, roughly tooled mortises appear within each of the depressed outlines, and these are deep at the ends, shallow in the centers. There were apparently four dowels on each foot to fit into the deeper ends of the mortises. The squared sides of the base are fairly smooth and the back and bottom are roughly tooled even. The back has a chiseled margin across the top edge. Limestone. 8.8 cm. by 25 cm. (24.5 cm. at the face) by 14.5 cm.

TC 1173 (Plate 85)

Statuette base with a three-line inscription filling the polished face: (1) *hn'm/bn/ḏkrkrb/ḏnḍ* (2) *ḥn/sqny/'nby/šymn/[ṣ]* (3) *lm/ḏhbn/m'mrs/br[ṣfm]*; see *JaPEHA*, pp. 199f., §351, in which the relative width of the base is exaggerated in the drawing, p. 248. The letters are 3.7 cm. high on the average; the face is damaged at the lower left. The top and sides of the base are chiseled fairly even. In the rear edge of the top, two cuttings *ca.* 1.5 cm. wide and 3.5 cm. deep are exposed, probably because the back has been split away; they were designed to hold the feet of a statuette. The bottom of the base is roughly tooled even and chiseled in a few places; the back is irregular in its present state. Light-colored, porous alabaster. 15.3 cm. by 23.5 cm. by 8.5 cm.

TC 1174 (Plate 85)

Base for two statuettes with a five-line inscription covering the polished face: (1) *sknm/wyšrḥ'm/bnw/[.......]* (2) *šymn/'d/rṣfm/slmy/ḏh[.....]* (3) *nby/'nfssmy/w'ḏnsmy[.....]* (4) *wkl/'wldsmy/w'qnysmy/[....]* (5) *[...ṣn]tm/wbḏt/z̧hrn/wb/mr[...]*. The approximate number of missing characters at the end of each line (indicated within the brackets) was determined on the assumption that the mortises in the top and the cuttings on the bottom of the base were symmetrical, although this does not allow room for Jamme's reconstructions: see *JaPEHA*, pp. 183f., §341. The entire left side of the base is broken away, and only a trace of one of the mortises for the statuette on the left is preserved; the face is also damaged at the lower right. The two foot-shaped mortises for the statuette on the right are fully preserved;

they are 3.3 cm. from front to back and *ca.* 1.4 cm. wide. The one for the right foot has a maximum depth of 1.9 cm., the other only 1.4 cm. They are 2 cm. apart, located about 1 cm. from the face of the base, 3 cm. from the right side.

Unusual cuttings occur on the bottom of the base. The face was left intact to a thickness of *ca.* 2 cm., forming a ridge with an evenly chiseled edge in front of the cuttings. Behind this ridge in the center part is a strip recessed *ca.* 1 cm. (extending right to the back of the base), at either end of which (i.e., in the lower corners of the base) is a much deeper cut or recess. Both of these corner recesses measured some 7 cm. deep (from the lower edge of the face). The one on the right is about 5 cm. wide (the left one was probably similar). The right side of the base is tooled fairly even and chiseled at the front and top. The back is rough, with long vertical tool marks. White alabaster. 14.8 cm. by 20.2 cm. (originally about 24 cm.) by 7.5 cm.

TC 1187 (Plate 86)

Fragment from center of base (for one or more statuettes) with a two-line inscription across the polished face reading (1)]*tkrbs/ lbnsmy/*[(2)]*lbʾm/wyšrḥ*ʾ[. On the top toward the left of the fragment and about 5 mm. back from the face is a foot-shaped mortise 3 cm. long and 1 cm. wide with a deeper cutting in the center filled with oxidized lead. At the fracture, 1.9 cm. to the left of this mortise, is a trace of the mortise (with a small cutting 1.2 cm. deep in the center) for the right foot of the statuette. Toward the right end of the fragment, *ca.* 1.2 cm. from the back of the base, is a roughly square (7 mm.) cutting 1 cm. deep, damaged at the front and sides. There is no indication of its purpose. The top of the base is polished, though not damaged; the bottom is tooled even and rounded at the rear. The back is chiseled even except at the left of the fragment where it projects out about 5 mm. and is only roughly tooled. White alabaster. 7.2 cm. by 12 cm. by 6 cm.

TC 1236 (Plate 86)

Statuette base with a two-line inscription on the polished face reading (1) *mʿmr/ʾl*[.] (2) *m/dndḥn*; see *JaPEHA*, p. 204, §359, but note that the relative width is exaggerated in the

drawing on p. 248. The upper tip of the last letter of the first line is damaged, and while there is scarcely room for the circle of *y*, a word divider makes no sense. The only alternatives, *l* or *g*, would be crowded. In the superficially smoothed top of the base are two foot-shaped depressions, each *ca.* 2.5 cm. long and 1 cm. wide. In the center of each is a deeper mortise filled with oxidized metal. The depressions are about 1 cm. apart, set back 1.2 cm. from the face, and both turned a little to the right side of the base. The right side of the base is chiseled fairly even, and the left side is partly chiseled, partly rough. The bottom, which slants up toward the rear, is roughly tooled except for a chiseled margin along the front. The back is smoothed, suggesting that this is a re-used piece. White alabaster. 8.7 cm. by 10 cm. by 6.5 cm.

TC 1298 (Plate 85)

Damaged right part of statuette base with a three-line inscription on the face reading (1) ʾ*nmrm/bn/drʾk*[*rb* (2) *ymn/ṣlm/dhbn/ bd*[*t* (3) *bnsww/drʾkrb/wʿ*[. The letters in the center line are crowded together more than those in the other two lines. There is no clear indication how many letters are missing at the end of each line. The left part of the base was deliberately cut off, as is indicated by the vertically chiseled cut at the fracture. Similarly, the lower edge of the face has been chiseled away 2.3 cm. from the bottom (a line of chisel marks is visible at the edge of the fracture immediately below the third line of the inscription). Part of one mortise (2.5 cm. deep, *ca.* 8 mm. wide) is preserved in the polished top of the base; the edges at the top of this mortise are chipped. A break across the back of the base removed all but the front part of the mortise. The right side of the base is polished. None of the right side or back is preserved. The small area of the bottom which is preserved is chiseled even and superficially smoothed. White alabaster. 11.8 cm. by 13.7 cm. by 9.9 cm.

TC 1303 (Plate 86)

Base for two statuettes (both sides broken away), bearing a three-line inscription on the polished face: (1)]/*sqny/ʾnby/šymn*[(2)]*s/ rtd/frʿm/ʾb*[*y* (3) *y*]*ḥrmʾl/wyšrḥ*ʾ[*l*. In the top of the fragment, toward the left end, are two foot-shaped cuttings each *ca.* 3.2 cm. long and 1.5 cm. wide. They are about 1 cm. apart and are set back 2.5 cm. from the face of the base. In the center of each is a deeper mortise filled with oxidized metal. Near the right end of the piece, partly removed by a fracture across the back, are traces of similar mortises for the second statuette. The deeper, center mortise of the left one of this pair is intact and empty; it measures 1 cm. square and is 1.5 cm. deep. The top of the base was polished but is now badly marred; none of the back or sides of the base is preserved. The bottom was partly chiseled even, partly tooled roughly. Grayish-white alabaster with darker streaks. 11 cm. by 20.5 cm. by 8.6 cm.

TC 1331 (Plate 84)

Fragment from the left end of a statuette base bearing a two-line inscription across the top of the polished face: (1) /]*ṣlm/d̲* (2)]/ *ḥwfʿm.* The front part of one mortise is preserved in the chiseled top of the base. This mortise is set back some 3 cm. from both the face and from the left side of the base; it is 1 cm. wide and 1.8 cm. deep. The left side of the base, which slants in toward the rear, is superficially chiseled over rough tooling. The small area of the bottom which is preserved is chiseled fairly even. Mottled grayish-white and rusty colored alabaster. 15 cm. by 7.7 cm. by 7.4 cm.

TC 1340 (Plate 86)

Right part of a statuette base with a short two-line inscription centered on the polished face: (1) *ʾn*[(2) *ḥd*[. Part of one mortise in the top is preserved; it is set back 3.3 cm. from the face and is 14.5 cm. from the right end of the base. It measures 2.5 cm. from front to back, a little more than 1 cm. wide, and nearly 2 cm. deep. Traces of oxidized lead cling to the interior, with green oxidized copper at one side. The top of the base is imperfectly polished (some long scratches were not removed); the back was chiseled even and smoothed. The right side, which slants in toward the bottom (the bottom corner is broken), is tooled. The bottom is roughly tooled and has a chiseled margin at the front. White alabaster. 7.5 cm. by 17.8 cm. by 7.7 cm.

TC 1344 (Plate 85)

Statuette base, badly damaged at the lower edge and corners of the front, with a two-line inscription on the polished face: (1) [..]*r/ʾb-mld*[.] (2) [.. *r ... b*]*r*[*y* ..]. The letters of the lower line were apparently shorter than those of the upper. In the polished top are two irregularly shaped mortises, 5 cm. apart and about the same distance from either side of the base. Each is *ca.* 1.5 cm. deep, *ca.* 2.3 cm. wide and *ca.* 3.5 cm. long, with a depression only *ca.* 5 mm. deep extending out in front for 1 cm. The left side of the base was smoothed; the right side was roughly chiseled. In its present state, the back is irregular. The bottom is rough and exhibits a few tool marks. Alabaster, mottled white with dark reddish-brown streaks. 7.5 cm. by 20.1 cm. by 8.9 cm.

TC 1389 (Plate 85)

Statuette base with a two-line inscription on the face reading (1) [*m*]*ʿmr/ʾmt/bnt/ʾ*[*b*] (2) [*ʾ*]*ns/wšmtt/d̲twh.* One line is on each of the upper two of three horizontal bands which run across the face and around the sides of the piece. The upper band is *ca.* 2.8 cm. wide, the center 3 cm., and lower 1.5 cm. Each of the upper two bands is recessed *ca.* 4 mm. behind the one below it (on the front, the faces of the upper two bands slant in toward the bottom to produce this offset). In the top of the base is a pair of small mortises, centered from the sides and set back 2.2 cm. from the face. The left one is 1.3 cm. deep, 1.5 cm. from front to back, and 1 cm. wide. The right one is slightly smaller and not quite as deep. The back of the base is chiseled even and superficially smoothed; the bottom is chiseled fairly even. Clear alabaster with slight grayish tint. 7.8 cm. by 12.5 cm. by 7 cm.

TC 1976 (Plate 86)

High statuette base, broken at the upper right corner, with a five-line inscription covering the smoothed face: (1) [...] *m/drbḥ/ wbn/* (2) [.]*db/sqny/ʾnby/* (3) *šymn/ṣlm/d̲hb* (4) *n/ḥgn/tkrbs/*[*l*] (5) *wlds/rt̲d/rgnm/*; see *JaPEHA*, pp. 191f., §347. There is no trace of a sixth line at the bottom (only 2.5 cm. remain, while each of the five lines above is 3 cm. high, with about 5 mm. between). Traces of reddening are visible on parts of the face. In the top of the base is an irregular depression, crudely tooled, in the bottom of which are two rectangular mortises, each measuring *ca.* 1.2 cm. in width, 2 cm. from front to back, and *ca.* 2.6 cm. deep. They are set back about 2.5 cm. from the face and are 2.2 cm. apart. The sides of the base are chiseled fairly even; the bottom was chiseled less carefully, while the back is irregular. Limestone. 19.5 cm. by 16.6 cm. by 9.8 cm.

TC 2080 (Plate 86)

Statuette base, broken at the left top, with a three-line inscription on the polished face reading (1) *m'mr[/']š[b]m[/]* (2) *brn/bn/'dbb* (3) *brṣfm*; *see JaPEHA*, p. 205, §361, Pl. XXII. Only a small area of the top is preserved at the right front corner. The bottom corner of a mortise 1.5 cm. deep is preserved 4.3 cm. from the right side, and 3.2 cm. from the face; its size and shape cannot be determined. The sides of the base are smoothed; the bottom is chiseled roughly even. The back is tooled even and has wide (*ca.* 3 cm.) chiseled margins at the sides and bottom. Yellowish alabaster. 13.5 cm. by 14.5 cm. by 8.8 cm.

TC 2241 (Plate 87)

Left end of statuette base with inscription on the front, of which only a final *ḥ* is preserved, and a monogram on the left side which is perhaps to be read *wdm* (a name occurring on potsherd TC 1247, described in *JaPEHA*, p. 218, §381). All the faces of the piece are chiseled even and all the edges are beveled at an angle of 45°. In the top, one complete mortise is preserved near the left side and part of another at the break; the complete one is rectangular, 2.3 cm. wide and 1.6 cm. from front to back. It is 2.7 cm. deep, 2.6 cm. from the left side, and 4.5 cm. from the face; the other mortise is 4.7 cm. to the right of the first. Sandstone, grayish and slightly crumbly. 8.3 cm. by 11 cm. by 11.6 cm.

TC 2276 (Plate 87)

Flat statuette base (?), broken at the right, with a one-line inscription across the polished front reading *]/dt/'krn/*. If it is assumed that the mortises in the top were symmetrically placed, five characters would be missing at the beginning of this inscription. The piece seems to be re-used, however, so this may be only part of a longer inscription. There are two

mortises, roughly circular, in the superficially smoothed top. Set back about 5 cm. from the front, they measure *ca.* 3 cm. in diameter and 1.8 cm. deep. One is very near the left side, while the break at the right runs through the middle of the other. The left side of the piece is chiseled fairly even with vertical marks visible; it slants in toward the top. As this side is much cruder than the other faces, it is clearly a secondary cut. The high polish on the bottom of the piece suggests that this was originally the upper surface of some larger object, perhaps a tabletop. The back is broken irregularly. Light-colored alabaster. 4.7 cm. by 16 cm. by 19.8 cm.

TC 2279 (Plate 86)

Left front corner of a statue base, with a three-line inscription on the face reading (1) *]mdkr/bn/'lšrḥ* (2) *]ḥfnm/w'twl/br* (3) *ṣfm*. Eight or nine letters seem to be missing at the beginning of the first two lines, but the short third line, which was apparently centered, seems to be complete. Traces of reddening are visible on the face. On the top of the base, coming within 1 cm. of the left side and 1.3 cm. of the face, is the front part of a foot-shaped cutting 2 mm. deep. As the cutting has a maximum width of 6 cm. and a length of *ca.* 13 cm. (estimated), the statue was about one-third life size. In the center of the cutting is a nearly square (1.6 cm. by 1.8 cm.) mortise 1.3 cm. deep; no trace of a similar cutting for the left foot of the statue is preserved. The left side of the base is smoothed; the bottom has a depression of about 2.5 cm. in the center, 3.5 cm. from the face, and 5.5 cm. from the left side. Limestone. 8.6 cm. by 14.8 cm. by 10.7 cm.

TC 2539 (Plate 86)

Fragment of a statuette base with a two-line inscription on the polished face. Only a small part of the first letter is preserved in the upper line, not enough to identify it. The second line reads *ḥdrn[/*. In the polished top, part of one mortise is preserved at the left edge of the fragment. The back of the piece is roughly tooled even at the right, more irregular over the surface of the protruding (*ca.* 1 cm) left part (i.e., what was apparently the center of the base). Light-colored alabaster. 11.5 cm. by 15 cm. by 6.6 cm.

STONE BOWLS AND SIMILAR VESSELS

While only a very limited number of complete or nearly complete stone vessels were found in the Timnaʻ Cemetery during the second campaign, fragments of a rather large number of bowls and similar vessels were found. The type of vessel represented by the fragment can be determined in most cases. The variety of forms is rather extensive, though the function of many of the forms can only be conjectured. The number of different kinds of stone used is greater in this group of objects than in any other, although some other groups have many more individual objects.

TC 515

Stem of a pedestal cup (or bowl) ringed by three horizontal ridges. The bottom of the bowl was nearly flat and was 9 mm. thick. Below the ridges the stem flared out. The inside of the stem was hollowed out, and tool marks are visible. This form is probably similar to one in pottery found at Ḥureiḍa; see G. Caton Thompson, *The Tombs and Moon Temple of Hureidha (Hadhramaut)* in *Reports of the Research Committee of the Society of Antiquaries of London*, No. XIII (Oxford, 1944), p. 74, Pl. xxxvii, 1; xlix, 7. Limestone. 2.8 cm. by 3.3 cm. by 3.7 cm.

TC 548 (Plate 86)

Fragment of a circular, flat-bottomed bowl, consisting of a section of the bottom and vertical wall (including rim). The top of the rim is cut off level and is polished. The outside of the wall of the vessel has been chiseled along the upper edge, tooled below. The bottom is roughly tooled. The interior is rough. The wall is 2 cm. thick, the bottom 2.5 cm. The total height of the vessel is 7 cm. This fragment measures 15.5 cm. by 9.5 cm. Alabaster.

TC 550 (Plate 86)

Small lid with a knob. On the under side is a flange *ca.* 3 mm. wide. There is a geometric design on the top of the lid. Beginning at the outside, we find a lightly-incised, scal-

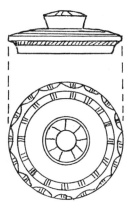

TC 550. Scale 1:1.

loped line with, typically, three radial lines in each scallop. Inside this is a band consisting of two uneven concentric circles with spaced groups of three radial lines between them. On the slightly convex top of the knob are two concentric circles with evenly spaced radial lines between. Limestone. Diameter 3 cm.; height (with knob) 1.1 cm.

For bands consisting of concentric circles with groups of incised lines between, cf. Robert S. Lamon and Geoffrey M. Shipton, *Megiddo I, Seasons of 1925–34, Strata I–V* (Chicago, 1939), Pl. 108:8.

TC 562

Rim of a large bowl, very similar in thickness (maximum 1.3 cm.) and section to TC 688, below. The thickness diminishes near the rim, the top of which is somewhat flattened. The inside of the fragment is somewhat smoother than the outside. Diameter of the bowl, judged from the curvature of this fragment, was about 50 cm. Steatite. 6.5 cm. (wide) by 4 cm. (high).

TC 591

Flat base of a small stone jar, discarded in the field after being drawn. 4.5 cm. in diameter.

TC 591. Scale 1:2.

TC 686

Fragment of the flat base of a cylindrical vessel. The bottom of the vessel averages 2.5 cm. in thickness; traces of the wall indicate that it varied in thickness between 1.5 cm. and 2 cm. The bottom of the interior was left rough with spot tool marks. The bottom of the base is likewise rough and somewhat concave; the outside appears to have been more smooth. Oölitic limestone. Diameter, 14.5 cm.

TC 688

Fragment from the side of a stone vessel. One end of a ledge-handle, 1.5 cm. thick and protruding 1.5 cm. from the wall, is preserved to a width of 4 cm. It was set 5.7 cm. below the brim (which is badly damaged, but recognizable). Chisel marks perpendicular to the wall were left when the top of the handle was evened; the bottom of it is rough with diagonal tool marks. The exterior of the wall has a patterned texture of generally oval hollows separated by shallow ridges; the interior is smoothed. The wall has a maximum thickness of 1.4 cm. Steatite. 8.3 cm. high by 6.2 cm. wide.

TC 694

Half of the flat base of a small jar. The walls of the jar are *ca.* 3 mm. thick. The interior has tiny tool marks; the exterior is polished. Alabaster. Diameter 3 cm.; total height of fragment, 1.3 cm.

TC 694. Scale 1:1.

TC 711

Fragment from the rim of a very large circular vessel. In profile, the rim is rounded on the outside and top, flush with the wall on the inside. On the interior, *ca.* 5.3 cm. below

TC 711. Scale 1:3.

the top of the rim and right at the break, is a lip, suggesting an incurving at this point. Reddish-brown marble. Thickness of the wall, 2.4 cm.; fragment measures 9.5 cm. wide, 5.4 cm. high.

TC 750

Fragment from the wall of a small vessel, with triangular lug-handle. For stance and form, cf. TC 1772. The wall has a maximum thickness of 8 mm. The lug is 1.6 cm. high, 1.2 cm. wide, and 9 mm. deep. Alabaster. 2.7 cm. by 1.5 cm. by 1.5 cm.

TC 814 (Plate 86)

Small, crude saucer-shaped object, roughly circular (tending to be squarish). An iron dowel exposed at one edge, once part of a repair, clearly indicates that this piece was made from a fragment of a large stone bowl. The bottom (originally the outside of the large bowl) is rough with large parallel tool marks. Steatite. Diameter, 5 cm.; maximum thickness, 1.2 cm.; maximum depth of depression, 8 mm.

TC 821

Bottom and stem of a miniature goblet. The exterior (except for the bottom of the

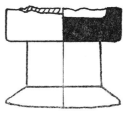

TC 821. Scale 1:1.

base, which is partly rough) is polished; the interior is smoothed. Alabaster. Preserved height, 2.5 cm.; diameter of the stem, 2 cm.; diameter of cup bottom, 3.4 cm.

TC 822

Fragment from the rim of a large stone basin or pot. Part of a ledge handle is preserved at the lower edge (6 cm. below the brim). Steatite with specks of brown oxide. Diameter at rim, about 42 cm. Thickness of wall at handle, *ca.* 1.8 cm.; near rim, *ca.* 1.2 cm. Over-all dimensions, 12 cm. by 8.5 cm.

TC 842

Fragment of a wall with the stump of a circular handle from a stone ladle. The handle, which slants upward, is 5 mm. below the small section of the rim which is preserved. Limestone. Maximum diameter of handle, 2 cm.; preserved length, 3.5 cm.; thickness of wall, 5 mm.

TC 843

Fragment of the side (including rim) and bottom of a flat dish. A ridge, now damaged, ran around the outside of the wall at the bottom. Above this is a section of vertical

TC 843. Scale 2:5.

wall (1.7 cm. wide); this then flares out to form a wide (1.4 cm.) rim, flat on the top (where it is polished). Horizontal marks on the interior of the wall and bottom indicate that the dish was turned. Alabaster. Thickness of wall, 8 mm.; height of vessel, 3.5 cm.; width of preserved section, 4.5 cm. at rim. Diameter at outer edge of rim, *ca.* 13 cm.

TC 892 (Plate 87)

Fragment from the side of a stone vessel. The rim is somewhat flattened on top. A ledge-handle, preserved to a width of *ca.* 6.5 cm., is 2.5 cm. below the brim; it projects 1.1 cm. from the wall of the vessel. The top and front of it are smoothed, the bottom rough and slanting. The interior of the vessel was smoothed. The exterior was smoothed above the level of the handle, but left rough (with diagonal tool marks) below. Steatite. Maximum thickness of wall, *ca.* 1.7 cm. (at bottom of fragment); the fragment measures 13 cm. (in width) by 6.5 cm. (in height).

TC 904

Fragment from the rim of an alabaster vessel. 2.3 cm. by 1.8 cm. (Missing.)

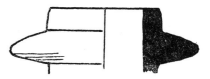

TC 904. Scale 1:1.

TC 905

Fragment from the side (including rim) of an alabaster vessel. 4 cm. by 3.5 cm. (Missing.)

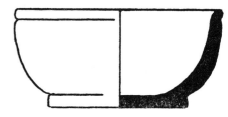

TC 905. Scale 1:1.

TC 906

Fragment from the rim of a shallow bowl. The body is *ca.* 1 cm. thick and has a broad (2.2 cm.) flat rim which extends *ca.* 1.5 cm. beyond the exterior of the wall, thus forming

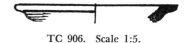

TC 906. Scale 1:5.

a flange tapering from 1 cm. in thickness at the body to *ca.* 6 mm. in thickness at the rounded outer edge. Polished alabaster. The diameter at the outer edge of the rim is *ca.* 22 cm. The fragment measures 13 cm. by 4 cm.

TC 919

Part of the flat bottom from a circular stone vessel. Two sections of a nearly vertical wall are preserved on opposite sides of the base fragment, one section to a maximum height of *ca.* 9 cm. The interior is smoothed, but somewhat uneven. The outside of the wall is smoothed above a band, some 2 cm. wide, of vertical tool marks running along the lower edge. The bottom has irregular, large tool marks, though they have been partly worn away by use. Steatite. The outside diameter of the base is 14 cm.; the bottom is 1.5 cm. thick. The wall is thinner, varying between 8 mm. on one side to 1.1 cm. on the other.

TC 935

Fragment of the rim and wall from a stone vessel. The interior is smoothed; the exterior is smoothed down to about 2 cm. from the rim, tooled below. The wall has a maximum thickness of 9 mm. Steatite. Diameter at rim, *ca.* 12 cm. The fragment measures 6 cm. by 5 cm.

TC 946

Fragment from the lower side of a flat-bottomed stone vessel. The wall is smoothed on both inside and outside, while the bottom is rough with tool marks on both the interior and exterior. The wall varies in thickness from 8 mm. (at the upper part of the fragment) to 1.5 cm. (near the base). Steatite. The outside diameter at the bottom, *ca.* 14 cm. Width, 9.5 cm.; height, 8 cm.

TC 959

Fragment of the rim and wall from a stone vessel. Although the fragment is narrow, the curvature of the rim provides the information, with relative certainty, that the piece comes from a bowl with sides that slanted outward slightly and that the rim diameter was about 11 cm. The wall is 5 mm. to 8 mm. thick. The rim is rounded, and there is a groove on the outside of it some 5 mm. below the top. The interior is somewhat uneven; the exterior and rim are polished. Alabaster. 4 cm. by 2.8 cm.

TC 975

Fragment of the rim and wall from a polished stone jar. This piece contrasts with TC 1951 in having a lip on the outside of the rim and in having a thicker wall near the top. The

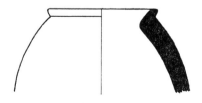

TC 975. Scale 1:2.

thickness of the wall varies from 6 mm. at the lower end of the fragment to 1 cm. near the rim. Alabaster. Outside rim diameter, slightly more than 6 cm. The fragment measures 4.5 cm. by 4 cm.

TC 979

Half of a miniature jar, polished except for the bottom of the interior. A vertical, pierced

TC 979. Scale 1:1.

handle, near the top, has been broken off. Alabaster. Maximum diameter, 2 cm.; height, 1.5 cm.

TC 988

Fragment of the rim and wall from a small bowl. On the inside the rim is flush with the body, but on the outside it is recessed and thus thinner than the wall below (which is *ca.* 5 mm. thick). A handle on the side of the bowl, 1.2 cm. below the rim, is 1.2 cm. high, with a slightly smaller width, and extends 6

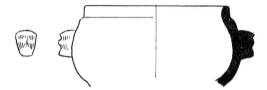

TC 988. Scale 2:3.

mm. out from the wall. It has a vertical groove down the center crossed by two horizontal grooves. The exterior is smooth, while the interior has horizontal ridges indicating that it was turned (there are also short tool marks near the top). Alabaster. 4.2 cm. by 3.1 cm.

TC 989

Small vase with much of the wall and rim broken away. The flat base has a ridge around it, above which the sides flare out toward the

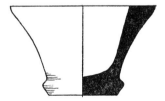

TC 989. Scale 1:2.

top, where they form a broad, flat rim. The wall is *ca.* 4 mm. thick near the center, while the top of the rim measures 1.4 cm. in width. Alabaster. Diameter at base, 3.8 cm.; outside diameter of rim, *ca.* 8.5 cm.; height, 5 cm.

TC 1053

Fragment of the rim and side from a flat dish. The ridge on the outside just below the flaring rim suggests a carinated prototype.

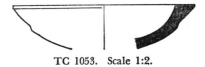

TC 1053. Scale 1:2.

Polished alabaster. Outside rim diameter, *ca.* 11 cm. The fragment measures 3.5 cm. by 4 cm.

TC 1054

Fragment of the rim and wall from an alabaster vessel. 4 cm. by 3 cm. (Discarded in the field.)

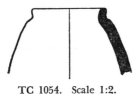

TC 1054. Scale 1:2.

TC 1077

Section of the flaring rim from a low dish, polished inside and out. On the broad (*ca.* 1.7 cm. wide), flat top of the rim is a crudely

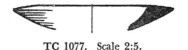

TC 1077. Scale 2:5.

inscribed Old South Arabic *m*; as it is near a break, it could well have been the first letter of a word or name. Alabaster. Outside rim diameter, *ca.* 11 cm. Over-all dimensions, 9 cm. by 3 cm.

TC 1103

Lug handle and section of the wall from a small vessel. The wall is 6 mm. thick. It is smoothed on the outside, and the inside has slightly irregular horizontal tool marks, partly worn away. The handle extends 2.2 cm. out from the wall and is 2.8 cm. wide and 7 mm. thick; the end of it is rounded. Steatite. Diameter of bowl, *ca.* 7 cm. The fragment measures 4.5 cm. by 2.5 cm.

TC 1129 (Plate 87)

Ladle or cup with a roughly circular bowl. The broad, flat handle, which is broken off 2 cm. from the body, is 4 cm. wide and 1.2 cm. thick (less at rounded edges). The walls, nearly vertical, are of unequal height, 4.8 cm.

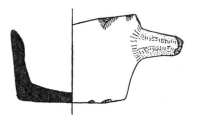

TC 1129. Scale 1:2.

on the handle side and 4 cm. on the side opposite. The bottom on the inside is concave. The walls are of irregular thickness, averaging *ca.* 6 mm. or 7 mm.; the inner face flares back at the top, leaving a narrow rim. All surfaces are partly smoothed, with only a few tool marks still visible. Rather dark gray steatite. Maximum diameter at rim, 7 cm.

TC 1134 (Plate 87)

Damaged stone bowl with narrow ledge-handles on opposite sides of the body. Most of the rim and much of one side are missing. Although the corners are very broadly rounded, the body has a very squarish appearance. The walls, varying in thickness from 7 mm. to 1.1 cm., are nearly vertical and are rounded into the flat bottom. The bottom is concave on the interior and only *ca.* 3 mm. thick in the center (where a hole has been broken). The handles are both *ca.* 8.5 cm. wide and extend *ca.* 1.5 cm. out from the body. They are not at the same height, as one is some 2.5 cm. below the rim, the other nearly 1.5 cm. higher. Steatite with mica and other material. Height, 8 cm.; outside rim diameter, 14 cm. to 14.5 cm.; maximum width (including handles), 17 cm.

TC 1206

Fragment of the base and wall from a small jar with a flat, vertical handle, which is pierced. This object was similar to TC 1951, but smaller. The wall is 6 mm. thick at the handle, thicker near the base; the bottom is somewhat rounded inside, flat outside. The jar was squarish rather than circular. Alabaster of poor quality. 4 cm. by 4 cm.

TC 1241

Fragment of the rim, side, and bottom from a low stone bowl. There is a groove just below the rim on the outside, leaving a margin 5 mm. wide at the rim. Maximum thickness of the side (near the bottom), 8 mm.; thickness at rim, 5 mm. Crystaline limestone. Outside rim diameter, *ca.* 8.5 cm. Fragment measures 5.5 cm. by 4 cm.

TC 1242

Section of the rim from a very large stone vessel, the walls of which slanted outward at about 30° from vertical. The sides were smoothed, but not completely even, on the inside and in a margin about 4 cm. wide along the top on the outside. Below this margin the outside is rough with large vertical tool marks. The top of the rim is chiseled flat. The wall is of uneven thickness, varying between 1.3 cm. and 2 cm. Steatite. Rim diameter nearly 60 cm. Width, 32 cm.; height, 12 cm.

TC 1244

Fragment of large vessel. The outside is roughly tooled; the inside, which is deeply burned, is smoothed. Near one edge is a bronze dowel or rivet which had been used in mending the broken vessel. (The method was to drill a hole on both sides of the break, insert a metal dowel in each, and connect the heads of the dowels on both sides with flat strips of bronze to form a bond.) The holes for two other dowels are exposed at breaks; they are *ca.* 7 mm. in diameter. The thickness of the fragment varies between 1.3 cm. and 1.7 cm. Steatite. 8.5 cm. by 5 cm.

TC 1245

Fragment similar to TC 1244 but smaller. There is one dowel in place. Steatite. Thickness, 1.7 cm. Over-all dimensions, 6.5 cm. by 4 cm.

TC 1246

Fragment similar to TC 1244. A dowel with a strip of bronze running to the break is in place. Steatite. 1.3 cm. in thickness. 4.5 cm. by 4 cm.

TC 1279

Battered cylindrical fragment with three narrow, rounded bands running around it. This piece seems to be the stem of a chalice; one end has a concave surface preserved in a small area which is taken as the bottom of the bowl. Alabaster. Diameter, 4 cm.; length, 4.5 cm.

TC 1318

Fragment of the wall and base from a small, cylindrical jar. A vertical pierced handle, *ca.* 1.8 cm. long, has been broken off at the top of the fragment. The bottom of the jar is 1.4 cm. thick; the side diminishes in thickness from *ca.* 1.3 cm. at the bottom to *ca.* 7 mm. at the top of the level of the handle. While the outer face is nearly vertical, therefore, the interior of the jar increases in diameter toward the top. Alabaster. Outside diameter, *ca.* 5 cm.; inside diameter at bottom, *ca.* 2.7 cm.; height of fragment, 5.7 cm.

TC 1332 (Plate 87)

Crude, heavy bowl (broken into two joining parts). The interior, 3.5 cm. deep and having a diameter of 12 cm., forms an almost perfect circle and has vertical walls and flat bottom, all chiseled even. The top of the rim is also chiseled off flat. The exterior was apparently not finished; half of the outside is roughly tooled, and the remainder is irregular. The bottom is roughly tooled flat. The wall varies in thickness from 1.7 cm. (on the part tooled) to *ca.* 2.8 cm. (on the irregular part); the bottom is *ca.* 3.8 cm. thick. Limestone. Maximum outside diameter, 16.7 cm.; height, 7.5 cm.

TC 1336 (Plate 87)

Very crude stone bowl, with about half of the wall missing. The bottom is very roughly tooled flat, the outside vertical. The top of the rim is chiseled flat, and there is red coloring on one section of it. The interior is merely an irregular cavity with a maximum depth of 3.8 cm. crudely tooled out; it has a diameter of *ca.* 8.5 cm. The wall measures between 2 cm. and 2.5 cm. in thickness at the rim. Limestone. Maximum diameter, 15.5 cm.; height, 8.5 cm.

TC 1346 (Plate 87)

Fragment from the side of a circular stone vessel. The vessel was flat-bottomed and had walls that slanted outward slightly toward the top. This fragment includes a large rounded rib, extending from rim to bottom, protruding into the inside of the vessel. This rib is 1.6 cm. wide at the bottom, slightly more at the top, and protrudes 1.1 cm. from the wall at the bottom, slightly more at the top. The top of the rib is cut off on a bevel, so that the innermost edge of it is *ca.* 8 mm. lower than the rim. A hole 7 mm. in diameter has been drilled down into the center of the rib to a depth of *ca.* 3 cm. The outside of the wall has incised geometric decorations in identical bands 1 cm. wide at top and bottom. Each consists of four evenly spaced horizontal lines with an irregular zigzag in the center space and groups of two and three vertical lines in the upper and lower spaces. Both the wall and bottom of the vessel are 6 mm. thick. Limestone. Outside diameter at bottom, *ca.* 9 cm.; 4.5 cm. (height) by 5 cm. (maximum preserved width of fragment) by 1.9 cm.

TC 1417

Fragment from the high (1.2 cm.) ring base of a stone vessel. Concentric lines on the bottom of the interior show that it was turned. The bottom is 5 mm. thick; the wall was about the same. The ring base is 7 mm. thick. Alabaster. Outer diameter of base, *ca.* 7.5 cm. Fragment measures 4.8 cm. by 3 cm. by 2.5 cm.

TC 1442 (Plate 87)

Fragment of the rim and upper wall from a small-mouthed jar. The lower break runs through a pierced lug handle, just below the drilled hole. From the mouth (outside rim diameter, *ca.* 6 cm.) the rounded body increases in diameter to at least 12 cm. The wall averages 1 cm. in thickness, diminishing toward the rim, which has a ridge on the outside. The interior is evened; the exterior and top of the rim are polished. The handle appears to be the stylization of an animal head, perhaps that of a bull. Alabaster. 5 cm. by 5 cm.

TC 1444

Miniature bowl, one side missing. It has a disc base (diameter, 2.5 cm.) and flaring sides (rim diameter, 5 cm.). The interior is smoothed, but not polished, except for the bottom, which is roughly tooled. The flat top of the rim, the outside, and the bottom are polished, but not well. The wall has an average thickness of *ca.* 6 mm. White alabaster. Height, 2 cm.

TC 1625 (Plate 87)

Small, crude stone bowl with one side and part of the bottom broken away. The interior diameter is 3.5 cm. at the flat bottom, 4.3 cm. at the top. The bottom and walls have a maximum thickness of *ca.* 1.8 cm. The bowl appears to have been somewhat oval. One side is about 1 cm. shorter than the other. Scora. Diameter, 7 cm.; height, 5.2 cm.

TC 1626 (Plate 87)

Square stone vessel with a circular depression in the top and a narrow vertical handle on the end. The half opposite the handle is formed by TC vi: 5, from the first campaign of excavation in the Timna' Cemetery. The hollow in the top, approximately semi-circular in cross section, is 2.1 cm. deep in the center and has a diameter of 5.4 cm. at the top; horizontal marks were left on the interior when it was turned. The top of the piece is mostly polished smooth. The sides are polished, but fine chisel marks remain, as on the sides of the handle; the bottom is more roughly chiseled. The handle, which is flush with the body at top and bottom, protrudes 1.8 cm., and it averages *ca.* 1 cm. wide, narrowing slightly toward the bottom. The horizontal hole drilled through it, *ca.* 3.5 mm. in diameter, is flush with the side of the body and is located 1.5 cm. below the top. Dark, mottled alabaster. Height, 4 cm.; width, 6.9 cm.; length, including handle, 8.8 cm.

TC 1648 (Plate 87)

Crude, porous stone bowl with the wall broken away on one side. The roughly circular depression in the top has a maximum depth of *ca.* 3 cm. The walls are some 2 cm. thick; the bottom is nearly 5 cm. thick. Very rough scora. Diameter, 13.5 cm.; height, 7.7 cm.

TC 1660 (Plate 87)

Crude circular stone object with a shallow (*ca.* 6 mm.) depression in the top. All surfaces are rough or irregular. Sandstone. Diameter, 8 cm.; height, 4.2 cm.

TC 1670

Fragment of the wall and bottom from a stone bowl with a flat bottom and vertical sides. The wall is 1 cm. thick at the upper break, but diminishes slightly before flaring out on the interior to meet the bottom. The bottom is 7 mm. thick. Alabaster. Outside diameter, *ca.* 14 cm.; preserved height, 6 cm.; width, 7 cm.

TC 1707 (Plate 88)

Rectangular stone vessel, broken anciently into two parts. It is divided into three compartments, circular ones on the ends and an irregular one between; cf. Oscar Reuther, *Die Innenstadt von Babylon (Merkes)*, Fig. 10:h,i, for roughly parallel clay vessels (with four compartments). On one of the ends (both of which are slightly concave in plan) is a vertical handle reaching from top to bottom; it is nearly semicircular in profile, V-shaped in section. On the sides, which flare out slightly at the ends, are raised **panels** (also concave), flush at top and bottom. They are 6.2 cm. wide, corresponding approximately to the width of the ends of the central compartment. The inner diameter of the circular compartments is 5.6 cm. at the top (one is slightly less at the bottom). The sides of the center compartment are formed by the curved walls (*ca.* 6 mm. thick) of the end compartments. Its minimum width is 3.4 cm., maximum *ca.* 5.5 cm.; its longer dimension (sideways across the object) is 6 cm. It is 2.6 cm. deep, slightly shallower than the 3 cm. of the circular compartments. Limestone, white except for the darkened patina. Total length (including 1.5 cm. handle), 18.5 cm.; width, 7.5 cm.; height, 4.4 cm.

TC 1738 (Plate 88)

Fragment of the rim and wall from a bowl, rounded in section. The wall varies in thickness from about 5 mm. at the rim to about 9 mm. lower down. A small handle occupies a position on the outside 2.3 cm. below the rim; it protrudes 8 mm. from the body, is

1 cm. thick and 3.6 cm. wide. The outside surface above the level of the handle is chiseled smooth; below, it is rough with vertical

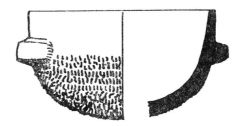

TC 1738. Scale 2:5.

and criss-cross tool marks. The interior is worn fairly smooth, but is not entirely even. Steatite. 8.5 cm. (preserved height) by 11.5 cm.

TC 1753 (Plate 88)

Fragment of the wall (with bit of rim preserved) from a large vessel. A ledge-handle (some 13 cm. long, 1.4 cm. wide, and protruding 1.8 cm.) is set 4.6 cm. below the rim. The underside of it has oblique tool marks, and the outer edge and top are roughly smoothed. The wall, with a maximum thickness of *ca.* 1.8 cm., is rough with tool marks on the outside below the level of the handle and smooth above. The interior is also smoothed; the wall diminishes to a thickness of *ca.* 5 mm. at the rounded rim. Steatite. The fragment is 10.5 cm. high by 20 cm. wide.

TC 1756

Fragment of base and wall from very small jar. The flat bottom and the vertical wall meet at a slightly rounded right angle. The bottom is 9 mm. thick, the wall *ca.* 7 mm. The outside is polished; the interior exhibits tool marks only partly obscured by smoothing. Alabaster. The diameter was slightly less than 5 cm. Height, 2.5 cm.; width, 4.3 cm.

TC 1771 (Plate 88)

Side of a miniature jar, including part of the base and a short section of the rim. The maximum diameter of the body was *ca.* 4 cm. (just below the middle); the disc-shaped base had a diameter of *ca.* 3 cm. The smooth inner surface of the wall blends into the rounded rim; on the outside the thin rim is set off by a recess or groove 4 mm. wide. The outside of the jar, including the bottom, is polished.

The walls and bottom have a thickness of about 5 mm. Alabaster. 4.8 cm. (height of the jar) by 3.7 cm.

TC 1771. Scale 2:3.

TC 1772 (Plate 88)

Fragment of the rim and wall from a thin-walled bowl. On the outside, 9 mm. below the rim and separated from it by three shallow horizontal grooves, is a triangular handle with glyphs (two horizontal, one vertical). The

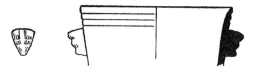

TC 1772. Scale 2:3.

form suggests an origin as an animal head (probably a bull's head; cf. **TC 2218** for similar stylization). It protrudes 6 mm. from the body and measures *ca.* 1 cm. by 1 cm. The wall has a maximum thickness of *ca* 3 mm.; it is polished on both the inside and the outside, though shallow tool marks are still faintly visible. White alabaster. 2.4 cm. (preserved height) by 2.7 cm.

TC 1802

Fragment of the base and lower part of the wall from a small jar (probably similar in form to TC 1951, though smaller). The flat bottom averages 1 cm. in thickness (the interior is slightly uneven), the vertical walls *ca.* 6 mm. The outside, including the bottom, is polished; the interior exhibits small tool marks, vertical on the sides. Alabaster. Diameter, about 5 cm.; the fragment measures 2.8 cm. in height, 4.5 cm. in width.

TC 1806

Section of the wall and rim from jar with small mouth and with body which flares out toward the bottom. The rim has a thickened

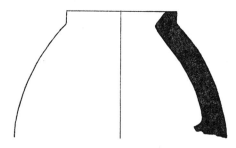

TC 1806. Scale 1:2.

lip on the outside. The wall has a thickness of *ca.* 1.3 cm. The outside of the body and top of the rim are polished; the interior of the body exhibits shallow tool marks. Alabaster. Inner rim diameter *ca.* 3.5 cm.; diameter of body near bottom, *ca.* 12 cm. Fragment measures 7.5 cm. in height, 9 cm. in width.

TC 1813 (Plate 88)

Two fragments forming most of a stone bowl (all of bottom and part of one side are missing), rounded in section. Two ledge-handles are set on opposite sides at a distance of 2.5 cm. and 2.8 cm. below the rim. They are 6 cm. and 5.5 cm. wide respectively and

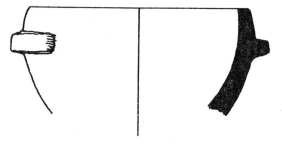

TC 1813. Scale 2:5.

protrude 1 cm. from the body. Below the level of the handles the outside of the bowl is rough with tool marks; above this level it is smooth, as is the interior. The walls have a maximum thickness of 1.5 cm., but diminish to *ca.* 7 mm. at the rounded rim. Steatite. Outside rim diameter, 15 cm.; greatest dimension (including handles), 18 cm.; maximum preserved height, 7.5 cm.

TC 1814 (Plate 88)

Broken stone lid with a vertical, cylindrical handle in the center. The lid is 7 mm. thick in the center, diminishing toward the scarcely preserved edges. The handle is 1.4 cm. in

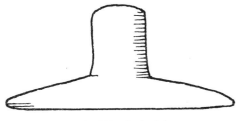

TC 1814. Scale 1:1.

diameter and 2 cm. high. Steatite. The original diameter was 6.5 cm. or more; preserved dimensions, 6 cm. by *ca.* 2.7 cm.

TC 1819 (Plate 88)

Fragment of the wall, bottom, and rim from small alabaster jar. The vessel is not symmetrical, as it tilts to one side so that the rim is not level and the wall on one side is nearly vertical, while the opposite wall slants in toward the top. The maximum rim diameter is 3.5 cm., while that of the base is *ca.* 5.5 cm. There is a groove on the outside below the rim; the inner edge of the rim is beveled, the outer rounded. The interior of the jar exhibits vertical **tool marks on the** sides; the exterior is smoothed, but not polished. Alabaster. 5.3 cm. (height) by 5 cm. by 2.7 cm.

TC 1826 (Plate 88)

Fragment of a shallow bowl, probably from a footed chalice, although the pedestal is broken off immediately below the body. The thickness of the bottom is equal to the depth of the interior (*ca.* 1.6 cm.); the walls taper to a thickness of about 5 mm. at the flat rim. The outside rim diameter was slightly less than 10 cm.; the pedestal was 3.1 cm. in di-

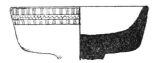

TC 1826. Scale 2:5.

ameter at the top. An incised band in geometric design 9 mm. wide runs around the outside of the bowl just below the rim. There are four evenly spaced horizontal lines. In the upper and lower spaces are vertical lines in groups of three, while the center space has a zigzag line. Limestone. 9 cm. by 4.6 cm. by 3 cm. (height).

TC 1867

Fragment of the rim from a stone jar with thin walls. The rim is broad (1.2 cm.) and flat, flush on the inside but with an overhanging lip on the outside about 6 mm. thick. The wall immediately below this lip is 7 mm. thick, but tapers to 4 mm. at a point 2.3 cm. below the brim. Below this point is

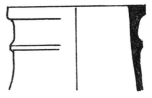

TC 1867. Scale 2:5.

a rounded ridge which runs around the vessel. The interior is well smoothed, but not polished; the top of the rim and the outside are polished. Alabaster with horizontal striations. Outside rim diameter, 9.5 cm. Fragment measures 5.8 cm. (height) by 6 cm.

TC 1905 (Plate 88)

Stone ladle with a circular bowl, which is rounded in section. On one side is a handle, now broken off 3.5 cm. from the body, which is flush with the brim at the top. It decreases in size from the body, where it is 2.7 cm. wide, outward to the break; at the break it is 2.1

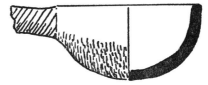

TC 1905. Scale 2:5.

cm. wide. It is flat on the top and sides (which are smoothed), rounded on the bottom (which is roughly tooled). At the body it measures 2 cm. in thickness. The interior of the bowl is smoothed, but not completely evened; the outside is the same from the rim down about 2 cm. The lower sides and bottom are rough with tool marks, mostly parallel and vertical, converging irregularly on the bottom. The walls have a thickness of *ca.* 8 mm. Steatite. Outside rim diameter, 9.6 cm.; height, 5 cm.; over-all length including handle, 15 cm.

TC 1906 (Plate 87)

Round stone vessel of a rather common type, broken only at one place on the rim.

The bottom is almost perfectly flat. The sides begin at the bottom almost vertical, then very gradually curve in slightly in cross section. There is no shoulder at the top, for the sides are simply cut off approximately level, leaving a mouth nearly as large as the interior. According to the field catalogue, there is a pottery lid or plug in the vessel, mortared in place with plaster, so that the contents would have been sealed in. Steatite. 9 cm. in height by 11 cm. in diameter (dimensions from field catalogue). (Carnegie Museum.)

TC 1909
Small alabaster jar with four triangular lugs on the sides. 3.7 cm. in height by 4.2 cm. in diameter (dimensions from field catalogue). (Carnegie Museum.)

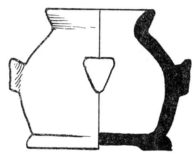

TC 1909. Scale 1:1.

TC 1910 (Plate 89)
Small limestone jar with nearly vertical walls, everted rim, and incised geometric design around the shoulder. The bottom is flat; a ring around the edge is chiseled even, within which the bottom is slightly concave and rough. Above a narrow flange at the outside

TC 1910. Scale 3:5.

bottom, the walls of the vessel widen from a diameter of 6.2 cm. at the bottom to 7 cm. at the beginning of the shoulder. The shoul-

der then is rounded inward to meet the rim; the diameter at the base of the flaring rim is 5 cm. The decoration on the shoulder (similar to that on TC 1826, but less regular) consists of four roughly parallel horizontal lines. In the center space formed by these lines is a zigzag; in the upper and lower spaces are groups of vertical lines. Crystalline limestone (white inside with tan patina). Height of vessel, 8 cm.

TC 1924
Fragment of the wall and rim from a miniature alabastron with a pierced, vertical handle. 5.2 cm. (height) by *ca.* 3.5 cm. (preserved width). (Missing.)

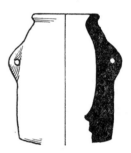

TC 1924. Scale 2:3.

TC 1946
Fragment from a stone vessel. This fragment seems to be a small part of the bottom (*ca.* 1 cm. thick) of a stemmed bowl with the upper part of the stem intact; although the interior (upper side of the fragment) is superficially polished smooth, there are still several deep tool marks at the center. White alabaster. 5 cm. by 3.5 cm. by 2.5 cm. (preserved height).

TC 1947 (Plate 88)
Small lid with a triangular knob-handle in the center. The rounded top is polished; the bottom is rough with parallel tool marks except for a polished margin *ca.* 4 mm. wide at the edge. Alabaster. Diameter, 3.5 cm.; height, 1.5 cm. (including handle).

TC 1951 (Plate 89)
Circular jar with pierced ear-handles, broken into several pieces but now repaired. The rim is of the hole-mouth variety, modified by a low, rounded ridge on the outside. From an inner rim diameter of 3.8 cm., the body increases in size to 7.7 cm. near the

TC 1951. Scale 1:2.

bottom. The walls have a maximum thickness of *ca.* 1 cm. toward the bottom, but they diminish to *ca.* 4 mm. near the rim; the tiny handles are some 2 cm. below the rim. The exterior and interior are both smoothed. Alabaster, gray with white, slightly wavy horizontal striations. Height, 7 cm.; maximum diameter, 8.1 cm.

TC 1952

Fragment from the rim of a large stone bowl. On the outside, 2.3 cm. below the rim is a wide (7.5 cm.), thin ledge-handle; it protrudes a maximum of 1.3 cm. from the wall (at the center). The top is squared, but the lower side slants so that the handle is wider at the wall than at the outer edge. The exterior of the wall is roughly tooled below the level of the handle; above this level it is chiseled smooth, as is the interior. The wall has a maximum thickness of 1.4 cm. Steatite. 13 cm. (preserved width) by 10.5 cm.

TC 1954 (Plate 88)

Crude miniature vessel of stone. An irregular margin was drafted around the outside of the rim. White limestone. 2.8 cm. (height) by 3.8 cm. (maximum diameter).

TC 1957 (Plate 89)

Flat-bottomed jar with the sides slanting inward so that the diameter diminishes from 12.2 cm. at the bottom to 9.5 cm. at the plain rim. The bottom and walls are both rather uniformly thin (*ca.* 6 mm.) and a hole has been broken in both at some time. The bottom is rough with long tool marks (crisscross except radial at the edges); at the lower edge of the outside is a margin (*ca.* 1 cm. wide) of vertical tool marks. The rest of the outside and the interior are chiseled somewhat more

even, though the surfaces are not entirely smooth. Steatite. Height, 11.2 cm.

TC 1957. Scale 2:5.

TC 2000 (Plate 89)

Fragment from the base and wall of a slender cylindrical vessel with a flat bottom. On the outside there is a band (*ca.* 1.5 cm. wide) of geometric decoration running around the piece. The main part of this decoration consists of four horizontal lines. The upper and lower spaces are very narrow (less than 2 mm.) and have groups of three vertical lines, while the center space is wider (nearly 7 mm.) and has upright triangles filled in with horizontal hatching (the intervening inverted triangles are empty). Below this main band of decoration is a pair of parallel wavy lines with groups of three vertical bars.

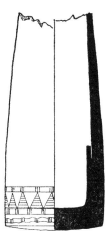

TC 2000. Scale 2:3.

The bottom of the vessel is 6 mm. thick, approximately the same as the lower portions of the walls. The upper part of the walls is less than 3 mm. thick down to within 2.5 cm. of the interior bottom, where there is an offset. A narrow groove extending *ca.* 1.5 cm. down into this offset, flush with the inner surface of the thinner part of the walls, indicates that the inside of the vessel was cut out with a cutting tool in the shape of a thin-walled tube. Crystalline limestone with calcium accretion. 4 cm. (diameter at bottom) by 8.5 cm. (preserved height of fragment).

TC 2023 (Plate 88)

Miniature stone pot with a small oval hole broken in one side. The outside is rough with short, deep tool marks, generally vertical; the bottom is flat, partly evened to make it level. The top and inside of the rim, which slants down to one side, are smoothed. The inside of the pot is fairly smooth. Limestone. Height, 3.8 cm.; maximum diameter, 4 cm.; inside rim diameter, 2.4 cm.

TC 2045 (Plate 89)

Crude vessel in the form of a cylinder diminishing in diameter from top (*ca.* 5.3 cm.) to bottom (*ca.* 4.4 cm.). There is a rounded hollow 1.8 cm. deep in the top. Porous limestone. Height, 5.2 cm.

TC 2063 (Plate 88)

Fragment of the base, wall, and rim from a stone jar. Above a flange around the outside bottom, the wall rises nearly vertically for 6.6 cm.; at this point is a carination. Above the shoulder (2 cm. wide) is a thin everted rim 1 cm. wide which meets the shoulder at a right angle. On the shoulder is a band of incised geometric decoration 1.5 cm. wide. The decoration consists of five horizontal

TC 2063. Scale 1:3.

lines with the spaces incised with geometric designs; the second space from the top has a zigzag. The other three have groups of three or four vertical lines. The bottom of the jar is *ca.* 8 mm. thick; the wall varies from 1 cm. (both at the bottom and at the carination) to

6 mm. (near the center), while the rim is only *ca.* 4 mm. thick. Limestone. Outside diameter at base, *ca.* 9.5 cm.; height, 8.6 cm.; preserved width of fragment, 10 cm.

TC 2221

Miniature jar lid. The bottom has a smoothed margin *ca.* 3 mm. wide around the edge to fit against the jar rim; inside this is a rough boss. The top of the lid is rounded, producing a thick center and thin edges. In the top center is a pointed handle (*ca.* 4 mm. by 8 mm.) pierced at the base. Grayish alabaster with white striations. Diameter, 2.3 cm.; total height, 1.5 cm.

TC 2243

Fragment from the base, wall, and rim of a stone bowl. The flat bottom varies from 1.2 cm. to 1.5 cm. in thickness. The nearly vertical wall (slanting out slightly toward the top) is 1.5 cm. thick. The rim is nearly flat on top. Very porous limestone. Diameter, *ca.* 16 cm.; height, 5.5 cm.; preserved width of fragment, 10.5 cm.

TC 2271

Fragment of the base and lower wall of a stone vessel. Both the outside of the wall and the flat bottom are polished. The interior is rough with tool marks. The wall is 1.1 cm. thick and is preserved to a height of only about 1 cm. above the interior bottom of the vessel. The bottom is *ca.* 3.5 cm. thick at the outside, 2.5 cm. at the inner break (estimated center of the vessel). Grayish alabaster with light-colored horizontal striations. Diameter, *ca.* 11.5 cm. Fragment is 4.6 cm. high, 6.5 cm. wide and 6 cm. along a diameter.

TC 2272

Fragment of the lower wall and ring-base of a stone vessel. The exterior face of the wall is vertical and smooth above a 5-mm. ridge around the lower edge. The wall diminishes in thickness from bottom to top of the fragment. At one end of the fragment it is *ca.* 2.3 cm. thick at the bottom, at the other *ca.* 1 cm., with a minimum of 5 mm. in thickness at the upper break. The bottom is *ca.* 1 cm. thick. Limestone. Outside base diameter, *ca.* 13.5 cm.; preserved height, 5 cm.; width, 6 cm.; length, 11 cm.

TC 2513 (Plate 89)

Fragment of the rim and handle from a stone vessel. The wall of the bowl curves in toward the bottom. Just above the lower break, the polished inner face makes a corner, and there is a horizontal surface *ca.* 5 mm. wide interrupted by the break. No complementary turn is preserved on the outer face. The handle, flush with the rim, is preserved to *ca.* 2.5 cm. from the body; on the under side of it, at the break, is a ridge indicating that the handle turned down sharply at this point. On top of the handle are two rounded ridges parallel to the rim and located beside it; perpendicular to these ridges are three shallow grooves, only the ends of which are preserved at the break. White alabaster. 3.5 cm. by 3.2 cm. by *ca.* 4 cm.

TC 2514 (Plate 89)

Fragment of the rim and wall (with most of a vertical handle) from a stone vessel. From a rim diameter of 7 cm., the body widens out somewhat as far down as preserved. The inner surface immediately above the break seems to begin curving in again. The handle, protruding a maximum of 1.1 cm. from the body, diminishes in size in a gradual curve toward the bottom and would have ended just below the break. It is preserved to a length of 5.2 cm. and is *ca.* 8 mm. thick at the body, 5 mm. at the outer edge; it begins 1.2 cm. below the rim. The wall of the vessel is *ca.* 7 mm. thick, except at the thinner rim. Steatite. 5.5 cm. wide (at rim) by 6.7 cm.

TC 2515

Fragment of the rim and wall (with horizontal ledge-handle) from a large stone vessel with a rim diameter of about 24 cm. The handle, located 3 cm. below the rim, protrudes *ca.* 9 mm. from the body; it is 7 cm. wide and 1.5 cm. thick. It is unevenly chiseled on the top and outer face, while the bottom bears oblique tool marks. Though the fragment is badly worn, the interior seems to have been at least superficially smoothed; the outside was chiseled unevenly above the level of the handle, partly tooled and partly chiseled below. There is a 5-mm. perforation about 2.5 cm. below the handle. The plain rim is flat on top. Steatite with impurities of iron oxide. Width of fragment, 8 cm.; height, 11 cm.

TC 2516

Fragment of the rim and upper wall from a well-made stone vessel. From an outside rim diameter of about 8 cm., the wall widens in a smooth curve and is almost vertical at the lower break, where the diameter is about 13 cm. The rim is thickened on the outside with a sort of lip; it is flat on the top at the outer edge and beveled on the inner side. The wall is 9 mm. thick just below the rim, then it widens immediately to 1 cm. before gradually diminishing to a thickness of 4 mm. at the lower break. The interior is somewhat smoothed, the rim is polished, and the exterior is highly polished. Alabaster with nearly horizontal striations of white and gray. 6.5 cm. (width) by 7.3 cm.

TC 2525 (Plate 88)

Flat stone vessel, broken at one edge, with an interior depth of *ca.* 7 mm. The bottom is *ca.* 1.2 cm. thick in the center, 9 mm. at the edges (the upper surface is convex). The low walls, slanting outward, taper from a thickness of *ca.* 6 mm. to a narrow rim. The piece is chiseled and superficially smoothed. Clear steatite. Diameter at rim, 8 cm.; height, 1.8 cm.

HAND MORTARS AND SIMILAR FORMS

Eleven stone objects from the second campaign, which appear to be hand mortars in most cases, are presently in the collection. All are approximately circular and rounded; otherwise, their size, shape, and material vary considerably.

TC 1118 (Plate 89)

Mortar with a flat bottom. The rounded sides are not very smooth, but the depression in the top (1 cm. deep) is quite smooth and fairly regular. Pinkish granite. Diameter, 10 cm.; height, 4 cm.; diameter of depression, *ca.* 6.5 cm.

TC 1119 (Plate 89)

Small mortar with the top completely occupied by a depression 8 mm. deep. The sides are rounded into the nearly flat bottom. Gray granite. Diameter, 4.2 cm.; height, 2.2 cm.

TC 1156 (Plate 89)

Round stone with one side cut off and containing a depression (*ca.* 1 cm. deep) for use as a mortar. The edges around the depression are irregular. Alabaster of poor quality. Diameter, 5.8 cm.; maximum height, 4.1 cm.

TC 1157 (Plate 89)

Mortar, not exactly circular, but irregularly so. The bottom approaches flatness, and the sides are rounded. The depression is relatively deep (*ca.* 1.6 cm.) and has a diameter of 4.5 cm. on the average. Granite. Height, 4.5 cm.

TC 1158 (Plate 89)

Mortar, somewhat ovoid in shape (8.5 cm. by 7.5 cm.), flattened in the center of the bottom. The sides are well rounded. The depression is *ca.* 1.2 cm. deep. Limestone. Height, 4 cm.

TC 1721

Mortar, rounded and having a shallow depression on one side. Pink granite. Diameter, 7 cm.; height, 4.2 cm.

TC 1833 (Plate 89)

Crude mortar (or shallow bowl?). The depression is nearly 2 cm. deep. Scora. Diameter, 7.5 cm.; height, 4 cm.

TC 1920 (Plate 89)

Small rounded mortar. Orthoquartzite sandstone, burned. Diameter, 5 cm.; height, 3 cm.

TC 1920. Scale 1:2.

TC 1956 (Plate 89)

Mortar (or burner?). This piece is round and has a deep (3 cm.) hollow in the top; the inside of this hollow is blackened from burning. Scora. Diameter, 9.5 cm.; height, 6.7 cm.

TC 2065

Crude mortar (or symbolic stone vessel?). Scora. Diameter, 5.5 cm.; height, 3 cm.

TC 2087 (Plate 89)

Flat-bottomed mortar (or crude miniature dish?). Scora. Diameter, 6.5 cm.; height, 3 cm.

TRIPOD OFFERING SAUCERS

Nine pieces from the second campaign, described in this chapter, are three-footed, circular vessels with a depression in the top. This form has been well described by G. Caton Thompson as a tripod offering saucer in *The Tombs and Moon Temple of Hureidha (Hadhramaut)*, pp. 88, 133. Most of those from the Timna' Cemetery are miniatures, though part of a full-sized one (TC 1100) and the leg of another (TC 1545) were also found. Most are of alabaster, but one (TC 1100) is of limestone. The decoration varies greatly, as does the detail of the shape, such as the size of the feet or legs, particularly in length.

This form has a wide distribution. In addition to examples previously known from South Arabia (G. Caton Thompson, *The Tombs and Moon Temple of Hureidha*, Pl. XXXVII: 5, 7–10; LVII: 1–5; *Sabaeica II*, p. 280, Photo 572–74); it is also known from Abyssinia (*Annales d'Ethiopie*, Vol. I, pp. 39ff.), Petra (Murray and Ellis, *A Street in Petra*, pp. 15f., Pl. XV), Samaria (*The Objects from Samaria* [*Samaria-Sebaste III*], Fig. 117:7, which was conjectured, probably erroneously, to have had four legs), Hazor (*Hazor II*, Pl. LXXVII: 2,3,4,5,6; Pl. CIV: 1,13; Pl. CLXIV: 2,6; here called mortars throughout), Hama (Riis, *Hama*, p. 182, B,E), Alalakh (Sir Leonard Woolley, *Alalakh* [1955], p. 293, Pl. LXXXIII: C), and Babylon (Reuther, *Babylon*, p. 25, Fig. 25:a,b).

TC 1100 (Plate 90)

Part of an offering saucer (larger than those from Hureida). One broad foot or leg (2 cm. long) is preserved and about one-third of the body. On top, within a flat margin 1.5 cm. wide, is a smooth concavity 1.7 cm. deep in the center. The outside of the foot (flush with the outside of the body and now damaged) and the bottom of it are smooth. The under side of the body is rough with large tool marks. Limestone. Diameter, 15 cm.; over-all height, 7 cm.

TC 1189 (Plate 90)

Small tripod offering saucer. The rim is battered at almost every point and preserved intact at no place. The surface of the circular depression (at least 1 cm. deep) has been superficially smoothed, but it is very rough with short tool marks. The outside of the object has an evened margin 2.5 cm. wide around the upper part; the band slants out slightly toward the top. The roughly tooled band below, covering the lower part of the body and the outside of the broad feet, is vertical and is set out slightly beyond the upper band. The bottom of the piece is very rough with large tool marks. Alabaster. Diameter, 7.1 cm.; height, 4.5 cm.

TC 1217 (Plate 90)

Miniature tripodal offering saucer, complete, except that the lower end and inner side of one leg are broken off obliquely. The top is occupied by a smooth shallow concavity. There is a simple decoration on the outside. Below a horizontal groove or scoring 2 mm. below the top are vertical grooves about 2 mm. apart completely around the outside of the body. A horizontal groove at the top of each leg (i.e., at the level of the bottom of the body) marks the lower limit of the decoration. The legs are flush with the outside of the body and smooth on the outer surface and on the bottom; the rest of the legs and the under side of the body are well evened. The body is 1.8 cm. thick (i.e., high); the

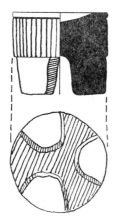

TC 1217. Scale 2:3.

legs are 1.4 cm. long and 1.7 cm. wide. Darkened alabaster (?). Diameter, 4.1 cm.; height, 3.2 cm.

TC 1263 (Plate 90)

Fragment, probably from a small offering saucer. The geometric design incised on the outside is similar to that on TC 1908. The depression in the top is *ca.* 6 mm. deep. The narrow walls, which came to a thin edge at the top, are mostly chipped away; the bottom of the depression is flat. The bottom of the body is about 1 cm. thick. There were probably three legs, though no certain indication of these remains. The outside and top are polished; the bottom is pecked even. Alabaster, blackened by fire. 5.8 cm. (diameter) by 2 cm. (preserved height).

TC 1545 (Plate 90)

Fragment of an offering saucer, consisting of a leg and a small part of the wall (not complete to the rim). At the lower end of the leg, on the outside only, was a low, rounded ridge, now battered. At 1.5 cm. above the bottom of the body of the vessel is a slight recess with a smooth face above. The leg is 3.5 cm. long and tapers in size from top (*ca.* 4 cm. wide) to bottom (*ca.* 3 cm.). The bottom of the body is *ca.* 9 mm. thick; the wall is less thick and apparently tapers toward the top. Nearly all the surfaces are polished, the inside especially well. Alabaster. 6.5 cm. by 6 cm. by 4 cm.

TC 1565 (Plate 90)

Miniature tripod offering saucer, badly battered around the top with the legs broken off. The top was similar to that of TC 1217. The only decoration is vertical grooves incised about 2 mm. apart around the outside of the body. Alabaster. 4.8 cm. (diameter) by 2 cm. (preserved height).

TC 1908 (Plate 90)

Miniature tripod offering saucer with one leg broken off. Above each leg on the side of the body is an incised X flanked on either side by a pair of vertical lines. On the outside of the lower end of each leg is a pair of

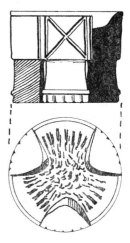

TC 1908. Scale 2:3.

rounded ridges; the outer face of each leg above this is recessed slightly. Much of the low, thin wall around the shallow, polished depression in the top is broken. The outside and top are polished; the bottom of the body is roughly tooled. Alabaster. 4.7 cm. (diameter) by 3.5 cm. (height).

TC 2019 (Plate 90)

Miniature tripod offering saucer. The legs are short (5 mm.) and the body is thick in proportion to the over-all size. A single groove runs around the outside of the body some 3 mm. below the top. There is a shallow depression in the top within a flat margin (*ca.* 5 mm. wide). All surfaces are fairly smooth, but not polished. Alabaster. 3.5 cm. (diameter) by 2.5 cm. (height).

TC 2020 (Plate 90)

Small tripod offering saucer, with one leg broken off. The concavity of the top is about 1 cm. deep in the center; the edges are chipped. A groove was incised around the outside *ca.* 3 mm. below the rim. Below this, the outside is smoothed evenly down to a ridge which encircles the lower edge; between the legs this ridge is notched. The outer face of the legs is flush with the ridge; this face ends at a ridge at the lower end of each leg. The legs are *ca.* 2.5 cm. long and taper from top (*ca.* 2.5 cm.) to bottom (*ca.* 1.8 cm.) in width. The underside of the body is roughly tooled. Alabaster. 6.5 cm. (diameter) by 6 cm. (height).

INCENSE BURNERS

Nine objects which apparently served as incense burners are present in the collection from the second campaign at Timna' Cemetery.[1] Seven are fairly complete, one is badly damaged, and only the corner of one is present. One of the burners (TC 1955) has a stone core covered with plaster. The others are of stone, limestone in most cases, except one (TC 1915), which is of pottery—this is also the only one without any trace of decoration. The decoration on the others consists of various types of geometric designs and recessed paneling imitating architectural features. Three of the burners (TC 536, 1751, and 1862) have letters inscribed. All, except TC 1708 and 1915 (which are legless), are four-legged; the legs are generally square and set at the corners flush with both faces of the body above.

TC 536 (Plate 90)

Two fragments (including TC 537), forming the corner of an incense burner (cf. *Ja-PEHA*, pp. 211f., §370) with one leg preserved, though damaged. (The oblique crack separating the two fragments forming this item runs through the leg.) The sides are incised with four horizontal bands of crude decoration (described from top to bottom): (1) a zigzag band, 1 cm. wide, just below the rim; (2) a band, 2.1 cm. wide, consisting of crude, recessed panels 3 mm. wide and 6 mm. to 7 mm. apart, on the side to the left of the corner; the corresponding band

on the adjacent face, to the right, is inscribed with the characters [ḥ]ḏk/; (3) a band, 1.6 cm. wide, divided into upper and lower registers of equal height with staggered panels; (4) a band of criss-crossing, covering the outer surfaces of the legs. Limestone. Height: 8 cm.; maximum preserved width of face: 6.5 cm., of side: 6.4 cm.; length of leg: 2.7 cm.; depth of cavity in top: *ca.* 3.5 cm.

TC 1708 (Plate 90)

Legless, rectangular incense burner with traces of burning inside the cavity in the top, specifically on the center of the front and back walls. The only decoration is on the front; below a slightly raised margin 1.1 cm. wide is a row of four raised tegular panels measuring *ca.* 1.6 cm. from top to bottom and having widths (from left to right) of *ca.* 1.9 cm., 2 cm., 2 cm., and 1.5 cm. (not including the glyphs *ca.* 5 mm. wide between them). The cavity in the top measures 6 cm. from side to side, 4 cm. from front to back, and 3 cm. in depth. Limestone. 7.2 cm. by 9 cm. by 7 cm.

TC 1731 (Plate 90)

Rectangular incense burner. One of the four legs is almost entirely missing. The incised geometric decoration around the outside of the body is obscured by weathering. It consisted of two parallel lines *ca.* 8 mm. apart near the top with vertical lines between, a similar band at the bottom, and apparently crude recessed panels in the register between. A dark rusty colored stain was applied to the surface before the decoration was incised. The cavity in the top is also rather crude; it measures *ca.* 5.2 cm. by 4 cm., and is *ca.* 2.2 cm. deep. The legs were about 1.5 cm. long and

[1] For references to similar objects see the following publications: Sir Flinders Petrie, *Gerar*, pp. 18f., Pl. XL, XLI, XLII: 5, 6; Reuther, *Die Innenstadt von Babylon (Merkes)*, p. 23, Fig. 20 (rectangular burner with four legs; of terra cotta; geometric design); Macalister, *Gezer*, III, Pl. CVII, 2 (cf. II, pp. 422 ff.); J. W. Crowfoot, *et al.*, *Samaria-Sebaste III*, Fig. 119:2 (plain, undecorated; under Hellenistic floor; compared with examples from *Gerar*).

2 cm. square. Porous stone. 6 cm. by 7 cm.
by 6.4 cm.

TC 1751 (Plate 91)

Square incense burner, badly damaged
(most of right side, front, and back are missing, as well as all of the legs except the stump
of one at the left rear). A hole *ca.* 3 mm. in
diameter, 8 mm. from the front face, and 7
mm. from the side, drilled 7 mm. up into the
body of the object where the left front leg is
broken off, probably indicates an ancient repair of this leg. On all outside faces, except
the front, the body was incised with decorations in three bands (described from top to
bottom): (1) a zigzag between parallel lines
8 mm. apart; (2) broad (5 mm.) vertical recessed bars (or panels) about 6 mm. apart,
between lines 1.3 cm. apart, separated from
upper and lower bands by a blank strip 3 mm.
wide; (3) bars similar to above, but shorter, as
they fit between lines only 8 mm. apart. A
fourth band had covered the exterior of the
legs (which are flush with the faces above),
but little remains. All the outside faces, as
well as the top of the rim, were stained a light
rusty color before the incising was done.

On the front face at the level of band 2 on
the sides were four incised letters. The first
(on the right) is entirely missing. The second, barely preserved at the center, is probably *r*. The third is in the form of a diamond
with a vertical line through it, so whether
ṭ, *ṭ*, or some other letter was intended is not
clear. The last letter is a clear *m*. The cavity
in the top, well formed and surrounded by
walls about 8 mm. thick, measures 5 cm.
square and is 2.1 cm. deep. Tool marks appear, though the interior has been partly
chiseled. Limestone. 5 cm. (preserved height
including broken leg on left rear) by 7 cm.
by 7 cm.

TC 1862 (Plate 90)

Square incense burner, weathered. Cf.
JaPEHA, p. 212, §371, where TC 1867 is a
typographical error. The front legs are broken
off at the body. The incised decoration on
the sides and back is in three bands: a zigzag
at both the top and bottom of body (the legs
are left undecorated) with crude panels (*ca.*
3 cm. from top to bottom and 5 mm. to 1 cm.
in width) between. On the front in the

central band are the inscribed letters, *d̲r'*, and
a broad bar or panel at each side. The cavity
in the top, *ca.* 5 cm. square, is 2.3 cm. deep.
Limestone. 7.2 cm. by 7 cm. by 7 cm.

TC 1915 (Plate 90)

Square incense burner without legs. The
sides are smooth and vertical; the bottom was
originally rough and is now damaged. The
object was entirely covered with a creamy
slip. The cavity in the top, *ca.* 1.4 cm. deep,
measures approximately 4.8 cm. by 5.1 cm.
The cavity and two adjacent sides of the
burner show traces of burning. A crack runs
down one burned side. Terra cotta with sand
grit. 5 cm. by 7 cm. by 7 cm.

TC 1955 (Plate 90)

Tall, square incense burner. Decorations
are incised in four bands (each demarked at
top and bottom by horizontal incised lines
ca. 4 mm. apart) around all four sides (described from top to bottom): (1) row of recessed triangles about 1.3 cm. high, five on all

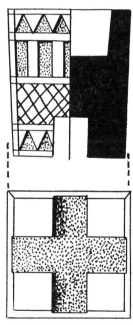

TC 1955. Scale 2:5.

sides but one, which has six; the zigzag on the
other burners is apparently related to this
band of triangles; (2) row of vertical recessed
panels 2.5 cm. from top to bottom and varying in width between 5 mm. and 1 cm.; (3)
criss-cross pattern with lines *ca.* 6 mm. apart,
extending down slightly onto the legs; (4)

triangles, as in band 1, two on each outer face of each leg. The top of the rim around the cavity was also incised with a criss-cross. The entire surface of all four sides, as well as the top of the rim, was stained a dark rusty color before being incised. The cavity in the top, 3 cm. deep, measures 5.8 cm. by 5.3 cm. Porous white stone (visible on the bottom and in the cavity) with the outside completely covered with hard lime plaster (on which the decoration is found); the plaster covers the rim also. 10 cm. by 8.2 cm. by 8.4 cm.

TC 2011 (Plate 91)

Square incense burner, the best made and largest in the collection. The center of one wall of the cavity in the top is broken out; three of the upper corners are battered to various extents. Nearly all of one leg is broken off, and an adjacent leg is chipped. The layout of the triply recessed panels, which serve as decoration, is the same on all four sides, though the exact dimensions vary slightly.

At either side of each face, extending down to cover the outer face of each leg, is a long (*ca.* 10.5 cm.) narrow (2.3 cm. to 2.5 cm.) recessed panel within which are, in each case, a pair of secondary recesses, the upper one being longer (5.2 cm.) than the lower (4.1 cm.) but equally wide (*ca.* 1.4 cm.). Within each upper secondary recess is a third plain recess, while within each lower secondary recess is a tertiary recess with a raised band across it just above the center. (This band is not flush with the secondary recess, but cut down to a thickness equal to about half the depth of the tertiary recess. Between the two long narrow panels is a wider one (varying from 3 cm. to 3.4 cm. on the several sides of the burner) entirely on the body of the object and equal in length to the upper second-

ary panels on the sides. These central panels are also characterized by a panel-within-a-panel-within-a-panel.

Below the central panel is an inverted T representing perhaps, as it is between the legs, a rung and a brace. This member is flush with the face of the body and legs but is only about one-third as thick as the legs. The legs are 3.2 cm. square, the same distance apart, and 4.7 cm. long. The bottom of the body between them, in the shape of a thick symmetrical cross, is tooled, while the inner sides of the legs have been chiseled and partly smoothed. The carefully made cavity in the top, surrounded by a 1-cm. wide rim, is 7.7 cm. square at the top and 6 cm. square at the bottom (as the walls slant in toward the bottom) and has a depth of 2.2 cm.; traces of burning cover most of the interior. Limestone. 11.5 cm. by 9.7 cm. by 9.7 cm.

TC 2012 (Plate 92)

Low, square incense burner of stone with elaborate recessed paneling as decoration on the sides. 5.5 cm. by 9.6 cm. by 9.6 cm. (dimensions from field catalogue). (Present location unknown.)

TC 2273 (Plate 90)

Crude incense burner, approximately square. Traces of incised lines on the sides indicate attempts at decoration, but the roughness of the piece precludes any interpretation. The cavity in the top measures about 5 cm. by 4.5 cm. at the top, but it diminishes in size toward the bottom, which is almost entirely covered with plaster. This suggests that the piece may have been used as the base for some sort of stele or sculpture. One of the four legs is broken off. Limestone. 5.8 cm. by 6.7 cm. by 6.9 cm.

XVI

OBJECTS OF BRONZE

TC 554

Bronze nail. 4 cm. long. (Disappeared while in Baltimore for study.)

TC 734

Bronze fragment, flat and irregular, with a ridge near one end. The fragment, which has an average thickness of *ca.* 5 mm., was shaped over a rounded surface. 5 cm. by 4 cm. by *ca.* 1 cm.

TC 742

Bronze nail or rivet with a broad flat head. The shaft is round (diameter, *ca.* 7 mm.) next to the head, but changes to a rectangular shape (*ca.* 4 mm. by *ca.* 7 mm.) less than a centimeter from the head. The diameter of the head is 1.8 cm.; it has a maximum thickness of 3 mm. or less. Total preserved length, 2.5 cm.

TC 805 (Plate 92)

Bronze door socket, broken at one corner, with two dowels on opposite sides of the bottom. The piece is approximately square, about 9.3 cm. by 9.6 cm. The circular depression in the top, *ca.* 1.2 cm. deep in the center, has a diameter of slightly more than 6.5 cm. It is placed nearer to one edge of the square than to the opposite (*ca.* 1 cm., compared with *ca.* 1.7 cm.). Below the center of the depression it is 1.4 cm. thick, so there is a large circular bulge on the bottom corresponding to the depression in the top. The thickness diminishes toward the edges of the depression, and the flange forming the square is only about 5 mm. thick. The dowels, also about 5 mm. thick, are flush with opposite edges of the flange; they are both *ca.* 1.2 cm. wide at the base. One widens at the outer end to *ca.* 2.2 cm., the other to *ca.* 1.8 cm. They are both some 2.5 cm. long. 3.1 cm. by 9.8 cm. by 9.5 cm.

TC 856

Small flat piece of bronze, *ca.* 3 mm. thick, which widens toward both ends. One end is broken off, the other appears to have a plain, original edge preserved for a short distance. On one corner next to the preserved edge is a perpendicular appendage, 1.2 cm. long, 1 cm. wide, and averaging *ca.* 2.5 mm. thick. 3 cm. by 3 cm. by 1.8 cm.

TC 894

Bronze ring, too badly corroded for detailed description. A thin piece of metal appears to have been wrapped around one side. The band itself appears to have been flat on the inside, but possesses a carination on the outside, while it is generally rounded. The band was *ca.* 3 mm. thick; the diameter is 2 cm. (outside measurement).

TC 902

Bronze fragment, representing the corner rim of some unidentified object. The rim was *ca.* 2 mm. thicker than the body in a band 7 mm. wide. The body is about 3 mm. thick. 2 cm. by 2.6 cm. by 1.1 cm.

TC 952

Flat bronze fragment, slightly curved, with a straight edge (possibly a rim) along one side. Near one end is a shallow ridge, after which the thickness of the metal diminishes. 2.5 cm. by 7.4 cm. by 4 mm.

TC 999

Fragment of bronze, perhaps a section of the rim of a bronze vessel. On the inside of the curve is a high (*ca.* 4 mm.) rounded ridge. On top of the rim is a pointed ridge, formed by the meeting of the rounded ridge and the incurving outer face. The body appears to have been less than 3 mm. thick. 1.5 cm. by 7.5 cm. by 7 mm.

TC 1003

Tiny rounded cup made of thin bronze. The edges are wavy from being bent into the present shape, and on the bottom is a minute button, as though there had been an attachment here. 1.2 cm. (diameter) by 7 mm. (depth).

TC 1040 (Plate 92)

Flaring, circular object of bronze. The larger end (diameter 10.1 cm.) has a flat, turned-in flange about 1 cm. wide. The smaller end (diameter 5.7 cm.) also has a flat flange inside. This flange has a roughly cut square hole in it measuring *ca.* 3.5 cm. by 3.3 cm. The bronze is about 2 mm. thick. On the inside near the top are some irregular bits of metal, apparently formed in casting. Height, 5.6 cm.

TC 1063 (Plate 91)

Bronze letter *n* with a dowel on the back near each end. This piece, designed for attachment to a flat surface, is rounded on the front and flat on the back (*ca.* 1.1 cm. wide) in cross section. The upper end is cut off square, the lower end at a slight angle. The central bar is almost horizontal, but the angles formed with the vertical members are slightly less than 90°. The dowels, 1.5 cm. long, are flat, 5 mm. by *ca.* 1 cm., and are placed *ca.* 8 mm. from the ends with the thinner dimension running vertically. 13.7 cm. by 4 cm. by 2.6 cm.

TC 1084

Bronze bar, triangular in cross section. The faces measure about 8 mm., 1 cm., and 1.1 cm. in width. The corners come to rather sharp angles. The bar tapers very slightly toward one end, and it is broken off at both ends. Length, 11 cm.

TC 1141

Long flat bronze piece, tapering slightly in width toward one end (from 2 cm. to 1.4 cm.).

On one side there is a decoration at the wider end; this consists of four wavy ridges *ca.* 2.3 cm. long, running off the end. The metal is about 3 mm. thick. 2 cm. by 12.4 cm.

TC 1142 (Plate 91)

Large, flat, circular object of bronze, perhaps a tray or possibly a mirror. The sheet of metal is *ca.* 2 mm. thick or slightly more. The piece is slightly concave and has a turned-back lip at the preserved edges. On the convex side along one edge is a strip of metal *ca.* 3 mm. thick measuring 2.5 cm. by 12 cm. This is attached with rivets. At one rivet and on an outer edge is another bit of flat metal which may have been part of a handle. The disc-like object was apparently in one piece when found, but was broken into more than a dozen fragments in transportation. Maximum diameter, 25.3 cm.

TC 1146 (Plate 91)

Bronze dagger blade. There are two corroded rivets *ca.* 9 mm. long in place through the corners of the broad end where the blade was attached to the handle. The maximum thickness of the blade, at the shallow ridge which runs longitudinally along the center on each face, is *ca.* 3 mm. The point of the blade is broken off at a point where the width has tapered to 7 mm. The blade measures 2.3 cm. by 11 cm.

TC 1183

Fragment of a large bronze handle, with a sort of tear-drop shape in cross section. At the end, a flange, designed to be placed against a flat surface, is preserved; it has a height of 6.5 cm. and a width of 5 cm. The body of the handle, preserved for *ca.* 5.5 cm. from the flanged end, is *ca.* 4 cm. by 3.5 cm. The metal of which the piece is made has a thickness of between 2 mm. and 3 mm. Maximum dimension of the fragment, 9.5 cm.

TC 1196 (Plate 92)

Fragment of a bronze statuette of a human, consisting of the left foot with a dowel on the bottom for attachment to a base and the leg up as far as the knee. The metal of which it is made seems to be *ca.* 4 mm. in thickness; the core is charcoal or a similar substance. The dowel is flat, running with the length of the foot. It is 2.2 cm. long, 1.5 cm. wide, and about 4 mm. thick. The foot is 3.5 cm. long. The total length of the fragment, including the dowel, is 8.4 cm.

TC 1197 (Plate 92)

Three double links of a bronze chain. Each link consists of two rings joined on the outer circumference at a half turn with a rather thick weld; thus one might at first describe the preserved section of the chain as consisting of six links. The solid metal of each ring is *ca.* 5 mm. thick and is round. The outside diameter of each ring is *ca.* 2.7 cm. The total length of the three links is 14 cm.

TC 1207

Flat bronze object. From the wider end, which is cut off obliquely, the piece tapers in width to slightly less than 7 mm. and then has a rounded enlargement on the end about 7 mm. thick, 9 mm. wide, and 7 mm. long. There is a low ridge along the longitudinal center on one side; the other side is flat. The thickness of the object (except for the bulbous enlargement on the end) is 5 mm. The maximum width is 1.7 cm., and the length is 5.3 cm.

TC 1208

Small cylindrical bronze piece with a large loop on the end, in a shape something like a miniature bucket with the bail up straight. The bottom, *ca.* 1.4 cm. in diameter, is flat; the body diminishes slightly in diameter toward the middle and then flares out again at the upper end, where the two ends of the upright loop are attached at opposite edges. The wire of which the loop is composed is *ca.* 3.5 mm. in diameter; the loop is 1.6 cm. high above the top of the body. Total length, 3.2 cm.

TC 1209

Fragment of bronze. This appears to be a rivet or dowel 1.6 cm. long and *ca.* 7 mm. in diameter with a flat strip of metal at each end, each strip being attached at the end and extending in the same direction. One strip is 1.6 cm., the other 2.7 cm., long; the shorter is *ca.* 7 mm. wide, the longer *ca.* 1 cm. Both are about 3 mm. thick. Such bronze rivets and strips were used in repairing broken stone

bowls; cf. TC 1244, 1245, and 1246 in Chapter XII. 2.7 cm. by 1.8 cm.

TC 1210

Small bronze disc, *ca.* 3 mm. thick and 2 cm. in diameter, with a perpendicular projection in the center of both faces. On one side, the projection, 1 cm. long, is round, tapering in diameter from *ca.* 6 mm. at the base to *ca.* 4 mm. near the rounded end. The other, 1.5 cm. long, is larger, *ca.* 8 mm. in diameter at the base, and it flattens out toward the end to a thickness of about 3 mm. and a width of 9.5 cm. Total length, 3 cm.

TC 1218

Flat bronze fragment with a perpendicular member resembling dowels seen on other objects of bronze. The main fragment, *ca.* 3 mm. thick, measures 2.8 cm. by 2.1 cm. and is broken at an angle on both ends. The flat dowel runs with the greater length and is at the edge of the more oblique break; it is 1.5 cm. long and *ca.* 4 mm. thick. Its width flares out from 1.3 cm. near the base to 1.8 cm. on the end, where the corners point outward. 2.8 cm. by 1.9 cm.

TC 1232

Fragment from shaft of a thick bronze spike (?), square in cross section. From a width of *ca.* 8 mm. on one end, it tapers to *ca.* 5 mm. on the other. Length, 5.8 cm.

TC 1233

Bronze fragment, consisting of the upper part of the letter *b* or possibly *d̪*. The upper bar and the parts preserved of the two uprights are rectangular in cross section, deeper than wide (5 mm. by 3 mm.). The upper corners of the letter form acute angles. The uprights have been slightly bent together. 1.7 cm. (preserved height) by 1.5 cm. (width) by 5 mm.

TC 1234 (Plate 92)

Small, solid bronze object, rather in the shape of a tall loaf with a small protrusion on one end and another on the top. The flat, rectangular bottom measures 2.4 cm. by 1.1 cm.; the sides and ends are nearly vertical for about 1 cm., then the piece is rounded off. The rounded upper part has four shallow ridges running around it. It is difficult to say what the small blob on top is. The protrusion on the end may have represented the neck and head of an animal, in which case the object may be a weight designated by an animal name. The object in its present state weighs some 25 gm. Total height, 2 cm.; over-all length, 2.8 cm.; width, 1.1 cm.

A much larger weight of a comparable sort was found in the early months of 1960 at Khôr Rûrī on the south central coast of the Arabian Peninsula. This larger weight has a rectangular body with an animal head on one end. It also has raised letters on the sides, apparently giving the name of some official, and the stubs of a large handle on the top. See "The 1960 American Archaeological Expedition to Dhofar," *Bulletin of the American Schools of Oriental Research*, No. 159 (October, 1960), pp. 21–23, Fig. 5.

TC 1256 (Plate 91)

Right forearm from a bronze statuette of a human, raised in salutation with the hand open (cf. TC 1776 for a relief with the arm in this position). The elbow itself is missing, but a bit of the upper arm is preserved at the end of the fragment. Diameter of wrist, 1 cm. Maximum diameter of forearm, 1.4 cm. Over-all length of fragment, 6.2 cm.

TC 1257

Fragment of a thin (2 mm.) bronze casting. This appears to be the lower side of the long garment and part of the leg from a statuette of a human; the fragment is bent out of shape at the top. The feature identified as a leg, preserved to a length of *ca.* 1 cm., has a diameter of *ca.* 1.5 cm. Fragment measures 5 cm. by 2.7 cm.

TC 1258

Fragment of bronze, interpreted as a solid handle and a piece of the vessel to which it belongs. In width, the handle narrows from 2.4 cm. where it is attached to 1.8 cm. at a distance 8 mm. from the body. It then continues in the same curve to flare out to an original width of 3.4 cm. (estimated), of which 3 cm. is now preserved, although the corners are broken off. The handle is about 1 cm. thick. The side of the vessel itself is

ca. 2 mm. thick. This is preserved only in an irregular section 1.5 cm. high and 3.5 cm. wide, which curves inward at the side of the handle. Maximum dimension of the fragment, 5 cm.

TC 1259

Solid bronze foot from the statuette of a human. On the bottom of the instep is the stub of a circular (diameter *ca.* 7 mm.) doweling for attachment to a base. The foot has a length of 3.1 cm. and is 1.3 cm. wide across the ball of the foot. From there it tapers in width to *ca.* 8 mm. at the heel; the preserved height is 1.6 cm.

TC 1269 (Plate 92)

Bronze foot, with a non-metallic core, from a statuette of a human. A sandal is represented. It has a thick (*ca.* 3 mm.) sole, a piece fitting around the sides and rear of the heel, and straps coming from the heel to the upper instep, where they are fastened with a buckle. Traces of a dowel can be seen on the bottom of the heel, though much of the bottom of the heel and instep is broken away. The length of the foot is 3.7 cm.; its greatest width, across the ball, is *ca.* 1.3 cm. The ankle is 1.5 cm. from front to rear, 1.3 cm. from side to side. Maximum height of the fragment, 3.3 cm.

TC 1289 (Plate 91)

Concave bronze disc possessing a flange or rim extending *ca.* 1 cm. to the rear from the outer edge. The piece is covered on the face with raised concentric circles as decoration and on the outside of the flange with a continuous frieze suggesting an archaic egg-and-tongue pattern. On the corner between the face and the flange is a narrow beaded border; outside and below this is a plain, thin, raised line. The diameters of the concentric circles on the face are *ca.* 3 mm., 1.7 cm., 2.8 cm., 3.2 cm., 8.2 cm., and 9.4 cm. Thus they are in two groups, one near the center, and the other some two-thirds of the way out toward the edge. The back is badly corroded, and it does not appear to have had any decoration. The outside height of the edge (i.e., the flange) of the disc is *ca.* 1.5 cm. The maximum diameter of the piece is 12.7 cm., and the metal of which it is made is *ca.* 2 mm. thick.

TC 1290 (Plate 92)

Unidentified bronze object. There is a "handle," preserved to a length of 3 cm. and measuring 8 mm. in width, 5 mm. in thickness. The rest of the piece is flattened, *ca.* 2 mm. thick. Next to the handle it widens out with a rounded shape to a maximum width of 2.6 cm., then curves back to a width of 9 mm. at a distance of *ca.* 7 mm. from the end. The end flares out like a fishtail to a width of 1.6 cm. Over-all length, 7 cm.

TC 1291

Miniature bronze ladle. The thick semi-spherical bowl, 1.3 cm. high and 1.8 cm. in diameter, is filled with an ashy substance. From the edge of the bowl, a handle, rounded in cross section (*ca.* 5 mm. thick), rises vertically for 3.3 cm. before it curves to the rear in a half circle and continues down straight for 5 mm., forming a hook with a gap of 3 mm. The over-all height of the ladle is 5 cm.

TC 1292

Unidentified bronze fragment, perhaps to be compared with TC 1290. A "handle," of which only 1.5 cm. in length is preserved, is 5 mm. thick and 1.3 cm. wide. The part of the fragment at the end of it is thinner. It widens out to a maximum width of 2.1 cm. in a rounded form, narrows again, then widens, with a loop at each side, to 2.3 cm. before narrowing to the end, on which is a pointed projection *ca.* 5 mm. long. Over-all length, 5 cm.

TC 1293

Small bronze object, perhaps a miniature ladle with the hook on the end of the 2-cm. handle bent to the side rather than toward the back. 3.9 cm. by 1.4 cm. by 1.3 cm.

TC 1348

Bronze rod, apparently solid, and *ca.* 6 mm. in diameter, with a very small flange not more than 1 mm. wide, running around each end. 8 mm. by 8.2 cm.

TC 1349

Miniature dish with a flat bottom and vertical sides, nearly 2 mm. thick. The piece, rather heavy for its size, is made of bronze, now badly corroded. Diameter, 2.5 cm.; height, 9 mm.

TC 1353

Two bronze tacks. The larger has a head 1 cm. in diameter, broken off on one side, and a shaft preserved to a length of 5 mm. The smaller has a head 7 mm. in diameter and a shaft only 3.5 mm. in length.

TC 1449 (Plate 93)

A bronze door socket. The circular cup, rounded in cross section, is about 1 cm. deep at the edges of the smaller depression in the center bottom. The main depression has a diameter of 4.5 cm., while the diameter of the smaller one, 5 mm. deep, is *ca.* 8 mm. Around the socket is a flange about 5 mm. thick measuring over-all 6.5 cm. by 7.5 cm. on the average (the edges are not quite parallel). The socket is within 4 mm. of the edge of this rectangular area on one side, 1.5 cm., 1.8 cm., and 1.2 cm. (moving clockwise) from the other edges. The socket has a maximum thickness of 1 cm. On the bottom (or top, if the socket were used at the top of a doorway) of the socket is a perpendicular doweling, 2.5 cm. long, 1 cm. thick, and flaring from a width of 1.5 cm. at the base to 2.7 cm. at the outer end, somewhat in the form of a swallowtail. 4.6 cm. (height) by 6.7 cm. by 7.6 cm.

TC 1636

Bronze tube, partly flattened and bent, possessing a longitudinal seam without overlap. The sheet of metal of which it is made is *ca.* 1 mm. thick or slightly more. The diameter seems to have been approximately 1 cm.; its maximum width in the present condition is 1.3 cm. Length, 6.2 cm.

TC 1746

Fragment of bronze. This appears to be the front and part of the bottom and side of a hoof from a bronze bull. It is made of metal about 1.5 mm. to 2 mm. thick. Preserved height, 3 cm.; length, 4.4 cm.

TC 1891

Bronze tube with a seam that overlapped *ca.* 2 mm. It is made of a sheet of metal *ca.* 1 mm. thick. Only one original end is preserved. The piece has been broken and repaired since being found. Diameter, *ca.* 1.1 cm. Preserved length, 5.4 cm.

TC 1918

Miniature bronze dish, made of very thin metal (*ca.* 1 mm.). The object is simply a concave piece of metal with a slight flaring at the rim; there is no suggestion of any kind of a base, for the bottom is rounded. Diameter, 2.7 cm.; height, 8 mm.

TC 1930

Miniature bronze dish or bowl, smaller than TC 1918, but made much heavier. This miniature appears to have been cast, and the body is *ca.* 2.5 mm. thick. It is roughly semicircular in cross section. Height, 1 cm.; diameter, 2.1 cm.

TC 1931

Tiny bronze object in the shape of a plumb bob with a neck *ca.* 2 mm. below the top and four incised lines running around it in the lower half. Maximum diameter, 9 mm.; length, 1.7 cm.

TC 1932

Small bronze object. The rectangular body, 1.5 cm. by *ca.* 1.2 cm., is 8 mm. high. There are two narrow depressions 6 mm. long running across the top about 3 mm. from the ends. On one end is a vertical loop handle, flush with the bottom of the body, but extending 2 mm. higher than the top of the body; the wire forming the loop is some 3.5 mm. in diameter. This object appears to be a miniature form, perhaps representing some object similar to TC 1626, which is of stone. Maximum height, 1.2 cm.; length, 2.3 cm.; width, 1.3 cm.

TC 1933

Five tiny fragments of very thin (less than 1 mm.) bronze. According to the field catalogue, the fragment found (and later broken into five pieces) had a diameter of 1.5 cm. and another dimension of 1 cm.

TC 2036

Small bronze object, apparently a miniature dipper with part of the handle broken off. The piece is made of metal averaging about 1.5 mm. in thickness. The circular bowl, which has a diameter of 1.8 cm. (outside measurement), is 1 cm. deep. The handle, semicircular in cross section, is merely a

smaller extension of one side of the bowl, and its top is flush with the rim of the bowl. The handle tapers in size away from the bowl. On the side of the bowl opposite the handle is a tiny vertical lug, which projects out *ca.* 3 mm.; it is just below the rim. Over-all length, 3.8 cm.

TC 2110

Miniature cup, cylindrical in form, made of thick bronze. The plain flat bottom is at an angle, so the object tilts to one side when placed on a flat surface. The walls are *ca.* 2.5 mm. thick. Height, 2.2 cm.; diameter, 1.7 cm.

TC 2111

Small rectangular bronze object with a vertical loop handle on one end, comparable to TC 1932. The body measures 1.6 cm. by 1.3 cm. and is 9 mm. high. In the top is a circular depression, about 1 mm. deep, with a diameter of about 7 mm. The outside diameter of the loop on the end is 9 mm., the same as the height of the body. The wire of the loop is *ca.* 3 mm. Over-all length, 2.2 cm.

TC 2112

Miniature bronze dish, identical in form to TC 1918, except that the present dish has no flaring rim. The metal of which the dish is made is *ca.* 2 mm. thick. Height, 8 mm.; diameter, 2.6 cm.

TC 2113

Miniature bronze dish or saucer, smaller and flatter than TC 1918 and TC 2112. Thickness of the metal, *ca.* 1.5 mm. Height, 5 mm.; diameter, 2.1 cm.

TC 2129 (Plate 93)

Miniature bronze bowl or kettle on an attached tripod. The bowl has a thickened rim, round in cross section, which is decorated with a row of raised dots, now mostly corroded away. On the top of the rim directly above each leg of the tripod is a blob of metal *ca.* 6 mm. wide. The diameter of the bowl inside the rim is 1.5 cm., while the maximum outside diameter is *ca.* 2.5 cm. The walls and bottom of the bowl are 3 mm., and in some places more, in thickness. The legs of the tripod, *ca.* 3.5 mm. thick, slant out from top to bottom. At the top they are joined to the underside of a ring on the bottom of the bowl, and this ring has an outside diameter of *ca.* 2.1 cm. At the bottom the legs are attached to the outside of another ring of approximately the same diameter; this lower ring, which has the function of bracing the legs, has a thickness of some 3 mm. The maximum spread of any two legs at the lower ends (outside measurement) is 3 cm., while at the top it is only 2 cm. The piece is badly corroded, and in many places the copper oxide is flaking off. Over-all height, 3.8 cm.

TC 2130 (Plate 91)

Rectangular object of bronze. The shape is a miniature box with vertical sides divided by a longitudinal partition into two narrow compartments, one of which is approximately twice as wide as the other (inside measurements, 7 mm. and *ca.* 3.5 mm. by a length of 3.2 cm.). On one end are two irregular projections which appear to be the stubs of a horizontal loop handle. All four walls of the wider compartment are 1.1 cm. high, but the walls of the narrower one, except for the common wall down the center, are some 2 mm. lower. Width, 1.7 cm.; over-all length, 4.2 cm.

TC 2131

Ear, apparently of solid bronze, from a representation of an animal. It is estimated that about 1 cm. of the length at the tip is broken off; it appears that at the base it was broken right at the head. The lower 1 cm. is completely oval (1.5 cm. by 1.2 cm.), then the rest has a wide groove in one side of *ca.* 4.5 mm. depth. The piece seems slender for the ear from a bull's head, but representations in other art forms suggest this interpretation. Preserved length, 5.1 cm. Maximum width (toward top), 1.8 cm.

TC 2132

Flat bronze piece, broken off square at one end and flaring in width at the other. At the flaring end, there were three points, one at each corner (one of these has been broken off) and one in the middle (*ca.* 3 mm. long). This piece can perhaps be compared with TC 1292. Thickness, from *ca.* 2 mm. to *ca.*

3 mm. Maximum width, 2.1 cm.; average width, 1.5 cm.; length, 4.3 cm.

TC 2166 (Plate 92)

Small bronze object, consisting of a rectangular body with a circular depression in the top and a vertical loop handle on one end (compare with TC 1932 and TC 2111). The body measures 1.4 cm. by 1.7 cm. and is 9 mm. high. The depression in the top, rounded in cross section, has a diameter of *ca.* 8 mm. and is *ca.* 2.5 mm. deep in the center. Much of the handle projects above the top of the body. In fact, the upper end is attached to the edge of the top, while the lower end reaches down at an angle nearly to the lower edge of the end. The handle is *ca.* 5 mm. thick. This object, except for the larger handle, is a miniature of the form found in stone in TC 1626. Over-all length, 2.4 cm.; maximum height, 1.5 cm.

TC 2172

Heavy bronze dish with a flat bottom rounded into vertical sides. The rough metal is *ca.* 3 mm. thick. On one side is a rough protrusion which may be the stub of a handle standing out horizontally. Diameter, 3.4 cm.; height, 1 cm.

TC 2208

Miniature bronze jar. The mouth and body, rather than being round, are oblong; the inside dimensions of the mouth are 1.3 cm. by 8 mm. The outside measurements of the body are 2.4 cm. by 1.9 cm. The bottom is flat, the sides slant out slightly toward the top up as far as the shoulder, 1.2 cm. from the bottom, and then the piece narrows to 2 cm. by 1.4 cm. There is no thickening at the rim. Height, 1.8 cm.

TC 2209 (Plate 93)

Miniature bronze ladle, similar to TC 1291, but with a longer handle and larger hook. The circular bowl, rounded in cross section, has a diameter of *ca.* 1.8 cm. and a height of 1.2 cm. The handle, *ca.* 4.5 mm. in diameter, rises vertically from the top of the rim of the bowl for about 4.2 cm., then curves back into a hook with a maximum gap of *ca.* 1.3 cm. Height, *ca.* 6.5 cm.

TC 2210 (Plate 93)

Small bronze object, perhaps a miniature mirror. At one end is a flat circular part with a thickness of slightly more than 1 mm. and a diameter of 2.5 cm. The "handle" is roughly round in cross section (*ca.* 5 mm.) and 3 cm. long. On the end opposite the flat circular member, the handle is bent on the end to form a projection extending out *ca.* 5 mm. Over-all length, 6.1 cm.

TC 2226 (Plate 92)

Miniature bronze mirror with a wooden handle attached by two rivets. The object was badly broken in transportation; the handle has been reassembled, and six fragments of the bronze oval, approximately 1 mm. thick, have been restored to form all of the mirror except the upper corner and center on one side. The handle, *ca.* 7 mm. thick, tapers in width from 1.3 cm. where it is attached to *ca.* 9 mm. near the middle. It then widens again to *ca.* 1.2 cm. at the lower end, where it is cut off on an angle of about 45°. The bronze mirror itself has a length of 4.8 cm.,

and its original width was *ca.* 4.3 cm. The oval of bronze is inserted some 7 mm. into a slot in the upper end of the handle and is held in place by two small rivets. Over-all length, 10 cm. Preserved width of mirror, 3.8 cm.

TC 2227 (Plate 92)

Cylindrical bronze object with a flange at each end. The diameter of the body of the piece tapers from *ca.* 1.6 cm. near one end to *ca.* 1.1 cm. at the other. At the thinner end the body flares out to form a rather oval flange 2 cm. by 2.3 cm., which is slightly concave on the end. The flange at the larger end of the piece is not quite round, measuring 2 cm. by 2.4 cm.; in the end of it is a hole *ca.* 7 mm. by *ca.* 9 mm. Length of the object, 4.7 cm.

TC 2526

Fragment of bronze from an unidentified object. This is of rather thin metal, *ca.* 2.5 mm. thick, with various features indicated. 8 cm. by 3.5 cm.

XVII

MARINE SHELLS

Although Timna' is more than 150 kilometers in a straight line—more along any passable routes—from the Gulf of 'Aden, which is the nearest body of seawater, a small number of marine shells were recorded as having been found in the necropolis of the city during the 1951 season of excavation. Four of these were pierced so that they could be strung, certainly as beads or necklaces. A fifth complete shell (TC 2128) had not been worked, but rather was carried inland in its natural state. Of the four fragments of shells, one (TC 1368) has been worked in a curious way. A piece of coral (TC 1347) has also been listed in this group. Several very small shells are included with the beads; see the following chapter.

A much larger number of seashells were recorded at Ḥureiḍa; see G. Caton Thompson, *The Tombs and Moon Temple of Hureidha (Hadhramaut)*, pp. 104f., Pl. XLI. Every type of seashell recorded from the second campaign in the Timna' Cemetery, exclusive of TC 1347 and 2128, is found in the Ḥureiḍa report. One may note that at both places they were in burials.

TC 528

Olive shell with apical perforation. The outside of the shell is polished smooth on the higher areas of the surface; whether this was done deliberately or by friction against the clothing or skin of the wearer cannot be determined. 3.2 cm. by 2 cm.

TC 635

Fragment of an ark shell, with part of the outer edge preserved. 4 cm. by 3.5 cm.

TC 693

Olive shell with apical perforation. This shell has not been polished at all, and the outside is a chalky white. There is a narrow spiral groove around the hole in the end. 3.2 cm. by 1.7 cm.

TC 796

Fragment of a large pecten shell, flaking apart rather badly. 6.5 cm. by 5 cm. by 8 mm.

TC 846

Highly polished olive shell with apical perforation and spiral groove around the hole. The side with the opening has been rubbed down to such a depth that the edge of the mantle is straight, and an oval hole, 1.6 cm. by 7 mm., has been worn through near the larger end of the shell. This effect would have been produced only if the shell had been rubbed on a flat surface, but the reason for such rubbing is difficult to find (among the shells found at Ḥureiḍa several varieties of specimens of the genus *Cypraea* had been rubbed down on the back, but none of the olive shells which were recorded). 3.5 cm. by 2 cm.

TC 896

Large fragment from a pecten shell with part of the edge preserved. 12 cm. by 6.8 cm. by *ca.* 8 mm.

This mollusk has been identified by Joseph Rosewater of the Smithsonian Institution as *Pecten baylei* Jousseaume, which "was described from 'subfossil' valves from the mountains of Aden, but is also thought to be living in the western Indian Ocean region today."

TC 1326

Olive shell with apical perforation. This shell was partly polished over most of its outer surface. 3.6 cm. by 2 cm.

This mollusk has been identified by Joseph Rosewater as *Oliva bulbosa* Röding, a gastropod found living in the Red Sea and East African regions.

TC 1347

Small piece of coral. 2.2 cm. by 2 cm.

TC 1368

The point and part of the side of a shell, perhaps of the genus *Trochus*. This shell appears to have been cut deliberately to the present shape, as it is fairly symmetrical. All the edges have since been worn smooth, as have the natural protrusions on both the outside and inside. 2.5 cm. by 2 cm.

TC 2128

Shell, complete or nearly complete. Diameter, 3 cm.; height, 2.2 cm.

This mollusk has been identified by Joseph Rosewater as *Lunella coronata* Gmelin, a gastropod found living in the Red Sea and East African regions.

BEADS

Compared with the collection of beads found by the excavators at Ḥureiḍa in 1938, which numbered "under 500 specimens,"[1] the number found during the 1951 campaign in the Timnaʻ Cemetery is insignificant, reaching only slightly more than fifty. Most of this group of beads from the necropolis at Timnaʻ appear to be paralleled by examples from Ḥureiḍa,[2] but the study of the beads from Timnaʻ cannot be completed without the aid of a specialist. This being the case, the beads of this group are planned for publication in a future volume on the Timnaʻ Cemetery.

Beads are small, light, and almost universally appealing, so no one should be surprised if it is found that the ancient beads from Beiḥân were carried or worn long distances, hundreds, if not thousands, of kilometers from their place of origin.

The beads in the collection are numbered TC 692, 1008, 1009, 1352 (23 beads), 1585, 1586, 1684 (six beads), 1693 (eight beads), 1935, 1936, 1937, 1938, 1939, 1940, 2224, and 2225 (seven beads).

[1] G. Caton Thompson, *The Tombs and Moon Temple of Hureidha (Hadhramaut)*, p. 94.
[2] *Ibid.*, pp. 94–101, Pl. XXXVIII–XL.

MISCELLANEOUS OBJECTS

TC 525

Badly battered stone which seems originally to have been a building block similar to TC 560. A slightly raised area 1.8 cm. by 10.8 cm. with a pecked design on the surface runs through the center of the face; in *The Tombs and Moon Temple of Hureidha (Hadhramaut)*, p. 56, G. Caton Thompson describes the raised band on a similar piece as a "vertical bar." She pictures three examples (Pl. xx, center) as though the band were vertical, but as none of the ten of the blocks thus decorated from Ḥureiḍa was found *in situ*, that description seems gratuitous, for the band could equally well have been horizontal. Two opposite edges of the block are preserved for part of their lengths, and these both slant in somewhat toward the rear. The other two sides are both broken off, and the back irregular. Sandstone. 12.7 cm. (between the preserved edges) by 11.8 cm. by 4 cm.

TC 560 (Plate 93)

Block of stone with a square face bearing a rectangular area (2.3 cm. by 9.4 cm.), slightly raised, across the middle of it. The pecked design on the surface of the rectangular area is in four rows running the long way. Except for this pecked area, the face of the block is plain, chiseled even and superficially smoothed. On the orientation of the pecked band, see TC 525, immediately above. Three sides of the block are chiseled even, and these sides all slant in slightly toward the rear. The fourth side, parallel to the length of the pecked band, is somewhat irregular and slants out slightly toward the rear. The side opposite the unfinished one has the broadest finished surface. This side would be the most likely choice for the bottom of the piece

if objects of this sort were not used as building blocks but for some purpose which did not require their attachment. In this case, the pecked band or bar would be horizontal. The back of the block is irregular. Sandstone. 11.5 cm. by 11.2 cm. by 6.2 cm.

TC 607

Terminus of a long bone. Length, 15 cm. Diameter of the shaft, 2.5 cm. Width of the joint, 5.5 cm.

This bone has been identified by Kent V. Flannery of the Smithsonian Institution as a metatarsal of *Bos taurus* (domestic).

TC 608

Tooth (lower second molar) of *Bos taurus* (domestic), identified by Kent V. Flannery. 5 cm. by 2.5 cm.

TC 632 (Plate 93)

Fragment from the corner of a plaque or tablet of stone. The thickness of the tablet tapers toward the edges, which are somewhat rounded. Both sides of the plaque are smooth, but only one has a decoration; this consists of three parallel grooves along the edges. The outer groove is *ca.* 4 mm. from the edge; at one edge the other two grooves are spaced about 4 mm. apart. At the other edge the outer space is 5 mm. wide and is filled with a pattern of Xs, and the inner space is 6 mm. wide and exhibits incised lines running from one groove to the other, forming triangular zones. Poor quality alabaster with flecks of mica. 7.9 cm. by 6.1 cm. by 2.5 cm.

TC 655 (Plate 93)

Small offering table, broken at the left rear corner, with the end of the spout missing. The top has a margin, raised *ca.* 5 mm. and averaging 1.7 cm. in width, running around the edge, leaving a rectangular depression with an extension leading through the center of the spout. This channel on the top of the spout is 3.5 cm. wide. In the bottom of the rectangular depression, 4 cm. from the rear of the offering table and 4.2 cm. from the preserved edge, is a mortise with its length running across the table. This mortise is 1.5 cm. wide and 1.3 cm. deep, and (if it was symmetrical) it was originally some 5 cm. long. The spout is 7.5 cm. wide at its base and tapers slightly in width in its maximum preserved length of 4 cm. Very porous stone. Width, as preserved, 13 cm. (originally probably *ca.* 14 cm.); length of the body, 11.5 cm.; total preserved length, 15.5 cm.; thickness, 5 cm.

TC 865
Fragment from an ostrich egg shell. Thickness, *ca.* 2 mm. 3.5 cm. by 3 cm.

TC 885 (Plate 93)
Oblong stone, with two adjoining circular depressions on both sides. The edges are rounded off. This piece was probably used for rubbing or pounding. Gabbro. 13 cm. by 7.5 cm. by 4.5 cm.

TC 916 (Plate 93)
Cone-shaped fossil of a marine shell, rounded at the top. What is actually preserved is the limestone-filled cavity of a snail; all parts of the snail shell have disappeared. Height, 6 cm. Maximum diameter, 5 cm.

TC 917 (Plate 93)
Object of greenish stone, perhaps the badly worn paw of a lion or other animal. Four large claws are visible on the wider end; across the top on the narrower end are two shallow grooves. The back is broken off diagonally. This object may have been re-used as a rubbing stone or a pestle. Maximum width, 7.5 cm.; length, 8.3 cm.; height, 4.8 cm.

TC 932 (Plate 93)
Rough core of obsidian. 11.5 cm. by 4.5 cm. by 6 cm.

TC 941 (Plate 93)
Fragment of plaster. The surface is smooth and covered with white paint; there are two parallel bands, about 3.5 mm. wide, of dark reddish-brown paint 1.5 cm. apart. Single layer of coarse plaster 1.7 cm. thick. 4.5 cm. by 3 cm.

TC 1002 (Plate 94)
Ring made of shell. There is a spiral groove on one side. The band is *ca.* 3 mm. thick and 3.5 mm. wide. Diameter, 2.2 cm.

TC 1010 (Plate 93)
Torso and head of a tiny faience figurine of a human. This is a representation of Horus sitting on the lap of Isis and being suckled; the hand supporting the head is present, with the arm broken off. The uraeus is visible on the forehead, and the "lock of youth" lies on the right shoulder. There is a prominent depression at the navel. The surface of the piece is pale green; the core is white. 1.5 cm. by 8 mm. For examples of the Horus child sitting on the knee of Isis, see *Catalogue général des antiquités égyptiennes du Musée du Caire: Nos. 38001–39384: Statues de divinités*, by Georges Daressy, Vol. I (Cairo, 1906), Pl. XLI, XLII.

TC 1011
Five irregular, more or less flat pieces of lead, brownish on the surface. Average thickness, *ca.* 5 mm. The largest piece measures 11 cm. by 6 cm.; others are 9 cm. by 4.5 cm., 6.8 cm. by 2.5 cm., 5 cm. by 4.2 cm., and 6.3 cm. by 2.4 cm.

TC 1034
Rather large cylindrical fragment of black basalt. There is a rounded ridge, broken off at one side, running around it near one end. Diameter around ridge, 7.5 cm., at opposite end, 5.5 cm. Maximum preserved length, 7 cm.

TC 1055
Small whetstone, broken off at one end. This piece, rectangular with rounded corners in cross section, tapers from 1.3 cm. by 1.1 cm. at the broken end to *ca.* 9 mm. by 6 mm. at the preserved end, which is somewhat rounded and cut off oblique. Length, 5.6 cm.

TC 1057 (Plate 93)
Fragment of a thin object of limestone. On one side is a recessed (*ca.* 1 mm.) panel

surrounded by a raised margin 4 mm. wide on one edge, 2 mm. and 3 mm. on the other preserved edges. On the other side is an incised geometric design; 2 mm. from one edge is a band composed of two parallel lines 4 mm. apart with short lines between alternately slanting one way and then the other. Perpendicular to this band are six other lines, one *ca.* 2 mm. from each of the adjacent edges, one *ca.* 1 cm. from each of the edges, and two 3 mm. apart in the center. A small hole is drilled through the piece 1.2 cm. from the edge next to the criss-cross band and 5 mm. from the adjacent edge. At the break on the edge opposite the hole is a ridge indicating that the piece had a projecting member there. As this edge is preserved for only 9 mm. and the opposite edge is preserved for 1.7 cm., there was no corresponding member on the opposite edge. Maximum thickness, *ca.* 3 mm. 4.1 cm. by 1.8 cm.

TC 1068 (Plate 94)

Stone phallus, broken on end toward the base. The prepuce, which extends partly up over the glans, ends in a ridge about 3 mm. wide. The piece is flat and without detail on the back. 7 cm. by 3.8 cm.

TC 1083 (Plate 93)

Conical fossil of a snail, similar to TC 916. The dark line which spirals from bottom to top has been crudely gouged out, leaving a rough groove in its place. Height, 6.5 cm.; maximum diameter, 5.5 cm.

TC 1086 (Plate 94)

Unusually shaped stone, with two roughly spherical parts separated by a neck or groove running around the piece. The smaller part has a maximum diameter of *ca.* 2.3 cm., and the larger a diameter of *ca.* 3.5 cm., while the neck between is *ca.* 2 cm. in diameter. Height, 4.2 cm.

TC 1104

A narrow, flat iron object with a hole near one end, broken off at the other end. From its width of slightly less than 1 cm. for most of the length, the piece narrows near the preserved end to *ca.* 5 mm., then less, and is bent around edgewise to form a loop, leaving a hole 5 mm. long and 1.5 mm. wide. Thickness, *ca.* 2 mm. Length, 6.3 cm.

TC 1278 (Plate 94)

Ornamental disc, flat on the bottom, convex on the top. The top is not entirely regular, so the vertical edge varies in width from 4 mm. to 6 mm. at various places. A hole *ca.* 2 mm. in diameter is drilled completely

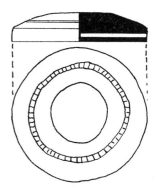

TC 1278. Scale 2:3.

through the disc from one edge to the opposite. The material of the disc appears to be a dark blue stone with a tan surface. In the center of the top is an inlay of almost white stone 1 mm. thick and 2.4 cm. in diameter. There is another inlay in a band about 2 mm. wide, averaging 5 mm. from the outer edge of the piece. Maximum diameter, 5.4 cm.; thickness at the center, 1.1 cm.

TC 1280

Decorated disc, broken into three pieces. From the drawing this object appears to be almost identical to TC 1278, above, but about

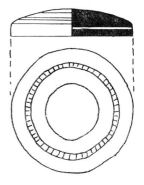

TC 1280. Scale 2:3.

5 mm. less in diameter. Both are described in the field catalogue as being made of blue glass. (Location unknown.)

TC 1351

Two obsidian flakes. One measuring 1.2 cm. by 1.4 cm., appears to be a waste flake. The other, 1.8 cm. by 6 mm., has sharp edges on the long sides and one end; the other end is broken off.

TC 1450

Broken tip of cylindrical object, rounded on the end. Alabaster. Diameter, 1.7 cm. (maximum); length, 1.5 cm.

TC 1548 (Plate 94)

Eye inlay, designed for human head of the type described in Chapter I. The back is flat; the front is nearly flat, but is slightly convex so that the piece is thinner at the pointed ends than at the center. In the approximate center is a cutting *ca.* 3 mm. deep and 1.2 cm. in diameter which appears to be intended for a secondary inlay to represent the iris. Limestone. 2.1 cm. by 3.7 cm. by 8 mm.

TC 1583 (Plate 94)

Small obsidian blade, apparently broken on both ends. Its maximum thickness of 3 mm. is attained at one end of the fragment, while the other end is only slightly more than 1 mm. thick. 1.8 cm. by 1.2 cm.

TC 1584

Flat piece of shell, crudely rounded into the shape of a disc. One side has the natural slight convexity of the original shell; the other side is polished and appears to have a depression worn into it. Thickness, *ca.* 4 mm. Diameter, 2.7 cm. (maximum).

TC 1683

Stone ball, about the size of a small marble. There are a few irregularities on it. Alabaster. Diameter, 1.5 cm.

TC 1685

Fragment of iron, very badly rusted. Length, 5.3 cm.; width, 1 cm.; thickness, 7 mm.

TC 1770 (Plate 94)

Whetstone. The top surface at one end was chipped off for a distance of about 3.5 cm. to a maximum depth of 5 mm., but the chip has been restored to its place. One side slants in a little toward the bottom, but the other

is square. The top and sides are very smooth; the back is even, but not polished, and is now chipped in several places. Greenish-gray stone with a streak of dark maroon. 12.9 cm. by 2.6 cm. by 1.3 cm.

TC 1870 (Plate 94)

Rectangular stone, fairly light and moderately porous. The edges and corners are all rounded somewhat, and all six sides are slightly convex and worn smooth. Perhaps this was a polishing stone. 2.1 cm. by 4.6 cm. by 3.8 cm.

TC 1916 (Plate 94)

Fragment from the corner of a well-made stone offering tray or similar object. The bottom of the object, 1.5 cm. thick, was flat; at the sides are walls with a height of 1.3 cm. above the inside bottom. These walls slant outward and then have a flange on the outside, so that the rim measures some 2.5 cm. in width; the inner edge is rounded, as is the lip on the outside edge. White alabaster with dark gray streak at one end. 3 cm. (total height) by 12.1 cm. by 5.7 cm.

TC 1934 (Plate 94)

Small flat decorated rectangle of hard wood. In the center is a hole (diameter 3.5 mm.), probably for attaching the piece to another surface. A band of circles (diameter *ca.* 4 mm.), with dots in the centers, forms a rectangle on one side of the piece; in all cases, these circles are *ca.* 2.5 mm. from the edge. They were apparently incised by some sort of drill, though they may merely have been pressed into the wood. The piece was broken into two fragments longitudinally with the break running through the hole in the center, but the two have been rejoined. 4.3 cm. by 3.5 cm.; thickness, *ca.* 3 mm.

TC 2001 (Plate 94)

Rectangular stone, similar to TC 1870 but larger. Some of the corners have been worn down to a considerable degree. This must have been some kind of a rubbing or polishing stone. 3.3 cm. by 7.8 cm. by 5 cm.

TC 2024 (Plate 94)

Stone object, nearly square, with a circular depression in the center of the top. The sides and bottom are even and fairly smooth. The depression in the top, which has a depth of *ca.* 1 cm., is flat on the bottom. The sides slant out toward the top, so that the diameter at the top is *ca.* 4.2 cm., while at the bottom it is 3.3 cm. Alabaster. 2.6 cm. by 6.8 cm. by 6.3 cm.

TC 2213 (Plate 94)

Piece of lime plaster, chipped at one end with one corner broken off. One side of the piece is smooth and was originally rectangular. The other side, thick in the middle and rounded up to the ends, is covered with crisscross incisions; it appears as though the plaster had been put into a depression to fill it up. 14 cm. by 5.7 cm.; maximum thickness, 2.4 cm.

TC 2219

Small rod of green glass. One end is crudely rounded off; the other has been broken off. The piece is oval in cross section, *ca.* 4 mm. by *ca.* 5 mm. Length, 3.9 cm.

TC 2222

Small cylindrical object, perhaps of ivory, with the ends cut off square. There are two holes drilled into the piece. One is a round hole *ca.* 2 mm. in diameter and 5 mm. deep in the center of one end; the other is oval in section, 2 mm. by 3 mm. and 6 mm. deep. This one is drilled straight into the side, *ca.* 8 mm. from one end, 1 cm. from the other; the two holes do not meet. Diameter, 9 mm.; length, 2.2 cm.

TC 2245 (Plate 94)

Fragment from a statuette of a kneeling animal, apparently a member of the cat family, perhaps a cheetah. The lower part of the body with complete hind legs stretched forward under it is all that is preserved. The forelegs appear to have been extended forward; a trace of the front of the body is visible above the broken left front leg. The surface of the animal is covered with incised marks. Limestone. 8 cm. by 4 cm. by 3.5 cm.

TC 2280 (Plate 94)

Small alabaster head of an animal. The ears are represented by low bumps; there is a slight offset where the eyes would be. Across the end of the snout are two parallel lines; between these are some five short incisions, perhaps to represent teeth. At the rear, there are slight ridges at the break indicating that the head either belonged to a statuette or that it was part of some plaque or other object. Maximum width, 2 cm.; length, 3 cm.

TC 2527 (Plate 94)

Flat piece, apparently of ivory, broken at both ends. Both edges are preserved; the piece tapers from a thickness of 3 mm. at one edge to *ca.* 1 mm. at the other, which is rounded. On one side, at a distance of 2.5 mm. from the thicker edge, is a shallow groove *ca.* 1 mm. wide; at 6 mm. from the edge is an offset where the thickness diminishes by *ca.* 0.5 mm.; thus in effect, there are two raised bands along the thicker edge of the piece. Width, 1.4 cm. Maximum length, 2.3 cm.

TC 2532 (Plate 94)

Four joining fragments forming a section of thick, coarse plaster, with a smooth white outer coat. One of the longer sides and both short sides of the section preserved are straight, having been formed against some architectural member or other object. On the surface there is a painted design, reddish-brown in color, in the form of the letter *t*, 10 cm. high. 18.5 cm. by 11.6 cm.; thickness, 2.6 cm. (The photograph shows only the largest fragment, 13 cm. by 10 cm.)

XX

WORKED STONES AND FRAGMENTS WITH ARCHITECTURAL SIGNIFICANCE

In this category have been placed stone objects and fragments exhibiting designs which appear to be the representations of architectural forms in diminutive. Most of this small group are stones which appear to have been used as blocks in construction of some kind, some of them forming corners. Others appear to be cut to represent small barred windows, and cuttings of this kind are of such an appearance that one is tempted to term them louvres, though this would hardly be correct. These diminutive representations of architectural forms are not out of keeping with the practice of placing miniature objects of various sorts in the cemetery area, for in addition to the miniature bronze pieces described above, there are numerous examples of tiny imitations of full-scale pottery forms.

By way of comparison, one may refer to panels carved in building blocks found by the excavators at Ḥujja,[1] the large recessed "window" panels in the entrance hall of the temple 'Awwâm at Mârib,[2] and the material brought together on this subject by Gus W. Van Beek and published in 1959 (including otherwise unpublished pieces from Wâdī Beiḥân).[3]

TC 545 (Plate 95)

Block finished on two adjacent sides with similar paneling, somewhat crudely done. One square end of the block is assumed to be the top (as the paneling suggests), and the sides are rectangles, higher than they are wide.

[1] See Carl Rathjens and Hermann von Wissmann, *Vorislamische Altertümer*, p. 52, Fig. 21–23.
[2] *Archaeological Discoveries in South Arabia*, p. 253, Fig. 165–66.
[3] "A New Interpretation of the So-Called South Arabian House Model," *American Journal of Archaeology*, Vol. 63 (1959), pp. 269–73, Pl. 69–70.

The bottom of the block is broken off, so the paneling is not fully preserved there. Inside an outer raised margin at the sides and top of each face is another margin (*ca.* 8 mm. wide); this surrounds a recessed area 3.3 cm. wide on the right side, 3 cm. on the left, and at least 7.5 cm. high. In this panel are placed four small recesses, *ca.* 1.7 cm. wide on the right side and 1.3 cm. on the left, in a vertical row. The first at the top is some 2 cm. high; the other three are about 6 mm. or 7 mm. high, i.e., narrow rectangles lying on their sides. Between the four small panels there are three dividing margins, and these are flush with the main panel. The two sides of the block without decoration are roughly tooled even. In the top is a mortise 2.4 cm. by 1.1 cm., cut 1.7 cm. deep at a distance of 2.4 cm. from each of the paneled faces. Alabaster, white with reddish streaks. 10.3 cm. by 7.2 cm. by 7.2 cm.

TC 642 (Plate 95)

Block of stone, rectangular at the finished face, bearing a panel of glyphs. This panel consists of a series of grooves, roughly V-shaped in section with narrow ridges between. The grooves run the short way across the face of the stone. The panel, placed near the center of the face (*ca.* 6 cm. from one end, 7.7 cm. from the other, and about 1.3 cm. from the sides), may have been intended to represent a window with slats or some kind of a grill (cf. remarks above at the beginning of this chapter). The "louvred" panel is 7.2 cm. high altogether and 6.4 cm. wide. Compare with TC 1190 and TC 1295. Crystalline rock. 20.9 cm. by 8.9 cm. (width) by 5 cm. (thickness).

138   *An Ancient South Arabian Necropolis*

TC 643A (Plate 95)

Corner fragment of TC 643, discarded in the field and designated as an "altar base." Three horizontal bands, *ca.* 9 mm. wide, each meeting neighboring bands in an offset of *ca.* 1 mm., belong to a part of the object over-hanging a lower, plain part. To the right of the corner, the overhang or offset is 1.2 cm., to the left 5 mm. Oölitic limestone. 5 cm. by 3.5 cm. by 3.4 cm.

TC 854 (Plate 94)

Fragment, from near upper right corner, of an architectural panel. Three dentils, 1.7 cm. long, 1.2 cm. wide, and 1 cm. deep at the lower end (*ca.* 8 mm. at the upper), are pre-served, with a reglet (6 mm. wide) and a fillet above. To the right of the row of dentils is a margin 1 cm. high, continuous with the reglet; below the dentils is a raised (3 mm.) margin 1.7 cm. wide at the side, 1.6 cm. at the top. Within this margin a bit of a flat panel is preserved; this appears to have been only 1 cm. wide, for the margin above runs down to the left. Badly burned alabaster. 8 cm. by 6 cm. by 5.5 cm. (thickness).

TC 1045 (Plate 95)

Large stone block, polished smooth on one of the broad sides, with paneling and a one-line inscription along the lower part of the front. The inscription, in large letters (5 cm. high), reads ʿmʿly/dyšrḥʾl/ddrʾn; cf. JaPEHA, p. 217, §379, Pl. ix, above. The piece is puzzling, for the highly polished surface, which, at first view, one would interpret as a table top or something similar, is on the bottom in relation to the inscription and the paneling. This situation strongly suggests that the block was re-used, though lack of information as to exactly how such a block was used does not exclude other possible explanations.

The front of the block, on which the in-scription is cut, is some 40 cm. wide and 9 cm. high, except at the left end, where a rectangular extension at the top (in line with the left edge) gives a height of 14.5 cm. A recessed panel extends up onto this rectangu-lar area, coming within 1 cm. of the top of it (which is chipped most of its width). The panel, which is 1.8 cm. from the left edge of

the face and the same distance from the right edge of the rectangular extension, has a height of slightly more than 7 cm. and a maximum depth of 7 mm. In this panel, the sides of which are beveled, is a margin running around the sides and top; this margin is some 1.3 cm. wide at the sides and 8 mm. at the top. Within this margin is a rectangular re-cess 5 cm. high and 2.2 cm. wide, recessed some 4 mm. Within this recess and across the upper end of it is a horizontal member, raised approximately half as much as the margin at the top and sides, nearly 1 cm. wide and possessing a surface which slants in slightly toward the top. This feature, along with the absence of a margin at the bottom, establishes the fact that the panel is right side up relative to the inscription. The lower 2.5 cm. of a similar panel is 1.7 cm. from the right edge of the face of the block; it apparently was cut through when the stone was re-used. Very little of the right side of the block is pre-served, as the whole upper right rear of the block has been broken away through a dark rusty colored banding. The part preserved is chiseled even for 1 cm. to 1.5 cm. along the front edge, roughly tooled even farther back. The left side of the block is roughly tooled even all over except for a margin *ca.* 1 cm. wide along the bottom.

The contour of the top, which displays long tool marks, follows the outline of the face. Behind the rectangular extension of the face is a large protrusion on the top, widening to about 10.5 cm. near the rear. A margin *ca.* 1.5 cm. wide is chiseled even across the top and down the side of the protrusion along the front; from the base of the protrusion toward the right the chiseled margin widens from *ca.* 2 cm. to *ca.* 4 cm. The chiseling in the area above the remains of the panel, which was cut in two, is finer than the chisel-ing elsewhere, suggesting again that the pro-trusion was cut off at a later time. Plaster fills a depression in this area also; the rear part of the top is somewhat irregular. The back of the block slants in toward the top; it is broken through a banding near the top, while near the bottom the solid stone is broken (not tooled) irregularly, so the rear edge of the polished bottom is not straight. Grayish alabaster. 15.5 cm. by 40.7 cm. by 27.5 cm.

TC 1190 (Plate 94)

Block of stone with a rectangular face more than half taken up by a series of five large glyphs. These glyphs or grooves, V-shaped in section with only thin fillets between, run across the longer dimension of the face. Each cutting is 4.5 cm. long, *ca.* 3.5 mm. deep, and *ca.* 1.4 cm. wide. The ends of the glyphs are about 1 cm. from the shorter edges of the block. At one side there is a polished flat surface 4.5 cm. wide, while at the other the pattern runs off the edge, which comes in the middle of what would have been a sixth groove if complete. The sides of the block are roughly trimmed near the face, but become increasingly more irregular, slanting in rather sharply, toward the rear. The back is irregular and exhibits several very large tool marks. White alabaster. 12.8 cm. by 17.2 cm., with a maximum thickness of 10 cm.

TC 1235 (Plate 95)

Rectangular block, squared on all sides and decorated with paneling on two adjacent sides, broken along the upper left edge, especially at the rear corner. The question of which end is the top was determined primarily by comparison of the paneled design with that of other examples, such as TC 1240 (the plain little "window" is always placed in the upper part of the panel). The broader decorated side, hereafter termed the "front," has an outer raised (3 mm. to 5 mm.) margin 1 cm. wide at the top, 1.2 cm. at the right, a maximum of 1.4 cm. at the left and 5 mm. at the bottom. Below the lower margin and along the bottom edge of the face is a slightly recessed band *ca.* 6 mm. wide with dentil-like members 1 cm. to 1.2 cm. wide separated by grooves. Inside the outer margin is another raised (3 mm.) margin about 1 cm. wide all the way around, but across the top, between the extension of the margins on the sides, it is recessed almost 1 mm. more than on the sides, producing an offset in line with the edges of the margin on the sides.

Within the second margin is a decorated panel 3.5 cm. wide and 7.5 cm. high; at the top of this panel is a small plain rectangular recess 1.7 cm. wide and 2.2 cm. high. Below this are two horizontal grooves, 1.7 cm. long, reminiscent in miniature of the grooved de-

sign on TC 1190 and other pieces. The lower 3.8 cm. of the panel is taken up with vertical recesses *ca.* 4 mm. wide and *ca.* 1 cm. apart, in each of which are five horizontal grooves which give the tiny areas between them the appearance of short horizontal slats. The paneling on the narrower side of the block, to the left of the front, is much simpler; there is an outer raised margin 1.1 cm. wide at the right (along the corner adjacent to the face), 1.5 cm. at the left, and 5 mm. at the bottom (the upper margin is broken off). Below the lower margin is a band of "dentils" as on the adjacent face. Inside this margin is another margin, 8 mm. wide at the right, 1 cm. at the left and bottom, and at least 1.2 cm. at the top, and this secondary margin is again recessed at the top *ca.* 1 mm. between the extended margins on the side. The plain, polished panel within the margins, recessed a total of 5 mm., measures 2 cm. wide and 7.5 cm. high.

In the top of the block is a roughly chiseled, somewhat circular depression 9 mm. deep; the sides of the depression are slanted outward at an angle of about 45°. The depression is a minimum of 8 mm. from the front of the block, *ca.* 3 mm. from the narrow undecorated side; there was no rear wall to this cutting. The narrow undecorated side is chiseled even along the face and bottom, otherwise it is rougher and exhibits tool marks. The back (broad undecorated surface) is chiseled fairly even, but is not at all polished. The bottom has been chiseled even at the edges, but the interior is rough. White alabaster, with a dark banding across the breadth at the upper edge. 12.8 cm. by 9 cm. by 7 cm.

TC 1240 (Plate 95)

Rectangular block of stone bearing similar paneled decorations on two adjacent sides, to be compared with the paneling on the front of TC 1235. The presence of small dentil-like features, which in the architecture of South Arabia are found at the top of windows or panels, with the free ends downward, determines the top of this piece. The paneling of the side to the left is slightly more than 1 cm. wider than that on the side to the right. The wider panel is surrounded by a raised (*ca.* 4 mm.) margin with a beveled inner edge. This is 1.3 cm. wide at the top, 1.6 cm. at the right side, 1.3 cm. at the left side, and 1.6 cm. at the bottom. Below this margin at the bottom is a band, *ca.* 7 mm. wide, of dentil-like members varying between 6 mm. and 8 mm. in width and separated by grooves some 2 mm. wide (this band is on a flange or ridge which protrudes some 6 mm. **lower than** the bottom of the block). Within the outer margin is a secondary raised margin, *ca.* 6 mm. wide at the top, 1.3 cm. on the left side, and 1.1 cm. on the right side (it does not appear at the bottom).

Within the beveled edges of the secondary margin is a panel measuring 11.5 cm. high and 2.6 cm. wide. At the top of it is a row of five dentils, each of which is 7 mm. long and *ca.* 4 mm. wide; these slant in toward the top. Centered 1 cm. below these is a small, plain, rectangular recess 2.3 cm. high and 1.3 cm. wide; 6 mm. below this is a row of five vertical grooves, each 8 mm. long and *ca.* 2 mm. wide. Another recess appears 2 mm. from the lower end of these, again centered vertically in the panel. This one 1 cm. wide and 6.5 cm. long, exhibiting five horizontal slats within its beveled edges; the upper slat is surrounded by a wide (*ca.* 7 mm.) groove. The four uppermost slats are each *ca.* 8 mm. wide, and the lower one is about half that width. The intervening grooves are all V-shaped and *ca.* 3 mm. wide, as is the groove below the lowest slat. The face to the right of the one described above is similar, but of narrower dimensions, and there are no projecting dentils at the bottom.

The upper margin is 1.5 cm. wide, the left is 1.5 cm. except near the bottom, where it is slightly less, and the lower margin is 1.5 cm. The right edge of the face is not even, so the width of the margin on that side varies from 1.7 cm. to 2.5 cm. The secondary raised margin is 1 cm. wide at the top and on the left side, but on the right it is slightly wider where it is bowed out near the middle. The panel inside the secondary margin is 11 cm. high and *ca.* 1.8 cm. wide; there are only three dentils at the top. The plain recess is only 8 mm. wide and 2 cm. high; there are four vertical grooves below this. The recess in which the slats are found is *ca.* 8 mm. wide; the slats are similar to those on the adjacent

face, but the grooves between are wider, and there is no extra space at the top.

The top of the block is chiseled even along the two finished faces, but exhibits tool marks elsewhere. The bottom is even, but rough with tool marks; it is chiseled even along the edge adjoining the right paneled face. Along the other paneled face is the projecting ridge bearing the dentil-like decorations. This ridge is some 5 mm. wide at the extremity, *ca.* 8 mm. at the base, as it is chiseled on a bevel on the inside. The side of the block adjacent to the face with the wider panel bears long horizontal tool marks except along the evenly chiseled front edge and the rougher rear edge; this side slants in slightly toward the back. The other unfinished side is somewhat irregular, though generally square with the adjacent finished face. Gray alabaster with rusty streaks. 16.5 cm. by 9 cm. by 8.9 cm.

TC 1295 (Plate 95)

Fragment which appears to be half of a decorated block of stone similar to TC 1190, broken off horizontally. Comparison with parallels indicates that the grooved design runs horizontally, but it remains uncertain whether this fragment is the upper or lower part of the block. The preserved face, except for a polished surface about 1 cm. wide at each edge, is entirely taken up by the series of parallel grooves or glyphs. There are three complete glyphs, V-shaped in section and placed immediately next to one another. Each is *ca.* 14 cm. long, 1.3 cm. wide, and 4 mm. deep; next to the preserved finished edge of the block, either top or bottom, there is a bevel, as though one half of another glyph were being indicated. The break at the opposite edge runs through the center of what was originally a fourth complete groove. The sides are chiseled fairly even for about 1 cm. along the front edge, but slant in toward the back irregularly otherwise. The finished long edge, either top or bottom, is generally even, chiseled along the front and to some extent elsewhere, though it is rougher toward the rear. The back of the fragment is irregular, protruding toward the finished edge; there is a rather deep horizontal row of tool marks at, or just below, the break. White alabaster. 6.4 cm. by 16.3 cm. by 6.1 cm.

TC 1423 (Plate 96)

Stone block which has the appearance of a diminutive pilaster capital. The decoration of the top and bottom halves of the front and sides is symmetrical, so it cannot actually be determined which is top and bottom. The decoration is in the form of various bands successively offset from a narrower center toward the ends of the block. At the center, where the block measures 7.5 cm. across the front, 6.4 cm. on the right side, and 6.1 cm. on the left, is a reglet 8 mm. wide. Above and below this reglet is a band of dentils some 3 mm. thick, each of which is *ca.* 1.2 cm. wide and 8 mm. to 9 mm. high (the width of the band is not entirely regular).

Next, proceeding toward the ends of the block, is another reglet or plain band, in this case meeting the dentils in an offset of *ca.* 3.5 mm., possessing a width averaging 1 cm. or slightly more, and slanting in toward the ends of the block; the next band, 2 cm. wide, vaguely resembles an archaic egg-and-tongue pattern without the tongue. The ovals are 1.5 cm. to 1.7 cm. wide, and an oval is spread around each corner. At each end of the block the ovals are surmounted by a raised reglet, 6 mm. wide at one end, 1 cm. at the other, where the block is slightly deeper. Both ends of the block are chiseled roughly even, and in the center of each is a mortise. On the end with the narrower reglet the mortise is 2 cm. square and 1.4 cm. deep, and the interior is chiseled even. On the other end the mortise measures 2.5 cm. by 2.8 cm. and is 1.9 cm. deep, and the interior is covered with tool marks. The back of the block is chiseled fairly even. Limestone. 10.6 cm. by 9.7 cm. by 8 cm.

TC 1424 (Plate 96)

Fragment, somewhat battered, from the upper corner of some stone object bearing decorations consisting of architectural forms in diminutive. The side to the right of the corner is preserved in a larger area and has part of a plain surface with a raised, undecorated horizontal band 1.6 cm. wide placed 3.8 cm. from the upper edge. Between this plain surface and the corner is a raised (8 mm.) panel 5.6 cm. wide. It possesses a raised horizontal reglet 6 mm. wide, the lower edge of which is in line with the lower edge of the

raised band on the plain surface to the right. Above this reglet is a series of six equally spaced vertical grooves 2.8 cm. long, which in effect form vertical slats between them. These slats are covered with red coloring. Below the reglet are four dentils, each 1.3 cm. long and a bit more than 1 cm. wide, also covered with reddening.

Below the dentils is a plain surface, *ca.* 4 mm. higher than the plain surface to the right with which it is not connected on this fragment. At the top, above the vertical grooves, are the traces of a notch cut some 7 mm. into the stone 4 cm. from the corner; there may have been another one between it and the corner, but the edge is not preserved here. To the left of the corner the decoration is identical, so far as preserved, with that on the raised panel to the right, except that there are only four vertical grooves. To the left of the fifth "slat" thus formed there are traces of a ridge at the break, indicating that there was a raised member there or that some surface projected out at right angles at that place. What remains on this fragment may be the representation of the capital of a column, a bit of a square pillar below, and adjoining members to the right. Limestone. 8.5 cm. by 12.5 cm. by 7.8 cm.

TC 1581 (Plate 95)

Stone fragment, burned on one side and the back after being broken, apparently from the capital of a column. On the lower half of the fragment the upper parts of two palmettes and traces of a third are seen. Some 7 mm. above the tops of the palmettes is a fillet *ca.*

TC 1581. Scale 1:3.

3 mm. wide surmounted by a round moulding 1 cm. wide, which stands out 5 mm. higher than the fillet. A feature 2 cm. wide above the round moulding is entirely missing; above this damaged area is a bit of polished surface. The original maximum diameter is estimated

to have been *ca.* 8 cm. Alabaster. 10 cm. by 4.7 cm. by 4.5 cm.

TC 2038 (Plate 96)

Fragment from the lower right corner of an inscription with paneling at the side and successively recessed bands below. The break at the left runs obliquely across the corner of the inscription, leaving only the letter *n* (incomplete at the top) and the lower tip of a second letter. The characters, estimated to have been 7 cm. high, are raised rather than incised. Below the two letters of which parts are preserved, and serving as a base for them, is a border 1.4 cm. wide which is raised 3.5 mm. above the panel containing the inscription and about 2 mm. above the surface of the raised letters. To the right of the preserved bit of the inscription is a rectangular paneled member 6.5 cm. wide and 9.7 cm. high, and the lower edge of this is in line with the lower edge of the raised margin below the inscription. The outer margin of this paneling stands out 1.3 cm. from the background of the inscription. This outer margin is 9 mm. wide at the left, 8 mm. at the top, 1.7 cm. at the right, and 1 cm. at the bottom.

Below this margin at the bottom is a band (7 mm. wide and recessed *ca.* 1 mm. behind the margin) which is divided by vertical grooves into dentils varying in width from 4 mm. to 6 mm. Inside the outer margin at the top is a similar band (*ca.* 5 mm. wide) divided into a dentil-like pattern. Below this band at the top and inside the outer margin on the sides, is a second margin, which is recessed *ca.* 2 mm. behind the outer one; this is 8 mm. wide at the left, 6 mm. at the top, and *ca.* 7 mm. at the right (it does not appear

at the bottom). Within this second margin is a third, approximately 6 mm. wide on the sides, 5 mm. wide at the top, and recessed some 1.5 mm. Within it is a narrow (*ca.* 9 mm.) recessed panel 5.3 cm. high, which has a slightly raised area at the bottom (8 mm. high) and at the top (1 cm. high).

Below the paneling and the margin below the inscription is a broad polished band 3.5 cm. wide which is flush at the right with the side of the paneling. This band is recessed 1.1 cm. behind the bottom of the paneling and 6 mm. behind the face of the band below the inscription. The face of the band slants out slightly toward the bottom, more in the left part than at the right end. Below this band and recessed 1.3 cm. behind it is another band, this one 3.6 cm. wide and ending 4.3 cm. from the end of the band above, leaving a large overhang. Below this band is a third, recessed 2 cm., which apparently ended on the right in line with the second, but this is not entirely certain, as the piece is broken in this area. The maximum preserved width of this band is 1.3 cm., and there remains no indication of its original width or of what was below it. The top of the piece is preserved in a small area above the paneling along the face. It was chiseled even, and this indicates that this block itself bore only one line of inscription. The right side is chiseled even along the front, but is rough and slants in toward the rear further back. None of the original bottom of the block is preserved. The back exhibits very long, thick tool marks running diagonally in the same direction as the break at the left. Alabaster, mottled in pale colors. 18.5 cm. by *ca.* 15 cm. by 11 cm.

XXI

STONE BLOCKS AND FRAGMENTS
BEARING INSCRIPTIONS

The rather large group of objects described below are not all of exactly the same type. Some are building blocks, whole or broken, which carry inscriptions of one kind or another. Others are fragments of monumental inscriptions, fragments of table tops bearing inscriptions, or pieces of unidentified inscribed objects of stone. As there remains at this point uncertainty as to how these objects and fragments should be subdivided into smaller groups, it was thought best simply to present them under one heading in numerical order. A few of the more complete inscriptions have already been published by A. Jamme in his *Pièces épigraphiques de Heid Bin ʿAqîl*, and in such cases reference is made to his publication.

TC 523

Fragment bearing the characters *n*/ and part of either *b* or *ġ* on the polished face. The letters are 4.5 cm. high, and there are guidelines at the top, center, and bottom of the line. The inscription is 1 cm. from the top of the piece, which is also polished. The back of the fragment is smooth and partly covered by a very thin layer of plaster which shows that the piece was placed against another flat surface. White alabaster. The slab was 4 cm. thick. The fragment measures 10.5 cm. by 7 cm.

TC 530

Fragment, apparently from the right edge of a large block. The inscription, as far as preserved, reads (1) ʿm'[(2) [*d*]*t*.[. Limestone. 9.5 cm. by 9.5 cm. by 8.3 cm.

TC 531

Block of stone, rectangular at the face, which is chiseled even and which bears an incised *s*. The sides are chiseled off square near the face, but the back of the block is quite irregular. 14.5 cm. by 11.7 cm. by 6 cm.

TC 543

Large inscribed fragment. At the top of the face is the lower part of three or four letters, badly damaged, the first of which is *t*; below this are the characters *y*/*b*, 6.5 cm. high. The lower 7 cm. of the face is blank. Conglomerate, somewhat friable. 20 cm. by 10 cm. by 9.5 cm.

TC 547 (Plate 96)

Porous block of stone, broken on right, with two lines of an inscription on the face. As preserved the inscription reads (1) [/]*md hm* (2) *dwb*/*y*; the lines of these letters are rather wide and deep. Just to the left of *d* in the second line is a faint and partly obliterated *y*, and under the *w* is a faint *g*. The letters of the first line are 4.5 cm. high, and those of the second slightly shorter. The lower 5.5 cm. of the face is blank. The entire face has traces of reddening. The top, bottom, and left side are chiseled roughly even at the front, but are irregular toward the rear, as is the back of the block; no part of the right side is preserved. Calcite. 15.3 cm. by 15.5 cm. by 7.3 cm.

TC 569 (Plate 96)

Rectangular block, broken at the right and along the top. Three lines of an inscription run the long way. The very top of the first line appears to have been on a stone or stones in the course above, and the stone is chipped so much that very little of it can be read. As preserved, the lines read (1) ...]n/r[ʿ... (2) ..]by/bḥtn/byd (3) d]b/šhr/ġyln/. The first half of line three is cut especially deep to obliterate earlier letters, none of which can be read with certainty except for an *l* under the *r*. The top of the block is rough with tool marks, but the sides and bottom were partly chiseled even, especially along the front. The back is somewhat irregular. Porous calcite. 13.3 cm. by 26.5 cm. by 7.6 cm.

TC 583 (Plate 96)

Inscribed block, broken at the left side and upper corner. The three lines of inscription, as preserved, read (1) t/.[... (2) yd"./[(3) .]yln[. The third character of line one is either ʾ or *s*. At the right edge on line three there seems to be the flag of *l*, the upright of which was on the neighboring stone. After the *n* of line three there is space for another letter, but no clear trace of one can be seen. The bottom of the block, the right side, and the small part of the top which is preserved are chiseled even and are square with the face. The back of the block is irregular. Porous calcite. 15.3 cm. by 12.7 cm. by 5.8 cm.

TC 589

Lower part of a block of stone, most likely a base of some kind. The lower line of an inscription of at least two lines (traces of the guidelines and tips of one character are visible above) is preserved on the face. The widely spaced letters, *ca.* 3 cm. high, read *ġrbm*; there are faint traces of reddening on the surface of the face. The bottom and sides of the piece, now badly battered, were chiseled square with the face. Porous calcite. 6.5 cm. by 11 cm. by 6.3 cm.

TC 598 (Plate 96)

Two joining fragments, including TC 2509, from a large stone slab inscribed on the face. TC 863 appears to belong to the same stone, but does not join. The lower tips of characters in one line are visible at the very top of the face, and parts of two lines of inscription are preserved below; as preserved, the inscription reads (1) .. (2)]y/ʾ[(3)]kb/b[. Line two runs right to left, but line three runs left to right (only the edge of *k* is preserved,

but is sufficient to indicate the direction). The characters are 7.6 cm. high. Lithographic limestone. 23 cm. by 15 cm. by 8.4 cm.

TC 630 (Plate 96)

Building block, with a rectangular face. Except for a margin around the edges, the face is covered with a tooled or pecked pattern; stone work of this type from South Arabia is discussed in some detail by Gus W. Van Beek, "Marginally Drafted, Pecked Masonry," in *Archaeological Discoveries in South Arabia*, pp. 287–95. On this block, the plain margin on three of the edges of the face is 1 cm. or less in width; on the fourth, a long side, the border is 3 cm. wide. The ends of the block are chiseled square with the face; on one end are five characters or symbols, consisting of *ḥ*, three vertical strokes, and *f*, all *ca.* 2.5 cm. high. The long sides of the block (probably the top and bottom) are also chiseled, but they slant in slightly toward the rear. The back is irregular. Limestone. 15.1 cm. by 17.5 cm. by 10.5 cm.

TC 639 (Plate 95)

Fragment of a large inscription, with a bit of the chiseled side of the block preserved at the left. Letters from only one line are preserved, and these read]ʿmġb.[; they are 6 cm. high. Conglomerate. 10 cm. by 14 cm. by 9 cm.

TC 647 (Plate 95)

Stone block, broken at the left side and along the bottom, bearing three lines from an inscription. As far as preserved, the inscription reads (1) yqnʿm/[bn... (2) rmm/sqn[y... (3) bmrʾhw/[...; cf. *JaPEHA*, pp. 172f., §332, Pl. ɪ, above. The top of the block is chiseled square with the face. The right side slants in toward the rear. The upper part of the back is a little more than 1 cm. thicker than the lower part, owing to a beveled offset; the back is rough with tool marks, but has been chiseled in places. Porous calcite. 17.6 cm. by 21 cm. by 6.2 cm.

TC 663 (Plate 97)

Stone block of the kind known as marginally drafted, pecked masonry (see TC 630, above). The margins are all narrow (*ca.* 7 mm.) except for one *ca.* 2.8 cm. wide along one of the long sides. The ends of the block, as were the top and bottom, were chiseled square with the face. On one end are three symbols, consisting of two lines perpendicular to the face and another symbol which looks like a sinistral, inverted *l* with a second flag at the center of the upright on the left side. The back of the block is irregular. Limestone. 13 cm. by 18 cm. by 8.5 cm.

TC 664 (Plate 96)

Fragment from the top of a large stone bearing an inscription. The parts of two lines which are preserved read (1)]*swḍ‘*[(2)]*fm*/*by*[; the characters are 5.5 cm. high. The top of the piece is chiseled square with the face. Porous calcite, friable. 15 cm. by 11.6 cm. by 8.3 cm.

TC 665

Fragment of a large inscribed stone with part of the upper edge preserved. The parts of the two lines of the inscription preserved read (1)].*/ḏšb‘*[(2)]*‘ly*[. The letters of the first line are 5.5 cm. high, while those of the second line are not complete at the bottom (the last character, in fact, could be *ṭ* rather than *y*). The top of the piece is square with the face, which has traces of reddening in the porous surface. Calcite, somewhat friable. 14.3 cm. by 18 cm. by 7.6 cm.

TC 676

Fragment from the lower edge of an inscribed stone. Part of one line of inscription, reading]*mn*/*ḍ.*[, is preserved; the letters are 3.2 cm. high, and the line is 1 cm. from the bottom of the stone. The bottom of the piece is square with the face. Blackened alabaster. 5.6 cm. by 8 cm. by 6.7 cm.

TC 678 (Plate 97)

Fragment from the upper right corner of a stone bearing an inscription. A large area of the right side, square with the face, but only a bit of the top, is preserved. Only the first two letters of two lines of inscription are preserved, and these read (1) ‘*š*[(2) ‘*s*[. The letters are 4.5 cm. high, and there were guidelines above and below; the surface of the face was covered with reddening before the guidelines and the inscription were cut. Limestone. 12 cm. by 4.3 cm. by 9.8 cm.

TC 681 (Plate 97)

Rectangular block of stone with a smoothed face on which a crude graffito has been scratched. The indistinct graffito appears to read *syṭm;* the first letter is about 2.5 cm. high, the others about 1.5 cm. The graffito is placed nearer to the top than the bottom and to the left of center. The sides and top of the block are chiseled even along the front, slanting in toward the rear, but are otherwise rough. The bottom, also slanting in toward the rear, is rough with tool marks. The back is irregular. White alabaster of poor quality. 15.6 cm. by 14.3 cm. by 5.8 cm.

TC 683 (Plate 96)

Tall, narrow block bearing part of an inscription in large characters. Across the top of the face are the lower parts (a little more than half) of the letters belonging to a line of inscription, and 2 cm. below this is part of another line. These read (1) *b*]*rṣ*[*f* (2)]/*bn*[*h*. The letters of the second line are 6.7 cm. high; below line two is a blank space of 6.5 cm. The top, sides, and bottom of the block are chiseled square with the face. The back is roughly chiseled flat except for a protrusion across the top. Porous calcite. 19.2 cm. by 9.8 cm. by 12 cm.

TC 684 (Plate 95)

Inscribed block, broken at the right side. The four letters evenly spaced across the face of the block are *rb‘n*. Only the extremities of the *r* are preserved, but it appears certain. The letters are 7.3 cm. high; 2.5 cm. above the inscription and 7 mm. below the upper edge of the face is a faint horizontal line of unknown purpose. The top of the block, now rough, slants down toward the rear. The sides, chiseled along the front edge, slant in toward the rear. The bottom is chiseled square with the face. The back is irregular. Porous calcite. 12.3 cm. by 20.8 cm. by 9.4 cm.

TC 699 (Plate 97)

Fragment of an inscribed stone plaque, broken on all sides. Parts of three lines of inscription, with guidelines at top and bottom, are preserved, and these read (1) *m‘*]*mr*/ *wd‘t*/*ḍt*/*byt*[/. (2)]*w‘bd’l*/*whllm*/*wġḍr*[(3)]*wbn*/*ḥḍrm*/*brsfm*/[; see *JaPEHA*, pp. 200f., §353, Pl. III, above, but the last preserved letter of line one, as shown by examination of the stone however, must be ', *s*, or *ṣ*. A bit of the original top of the stone appears to be preserved in a small area some 2.5 cm. above the first line of the inscription. It may be noted also that near the end of line one is preserved 1.5 cm. of blank space, although the lines are otherwise less than 1 cm. apart. The back of the stone is very roughly chiseled even, except for a strip some 5 cm. wide at the right edge, which would have been near the edge of the inscription in all probability. This strip is recessed *ca.* 6 mm. and bears rough tooling, especially along the offset, as well as some chisel marks. Alabaster. 15.5 cm. by 20.6 cm. by 5.2 cm.

TC 700

Small fragment of an inscription. Part of one line, reading]'*m*/*w*[*b*. ., is preserved. The character following the almost certain *b* may be *y* and the next one is either ' or *s*. Under the *w* are traces of a lightly incised ' which was partly obliterated. Above and below this line are tips of letters in other lines, but none of them is certain, though there seems to be an *r*, preceded, possibly, by a *t*. The preserved letters are 3.2 cm. high. Alabaster. 7 cm. by 7.7 cm. by 4 cm.

TC 701 (Plate 97)

Badly damaged block of stone with an inscription on the face. Two very broad but shallow horizontal grooves divide the face into three bands of approximately equal width. One line of inscription is visible on each of the upper two bands, and these read (1) *tw*[*b* .] (2) *hr*[.]; see *JaPEHA*, p. 141, §284. Note that *n* was apparently still preserved at the end of line two when the piece was discovered. Only the lower tip of the letter which is probably *m*, at the end of line one, is preserved. The letters are very widely spaced, especially in line two. The sides, top, and bottom appear to have been chiseled along the front. The back is irregular. Calcite. 12 cm. by 14.3 cm. by 5.6 cm.

TC 702 (Plate 97)

Fragment from the lower left corner of an inscribed stone. Parts of two lines of inscription are preserved, and these read (1)]./*ywm*[(2) .]*wds*/'[. The surface is badly worn on

the second line, and the *s*/ is not completely clear; there is space before the *w* of line two for a character, but none is visible. The pits in the surface of the face have traces of reddening. The side and the bottom of the block are chiseled square with the face. The back is irregular and displays two very large tool marks. Porous calcite, very friable. 13 cm. by 14 cm. by 7.5 cm.

TC 703 (Plate 97)

Large fragment from the top of an inscribed slab of stone. The face of the fragment is damaged extensively on the left and also at the upper right corner, so that much of the inscription cannot be read. The parts of the three lines of inscription, as preserved, read (1)]. . .*rn*/. .*rm*[(2)]/*kl*/.'*db*/*rṣ*[(3) ']*nb*[*y*/; the third line is only preserved at the right. The characters are 5.5 cm. high. The top of the fragment is square with the face. The entire back of the fragment seems to have been split off. Porous calcite, friable. 19 cm. by 23 cm. by 5.5 cm.

TC 704 (Plate 97)

Large fragment from the upper right corner of a slab bearing part of an inscription, broken obliquely from the upper left down to the lower right. Parts of two lines of inscription are preserved, and these read (1)]/*dhgrnhn*[/ (2) '*n*]*by*/*kl*/[. Only the upper tips of the first two characters (restored as '*n*) of line two, which runs left to right, are preserved. The *k* has two upper diagonals crossing each other, and it may be assumed that the normal form was made first, then corrected to the left-to-right form. The full-length letters are all 9 cm. high and the wide letters are 3.5 cm. in width; the lines are separated by *ca.* 7 mm. The first line comes within 8 mm. of the upper margin, which is raised *ca.* 5 mm. and which varies between 1.2 cm. and 3.5 cm. in width. The top and right side of the piece are nearly square with the face. The back is flat, and it exhibits large tool marks. Limestone of good quality. 29.5 cm. by 36.3 cm. by 8.4 cm.

The assertion, made in *JaPEHA*, pp. 175ff., §335, that this fragment belongs to the same inscription as TC 791 and 1046 (see below) is most difficult. If the curve of the upper margin in this piece is matched with that of

TC 791, the first line of the inscription does not match. In any case, the margin on TC 791 is not as high, and the edge of the margin is almost vertical, while the margin of TC 704 is beveled at an angle of about 45° on the edge. The letters of TC 704 are about 5 mm. higher and 7 mm. wider than those on TC 791, and the cuts making up the letters are also wider on TC 704. Furthermore, on TC 791, there is no indication of a second line coming as close below the first as on TC 704. The third fragment, TC 1046, has much smaller letters than either of the other two, and there is nothing but the similarity of the raised upper margin to suggest that it belongs to the same inscription.

TC 705 (Plate 97)

Inscribed stone block, broken at right side and at both upper and lower left corners. The part of one line of inscription which is preserved reads]*rqm/wm*[. The letters vary between 8 cm. and 8.5 cm. in height; only the extremities of the *r* are preserved. The inscription is some 4 cm. from the lower edge of the face. The bottom of the block is square with the face. The left side and the top are not entirely regular, and they slant in toward the rear. The back is irregular. Limestone. 13.6 cm. by 19.8 cm. by 6 cm.

TC 707

Fragment from the top of an inscribed stone. The preserved part of the inscription reads]*'n*/[. The lower tips of the characters are missing, but it seems that they were originally *ca.* 3 cm. high. The top of the piece is smoothed, and it slants up slightly toward the rear. White calcite. 3.8 cm. by 5.5 cm. by 2.8 cm.

TC 710 (Plate 97)

Fragment from the top of an inscribed stone. Parts of two lines of inscription are preserved, and these read (1) ']*ymn*/'*myṯ*/*sq*[(2)]./*w'nby*[/. ; the characters of the first line are 3.1 cm. high. None of the second line is fully preserved at the bottom. The top of the piece is preserved for a maximum distance of 6.7 cm. from the face; it is polished smooth. No other original surfaces of the block are preserved. Light gray alabaster. 6.6 cm. by 13.2 cm. by 8.9 cm.

TC 721 (Plate 97)

Fragment from the top of an inscribed stone. Part of one line of inscription, coming within 5 mm. of the top of the face, is preserved. This reads]*'ln'd*[; the letters are some 4.7 cm. high. The smoothed top of the piece, square with the face, is preserved to a maximum distance of 4.2 cm. behind the face. Hard stone. 5.7 cm. by 10.8 cm. by 4.7 cm.

TC 723 (Plate 98)

Inscribed stone block. Parts of two lines of inscription, reading (1)]*kw*[(2)].*l*[, are preserved. The letters of the second line are 7 cm. high; *k* in line one is not complete at the top. The top, bottom, and right edge of the stone are chiseled square with the face, but the left side is rougher and bears several tool marks, as though a secondary cut had been made on this side, which is not exactly vertical (the top of the piece is nearly 1 cm. narrower than the bottom). The back is somewhat irregular. Porous calcite. 15.4 cm. by 8.2 cm. by 4.3 cm.

TC 755 (Plate 97)

Inscribed block, broken obliquely at the right. Parts of three lines of an inscription run across the face, and these read (1)]*'m*/ *bny*/*dr*..[(2)]*qn*/*bḏtm*/*tkr*.[(3)]*ns*/*wkl* /*w*[; see *JaPEHA*, pp. 174f., §334. The letters of the third line are more widely spaced than those in the other two lines. Below the lowest line of inscription is a space of about 2 cm. which has faint traces of more characters. The left side of the block is rough, but square with the face. The top and bottom are also rough, and they slant in at an angle of *ca.* 45° toward the rear. The back is irregular. The stone is somewhat friable; it is tan and white with particles of dark green. 14.5 cm. by 19 cm. by 7.7 cm.

TC 756

Inscribed fragment. The letters *ḥdr*, followed by what must be the lower end of the word divider, are preserved in a single line; there is space before the *ḥ* for another character, but there is no trace of one. The fragment is from some kind of a plaque 3.8 cm. thick, but none of the edges is preserved. The back bears large vertical tool marks. Light tan alabaster. 6.5 cm. by 9.5 cm. by 3.8 cm.

TC 764 (Plate 98)

Block of marginally drafted, pecked masonry (see TC 630 and 663, above). On this block, the margin varies in width, being 8 mm. wide on one short side, 5 mm. on the other short side, *ca.* 1 cm. on one long side, and 2.2 cm. on the opposite long side, which is assumed to be either the top or the bottom. The ends of the block are chiseled fairly even, with chisel marks running in several directions, and the ends are square with the face. On the end which is thickest are incised marks, perpendicular to the face, which consist of three parallel straight lines and a symbol in the form of a Y with the head toward the back of the block. The top and bottom of the block, which slant in slightly toward the rear, are also chiseled even. The back is irregular. Limestone. 13.2 cm. by 18.6 cm. by 9.8 cm.

TC 791 (Plate 97)

Fragment from the upper right corner of a large inscription. The beginning of the first line, reading ʼmgsm[, is all that is preserved of the inscription; cf. *JaPEHA*, pp. 175ff., §335, but also see remarks at the end of the description of TC 704, above. The top of the piece curves up toward the right corner, and it may be assumed that the complete monument had a bowed top comparable to those of some of the plaques on memorial stelae described above. Along the upper edge of the face is a raised (*ca.* 4 mm.) margin varying in width from 3.2 cm. at the corner to 2.6 cm. at the break on the left. The right side of the piece is vertical, and along this edge on the face is a continuation of the raised margin, which is *ca.* 3.3 cm. wide here. The top and side are chiseled even except at the rear, where they slant in and become rough. The back is irregular. Sandstone. 15.5 cm. by 24.5 cm. by 9 cm.

TC 793

Fragment from a flat stone object with a worn inscription on the edge. As preserved, the inscription reads].yṯʻt[; the letters almost entirely fill the edge of the fragment. On top of the fragment, along the front edge, are several large tool marks. The small section of the bottom, as preserved, is more even. 3.7 cm. by 8.4 cm. by **7 cm.**

TC 807 (Plate 97)

Rectangular building block, inscribed on the face. Half of *b* and a complete *m* and *r* are preserved; these letters have heavy deep lines, and they are 11 cm. high, touching the upper edge of the face and leaving a blank space of about 3.5 cm. at the bottom. The top, bottom, and sides of the block are chiseled even. The back is irregular. Porous calcite. 15.2 cm. by 17.1 cm. by 6.2 cm.

TC 808 (Plate 97)

Two fragments (including TC 810) from the upper right corner of an inscribed block. The characters preserved along the upper part of the face read]n/ʼlṣdq[/w. These are 8.3 cm. high, and there are guidelines at the top, middle, and bottom; 7 mm. below is the upper guideline of another line of inscription, along with the tips of several characters of which only ʼ can be identified (below *q* in the upper line). The fragment to the right (TC 808) has the top and right side preserved, and these are chiseled roughly even near the front; the fragment to the left is broken off along the top, and it has no original edges preserved. Limestone. *Ca.* 12 cm. by 26.5 cm. by 10.4 cm.

TC 809 (Plate 97)

Inscribed fragment from the curved edge of a tabletop. The part of the one line of inscription which runs along the front edge which is preserved reads smhrm/bn[. There is space on the fragment for another character at the beginning, but it is left blank; the characters vary in height from 4.8 cm. to 5.2 cm. The top of the piece is flat and polished; along the edge is a border some 2.5 cm. wide, which is raised about 3 mm. The small section of the bottom which is preserved indicates that it was chiseled even. Alabaster of poor quality. 6.5 cm. by 18.3 cm. by 10.5 cm.

TC 820

Inscribed fragment from unidentified object. Along the top of the face, below a slightly raised margin *ca.* 6 mm. wide, is a line of inscription in raised letters 2.6 cm. high, reading].f/yṣ[. Immediately below these raised characters is a beveled offset transitional to a face standing out some 5 mm. from the background of the upper line of inscription. Here again is a raised margin *ca.* 6 mm. wide, and below are the tips of more raised characters or of figures in a relief. The small section of the top which is preserved is polished. The rear of the fragment appears to be the tooled front wall of a mortise of some kind, for at the right is a ridge at the break suggesting the end of a mortise. White alabaster with red streaks. 4.8 cm. by 8.2 cm. by 2.8 cm.

TC 829 (Plate 98)

Inscribed block of marginally drafted, pecked masonry. The margin at the right is 2.3 cm. wide, at the bottom 8 mm. At the left there are only slight traces of a very narrow margin, and at the top there is none. The block appears to have been re-used at the time the inscription was added, for the wide margin, at the right in reference to the inscription, would presumably have been either at the top or bottom originally (cf. TC 630, above). The letter ' appears on the face, some 8.7 cm. high, at a distance of 5 cm. from the left side. At the very edge of the face is the full-length upright of another letter; the inscription is a little below the horizontal center of the face. All four sides of the block have been chiseled roughly even. The back is irregular. 17.7 cm. by 20.8 cm. by 9 cm.

TC 835

Chip from the surface of an inscription bearing the characters]*.n/sfl.*[; the letters are 1 cm. high. No original edges are preserved. 5.3 cm. by 8.6 cm. by 1.9 cm.

TC 847

Fragment of a flat piece with a line of inscription on the front edge. The characters preserved in whole or in part read]*rm/nw*[. The letters are *ca.* 4.5 cm. high, filling the space almost entirely. The top of the fragment is chiseled fairly even. The bottom is also generally even; at the break on the left are the remains of a circular hole 1.5 cm. or more deep with a diameter at the surface of about 2 cm. Even with the hole in the bottom the face of the fragment begins to curve out at the lower left. Porous calcite. 4.8 cm. by 13.3 cm. by 5 cm.

TC 848 (Plate 97)

Inscribed block, broken at the bottom. The surface is badly pitted, so the two lines of inscription deeply incised on the face have a crude appearance. The first line reads]*h'll/ bn*[/; the lower part of the second line is broken away, but it seems safe to read it]*ny/'nby*[. Porous calcite. 8.8 cm. by 16.7 cm. by 7 cm.

TC 861 (Plate 98)

Inscribed block, broken at the right. The first three characters of the crude inscription are *m/d̲* ,but the fourth cannot be read. The inscription is near the top of the face in one line; the letters are about 3 cm. high. This block is of the kind described above (e.g., TC 630) as marginally drafted, pecked masonry, but is smaller than the four examples described above. The top, the left side, and the bottom of the block have been chiseled fairly even, and they slant in slightly toward the rear. The back is irregular. Limestone. 8.3 cm. by 11 cm. by 5.8 cm.

TC 863

Fragment from a large, inscribed stone, almost certainly the same stone to which TC 598 belongs, though the two do not join. The lower tips of two adjacent letters at the top of the face are distinguishable as]*mm*[; the line below has]*b/wy*[, the last letter only in traces at the break. At the edge of the break below the *b* is part of the upper circle of *y* or *t̲*; the *b* and the word divider are 7.5 cm. high, and the *b* is 3.7 cm. wide. No original edges of the block are preserved on this thick fragment. 17 cm. by 18 cm. by 8.3 cm.

TC 874 (Plate 98)

Two fragments (including TC 1022) from the lower edge of a stone object, inscribed on the face. Legible parts of two lines of inscription, the lower two on the face, are preserved, and on the left fragment are unidentifiable traces of another line above them. These read (1)]..[(2)]..*my/d̲hbn.*[..]..*smy/ywm/.*[(3)]*yd/'nby/nfss/w'd̲ns/wqn*[. The characters of line two are *ca.* 2.8 cm. high, but those of the third line are only 2.5 cm. high. The lines are separated by a space of *ca.* 7 mm.; the bottom of the last line is 1 cm. from the bottom edge of the block. The face of the stone is polished smooth, but the characters are cut somewhat crudely.

The bottom of the stone is square with the face; the surface of it is rough, exhibiting some tool marks, except at the front edge where it has been chiseled quite even. The back of the right fragment is rough with tool and chisel marks, but the back of the left fragment is polished smooth, though now chipped in places. A gap exists at the back between the two fragments, so the juncture of the two areas is not preserved. In the top of each fragment is the lower part of a mortise; these are some 9 cm. apart and 3 cm. behind the face. The one on the left is best preserved and has an oval section; only a trace of the one on the right remains. These mortises suggest that these fragments may be part of the base for a statuette. Alabaster, pale rusty in color. 10.2 cm. by 19.5 cm. by 8.9 cm.

TC 875 (Plate 98)
Two joining fragments (including TC 930) from an inscribed stone object. Parts of three lines are preserved on the polished face, which curves slightly in horizontal cross section as though the fragments belong to a cylindrical object. These lines read (1)]./ₐr.....q[(2)]ts/rṯdt/'[(3)]/w'mr'[; the characters of line two, 2.2 cm. high, are the only ones preserved to full height. Pale alabaster. 7 cm. by 8.5 cm. by 5.8 cm.

TC 876
Upper left corner of an inscribed block. Parts of two lines of inscription are preserved, and these read (1)]m'mr[(2)].bḥm[. Approximately the upper third of the letters of the first line were written on the stone above; two of the letters of the second line appear to be preserved to their full height (4 cm.). The top and left side of the piece, which have tool marks perpendicular to the face, slant in slightly toward the rear. The back is irregular. Limestone. 8.5 cm. by 6.9 cm. by 5.7 cm.

TC 877
Fragment from an inscribed stone, apparently with no original surfaces preserved other than the face. Part of one line of inscription runs diagonally across the face, nearly filling it; this reads /]'nb[y. The center part of the word divider is preserved, and the upper circle of the y. The other three

letters, which are complete, are 5.5 cm. high. Traces of reddening appear on the surface of the face. Limestone. 10.3 cm. by 10 cm. by 4.5 cm.

TC 887
Fragment from the right edge of an inscribed stone. Part of one line of inscription is preserved across the top of the fragment; this reads]b/mlk[/. The tips of all the characters are broken off at the top, but the original height can be determined at *ca.* 4 cm. Below the line of inscription a blank space is preserved to a maximum of 4 cm. The right side of the piece, as the face, has been smoothed; it is square with the face. No other original surfaces of the piece are preserved. Limestone. 7.9 cm. by 9 cm. by 3.1 cm.

TC 891 (Plate 98)
Inscribed block of stone, broken off at the left. Parts of two lines of inscription are preserved. These read (1)]'byṯ[(2)]wkl.[; the characters are *ca.* 8.3 cm. high. The top, right side, and bottom of the piece are chiseled roughly even, and they slant in slightly toward the rear. The back is irregular. Conglomerate. 19.3 cm. by 17.6 cm. by 8.3 cm.

TC 898 (Plate 98)
Fragment from the lower right corner of a block of stone inscribed on the face. The parts of four lines which are preserved read (1) sq..[(2) n/ṣlm..[(3) g/šfts[/. (4) bns/'[; see *JaPEHA*, pp. 177f., §336. The letters are about 3.7 cm. high, and the lines are about 2.5 mm. apart. The right side of the piece, now chipped, was chiseled even, and it was square with the face. The bottom was also chiseled square with the face, but some tool marks are still visible. The back exhibits numerous tool marks. White alabaster. 11 cm. by 10.5 cm. by 6.2 cm.

TC 899 (Plate 98)
Fragment from the upper right corner of a stone block inscribed on the polished face. The beginnings of three lines are preserved, and these read (1) ṯw[b'l/ (2) qny/'.[(3) ḥg[t. The letters are 2.5 cm. high, and the lines are separated by a space of *ca.* 4 mm. The right side of the piece is polished smooth in a band about 1.5 cm. wide along the front edge, but

is otherwise rough with fairly large tool marks. The band along the front is square with the face, but the remainder slants in toward the rear. The top, broken along the front, is highly polished and is square with the face. A little more than 6 cm. from the side are traces of a shallow cutting, the bottom of which is roughly chiseled. This stone may have been the base for a rather large bronze statuette, as this cutting, as preserved, may be the edge of a foot-shaped cutting similar to those found on TC 1172, above. Alabaster, light colored with rusty streaks. 9.8 cm. by 8 cm. by 11 cm.

TC 908

Inscribed fragment from the upper left corner of a plaque with raised borders. Only the end of a one-line inscription, reading]*gr*, is preserved on the upper border; the letters are about 2 cm. high. The upper border is *ca.* 3 cm. wide at the base (the inner edge is beveled, so the face of the border is not so wide) and raised about 1.1 cm. above the small section of background which is preserved. At the same height as the upper margin and continuous with it is a border 2 cm. wide along the left edge of the piece; within this border is a second one, also about 2 cm. wide, which is recessed nearly 2 mm. The small bit of the background preserved is polished, as are the borders, and it slopes inward away from the margins. The top and side of the piece are chiseled even and square with the face, but these surfaces are now chipped. The small area of the back preserved is rough. White alabaster. 5.8 cm. by 8.6 cm. by 5.5 cm.

TC 909

Fragment chipped from the upper edge of an inscribed stone. The only parts of two lines of inscription preserved on the polished face read (1)]/'.[(2)]*m*..[. The top of the piece is polished and is square with the face. Pale alabaster. 7.6 cm. by 6.5 cm. by 2.3 cm.

TC 910 (Plate 96)

Flat stone block, inscribed on the polished front edge and broken off on the left. The one line of inscription reads *yšrḥ'l/d̲*[; the letters are 3.2 cm. high. The upper parts of the first four are damaged. The top and bottom of the piece are polished. The right side

and the back are chiseled fairly even, but some tool marks remain. Gray alabaster. 3.9 cm. by 12 cm. by 9.4 cm.

TC 911

Fragment from the upper right corner of a stone block inscribed on the face. The parts of two lines of inscription preserved read (1) *n'mm*[(2) *hlm*/.[; the characters are 2.8 cm. high. The lines are 8 mm. apart, and the first line is 8 mm. from the top of the face. The top and right side of the piece are both smooth and square with the face. At the upper left rear of the fragment is the corner of a mortise of undetermined size. Limestone. 7.6 cm. by 5.7 cm. by 5.1 cm.

TC 912

Fragment from the right side of a stone inscribed on the face. The parts of three lines of inscription preserved read (1) *rm*[(2) *kl*/[(3) *ymn*[. Only the lower tips of the two letters of line one are preserved. The complete letters of line two are 4.5 cm. high; the lower tips of the letters in line three are missing. The right side of the piece is even. Limestone. 13 cm. by 5.9 cm. by 6.1 cm.

TC 913 (Plate 98)

Fragment from a stone object inscribed on the top and on the face. The parts of three lines of inscription preserved read (1)]*by*/' *nfss*.[(2)]'*d'l*/*d̲ḥw*.'*m*[(3)].'*n*. ./*šymn*/.[; see *JaPEHA*, pp. 178f., §337, but note that the beginning of line three seems to have been further damaged since the piece was discovered. Line one is on a raised margin along the front edge of the top of the object, while the other two lines are on the face; in all cases the letters are *ca.* 3.2 cm. high. Line two is only 4 mm. below the upper edge of the face, and line three is separated from line two by a space of 5 mm. Guidelines appear at the top and bottom of lines two and three; contrary to *JaPEHA*, the lettering on this fragment is rather different from that on TC 654 (Chapter XI), especially regarding the width of the letters. The margin along the front edge of the top of the object is some 4 cm. wide and is raised 4 mm. above the flat surface behind it. The bottom of the fragment shows some long chisel marks, especially near the front, but it is somewhat rough. This fragment is probably to be interpreted as part of a tabletop of some sort. Limestone. 7.3 cm. by 16.8 cm. by 8.5 cm.

TC 922 (Plate 99)

Fragment from the corner of a stone tabletop, inscribed on the two adjacent edges. This fragment appears to belong to the same object as TC 1050, but does not join it. The one line of inscription, which runs right to left around the corner, reads].sww/lhyʿ[. The first word and the divider are to the right of the corner, and the other four letters are to the left. The characters are about 5 cm. high, though they are not all exactly the same in height. The faces on which the inscription is incised are polished smooth. On the top of the piece, a raised (ca. 4 mm.) margin runs along the edges above the inscription. This margin is 2.8 cm. wide to the right of the corner and 3 cm. wide to the left; the sides of it are rounded. The flat area inside the border, like the border itself, is polished smooth. The bottom is rough with tool marks, except along the outer edges where it is chiseled even; 3.2 cm. in from the right face and 4 cm. in from the left is the corner of a recessed area ca. 3 cm. deep. The sides and bottom of this are covered with tool marks, but are generally even. White alabaster. 6.8 cm. by 11.6 cm. (along right face) by 9.5 cm. (along left face).

TC 924 (Plate 99)

Two joining fragments which form the bottom and upper left part of a block of stone inscribed on the face. The inscription is unusual, in that the part on the right fragment has larger letters than the part on the left fragment and is not in line with it. The parts of two lines preserved on the right fragment read (1)].r...[(2)].t/dwygr/.r.[. The parts of two lines preserved on the left fragment read (1)].šyr (2)]m..ygr. The characters of line 2 on the right fragment are ca. 2.7 cm. high, while those on the left part are only about 2 cm. high. On the right fragment, the inscription begins at the very edge of the block, but line one on the left fragment ends some 8 cm. from the left edge of the face, line two some 8.5 cm. Line two of the right part is 3.8 cm. from the bottom edge of the face, but line two of the left fragment is 4.7 cm. from the lower

edge. The face of the block has been smoothed even. The top and sides are chiseled even. The back is also even, but rougher. The bottom exhibits tool marks, but is chiseled along the front and rear edges. Limestone. 10.2 cm. by 29.5 cm. by 9 cm.

TC 925

Fragment from the edge of a re-used block of stone, inscribed on one face. Along the edge are the lower tips of characters belonging to a line of inscription and below this is a segment of another line. These read (1)]fm ...[(2)]b/dt/.[; the characters of line two are 3.4 cm. high. Guidelines are visible at the bottom of line one, at the top and bottom of line two, and in the space below line two, as though more lines of inscription had been planned. The lines of inscription are ca. 5 mm. apart, and similar spacing is left between the guidelines below for the two additional lines indicated. The face is chiseled even, and there are traces of reddening here and there over the surface. The face above the inscribed face has a pecked surface with marginal drafting (cf. TC 630, above); the chiseled margin along the edge is 1.7 cm. wide. Limestone. The inscribed face measures 11 cm. by 15 cm., and the adjacent pecked and drafted face measures 4.5 cm. by 14 cm.

TC 926 (Plate 99)

Inscribed fragment. This appears to belong to TC 929, but does not join it. The parts of two lines preserved on the face read (1)]t/d (2)].fm; the letters are about 1.2 cm. high. Guidelines appear at the top and bottom of each line. The face and the top of the piece are polished. The bottom is chiseled even. White alabaster. 4.7 cm. by 6 cm. by 3.3 cm.

TC 929 (Plate 99)

Fragment from the right part of a flat stone, inscribed on the polished front edge. The parts of the two lines of inscription preserved read (1) mʿmr/fr[(2) rhn[. The letters are of the same style and size as those on TC 926, which must form the left end of the inscribed face. Guidelines also are plainly visible at the top and bottom of each line. The top of the piece is polished smooth. The right end is chiseled even along the front and top in a band about 1 cm. wide, but inside this band there is a depression covered with tool marks. This side slants in slightly toward the rear. The bottom is chiseled even in a band along the front varying in width from 2.5 cm. to 3 cm.; farther back, there are very large tool marks. White alabaster with a rusty colored streak at the upper right. 4.8 cm. by 11.2 cm. by 7.7 cm.

TC 939

Fragment from a stone slab inscribed on the polished face. The parts of four lines of inscription preserved read (1)]/*dt*/[(2)]*..w*/ *yd*[(3)]*.kw*/*qt.*[(4)]*mʿhr*/*q.* *.*[. The characters of lines two and three are 3.7 cm. high (those of the other lines are not preserved to their full height). The lines are about 5 mm. apart. The back of the piece exhibits extremely large tool marks. No other original finished surfaces are preserved. White alabaster. 14.8 cm. by *ca.* 9 cm. by 5.7 cm.

TC 943

Fragment from the upper part of an inscribed stone. The parts of two lines of inscription preserved on the smooth face read (1)]*mʿmr*/[(2)]*.t.* *.*[. The letters of line 1 are 3.8 cm. high; only the upper ends of the letters of line 2 are preserved. The face is covered with reddening. The top of the piece is chiseled even. Limestone. 6.9 cm. by 7.2 cm. by 2.5 cm.

TC 947 (Plate 99)

Fragment from the upper left corner of a stone slab inscribed on the face. The parts of four lines of inscription preserved read (1)]*.ʾysmy*/*bdtm*/ (2)]*.*/*wbnsww*/*whb* (3)]*qny sm*/*wbmr* (4)]*.k*/*qt.*[. The characters are 5 cm. high; the letters of line 4 are more widely spaced than those in the first three lines. The first line is 2 cm. below the upper edge of the face; the lines are some 7 mm. apart. Guidelines are visible at the top, center, and bottom of each line, and also through the center of the spaces between the lines. The left edge of the slab is smooth and is square with the face. The top is square with the face, but is rough. The back is flat, but rough with very large diagonal tool marks. Limestone. 28.5 cm. by 22.5 cm. by 7.1 cm.

TC 951

Fragment from upper part of an inscribed stone. Parts of three lines of inscription are preserved on the face; these read (1)]*wstʿn*/*w*[(2)]*mbhl*[(3)]*sgʿ.*[; the characters are 2.5 cm. high. The top of the fragment is polished smooth. Rusty colored alabaster. 9 cm. by 7.2 cm. by 3.7 cm.

TC 956 (Plate 99)

Fragment from the left front corner of a tabletop, inscribed on the face and side. Parts of two lines of inscription are preserved on the face, the second of which runs around to the side. These read (1)]/*ḥn* (2)]*./ʾnby*/*nf*[; the corner comes between the *b* and the *y* of line two. The letters of line two are 4 cm. high, but those of line one seem to have been slightly shorter (the upper ends are not entirely clear). On the top there is a raised (*ca.* 5 mm.) border along the front and side; this is about 2.8 cm. wide and bears chisel marks on it. The surface within this border is flat. All of the surfaces of the fragment have flaked away to some extent. Limestone. 12 cm. by 12 cm. by 9.4 cm.

TC 991 (Plate 99)

Fragment from the front of a tabletop inscribed on the front edge. The part of one line of inscription preserved on the polished face reads]*t*/*ʾrglm*/*šʿb.* *.*[. The characters are 3.8 cm. high and are placed 5 mm. from the upper edge of the face, 1 cm. from the lower edge. On the top there is a raised (5 mm.) margin along the front 6.7 cm. wide at the surface (the inner side is beveled, so the margin is about 5 mm. wider at the base). Behind this border the flat surface is polished, as is the surface of the margin. The bottom is roughly chiseled even along the front in a band 3.5 cm. to 4.5 cm. wide. Behind this the surface is rough with tool marks. White alabaster with several rusty-orange streaks. 5.4 cm. by 15.5 cm. by 14.4 cm.

TC 992

Fragment from the front edge of a stone block inscribed on the face. The parts of two lines preserved read (1)]*dq*/*dwšḥ.* *.*[(2)]*mn*/ *m.* *.*[; the characters are *ca.* 3.4 cm. high. The top, like the face, has been smoothed fairly even, but it is now chipped. Limestone. 8.5 cm. by 14.5 cm. by 7 cm.

TC 994 (Plates 98 and 99)

Part of a large circular stone tabletop. One line of inscription runs around the edge of the top, just inside the rounded molding; the part of this line preserved reads]*wkl/'wldsm/ bmr'ḥm*[. A second line of inscription runs along the edge of the tabletop, below the rounded molding which protrudes from the corner where the top and the edge meet. This reads, as far as preserved,]*/bn/'nṣrm/ḏtw/ dnm/sqnyw/'n*[. The characters of the inscription on the top are 3 cm. high, those on the edge 2.8 cm. The protruding, rounded molding has a diameter of some 2.5 cm. It rises 1 cm. above the surface of the top and projects 7 mm. out beyond the edge of the piece on which the second line of inscription is located. The top is flat and is highly polished, as are the molding and the front edge. The bottom exhibits large tool marks; a band some 4 cm. wide has been superficially chiseled along the edge. The curve of the edge indicates a diameter of about 50 cm., but the piece may not have formed a complete circle in its original state. TC 1262 belongs to the same tabletop, but does not join this fragment. White alabaster with brown streaks. 5.5 cm. by 29 cm. by 18.3 cm.

TC 995 (Plate 99)

Part of a block of stone, inscribed on the polished face. The parts of four lines preserved read (1)]..*rn/w. .mr*[(2)]'*ḥw/yd"b/ḏ*[(3)]*byn/yhn'm/m*[(4)]*lk/qt...*.[. The characters of lines two and three, the only ones preserved to their full height, are 3.4 cm. high, and the space between the lines is *ca.* 5 mm. The piece appears to have had at least two periods of use, and the inscription belongs to an earlier one. The left side is square with the face and is polished. The right side has been cut off so that it slants in toward the rear, and it is rough with tool marks, though it has been chiseled sparingly along the front. The bottom has been cut into the last line of inscription, with the right part extending *ca.* 1.4 cm. lower than the left. The offset between the two parts is nearly vertical, but now damaged. All of the bottom is rough with tool marks and chipped areas, but the left edge and the front have been chiseled in a band about 1.5 cm. wide. The top of the block has been broken off. The back has large tool marks and has been chiseled along the left side, where the stone is thicker than on the right. Alabaster. 13.5 cm. by 14.8 cm. by 6.5 cm.

TC 1001 (Plate 100)

Left part of a stone slab inscribed on the face. The parts of five lines of inscription preserved read (1)]'*nby/šym* (2)].*tm/rtdw/* (3)]"*dnsmy/b* (4)]*yhn'm/mlk/* (5)]*bn*[9.2 cm. blank space]*nyḥ/*. The characters are 5.7 cm. high except those of line two, which are only 5.2 cm. high. Guidelines are visible at the top, middle, and bottom of each line; the first line is 1.2 cm. from the upper edge of the face. The lines are 5 mm. to 6 mm. apart. Below the last line is a blank space of *ca.* 6.5 cm. The face, now somewhat damaged in places, is covered with reddening. The top of the slab is partly chiseled, partly irregular. The left side is smooth and square with the face. The bottom is rough, and it slants up toward the rear. The back is roughly chiseled even along the left, but elsewhere it is very rough. The center and upper part of the back is recessed about 1 cm. behind the left and lower parts. Limestone. 38 cm. by 27 cm. by 6.7 cm.

TC 1013 (Plate 101)

Two joining fragments (including the larger fragment TC 1070 on the left) from the flat side of a stone trough or similar object, inscribed on the outside. The parts of the two lines of inscription preserved read (1)]'*m/ḏḏrḥn/sqny/'nby/mqldn.*[(2)]'*ts/frḏm/*. Line two ends 18 cm. from the right edge of the part of the stone preserved; the characters in both lines are *ca.* 4 cm. high. The top edges of the fragments are somewhat wavy, but generally even. The backs of the fragments, which would have been the inside of a trough, are fairly straight, and are largely covered with what appears to be an accretion of lime. Porous calcite. 15.5 cm. by 44.5 cm. by 4.6 cm.

TC 1014 (Plate 99)

Fragment from the upper face of a large stone block, inscribed on the front. The parts of the two lines of inscription which are preserved read (1)]*n/bn/fr'krb/*[(2)]*r/q.n/ršw.*[. In line two the second letter of the middle word is probably *y*, but the lower part is missing. The characters of line one are 5.7 cm. high, while none of the letters of line two are preserved fully at the bottom. The lines are *ca.* 6 mm. apart, and the first line is 1.3 cm. from the upper edge of the face. The surface of the face is smooth, and there are a few traces of reddening on it. The top, square with the face, has been chiseled even. Limestone. 13.1 cm. by 17.6 cm. by 4.9 cm.

TC 1015 (Plate 100)

Three fragments (including TC 1026 and TC 1027) from a circular stone flat on the top and bottom. Four lines of inscription run half way around the outside of the object. The preserved parts of these read (1) *'l*[about fifteen letters] *by/šym/* (2) *ṣlm/ḏ*[about eleven letters]*r.s/lb* (3) *ns/rḏw'*[about seven letters]*nby/'ḏns* (4) *wbns/rḏ*[about four letters]*wkl/wlds*. The characters are *ca.* 2.6 cm. high, except those in line three, which are between 2.8 cm. and 3 cm. The top of the object is preserved in only two small areas, and these are polished smooth. The bottom has been chiseled even in a band about 2.5 cm. wide around the edge; the interior is rough with tool marks. White alabaster with a few light-colored streaks. 14.4 cm. (height) by 18.5 cm. (diameter).

TC 1017 (Plate 101)

Fragment from the upper left corner of an inscribed block of stone. Parts of two lines of inscription are preserved across a wide raised margin on the upper part of the face. These read (1)]*yhrm/ḏ.* (2)]*/brṣfm*; the characters are 2.4 cm. high. The margin on which the inscription is found is 4 mm. higher than the flat surface below, and it is 6.2 cm. wide. It continues down the left edge of the block as a margin 3.5 cm. wide. Near the break on the right there seems to be the edge of another margin of the same height. The flat surface inside the raised borders is 5 cm. wide and is preserved for a distance of 5.5 cm. from top to bottom. The left side of the block is polished, as are all of the surfaces of the face. The top of the fragment has been superficially smoothed, but tool marks are visible in places; it is now badly chipped. The back is irregular except for a chiseled band 3 cm. wide along

the left. Light-colored alabaster. 12.5 cm. by 10.9 cm. by 9 cm.

TC 1018

Fragment from the inscribed face of a stone object, curved in horizontal section. The beginnings of two lines of the inscription are preserved, and these read (1) *n'm.*[(2) *šym.*[. The characters of line two are 2.3 cm. high; those of line one are not preserved to their full height. The face of the object is polished, as is the small area of the top which is preserved. White alabaster with darker streaks. 9.6 cm. by 8 cm. by 4.1 cm.

TC 1028 (Plate 100)

Fragment from the top of a stone object inscribed on the polished front. The part of the first line of inscription preserved reads]*'mbrl/ ḏt/thṭ.*[; the fourth letter of the last word appears to have been *k*. This line is 8 mm. below the upper edge of the face, and the characters of it are 3 cm. high; 6 mm. below the first line are the upper tips of the letters of a second line, the second and third letters of which are *kr*. No other letters can be identified. The top of the fragment has unusual cuttings. Behind a polished strip 2.7 cm. wide (now badly chipped) is a cutting 1.5 cm. deep and some 2 cm. wide parallel to the face. The interior of this cutting is rough with small, closely spaced tool marks. At the left edge of the fragment this cutting makes a 90° turn and continues toward the rear break. Within the two parts of this cutting is a flat area about 1 cm. higher than the bottom of the cuttings; this surface has been smoothed. No other original surfaces of the object are preserved. Alabaster, mottled gray and tan. 5.7 cm. by 15.5 cm. by 14 cm.

TC 1029 (Plate 99)

Fragment from the front edge of a stone tabletop inscribed on the face. The parts of the two lines of the rather crude, preserved inscription read (1)]*./bn/ḏll/sqny/'*[(2)]*./wr[ṭ]d/'nby/bn*[; the characters average about 2.6 cm. in height. The space between the two lines is barely 3 mm. The face of the piece is weather-beaten. The top has a raised (*ca.* 4 mm.) margin 2 cm. wide along the front edge; behind this is a plain, flat surface. The top is rather battered and worn, though it was apparently once polished. The bottom is rough, but has been superficially chiseled. Alabaster of poor quality, light in color except for a dark banding across the bottom of the fragment. 6.1 cm. by 20.5 cm. by 10.3 cm.

TC 1046 (Plate 101)

Large fragment from the upper left corner of a flat stone monument inscribed on the face. The parts of two lines of inscription preserved on the smooth face read (1)]m/bn/ y'dr' (2) l/'gr/šhr/w[; the second line runs left to right. The characters of the first line toward the right of the fragment are 5 cm. high, while those toward the left reach 5.4 cm. in height. None of the letters of line two is preserved to its full height; the lines are *ca.* 1 cm. apart. A raised (7 mm.) margin runs along the left side and the top of the face. The margin across the top, *ca.* 3.5 cm. wide at the face, follows the curve of the bowed (concave) top; the vertical margin on the left is *ca.* 3.3 cm. wide at the face. The inner edges on both margins are beveled. The first line of the inscription comes within 6 mm. of the base of the upper margin at the center of the bow. The left side of the stone and the bowed top are chiseled even along the front, but are somewhat irregular and slanting inward farther back. The back of the fragment is generally flat, but extremely rough. Limestone. 24.5 cm. by 36.7 cm. by 8 cm. See note at end of description of TC 704, above.

TC 1048 (Plate 100)

Fragment from the left corner of a stone object inscribed on the face and side. The parts of two lines of inscription preserved on the face read (1)].drš (2)]rh. Line two continues on the left side of the stone, reading '/brsfm; the characters are about 3 cm. high. The face of the piece, which is chiseled fairly even, bears traces of reddening. The left side has been chiseled, but is not as even as the face. A hole 1.5 cm. in diameter at the surface and 1.2 cm. deep is cut into the side 2.9 cm. behind the face and 1.6 cm. below the top. The top is square with the face and side. The surface of it has a pecked appearance, and there is an irregular cutting *ca.* 1.8 cm. wide and 2.3 cm. long in it. A small section of the smooth bottom of the piece is preserved. Limestone. 8 cm. by 4.8 cm. by 9.9 cm.

TC 1049 (Plate 98)

Fragment from the edge of a stone tabletop inscribed on the curved front. The part of a one-line inscription preserved reads]swfy/ 'n[; the characters are *ca.* 2.2 cm. high. The surface of the front has been polished, but is now chipped. The upper surface of the tabletop was polished. Along the front edge is a raised (6 mm.) margin *ca.* 2.1 cm. wide with rounded edges. The bottom has been chiseled superficially, but it is still somewhat rough with tool marks. White alabaster with tan and rusty colored streaks. 4.2 cm. by 11.4 cm. by 15 cm.

TC 1050

Fragment from a corner of a tabletop inscribed on the front. This fragment belongs to the same object as TC 922, but does not join it. The part of a one-line inscription preserved reads].sqn. White alabaster. 6.5 cm. by 9.4 cm. by 8.1 cm.

TC 1051

Fragment from the right corner of a stone object inscribed on the face. The parts of the two-line inscription preserved read (1) [.]t/ 't.[(2) .qs/br[; the characters are 2 cm. high. The two lines of inscription are on separate bands which run across the face and around the right side. The lower band is raised *ca.* 1 mm. beyond the upper, and there is a shallow offset between them. Both the face and the side of the piece are polished. The top has been partly smoothed even, but tool marks are still visible; *ca.* 1.7 cm. in from the front and side is the edge of a depression some 5 mm. deep with a roughly tooled interior. The bottom is rough, but flat. Alabaster, light-colored with brown streaks at the top and bottom. 5.2 cm. by 6.8 cm. by 8.5 cm.

TC 1069 (Plate 100)

Large fragment from the left corner of a stone tabletop inscribed on the polished front edge. The last part of a one-line inscription is preserved. This reads]bn/tmr/nbt'm; the characters are 4.4 cm. high. The last letter is 3.7 cm. from the corner. On the top of the piece there is a raised (5 mm.) margin *ca.* 3 cm. wide, which was originally polished but is now defaced by a chiseled strip about 1.5 cm. wide over the entire length of it. The inner edge of the margin is beveled; behind the margin is a flat surface which has been smoothed even. The left edge of the piece is chiseled even along the front and top but is otherwise rough and slants in toward the bottom. The bottom has an evenly chiseled band *ca.* 3 cm. wide along the front. Behind this the surface is very rough with short tool marks, but is generally even for some 13 cm. from the front. Behind the front, the small area preserved on the fragment indicates a much more irregular surface with larger tool marks. White alabaster with rusty-tan streaks. 6.4 cm. by 22.7 cm. by 19.8 cm.

TC 1073 (Plate 97)

Right front corner of a flat stone block inscribed on the front edge. The part of the one-line inscription preserved reads *m'mr/flm/*[; the characters are 3.5 cm. high. The top of the piece is smoothed even. The right side is chiseled square with the top and the face. The bottom is generally even, though chiseled only superficially. Limestone. 4.7 cm. by 14 cm. by 8.6 cm.

TC 1075 (Plate 101)

Fragment from the corner of a stone block inscribed on two adjacent, marginally drafted, pecked faces. The part of the one-line inscription preserved reads]*bn/h*[. The first letter is on the face to the right of the corner; the second letter has the lower vertical stroke on the right, but the rest of the character is on the left of the corner. There is also a more shallow lower vertical stroke to the left of the corner, and a second upper vertical stroke slightly to the right of the deeper one, so the intentions of the cutter are not entirely clear. The characters are *ca.* 11.6 cm high. Both the top and bottom of the fragment are chiseled fairly even. Limestone. 18 cm. by 6 cm. by 8.8 cm.

TC 1076

Fragment from the upper edge of some stone object, inscribed along the top of the polished face. The part of the one-line inscription preserved reads]*m/dr*[; the characters are 4.3 cm. high. The top of the piece is polished in a band 3 cm. wide along the front; behind this is a vertical offset 2.7 cm. deep, rough with tool marks. The back of

the fragment is very rough with large tool marks. Alabaster. 12.7 cm. by 10.5 cm. by 5.4 cm.

TC 1078 (Plate 101)

Right part of a stone block inscribed on the polished face. The parts of two lines of inscription preserved read (1) *m'mr/db'.*[(2) *b/wy'zz/dt*[; the characters are 3.8 cm. high. The first line is 2.1 cm. from the top of the face, and the lines are separated by a space of 8 mm. The lower 6.6 cm. of the face is blank. The top of the piece is partly polished. The right side and the bottom are square with the face. They are chiseled even along the front edges, but left rough with tool marks otherwise. The back, which exhibits very large tool marks, is somewhat irregular. Alabaster. 17.2 cm. by 13.6 cm. by 9.5 cm.

TC 1108

Rectangular block of stone, inscribed on the rough face. The parts of three lines of inscription preserved read (1)]*.rb/w*[(2)]*'b/dby*[(3)]*dmrk.*[; the characters are slightly more than 4 cm. high. The top, sides, and bottom of the piece have been roughly chiseled square with the face. The back is flat, but rough with large tool marks except along the left side where it is chiseled. The upper right corner is broken off. Very porous calcite. 16.5 cm. by 13.7 cm. by 4.8 cm.

TC 1114 (Plate 101)

Unidentified stone object, inscribed on the front. The one-line inscription reads *td'/dt/'ygn*; the characters are 1.5 cm. high. The inscription is on the upper register of the polished face; the lower register is *ca.* 2 cm. wide. The top of the piece has a polished strip 1.5 cm. wide along the front; behind this is a recess *ca.* 5 cm. from front to rear running the entire width of the piece. The interior of it is covered with tool marks, those in the bottom running mostly from front to back. Behind this is another raised (*ca.* 5 mm.) band, this one *ca.* 1 cm. wide, polished superficially on the top. The left side of the block is square with the face and the top; it is very superficially polished smooth. Only a tiny bit of the right side is preserved. The back is partly chiseled even, partly rough with tool marks. The bottom is very rough with tool marks; a band along the front is chiseled even. Alabaster. 4.8 cm. by 13 cm. by 8.6 cm.

TC 1130 (Plate 99)

Rectangular stone block inscribed on the face. The part of one line of inscription which is preserved reads]bn/'[; the characters are 10.5 cm. high. Reddening had been applied to the porous face before the letters were cut. The top, bottom, and sides of the piece have been roughly chiseled even along the front, but are otherwise irregular. The back is irregular, though generally flat. Porous calcite. 15.7 cm. by 19.4 cm. by 6.4 cm.

TC 1131 (Plate 102)

Stone block, broken at the left, inscribed on the face. Sections of two lines of inscription and the upper tips of the characters in a third line are preserved. The lines read (1)]s/w'd̲ns/w[(2)]n'/ywm/swf[; the characters are 7.4 cm. high, and the lines are 8 mm. apart. The face, which is badly pitted, is covered with reddening. The top, right side, and bottom are chiseled even along the front; farther back they are irregular and slant inward. The back is irregular. Porous calcite. 19.2 cm. by 26.3 cm. by 7 cm.

TC 1152 (Plate 99)

Inscribed piece of stone, broken at the top. The two-line inscription reads (1) m'mr/'lyt (2) d̲r'n/; see *JaPEHA*, pp. 202f., §356, Pl. x, above. The letters of the first line are *ca.* 1.7 cm. high, those of the second line 2.3 cm. high. There is no space between the two lines; therefore the lower guideline of the upper line serves as the upper guideline of the lower line. The sides and bottom have been roughly chiseled. The back is irregular and has large tool marks. Alabaster, light-colored with a dark brown streak at the upper rear. 6 cm. by 9.2 cm. by 3.2 cm.

TC 1154 (Plate 100)

Fragment from the corner of a stone table-top, inscribed on two adjacent sides. The part of the one-line of inscription preserved reads]y/nfs[; the characters are 4.5 cm. high. The first three characters are on the right side of the corner, the other two on the left. On the top of the fragment there is a low, raised margin about 2 cm. wide along the edges

adjacent to the inscribed faces; the top is otherwise plain and flat. Some 4 cm. to the left of the corner is a protrusion at the break indicating that there was some kind of a neck on the table. The raised margin on the top also follows this pattern; this was probably the front of the object. The bottom of the fragment is generally flat and even. Limestone. 7.9 cm. by 13.5 cm. by 8.5 cm.

TC 1155 (Plate 102)

Fragment from the left side of a stone slab which was inscribed on the face. The parts of the two preserved lines read (1)]brn/f (2)]'ṭbn; the characters, rather crudely incised, are *ca.* 3 cm. high. There are traces of a faintly incised letter above line one, so there may have been another line there. A blank space of 7 cm. is preserved below line two. The face is chiseled even. The left side has been roughly chiseled, and it is square with the face. The back is flat, but rough with tool marks; it has been superficially chiseled in places. There are two holes which were drilled into the right side, and these are now exposed in the break. These are 1.5 cm. back from the face and are *ca.* 6.8 cm. apart. The upper one is 3.9 cm. deep, the lower one the same; these holes were probably intended as dowel holes to be used in joining the fragment to the neighboring fragment. Limestone. 20 cm. by 8 cm. by 6.2 cm.

TC 1176 (Plate 102)

Fragment from a stone slab inscribed on the polished face. The parts of three preserved lines of inscription read (1)]bn/yd''b/ m.r.[(2)]wkm/d̲'mr/wšmr/q.[(3)]śhr/wrby/ 'm/ry'n.[. The upper tips of three letters in a fourth line are visible, but they cannot be identified; the characters are 3.4 cm. high. The first line is 1.3 cm. below the edge of a raised (7 mm.) margin at the top of the face, preserved only to a width of *ca.* 1 cm. in a small area to the right. The lines are *ca.* 6 mm. apart. The back of the piece is somewhat irregular. Light-colored alabaster. 14.5 cm. by 18 cm. by 6 cm.

TC 1185

Fragment from the upper left corner and end of a stone block inscribed on the front edge. The part of the inscription preserved reads]*ṣbḥ*; the lower ends of the letters are missing. The top of the piece is smooth. The left side has been chiseled fairly even, and it is square with the face and with the top. The small section of the back edge preserved indicates that it was chiseled also. Limestone. 6 cm. by 13.4 cm. by 21.8 cm.

TC 1201 (Plate 100)

Fragment from the left front corner of what appears to have been a stone trough, inscribed on the front and side. The preserved part of the one-line inscription on the front reads].*y*/'.[; the characters were 8.8 cm. high. Only the lower end of the final letter is preserved. The continuation of the inscription on the adjacent side is].*y*.[. The lower ends of vertical strokes of the first and last letters are preserved, so it may be safe to reconstruct the text represented as *sqn*]*y*/'[*nb*]*y*[/. The front wall of the fragment is about 4 cm. thick in the upper part, but only about 2.5 cm. near the interior bottom. The wall on the left side had a similar thickness; the top was chiseled off flat. The bottom was roughly chiseled off flat. Limestone. 13.5 cm. by 16.8 cm. by 12.1 cm.

TC 1225

Fragment from the inscribed face of a stone. The parts of two lines of inscription preserved read (1)]/*fy*[(2)]*m*/*b*[. The characters are 3.7 cm. high, and the lines are separated by a space of 1 cm. Guidelines appear at the top and bottom of both lines, and another guideline below the second line indicates that there was another line of inscription below. No original surfaces other than the face are preserved. Limestone. 11.8 cm. by 5.5 cm. by 3.4 cm.

TC 1227 (Plate 102)

Block of stone inscribed on the face. The parts of the two lines of inscription preserved are not entirely clear, as the stone is rough and the lettering crude. The upper part of the first line is damaged, and only *f* at the beginning (right end) and a *q* near the end can be identified. The second line seems to read]'*b*/*yglm*[, but the *m* is backwards, and the diagonal stroke of *l* is crowded into it. The characters of line 2 are *ca.* 4 cm. high.

In the blank space below line two (some 5.5 cm. wide) are traces of a graffito—or more likely modern scratchings; the surface of the face was covered with reddening before the inscription was cut. The right side of the block and the bottom are chiseled even, but the other two edges are rough. The back exhibits very large tool marks. Porous calcite. 13 cm. by 15.5 cm. by 6.5 cm.

TC 1239 (Plate 100)

Fragment from the lower right corner of a stone object inscribed on the front. The part of the one-line inscription preserved reads *fyšt*/[; the characters, which are rather crude, are 2.5 cm. high. The polished surface into which they are cut appears to be the face of a high (2.5 cm.) margin of some kind, for at the top of the fragment is a small area of the background of some kind of a plaque. At the break on the upper left of this background is a ridge suggesting that there may have been a relief. The right side of the fragment is partly evened, slanting in toward the rear. The bottom has also been partly chiseled even. The back is rough with tool marks. Alabaster, blackened by fire. 5.4 cm. by 9.5 cm. by 5 cm.

TC 1262 (Plate 102)

Fragment from the edge of a tabletop. This fragment belongs to the same tabletop as TC 994, but does not join it. The part of the one line of inscription preserved on the top reads].*wbn*[. The part of the one line of inscription on the edge preserved reads]'*tsm*/ *brṣf*[; the letters on the top are 3 cm. high, those on the edge *ca.* 2.8 cm. high. Alabaster. 5.5 cm. by 10 cm. by 7.8 cm.

TC 1297

Fragment from the lower left corner of a stone block, inscribed on the polished front. The part of the one line of inscription preserved reads].*ds*/*wqn*..; none of the characters are preserved to their full height at the top, but it is estimated at *ca.* 2.4 cm. The left side is square with the face and is polished smooth. The bottom is chiseled entirely even as far as preserved. No other original surfaces are preserved. White alabaster. 4.8 cm. by 11.3 cm. by 10.9 cm.

TC 1299

Fragment from the left front corner of a stone block, inscribed on the polished face. The ends of two lines of inscription are preserved, and these read (1)]ḥbm (2)]m. The letters of the upper line are 3.3 cm. high, the letter of the lower line only 3 cm. The top of the piece is polished smooth and is square with the face. The left side is square with the top and face, but it is only superficially smoothed and exhibits rough spots toward the center. The bottom was chiseled even for about 2 cm. along the front edge; elsewhere it is very rough. White alabaster with darker streaks. 8.8 cm. by 5.1 cm. by 9.3 cm.

TC 1314 (Plate 102)

Right end of an irregularly shaped stone block, inscribed on the polished face. The parts of the two-line inscription which are preserved read (1) *m'mr/*[(2) *ḥḍrn*[; the characters are 3 cm. high. Guidelines appear at the top and bottom of each line. The lines are separated by a space of *ca.* 4 mm., and there is a blank space of *ca.* 1.5 cm. at the bottom of the face and 7 mm. at the top of the face. Above the surface referred to as the face is an offset square with it. This offset is 5.9 cm. deep, and above it is another vertical surface 7.8 cm. from top to bottom; both this surface and the offset are roughly chiseled even. The top, back, bottom, and right side of the block now are chipped, especially at the corners, and all exhibit tool marks. A little more than 6 cm. from the right edge and 5 cm. from the back, there is the edge of what may have been a mortise in the top of the block. This suggests, as does the inscription, that the piece was the base or pedestal of a statuette, but the step cut along the front corner cannot be explained. Light-colored alabaster. 17 cm. by 7.7 cm. by 16.2 cm.

TC 1334 (Plate 102)

Large fragment from a stone slab of undetermined size inscribed on the polished front edge. The preserved parts of the two lines of inscription are to be read (1) *z'bt/ḏt/byt/f*[(2) *mn/m'mrs/brṣf.*[; see *JaPEHA*, pp. 204 f., §360. A very deep vertical groove, flaring at the bottom, is partly preserved at the right edge of the face, and this indicates that the beginnings of the two lines are intact. The characters are *ca.* 2.5 cm. high (they vary about 1 mm. in either direction). TC 1343, below, belongs to this same slab, though it does not join this larger fragment, and the parts of two lines of inscription preserved on it apparently are to be placed to the left of the inscription on this fragment. The preserved part of the slab extends diagonally back to the left from the face, and the rear edge is preserved for a distance of some 7 cm., but no part of either side is now preserved.

The top of the object is polished smooth. At the break on the right is the edge of a mortise 2.2 cm. deep and 5.7 cm. from the face; extending out to the left from the front of this mortise is a crude groove 3 cm. long. At the rear, just to left of the preserved section of the back edge, is a shallow (*ca.* 5 mm.) cutting *ca.* 2.5 cm. by 3 cm. rounded at the front and flat on the bottom, which ran off the back edge. The back has been chiseled a little near the top, but is rough. The bottom has been chiseled even superficially over large tool marks except for an irregular protruding strip about 7 cm. wide along the rear. Light-colored alabaster, somewhat mottled and with a darker horizontal streak running through the entire fragment. 8.5 cm. (near rear) by 17.5 cm. (across the face) by 28.2 cm. (distance between the face and the back edge).

TC 1335 (Plate 103)

Large fragment from the left side and upper left corner of a stone block inscribed on the polished face. The parts of the nine lines of inscription preserved read (1)]./qyl (2)]bn/ḥg (3)]wḥb'l/ (4)].ḥy'tt/w (5)].sm/w'byt (6)].by/wb/bšmm (7)]./ḏt/zhrn/ wb (8)].n/'šr/šb' (9)].wrn. The characters are 3 cm. high. The first line is 8 mm. from the upper edge of the face; the lines are between 3 mm. and 4 mm. apart. The letters of line nine are more widely spaced than those in the other lines; a blank space of 1.7 cm. is preserved below line nine. The left side of the block is square with the face; it has been roughly chiseled even along the front edge, but is otherwise rough with tool marks. The very small preserved area of the top was polished smooth, though it is now badly battered. The back is generally flat, and is very rough with large diagonal tool marks; the lower 8 cm. preserved slants in sharply toward the bottom, and the tool marks in this lower area are horizontal. The piece is only 5 cm. thick at the lower corner of the fragment. White alabaster without any flaws. 32.5 cm. by 13.5 cm. by 10.3 cm.

TC 1337 (Plate 101)
Irregular stone inscribed on the fairly even face. The one-line inscription reads *hn't/ hḥrm*; see *JaPEHA*, pp. 138f., §280. The characters are all about 4.5 cm. high, but their alignment is uneven. As the piece rests on its flat bottom, the face slants in toward the top. The sides and top are irregular. Greenish stone, very hard. 8 cm. by 24 cm. by 12 cm.

TC 1338 (Plate 99)
Right end of a flat stone block inscribed on the polished front edge. Only the first three letters, reading *m'm[*, are preserved of the one-line inscription. The first letter, the only one of the tall letters fully preserved, is 3.6 cm. high. The flat top of the block is polished smooth; 8.5 cm. from the right edge and *ca.* 8 cm. from the line of the face, is the edge of a mortise 1.4 cm. deep. This mortise, along with the inscription, suggests that the block was the base for a statuette.

The right side of the block is approximately square with the top and the face, but has two bosses left in the evenly chiseled surface. The first, *ca.* 1.3 cm. wide, is a vertical one flush with the front edge. The second boss is 3.5 cm. from the front edge and is *ca.* 2 cm. wide: it does not extend clear to the top, but ends *ca.* 8 mm. from it in a rounded end. The purpose of these bosses, neither of which is more than 6 mm. high, is not at all clear. The back of the block is tooled roughly even, and it is square with the top and with the right side. The bottom is tooled even also, and it has been chiseled even in a band *ca.* 2 cm. wide along the front edge. Alabaster, very light gray. 5.6 cm. by 11 cm. by 13.6 cm.

TC 1339 (Plate 100)
Left end of a flat stone block inscribed on the superficially polished front edge. The end of the one-line inscription reads *]brṣfm/*; the characters are 2.7 cm. high. The final word divider is 3.7 cm. from the left edge of the face. The *r* and the *f* have reddening in them. The flat top of the stone has been su-

perficially smoothed, but it is still rough and tool marks are visible. The left side has been very roughly chiseled even, square with the face and top, but is irregular along the bottom. The back is nearly all broken away. The bottom has tool marks and a chiseled band 1.5 cm. wide along the front; traces of plaster still adhere to areas of the bottom. White alabaster. 4.8 cm. by 11.7 cm. by 11.3 cm.

TC 1343 (Plate 101)
Fragment from the same stone slab as TC 1334, above. The preserved parts of the two lines of inscription read (1) *]./'nby/ṧy[* (2) *].m/m[*. The first letter of line one is preserved only at the top, and it is probably *y*; the surface is damaged at the end of line one, and it is not possible to know whether there were additional letters or not. Only the upper tips of the characters of line two are preserved, and they are near the end of line one; the characters of line one which are fully preserved are *ca.* 2.5 cm. high. At the right break of the polished top, at a distance of *ca.* 5 cm. from the face, is the edge of a mortise with a crude groove extending to the left; this is to be compared with similar cuttings at the right break of TC 1334. Alabaster, same as TC 1334. 6.6 cm. by 13.5 cm. by 12.3 cm.

TC 1345 (Plate 102)
Fragment from the corner of a stone table-top inscribed on the polished edges. The one-line inscription, as far as preserved, reads *]..byn/yhrgb*. This inscription is on the front edge, except for the last three letters, which are on the side, followed by a blank space preserved to a width of 11.5 cm. The characters are 5 cm. high and are located *ca.* 1.2 cm. from the upper edge of the face, 1.7 cm. from the lower edge. On the top there is a raised (*ca.* 3 mm.) margin around the edges at the front and side. This margin, which has rounded edges, is about 3.5 cm. wide; the surface within the border is polished, as is the margin itself. The relatively small preserved area of the bottom (maximum of 5.5 cm. wide along the side) is chiseled even. At about 11 cm. from the face there is an offset of some 5 mm. in it; 4 cm. from the face and 3.8 cm. from the side is the end of a rec-

tangular mortise 2.5 cm. deep and 3.3 cm. from front to rear. White marble. 7.7 cm. by 12.2 cm. by 17.8 cm.

TC 1356

Rough fragment from the right front corner of a block of stone inscribed on the front edge. The one-line inscription, as preserved, reads '*lt̲'*[. The letters, nearly 5 cm. high, run from the top to the bottom of the face. The top of the block is badly damaged, but there are indications of a raised border along the front and right side; this border was *ca.* 1 cm. wide at the front, 3 cm. wide at the side. The right side of the block is chiseled even. The bottom is flat, but very rough. Porous calcite. 5.7 cm. by 13.6 cm. by 11 cm.

TC 1357

Fragment from the upper left corner of a stone plaque inscribed across the top of the smooth face. The part of the one-line inscription preserved reads]*ṣṣ*/; the crudely incised characters are 2.5 cm. high. The top of the piece is square with the face and is generally even. The left side is rough and somewhat rounded. The back is smooth. White marble. 11.3 cm. by 8 cm. by 4 cm.

TC 1375

Triangular fragment from a large stone slab inscribed on the smooth face. At the upper point of the fragment is the lower tip of a vertical stroke of one character. Part of a line of inscription below this, running left to right, reads].*tbn*.[; the letters are 7.8 cm. high. Limestone. 16.5 cm. by 15.5 cm. by 7.8 cm.

TC 1379 (Plate 101)

Fragment from the lower right corner of a stone object, inscribed on the top and the front edge. On the top are the letters *dm*[; on the front are the letters *bhy*[. The third letter on the front may possibly be *t̲*, as it is damaged at the bottom. The surfaces of the top and front were both originally polished smooth, but they are now badly chipped. In the top there is the corner of a mortise 2.6 cm. deep; this is 2.6 cm. from the front and 2.9 cm. from the side. The side and back both are rough with tool marks. Alabaster with a rusty tint. 6 cm. by 7 cm. by 6.8 cm.

TC 1388 (Plate 102)

Rectangular block of stone inscribed on the face. The parts of the three lines of inscription preserved read (1)]. .*y'm/bn*[(2)]'*z/d̲rdm/k*[(3)]'*nby/b*.[; the characters are about 4 cm. high. The *d* in line two was made over an *m*. The top, sides and bottom of the block have all been chiseled to some extent; they all slant in slightly toward the rear. The back is irregular. Limestone. 13.8 cm. by 19.4 cm. by 6.8 cm.

TC 1395 (Plate 105)

Fragment from the upper part of a stone block inscribed on the polished face. The parts of the four lines of inscription preserved read (1)].*nsww.* .[(2)].*by/šym*[(3)]/*wb̲d̲*.[(4)].*qtbn*[; the letters are *ca.* 2.3 cm. high. A very small bit of the polished top of the block is preserved, and this indicates that our line one is the first of the inscription. Nearly 5 cm. from the face is the lower tip of a narrow mortise which was *ca.* 2.4 cm. deep, suggesting that this is a fragment of the inscribed base for a statuette. Mottled alabaster. 12.3 cm. by 8.5 cm. by 7.4 cm.

TC 1396 (Plate 105)

Block of stone, roughly rectangular with rounded corners, inscribed on two adjacent sides. On the top is the letter ' and on the front the letter *r*; the diameter of the former is 1.5 cm., the height of the latter 5 cm. Limestone. 6.7 cm. by 9 cm. by 6.8 cm.

TC 1402

Fragment from the upper edge of a stone slab inscribed on the face. The preserved part of the first line of the inscription reads]*mh*.[; the third letter is either *y* or *t̲*, but only part of the upper circle is preserved. None of the letters is preserved fully. Along the upper edge of the face is a raised (*ca.* 3 mm.) margin some 5 cm. wide; the inscription is on the flat surface immediately below this border. The top of the piece has been chiseled even; on the break at the left is a mortise or cutting of some kind *ca.* 2.7 cm. deep and 2 cm. behind the face. Sandstone. 12.7 cm. by 11.5 cm. by 6.1 cm.

TC 1447

Fragment from the lower part of a stone object inscribed on the front edge. The preserved part of the one-line inscription reads]/*bn*/‘*m*[; the characters are 2.3 cm. high. This fragment appears to be from some kind of a plaque (2.8 cm. thick) with a lower margin 3.1 cm. high extending out 4.8 cm. from its face. This deep margin is polished on the top and front, and it is on the front edge that the inscription is found. The bottom of the piece is rather rough, but it has been chiseled along the front. The small section of the back of the plaque which is preserved is rough with tool marks. White alabaster, burned on the front edge and part of the top of the high margin. 4.2 cm. by 7.6 cm. by 7.2 cm.

TC 1508

Fragment from the right edge of a stone block inscribed on the face. The parts of the two lines of inscription preserved read (1) *brm*[(2) .*r*/*d*[; none of the letters is preserved fully. The face and the right side are both smooth, and the corner between them is rounded, though now badly chipped. 10.1 cm. by 8.3 cm. by 5 cm.

TC 1578

Fragment from the lower edge of a stone block inscribed on the smooth face. The parts of the two lines of inscription preserved read (1)].*t*.[(2)]*dt*[; only the lower tips of three characters in the upper line are preserved. The letters of the bottom line, 5.4 cm. high, are slightly more than 5 cm. apart, though those of the line above are very close together. The bottom is chiseled even in a band *ca.* 2.5 cm. wide along the front edge; this band is raised *ca.* 6 mm. above the surface behind it (the possibility exists that this is actually the top.) Hard stone. 10.9 cm. by 14.7 cm. by 6.3 cm.

TC 1620 (Plate 105)

Stone block inscribed on the porous face. The parts of the two lines of inscription preserved read (1)]*m‘dkrb*/*bn*/*nbṭ*‘[(2)].*n*/*by.*“*b*/*ygl*[; the characters of the upper line are nearly 6 cm. high. Those of the lower line are not fully preserved at the bottom, where they apparently ran onto another stone. The top and sides of the block are chiseled even, and they slant in toward the rear. The bottom is now badly battered, but

it also appears to have been chiseled. The back is irregular. Porous calcite. 11.6 cm. by 30.5 cm. by 7.5 cm.

TC 1644

Fragment from the front edge of a flat stone. The preserved part of the one-line inscription reads]*hl*/*dt*/[. The porous surface of the face had been covered with reddening before the inscription was cut. The top is square with the face and is even. Porous calcite. 4.8 cm. by 10 cm. by 7.2 cm.

TC 1649

Fragment from upper right corner of a stone block with a raised inscription on the face. The part of the one line of inscription preserved reads ’*lw*.[; the characters are *ca.* 2.3 cm. high. The small part of the top and side of the stone preserved are polished smooth. Alabaster. 3.1 cm. by 5.1 cm. by 2.6 cm.

TC 1730

Inscribed fragment from the face of a stone block or slab. The parts of the two lines of inscription preserved read (1)].*m*[(2)]*qḥl*[; the letters of line two are 3.5 cm. high. Only the lower tips of those in line one are preserved; the lines are *ca.* 5 mm. apart, and below line two is a blank space of almost 3 cm. preserved on the fragment. No original surface other than the polished face is preserved. Light colored alabaster with a red streak through the center. 10.8 cm. by 8.6 cm. by 4.7 cm.

TC 1748 (Plate 102)

Rectangular block of stone inscribed on the face. The two lines of crudely incised inscription across the lower part of the face read (1) *yṭ‘t*/*msk*/*fyšmġ* (2) *rbm*. The characters of line one become smaller and more closely spaced toward the end of the line, and those of line two are small and crowded into a narrow space in the center below line one. The origin of this inscription is somewhat dubious, especially in view of the missing word divider before the last letter of the first line. The top, bottom, and sides of the block are chiseled roughly even, and they slant in toward the rear. The back is irregular, and there is a letter *ḥ* incised on it. White marble with a blue banding across the back. 10.1 cm. by 18.4 cm. by 3.5 cm.

TC 1778 (Plate 104)

Very large block of stone, inscribed on two adjacent faces. See *JaPEHA*, pp. 185–89, §343. Four lines of inscription appear on each of these faces, and the common corner between them is at the bottom of each inscription. The texts are nearly identical. The text on side A reads (1) 'šhrm/bnlḥyn/wškrm/bn/ 'm'ly/wš'bm/bn/nbṭ'l[y or /] (2) ḏtwġr[b]m/ 'syw / ẓrbw / bnyw / qrbsm /nfsm / wmśwds/ wnfshy (3) w/glm/bḫg/ 'nby/w'l/t'ly/wkwn/ l'šhrm/bn/ḏt/qbrn/ (4) wmśwds/wnfshsyw/ šltt/ 'ḳmsm/ wl/ škrm/ wš'bm/ṯnw/ ḳmsmyw. The very top of the last character of the first line is chipped, but there does not appear to be space enough for the circle of the expected *y*. After the fourth letter of line two there is a circular hole which was cut into the stone after the inscription was incised, and only the lower tips of the three letters *rbm* are preserved. Although the *k* in line one is normal for a right-to-left inscription, the occurrences in lines three and four are reversed.

The text on side B reads (1) 'šhrm[/bn/] lḥyn/wškrm/bn/ 'm'ly/wš'bm/bn/nbṭ'ly/ḏtw (2) ġrbm / 'syw / ẓrbw / bnyw / qbrsm / nfsm / wmśwds/wnfshsyw/glm / (3) bḫg / 'nby / w'l/ t'ly / wkwn/l'šrm/bn/ḏt/qbrn/wmśwds / wnf (4) shsyw / šltt /' ḳmsm / wl/škrm/wš'bm/ṯnw/ ḳmsmyw/wḥrmt. After the fourth letter of line one there is a circular hole cut into the inscription that leaves only the lower end of the *m* and none of the following four characters intact. The word divider at the end of line two, omitted in *JaPEHA*, is entirely clear, though it is at the edge of a chipped area. The first word divider in line three was originally *m*, a word divider occupied part of the place where the ' is, and the letter ' overlapped with the present *n*. The engraver then apparently realized his error and tried to obliterate all of the *m* except the vertical and the other three incorrect characters, but they are still visible in the background of the present characters.

The characters of side A vary in height between 4.5 cm. (lowest line) to nearly 6 cm. (first line); those of side B are *ca.* 3.5 cm. high. *JaPEHA* (p. 189) considers text B as a defective copy of text A, but this may be doubted, especially because of the extra word at the end of text B. It may be noted in this connection that the second *s* in the last word of line two of text A is omitted on the stone, though included in the transliteration in *JaPEHA* (p. 185). It is true that inscription B was engraved after the lower center had been chipped, but the circular cuttings on both sides were made after the inscriptions had been engraved. In any case, the addition of the inscription on face A represents a re-use of the stone, for the paneling (see below) was not designed to receive it.

The circular hole at the upper right of side A is located 5.5 cm. from the upper edge and 8 cm. from the right side of the face. This cutting has a diameter of 6 cm. to 6.5 cm. (it is not a perfect circle) and a depth of 5 cm. The interior, covered with tool marks, is rounded somewhat where the walls meet the bottom. A panel measuring 10.5 cm. by 72 cm. and recessed *ca.* 6 mm. runs along the bottom of this side, equidistant from either end of the block; the walls of this panel are beveled. The first two lines of the inscription are above this panel, and the characters of these lines were made high enough to fill the space. The lower two lines of the inscription run across the areas at the sides of the panel and on the panel. At the beginning of each of these two lines three letters are on the higher surface and at the end only two are. There is a large chipped area along the upper edge of the face at the right extending some 18 cm. to the left from the corner.

Side B of the block is flat; it has a circular hole 8.5 cm. from the right edge (i.e., at the opposite end of the block from the hole on side A) and this hole is partly exposed at the top. This cutting is *ca.* 6.5 cm. in diameter and *ca.* 5 cm. deep; the bottom of it is now filled with plaster to a depth of about 1.5 cm. to 2 cm. The face is chipped between this hole and the upper corner. The side of the block at the top of side A slants in rather markedly toward the rear, and it is rough with large short tool marks. The side extending back from the top of side B is square with that face. There are raised members at either end flush with the face and the ends of the block (cf. a similar member on one end of TC 1045, above). These protrusions are 4 cm. higher than the area between them. The one at the left is 13.5 cm. wide and is chiseled square on the inner side (i.e., at the offset). The one on the right has a maximum width of *ca.* 12 cm., but is narrower (*ca.* 9.5 cm.) at the face due to interference from the circular hole. A band *ca.* 2.5 cm. wide is chiseled even along the front edge of this entire side of the stone, and in addition the protruding member on the left has such a band at each side; the surface is otherwise rough with tool marks. Limestone. Length, 84 cm.; width on side A, 24.5 cm.; width on side B, 21 cm.

TC 1780 (Plate 101)

Fragment from the right part of a stone block inscribed on the face. The preserved parts of two lines of inscription read (1)]*m*/ *bn*/ (2)].*wrw'*[. Line two runs left to right; the *r* in line two, the only long character fully preserved, is 6.5 cm. high. The top of the block, preserved only in a very small area, is chiseled even. The bottom has been very roughly chiseled even. The right side is straight and vertical, but rough. The back is irregular. Limestone. 16.4 cm. by 13.6 cm. by 7.3 cm.

TC 1824 (Plate 103)

Fragment from the front edge of a stone slab forming a tabletop, inscribed on the polished face. The part preserved of the one-line of inscription reads]*fss*/*w'dns*/*wbnts*/*skyn*[; see *JaPEHA*, p. 190, §345. The characters, with heavy guidelines at the top and bottom, are 3.1 cm. high; the line of inscription is 1.4 cm. from the top of the piece, and there is a blank space of 2.1 cm. below. On the top, there is a raised margin along the front edge. This is a maximum of 6 mm. higher than the flat polished surface behind it and is *ca.* 2.5 cm. wide at the flat top (the inner edge is beveled). The edges are rounded, and all surfaces of the margin are polished. The bottom of the fragment is roughly chiseled even along the front in a band varying in width from 6.5 cm. to nearly 8 cm. Behind this there is a rough irregular protrusion in the small area preserved. The left side of the piece has also been partly chiseled even, especially toward the top. This side slants in somewhat toward the bottom edge, where it is badly chipped. At 6.6 cm. from the face there is a vertical offset of nearly 5 mm., as though to fit against

another stone with a protruding offset at this point. Mottled alabaster with a dark brown banding at the rear break. 6.6 cm. by 26 cm. by 10.5 cm.

TC 1825 (Plate 105)

Upper left corner of a stone block inscribed on the polished face. The ends of two lines of inscription are preserved, and these read (1)]*kwkbm*/*wšhr*/*wdt*/*mly* (2)]*rf'm*/*sqnyt*/ *'nby*/*šy*; see *JaPEHA*, pp. 190f., §346. At the lower edge of the fragment near the right side is the trace of the upper circle of a letter in a third line of inscription. The characters are 3.3 cm. high. Line one is 3 cm. from the upper edge of the face, and both lines end 5.3 cm. from the left edge. The polished left side of the stone is square with the face, which it meets in a rounded corner. The top, which has been chiseled even along the front and left side but otherwise left rough, slants down toward the rear. At the left end, the back is trimmed off flat for a distance of some 8 cm. from the side, giving the stone a thickness of 5.1 cm. at this side. The surface of this part of the back has large horizontal tool marks, except along the edge where it has been chiseled even; the remainder of the back is irregular and much higher. Alabaster, white at the front with darker banding across the back. 11 cm. by 24.5 cm. by 8.9 cm.

TC 1874 (Plate 103)

Fragment from the front and right corner of some kind of stone trough, inscribed crudely on the chiseled face of one side. The preserved parts of the two-line inscription read (1) *mqf*/.[(2) '/*dt*/*'šy*[; the letters vary in height between 3 cm. and 4 cm. The interior of the vessel, with a flat bottom, vertical sides and rounded corners, is 6 cm. deep. The bottom is 3.3 cm. thick, the walls 3 cm. The top of the front wall is roughly chiseled flat; the bottom of the piece is uneven. At the right side of it is a crude cutting 1.8 cm. deep, 3 cm. wide and 5.5 cm. from front to rear. Another crude cutting is at the break on the left; it is 2.8 cm. deep, but smaller. Limestone. 9.5 cm. by 18 cm. by 8 cm.

TC 1983

Small fragment from the lower edge of a stone object inscribed on the polished face.

The part of the one line of inscription preserved reads]/ġrbm[; the letters were *ca.* 2.5 cm. in height, but are not now fully preserved. The bottom of the fragment is chiseled even. White alabaster. 3 cm. by 6.7 cm. by 2.1 cm.

TC 1993

Fragment from the upper left corner of a stone object inscribed on the flat face. The parts of the two lines of inscription preserved read (1)]n't (2)].m; the characters are 2.7 cm. high. Guidelines appear at the top, center, and bottom of each line. The top of the piece was smooth. The left side was roughly chiseled even. Hard stone. 7.3 cm. by 8.5 cm. by 2.5 cm.

TC 2114 (Plate 105)

Large block of stone, broken at the left end. The preserved parts of three lines of inscription on the face read (1) r[']b['t̲]t/bn/ 'lwkl/d̲[d]ḥsm/'s (2) hw / m[ḫ]rm / wmś́wds/ wnfshsyw/g[(3) 'l/t'ly/; see *JaPEHA*, pp. 189f., §344. Part of the first word has been obliterated by chiseling in a circular area which extends down into the upper part of line two. Other letters in the first line and one in the second line have been damaged in the same way. Line three begins 28 cm. from the right end of the block, perhaps to center it on the panel; the characters are 5.5 cm. high. Along the lower edge of the face, coming within 4 cm. of the right edge, is a panel recessed *ca.* 8 mm. This panel measures slightly less than 8 cm. from top to bottom; the third line of the inscription is in the panel, the other two are above it.

The top of the block is rough; it has been chiseled along the front in a band of irregular width (3 cm. to 8 cm.). The right end of the block is partly chiseled, partly rough. The bottom, square with the face, is chiseled even at the front, but left rough toward the rear; *ca.* 14 cm. from the right edge is an offset of *ca.* 1 cm. The surface to the right of this is recessed in comparison with the rest of the bottom. The back of the block is rather irregular. The break at the left exposes the right side of a cutting open on the back and bottom; this cutting is 4 cm. from the face and 12.5 cm. from the top. The flat, vertical side of it, covered with tool marks, slants to the right toward the rear; its presence may account for the stone's breaking at this point. Limestone. 24.8 cm. by 60 cm. by 18.5 cm.

TC 2120

Battered fragment from a large stone inscribed on the face. The parts of the two lines of inscription preserved read (1)]š́w[(2)]m/h[. The upper line runs from left to right, the lower one from right to left; none of the characters is preserved to full height, but it is estimated at about 7.5 cm. Limestone. 17.5 cm. by 7.5 cm. by 6.4 cm.

TC 2160 (Plate 105)

Fragment from the upper edge of a large stone slab decorated with a double border and inscribed on the polished face. The part of one line of inscription which is preserved reads].mkrb/qtbn/[; the characters are 3.4 cm. high. The upper tips, unidentifiable, of two letters in a second line of inscription are preserved. The first line of the inscription is 1.3 cm. below the margin, and the second line is separated from the first by a space of *ca.* 6 mm. The uppermost margin is 4 cm. wide and is raised *ca.* 5 mm. above the face of the broad margin below, which it meets in a square offset. The second margin is 7.2 cm. wide and is raised nearly 7 mm. above the face in which the inscription is engraved. The offset here is very slightly beveled, and the face of the second margin slants in slightly toward the top. Both margins are polished smooth, and their lower edges are rounded off smoothly. The top of the fragment is roughly chiseled in a band 3 cm. to 4 cm. wide along the front; farther back it is rough and irregular. The back is partly rough with very large tool marks, partly taken up with an exposed natural banding. White alabaster with a few rusty colored streaks, as well as the dark banding over part of the back. 17.5 cm. by 21.8 cm. by 7.1 cm.

TC 2501 (Plate 103)

Large stone block inscribed on the face. The parts of the two lines of inscription preserved read (1)].rṣfm/[b]yt/.[(2)]t/wḥḍrmt/ wb[; line one runs right to left, line two left to right. None of the characters is preserved to full height, but it is estimated to have been 7.5 cm. or slightly more. The smooth face is damaged at the upper right, and the last letters of line two at this side appear to have been chiseled away. The top is rough with pick marks, and it slopes gently from the left down toward the right. This surface indicates a re-use, as the inscription was cut into irregularly when the surface was reworked.

The right end of the block is square with the face and bottom, and it has been chiseled over all of its surface. The left end was partly chiseled, but is rough toward the rear; the lower rear corner has been broken off. The bottom was chiseled even very carefully along the front edge and along the right end but is elsewhere somewhat rough; this pattern perhaps suggests that this stone was used at a corner at one time. The back is somewhat irregular except for *ca.* 8 cm. at the right end where it has been carefully chiseled even; the block is a little more than 1.5 cm. narrower at this end than near the other. Limestone. 15.2 cm. by 41.4 cm. by 21 cm.

TC 2508 (Plate 103)

The left part of a stone block inscribed on the face. The parts preserved of the three lines of inscription read (1)]..fṣ (2)]rm/br (3)]fm; the characters are *ca.* 2.5 cm. high. The two letters of the lowest line are more widely spaced than those in the other lines. The face of the block was polished smooth, but it is now badly chipped at the edges and has numerous scratches. The top was also polished. The left side and bottom have been chiseled and superficially polished, but are still rough, and some tool marks are visible on them. The back is rough with tool marks. Alabaster, light in color except for the dark brown banding exposed across the back. 9.2 cm. by 8.3 cm. by 5.4 cm.

TC 2510

Rectangular stone block inscribed on the face. The part of the one line of inscription which is present reads]ntm[; the letters are *ca.* 8.7 cm. high. The face, which had been chiseled even, is quite weathered. The top, bottom, and sides of the block were all chiseled rather even; they slant in slightly toward

the rear. The back is entirely irregular. Conglomerate, in limestone matrix. 15.9 cm. by 13.3 cm. by 5.3 cm.

TC 2511 (Plate 103)

Flat slab of stone inscribed on the front edge. The one-line inscription reads ʾlsʿd/ḏ ḥḏrn; see *JaPEHA*, p. 219, §383. The inscription begins 6.8 cm. from the right end of the stone and ends 6.1 cm. from the left end. The smooth face had been covered with reddening before the engraving was done. The top of the slab has been chiseled over all of its surface, but there are still many pits and blemishes in it. The edges, especially at the left end, are irregular; bits of plaster adhere in some of the pits and at the edges. The bottom is a completely finished face, smooth in every part. The edges of this face are all straight and carefully finished. The stone must have been used in such a position that only the front and bottom were visible to the viewer. The ends and back of the slab, except for the chiseling along the bottom edges, are irregular; plaster still adheres to much of the back edge. Fossiliferous limestone. The slab was broken through the center (front to rear), but the two parts have now been rejoined. 4.5 cm. by 33 cm. by 20.2 cm.

TC 2529 (Plate 105)

Fragment from the left edge of a stone slab decorated with a double-stepped margin and inscribed on the polished face within the border. The parts of the two lines of inscription preserved read (1)].rw/ʿm (2)].l/t; the characters were *ca.* 4.5 cm. high. The lines of inscription are separated by a space of 6 mm. The outer raised margin is 3.8 cm. wide and is raised 1 cm. above the face of the second margin. The second margin is 4.1 cm. wide and is raised 1.1 cm. above the face of the panel into which the inscription is engraved. Both steps of the double margin are polished smooth. The left side of the piece is chiseled even in a band *ca.* 2.5 cm. wide along the front but is otherwise rough with tool marks. The back is very rough with extremely large tool marks. White alabaster. 13 cm. by 14.4 cm. by 6.5 cm.

XXII

STONE HOUSINGS FOR MEMORIAL OBJECTS

Some ten stone housings for memorial objects or fragments of them were discovered during the second campaign in the Timnaʻ Cemetery.[1] These housings are in the form of a box stood on end and are sometimes inscribed with a formula beginning with the word *mqf*. Some of these housings were made from a single piece of stone, but others were made with separate flat slabs forming the top, bottom, sides, and rear. The inscription is most frequently on the front edge of the upper end. As most of them were found empty, as well as broken, the exact range of memorial objects which were placed in them remains uncertain. One of them (TC 1881) has the damaged base for a memorial plaque (whether for a plain plaque or one bearing a relief cannot be determined) preserved in place. If the large stone blocks with sculptured human heads placed in niches from Marib[2] can be adduced as parallels, we may assume that these housings also sometimes contained sculptured heads. Some of the fragments and parts preserved in our present collection also indicate that there were doors on the fronts of these housings and that these doors could at least in some cases be opened and closed.

TC 1238 (Plate 105)

Fragment from the right end of a stone which formed the top of the housing for a memorial object (cf. TC 1530, below). The preserved part of the one-line inscription on the face reads *tśwt*/[; the characters are *ca.* 3

cm. high. The surface of the face around the incised characters is tinted with reddening; the face is damaged along the upper edge and at the right. The bottom of the stone appears to have been flat. Coming within *ca.* 3.5 cm. of the right side is a cutting 4 cm. wide (front to rear) and 1.7 cm. deep along the front of the bottom. The back of this cutting served as the door stop for the putative door. A squarish hole some 3 cm. deep, 3 cm. wide, and 2.6 cm. from front to rear in the rear corner of the cutting formed the door socket for the right leaf of the door. The right side of the piece, now badly battered, was chiseled square with the face and bottom. The top is now irregular, as is the back. Near the rear of the break on the left a hollow, *ca.* 4 cm. in diameter and *ca.* 2 cm. deep, has been hollowed out; its purpose remains obscure. Porous calcite. 9 cm. by 11.5 cm. by 14 cm.

TC 1530 (Plate 106)

Inscribed stone block which formed the top of the housing for a memorial object. The one-line inscription across the front reads *mʻdrdm nʻmn*; see *JaPEHA*, pp. 214f., §375. The two parts of the inscription are separated by a cutting 3.2 cm. wide which is described below; the characters are 4.7 cm. high. Both the left and right ends of the face are raised in relation to the center section. The raised area at the right, bearing the first three letters of the inscription, is slightly less than 7 cm. wide. That at the left, bearing the final letter of the inscription, is slightly more than 7 cm. wide. The offset between the end panels and the center section is about 4 mm. deep. The surface of the face, which exhibits chisel marks running in various directions, has heavy traces of reddening.

[1] Professor A. M. Honeyman, who earlier recognized the significance of these housings, is planning to publish a more detailed study of them.
[2] See, for example, the photograph in Wendell Phillips, *Qataban and Sheba*, p. 239, below (opposite page 224, above, in the London edition).

168

In the center of the face is a cutting, open at the top, which is *ca.* 3.2 cm. wide, 3.4 cm. deep, and 4.5 cm. high at the front. In the lower rear it is cut through to the bottom of the stone in an area measuring *ca.* 1.7 cm. from front to rear, leaving a bridge 1.5 cm. thick at the face; this cutting was apparently designed to hold a sliding pin which locked the doors below shut. The top of the piece is very rough with large tool marks. The front edge along the top of the recessed center section of the face has been chiseled even on a plane a little lower than the rest of the top so that there are offsets at either side of this section in line with the offsets on the face.

The bottom of the stone is chiseled and superficially polished quite even. At the front is a recess 2.5 cm. deep, nearly 26 cm. from side to side, and 5.3 cm. from front to rear (maximum). In the rear corner of each end is a circular hole with a diameter of roughly 3.5 cm. and a depth of more than 2 cm. (measured from the bottom of the recessed area). These holes were sockets for the doors of the housing, and the offset at the rear of the recess served as a door stop. The ends of the block are roughly chiseled even. The back is rough but has been chiseled in places. Limestone. 10.3 cm. by 33.2 cm. by 21.5 cm.

TC 1532 (Plate 106)
Flat stone, inscribed on the front edge, which may have formed the top of the housing for a memorial object. The one-line inscription reads *mqf/l[ẖ]yʿm/nʿmn*; see *Ja-PEHA*, pp. 206f., §363. The characters are *ca.* 4 cm. high, filling the entire height of the face on which they are inscribed; traces of reddening are visible on the surface of the face around the inscription. The top of the piece has been chiseled roughly even in a band about 7.5 cm. wide along the front; farther back, the top is very rough. The vertical ends of the slab are chiseled even, and they are square with the face. The bottom is chiseled even overall. The back, broken away in the right part, was chiseled even; it slants in toward the top.

There are several cuttings in the stone; 12 cm. from the left end and 1 cm. from the upper edge, a circular hole with a diameter of *ca.* 8 mm. is drilled straight into the face. This hole continues back until it opens into

a rectangular cutting 4.2 cm. from the face which goes completely through the stone. This cutting measures 3.5 cm. from left to right and 1.3 cm. from front to rear. A similar cutting in the center of the stone and about 2 cm. behind the face has been filled with plaster; a small circular hole also leads from the face to it. Another square hole in the top 1 cm. from the face and 4.2 cm. from the right end is partly filled with plaster. Porous calcite. 4.3 cm. by 37.5 cm. by 15 cm.

TC 1607 (Plate 106)
Left part of a stone block which formed the top of the housing for a memorial object. Part of a one-line inscription is preserved on the front face, and this reads *]wkn/y.[*. The face is 4 cm. from top to bottom, and the rather crude characters nearly fill this space. The bottom of the stone is flat. Along the front edge is a cut 3 cm. wide and 2.5 cm. deep which comes within *ca.* 3 cm. of the left side of the stone. This cut or recess was designed to serve as the door stop for the door which would have closed the housing on the front. No socket for the door is preserved, but it may be presumed to have been on the right part of the piece, which is missing.

Slightly more than 1 cm. from the left edge, a rectangular hole 1.5 cm. from side to side, 3 cm. from front to rear, and 3.5 cm. deep has been cut. This hole is some 10 cm. from the front of the stone, and its purpose is not clear, though it may have served as a means of attaching the top to the rest of the housing. The top of the block is rough, but flat; 1 cm. behind the face and 4.5 cm. from the left side is a circular hole (diameter *ca.* 1.7 cm.) which is some 2 cm. deep. The surface between it and the corner is damaged. At the corner a notch has been cut out of the stone; this is slightly more than 4 cm. from front to rear, 2.5 cm. wide, and 3 cm. deep. The left side and back of the block are fairly even. Porous calcite. 6.5 cm. by 19.7 cm. by 23 cm.

TC 1613 (Plate 107)
Inscribed stone housing for a memorial object. The one-line inscription across the front of the upper end reads *yṣrʿm[ ]ẖn*; see *Ja-PEHA*, p. 219, §382. The characters average *ca.* 4.8 cm. high; the lacuna in the text results from a damaged section which has been filled

with mortar. The hollowed-out interior of the housing has a maximum width of nearly 15 cm., a height of some 37 cm., and a depth of *ca.* 10 cm. The lower end is 8.5 cm. thick, the upper end *ca.* 7 cm. at the center, the right side nearly 3 cm., and the left side *ca.* 3.5 cm. Most of the interior is somewhat rough. A band 3 cm. wide along the front edge of the interior surface of the lower end is fairly smooth. At the left end of this smooth band is a shallow (*ca.* 8 mm.) circular (diameter *ca.* 3 cm.) depression which appears to have been a door socket.

At the upper left rear corner of the interior of the housing is a large hole going completely through the upper end. This hole has a maximum width of *ca.* 4.5 cm. and is *ca.* 4 cm. from front to rear. The front of the hole is formed by a mass of mortar, as the stone of the upper end is missing at this side. On the exterior of this box-like housing, the sides are roughly evened. The bottom is fairly even in the front part, slanting up toward the rear, but the rear part is irregular and slants up toward the rear at a sharper angle. The top is similar to the bottom. The back is irregular. Porous calcite. 53 cm. by 20.5 cm. by 18 cm.

TC 1747 (Plate 107)

Flat stone block, inscribed, which formed the top of the housing for a memorial object. The one-line inscription on the front edge reads *škrm/ʿtbm/*; see *JaPEHA*, pp. 215f., §376. The characters vary between 2.5 cm. and 3 cm. in height; the face into which they are cut was chiseled even. The bottom of the piece is generally flat and rough. At the front edge is a recessed area, rectangular in shape, which measures 14 cm. from side to side, 4.7 cm. from front to rear, and *ca.* 1.1 cm. in depth; the interior of this recess is chiseled even. In the right rear corner of it is a hole, approximately square (1.7 cm.), which is partly filled with very coarse mortar. This hole appears to have been intended as a door socket. In the center of the recess, 1.6 cm. behind the face of the stone, is a rectangular hole, 1.5 cm. from front to rear and 2.3 cm. wide, which goes through the stone to the top. This hole appears to have received a sliding pin to hold the door below shut. The ends of the block are square with the face, but are not entirely regular. The top is gen-

erally flat, but has some irregularities at the right and rear. Limestone. 5.7 cm. by 22.5 cm. by 16.2 cm.

TC 1785 (Plate 106)

Inscribed stone, broken at the right, which formed the top of the housing for a memorial object. The one line of inscription which runs across the polished front edge reads]ʿkrb/*ḏǧrbm*/; see *JaPEHA*, p. 216, §377. The characters have a height of *ca.* 2.2 cm. The top is very roughly tooled even in a strip *ca.* 7 cm. wide along the front; the rear part of the top protrudes irregularly. The left end of the stone has been chiseled even; it is square with the bottom and with the front. The surface of the flat bottom is chiseled fairly even; at the front, coming within 3.6 cm. of the left end of the stone, is a recessed area 3.6 cm. wide and 1.4 cm. deep. At the left rear corner of this recess is a hole, roughly circular with a diameter of *ca.* 2 cm., which goes through to the top of the stone. About 5 mm. behind the recess and 10.2 cm. from the left end of the stone is another hole, this one nearly rectangular and measuring 2.8 cm. from side to side and *ca.* 2.6 cm. from front to rear. It also goes completely through the stone; it slants to the rear toward the top slightly, and on the top is 4.4 cm. from the front of the stone. The back edge of the stone is somewhat irregular, and it slants in toward the bottom. Gray alabaster of poor quality. 6.5 cm. by 21 cm. by 18 cm.

TC 1823 (Plate 107)

Fragment from the lower right corner of a block of stone which formed the top of the housing for a memorial object, inscribed on the face. The preserved part of the one-line inscription reads *mqf*[; the characters are 4.5 cm. high and widely spaced. Above the register into which the inscription is cut is the lower end of a recessed (*ca.* 2.5 mm.) panel some 4 cm. wide with an intermediate margin at each side (comparable to those on TC 1045, above). The right side of the fragment is chiseled even, and it has a slightly recessed margin slightly less than 1 cm. wide at the front and lower edges. The bottom is also even. The fragment has a square cutting 4 cm. from the right side. This cutting is squared, and it is 2.5 cm. from the line of the bottom of the fragment to the top, 3.9 cm. deep. In the roof of this cutting, coming within 1.7 cm. of the face, is another cutting which extends at least 3.2 cm. up into the stone. It is flush at the right and back with the squared cutting below, but as the break runs through it, little more can be said about it. These cuttings probably indicate that this fragment belonged to the small-scale representation of a lintel with door stop and socket. Porous calcite. 10 cm. by 8.6 cm. by 9.6 cm.

TC 1844 (Plate 107)

Fragment from the front of a flat slab of stone which formed the top of the housing for a memorial object. The preserved part of a one-line inscription on the front edge reads *m]qf/lḥy.[*. The letters are rather crude, and the face on which they appear is chiseled even. The flat top of the stone is rough, though it has been chiseled along the front. Most of the surface of the bottom has been chiseled superficially. Near the break on the right and *ca.* 8 mm. behind the face is an oval hole running through the stone from top to bottom. It measures 2 cm. from front to rear and is 2.5 cm. wide. Limestone. 2.6 cm. by 13.2 cm. by 11.5 cm.

TC 1881 (Plate 107)

Large inscribed stone housing for a memorial object, broken into two parts horizontally. The one-line inscription across the front of the upper end reads *mqf/yṣr'm/ dg̱rbm*; see *JaPEHA*, pp. 208f., §366. The characters, bounded at top and bottom by guidelines, are 4.9 cm. high; the face into which they are cut is fairly smooth, but not entirely even. The hollowed-out interior of the housing measures *ca.* 21 cm. wide, 56 cm. high, and 16 cm. deep. At the top, bottom, and sides there is a recessed margin *ca.* 4 cm. wide along the front edge. At the top and bottom, the offset at the inner edge of this margin is roughly square and is *ca.* 1 cm. deep; on the left side the offset is not so distinct and is not so deep.

The offsets at the top and bottom functioned as door stops for the single-leafed door (not extant) for which there is a socket at the upper right. This door socket, in line with the offset, has a diameter of about 3 cm. and goes completely through the upper end of the housing. There is also a smaller hole bored through the upper end in the rear center; the inner end of this hole is flush with the back of the interior of the housing, and the hole slants back toward the rear. Packed in mortar at the bottom of the interior of the housing is a stele base, damaged at the top (the original surface of the top of it is preserved only in a small area at the right side).

The base is of the type with three horizontal, successively recessed bands across the front and around the sides (cf. TC 1568, above). The central band on the face, 2.5 cm. wide, bears the inscription *dg̱rbm*, and the upper band presumably bore the name *yṣr'm* as at the top of the housing. A mortise, *ca.* 1.7 cm. behind the face of the base, is partly preserved; it measures *ca.* 12.3 cm. from side to side and 2.7 cm. from front to rear. It was *ca.* 3 cm. deep, and most of the bottom of it is covered with the mortar which held some sort of plaque in place. The base, made of gray alabaster with rusty-brown streaks, measures at least 7.5 cm. high (the bottom is buried in mortar) by 16.5 cm. by 8.5 cm. The left side of the housing is 2.8 cm. thick at the even face, the lower end is 5.5 cm. thick, the upper end is 6 cm. thick, and the right side is not preserved at the face. The outer surfaces of the housing, except for the front, are all rough. Limestone. 66.5 cm. by 27 cm. by 23.5 cm.

Plates

TC 539

Plate 1

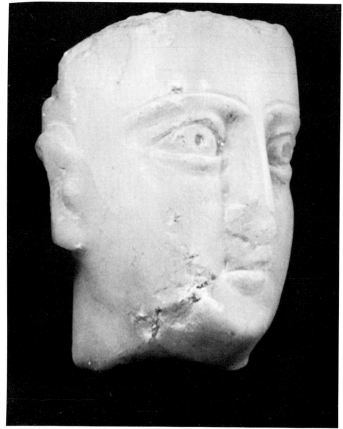

TC 539

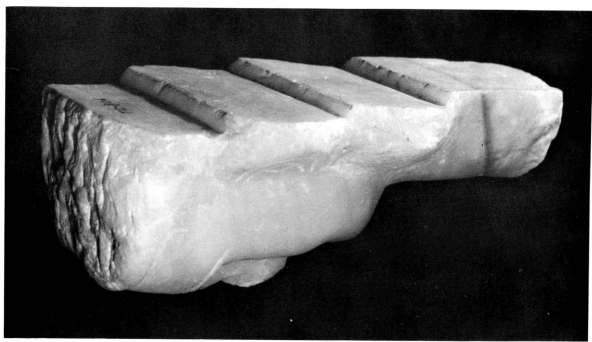

TC 806

PLATE 2

TC 806

PLATE 3

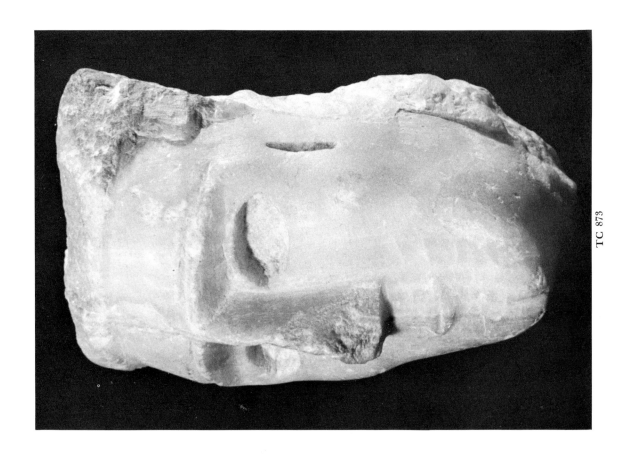

TC 873

TC 873

PLATE 4

TC 1230

PLATE 5

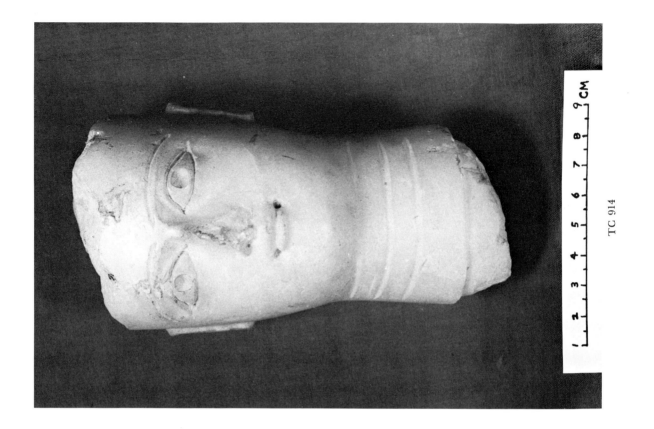

TC 914

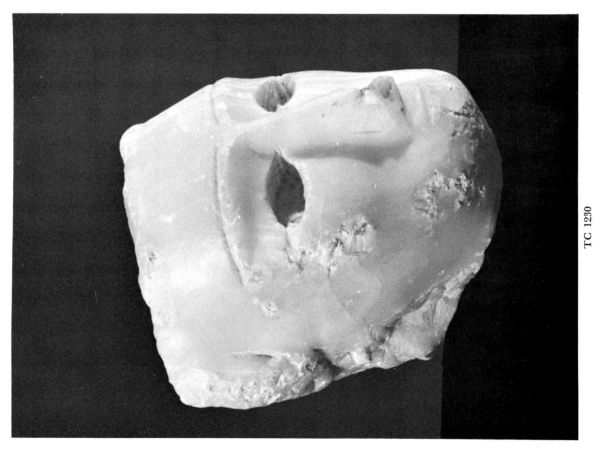

TC 1230

PLATE 6

TC 1316

PLATE 7

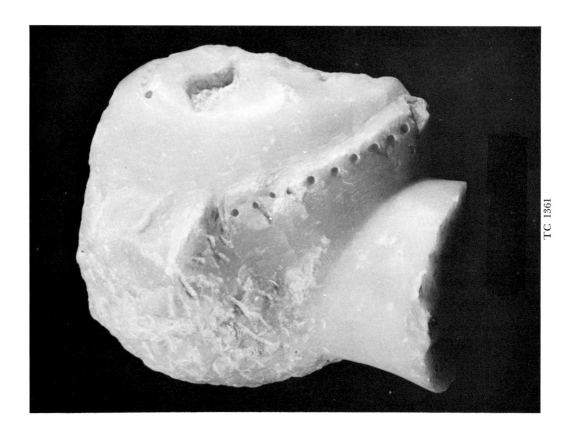

TC 1361

TC 1329

PLATE 8

TC 1361

PLATE 9

TC 1543

TC 1381

TC 1381

PLATE 10

TC 1543

Plate 11

TC 1556

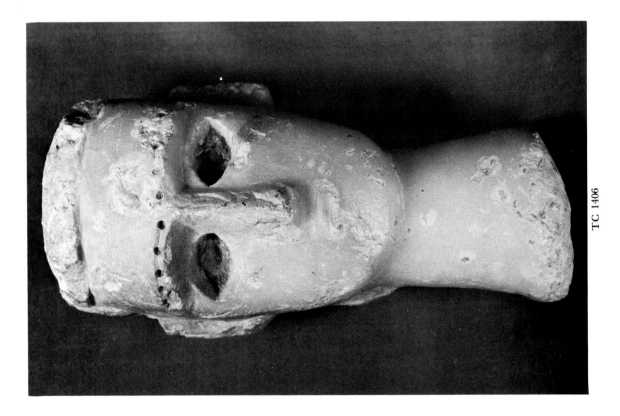

TC 1406

PLATE 12

TC 1588

PLATE 13

TC 1589

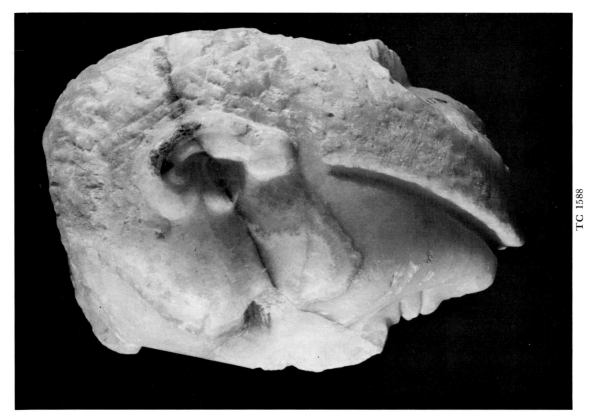

TC 1588

PLATE 14

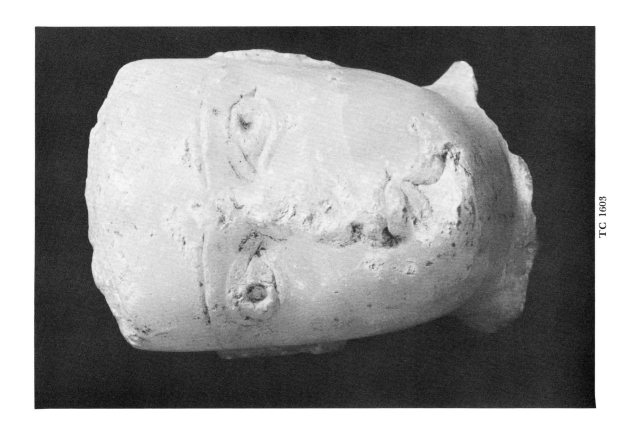

TC 1603

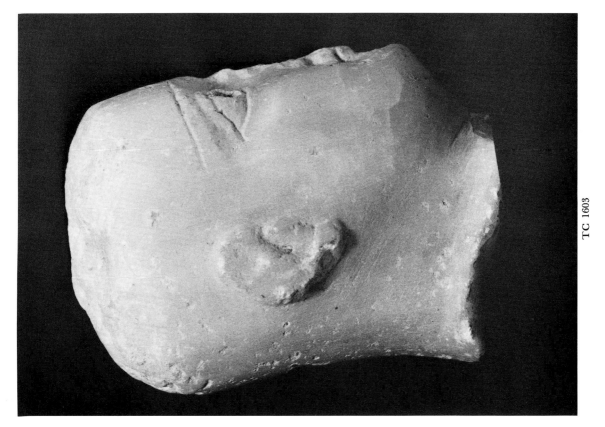

TC 1603

PLATE 15

TC 1882

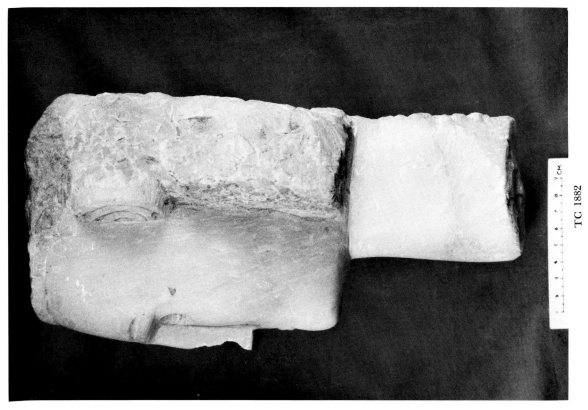

TC 1882

PLATE 16

TC 1795

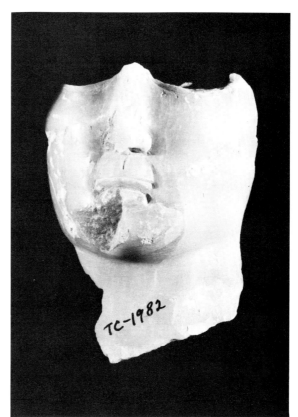

TC 1982

TC 1999

TC 1999

PLATE 17

TC 1975

PLATE 18

TC 2041

PLATE 19

TC 2270

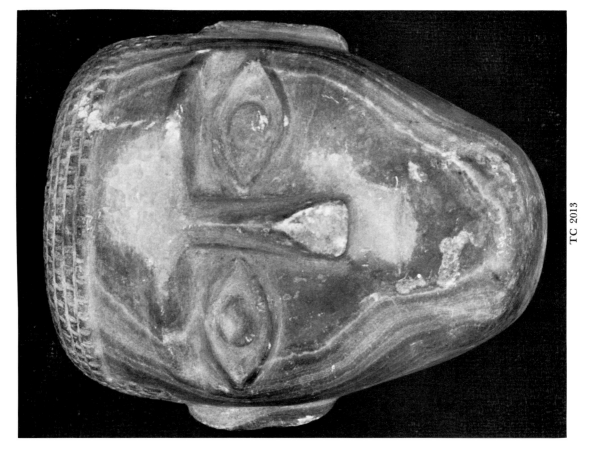

TC 2013

PLATE 20

TC 2043

PLATE 21

TC 2184

TC 2184

PLATE 22

TC 2259

PLATE 23

TC 1884

PLATE 24

TC 1884

PLATE 25

TC 540

TC 1559

TC 1998

TC 2053

TC 2053

PLATE 26

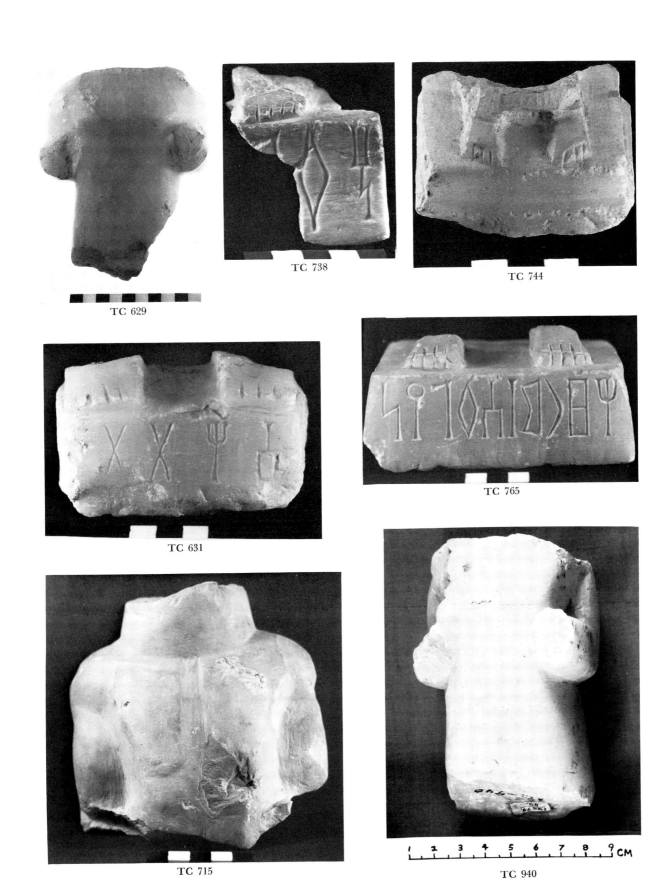

TC 629

TC 738

TC 744

TC 631

TC 765

TC 715

TC 940

Plate 27

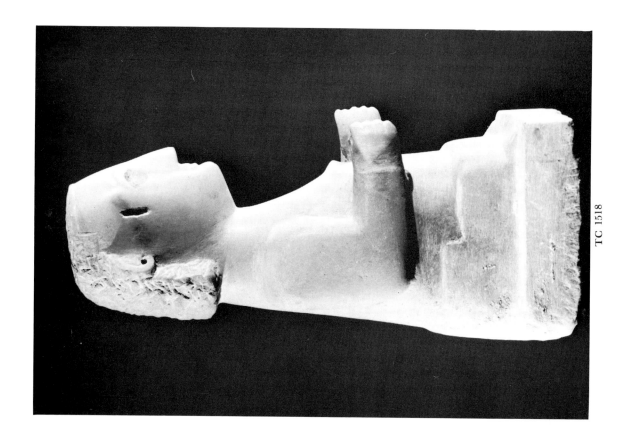

TC 1518

TC 1518

PLATE 28

TC 1518

PLATE 29

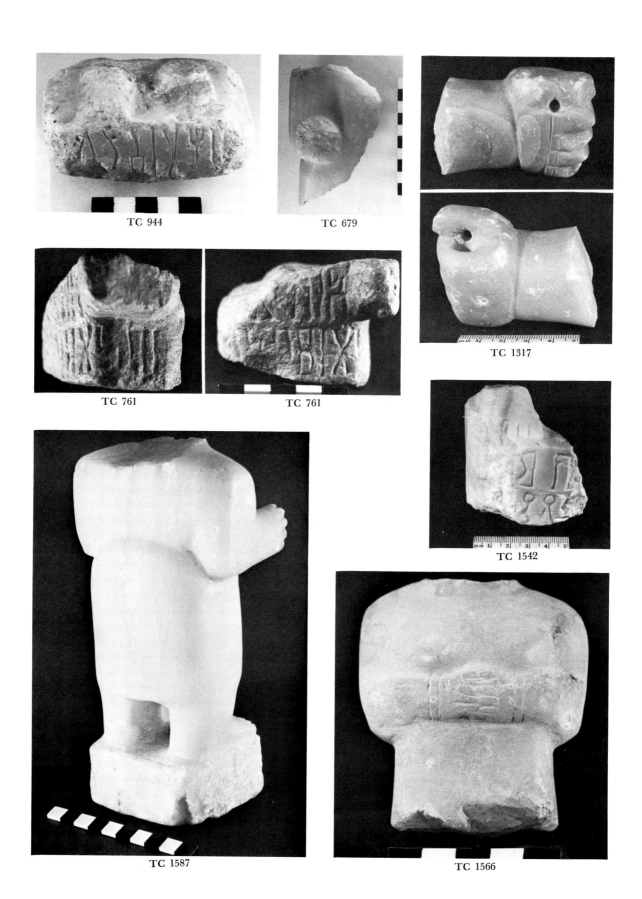

TC 944

TC 679

TC 1317

TC 761

TC 761

TC 1542

TC 1587

TC 1566

PLATE 30

TC 1587

PLATE 31

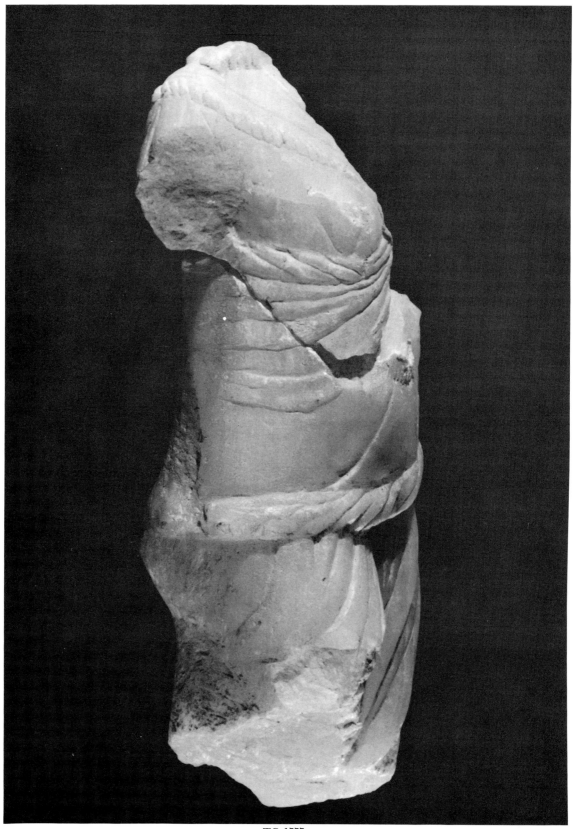

TC 1777

PLATE 32

TC 1777

PLATE 33

TC 1777 (upper fragment)

TC 1777 (lower fragment)

PLATE 34

TC 1816

TC 2064

TC 1890

TC 1981

TC 1818

TC 2533

TC 2531

TC 1885

TC 2531

Plate 35

TC 2064

TC 504

TC 1574

TC 675

PLATE 36

TC 1822

TC 2008

TC 1668

TC 831

Plate 37

TC 1692

TC 920

TC 1074

PLATE 38

TC 1366

TC 2039

TC 1604

TC 1645

TC 1638

PLATE 39

TC 1709

TC 1276

TC 1744

PLATE 40

TC 553

TC 709

TC 726

TC 648

TC 1662

TC 1358

PLATE 41

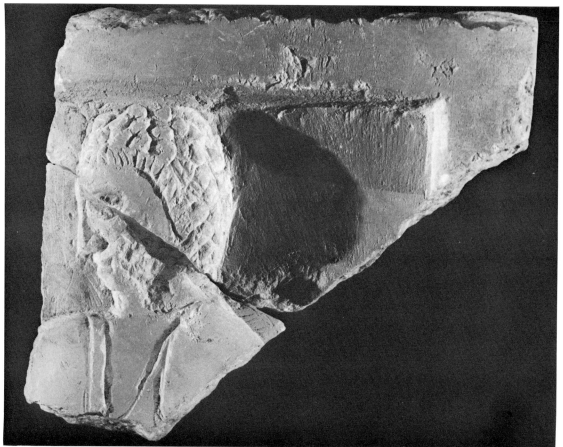

TC 870

TC 1117

PLATE 42

TC 1294

PLATE 43

TC 1307

PLATE 44

TC 1557

PLATE 45

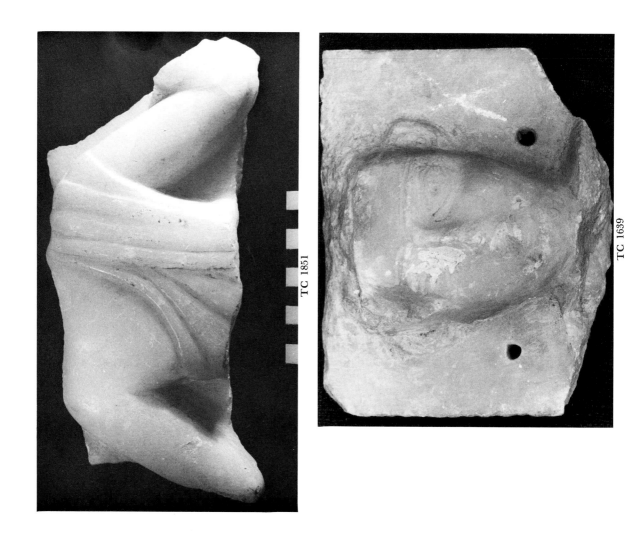

TC 1851

TC 1639

TC 1619

PLATE 46

TC 1663

TC 1847

PLATE 47

TC 1567

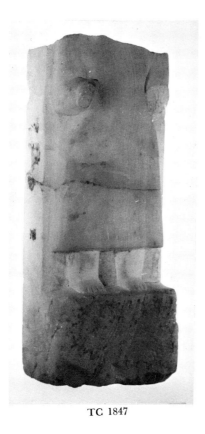

TC 1847

TC 1852

PLATE 48

TC 1776

PLATE 49

TC 1846

PLATE 50

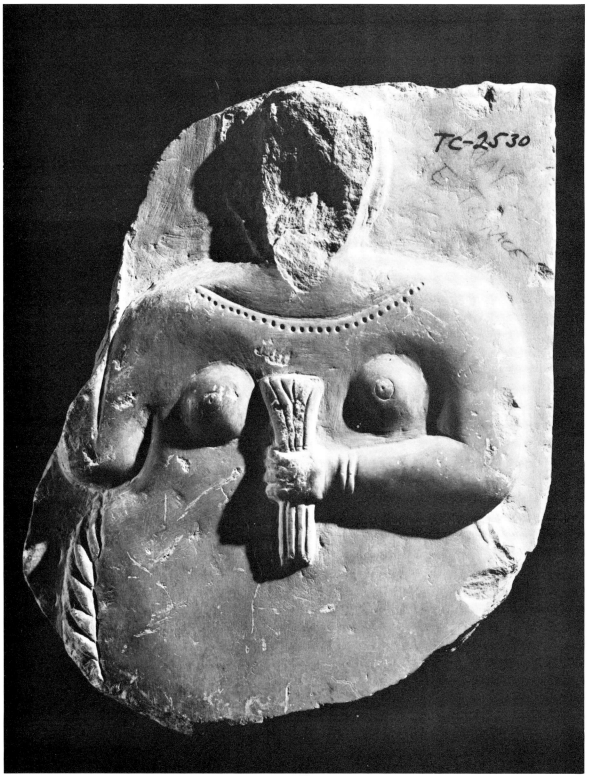

TC 2530

PLATE 51

TC 2173

TC 1664

TC 2108

TC 1664

TC 853

TC 933

PLATE 52

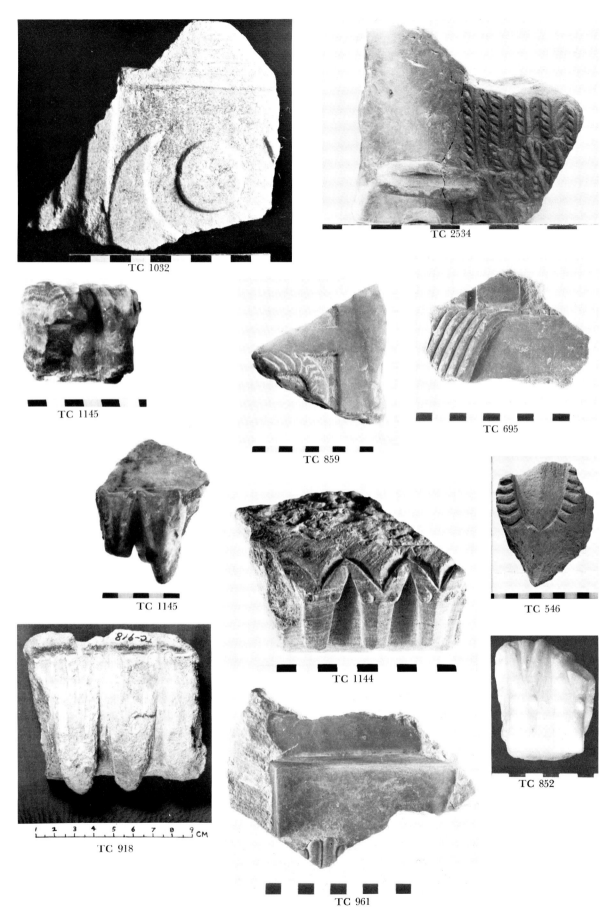

TC 1032

TC 2534

TC 1145

TC 859

TC 695

TC 1145

TC 1144

TC 546

TC 852

TC 918

TC 961

PLATE 53

TC 900

PLATE 54

TC 1071

PLATE 55

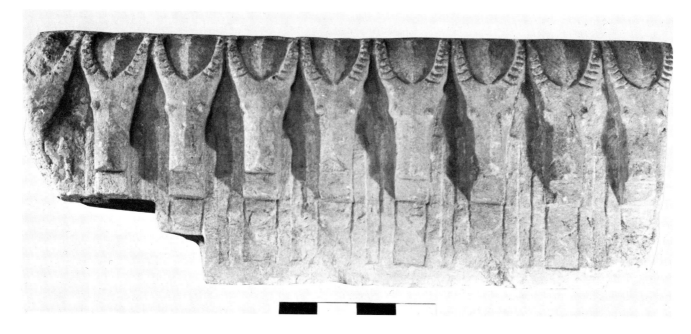

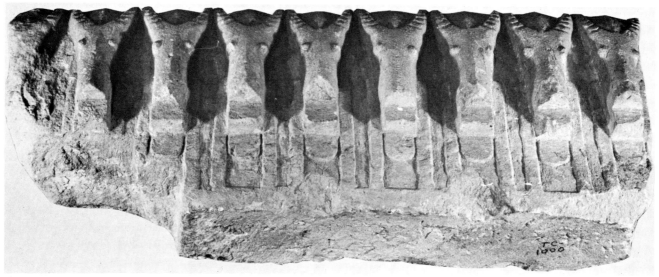

TC 1000 (three views; total length of scale, 20 cm.)

PLATE 56

TC 962 (total length of scale, 20 cm.)

TC 962

TC 1047

Plate 57

TC 1093

PLATE 58

TC 1095

TC 1093

TC 1095

PLATE 59

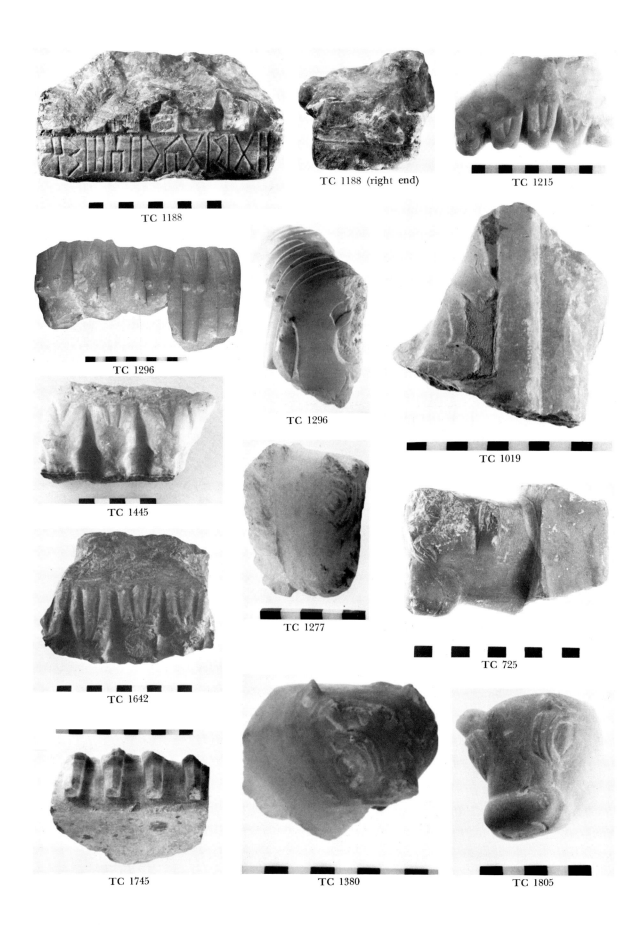

TC 1188 (right end)

TC 1215

TC 1188

TC 1296

TC 1296

TC 1019

TC 1445

TC 1277

TC 725

TC 1642

TC 1745

TC 1380

TC 1805

PLATE 60

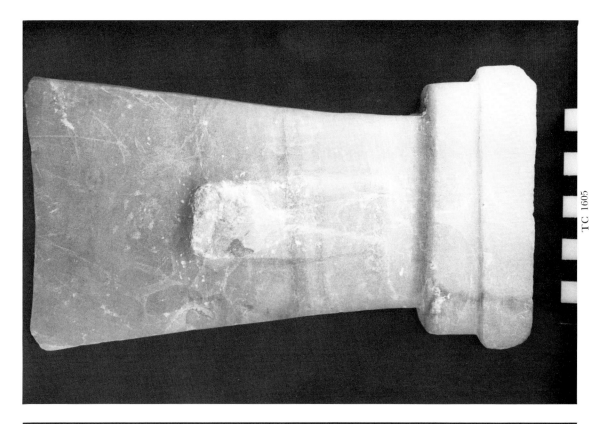

TC 1695

TC 696

PLATE 61

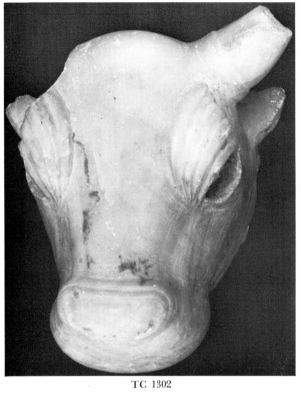

TC 1302

TC 1312

TC 1309

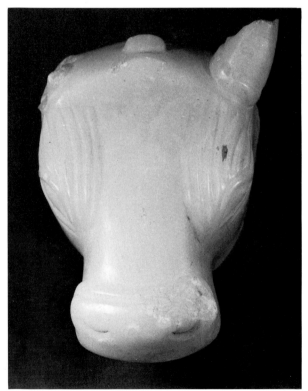

TC 1309

PLATE 62

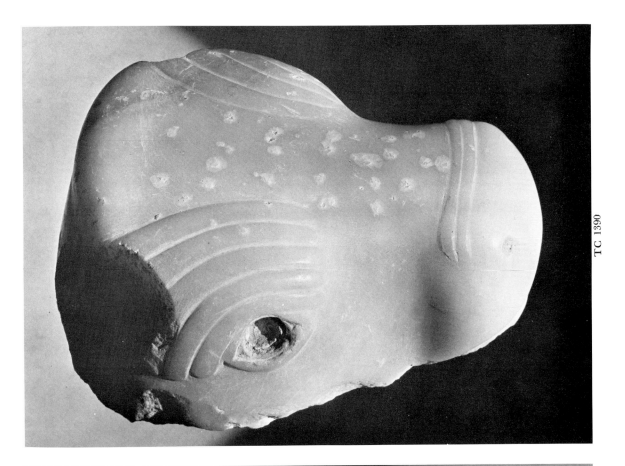

TC 1390

TC 1311

PLATE 63

TC 1519

PLATE 64

TC 1686

PLATE 65

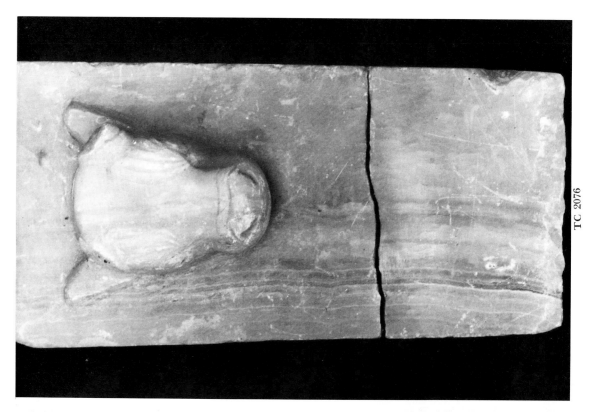

TC 2076

TC 1880

PLATE 66

TC 2182

PLATE 67

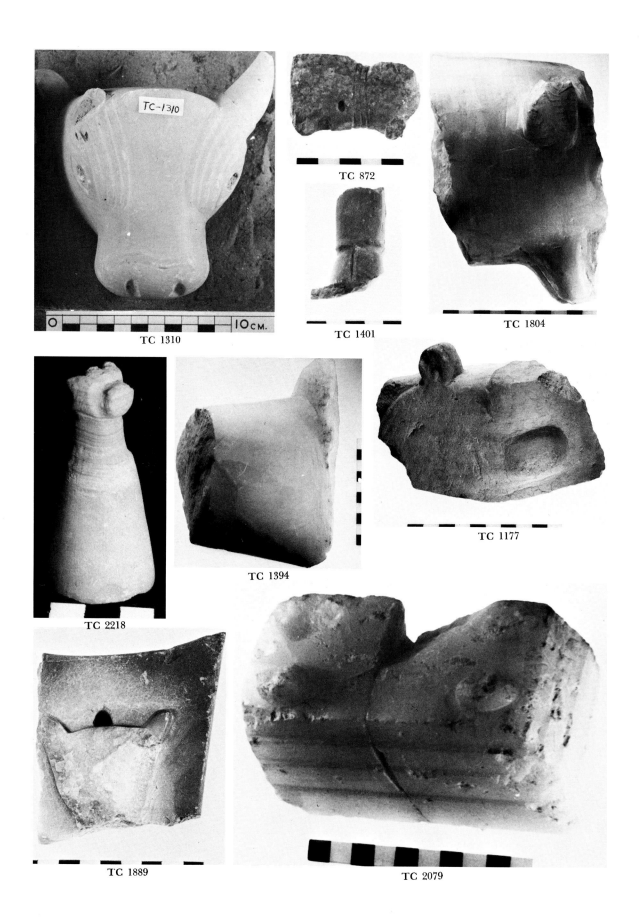

TC 1310

TC 872

TC 1401

TC 1804

TC 2218

TC 1394

TC 1177

TC 1889

TC 2079

PLATE 68

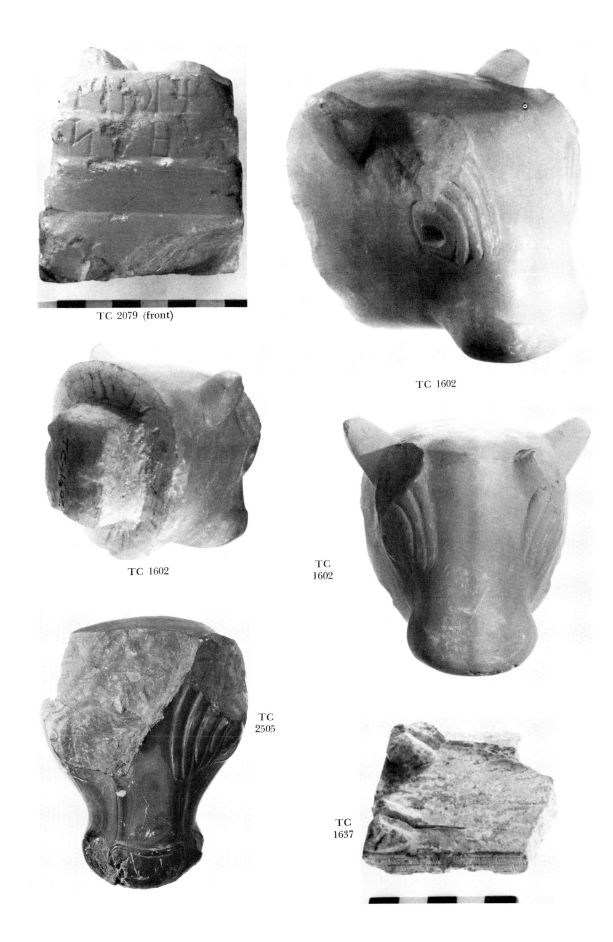

TC 2079 (front)

TC 1602

TC 1602

TC
1602

TC
2505

TC
1637

PLATE 69

TC 685

TC 714

TC 741

TC 990

TC 1107

TC 1333

TC 1573

TC 1213

TC 1378

TC 1364

TC 1541

TC 1873

TC 1691

PLATE 70

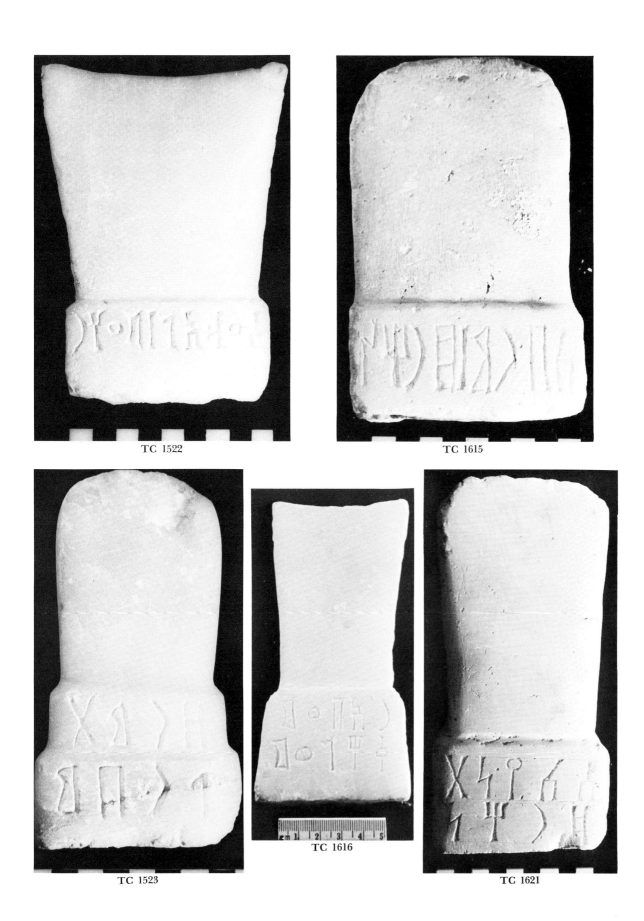

TC 1522

TC 1615

TC 1523

TC 1616

TC 1621

PLATE 71

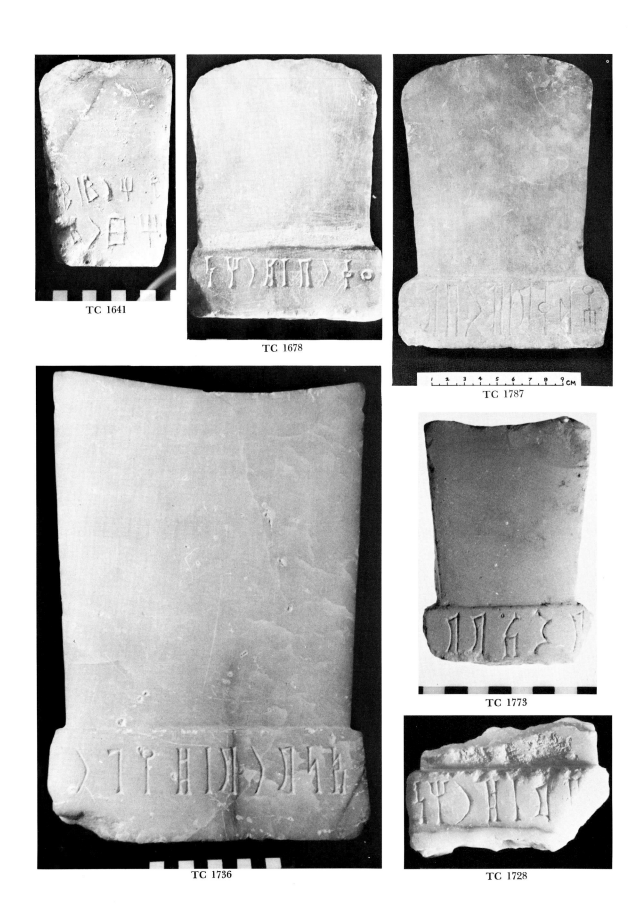

TC 1641

TC 1678

TC 1787

TC 1773

TC 1736

TC 1728

PLATE 72

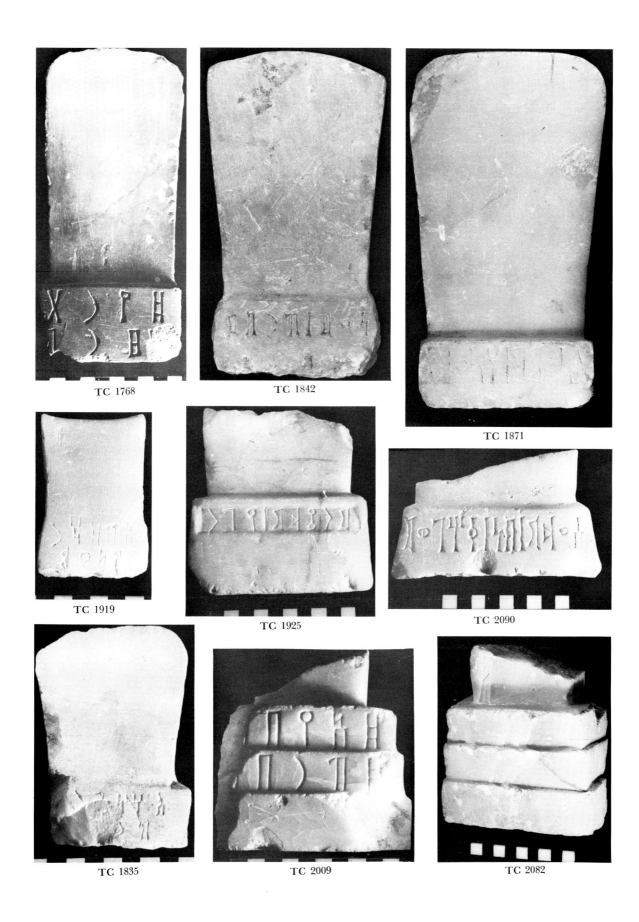

TC 1768

TC 1842

TC 1871

TC 1919

TC 1925

TC 2090

TC 1835

TC 2009

TC 2082

PLATE 73

TC 2078

TC 2183

PLATE 74

TC 1948

TC 2240

TC 1872

TC 1524

TC 1535

TC 1525 (front)   TC 1525 (back)

TC 1568 (back)

TC 1535 (back)

TC 1569

TC 1568 (front)

TC 1617 (front)

TC 1617 (back)

TC 1640

PLATE 75

TC 1521

PLATE 76

TC 1536

TC 1667

TC 1572

TC 1654

TC 2170

TC
1868

TC
1572
(side
and
back)

TC 1917

TC 1917

TC 1907

TC 503

PLATE 77

TC 535

TC 556

TC 653

TC 674

TC 697

TC 716

TC 724

TC 727

TC 766

TC 784

TC 785

TC 786

TC 788

TC 812

TC 818

TC 893

TC 958

TC 928

TC 927

TC 857

TC 1031

TC 964

TC 1030

PLATE 78

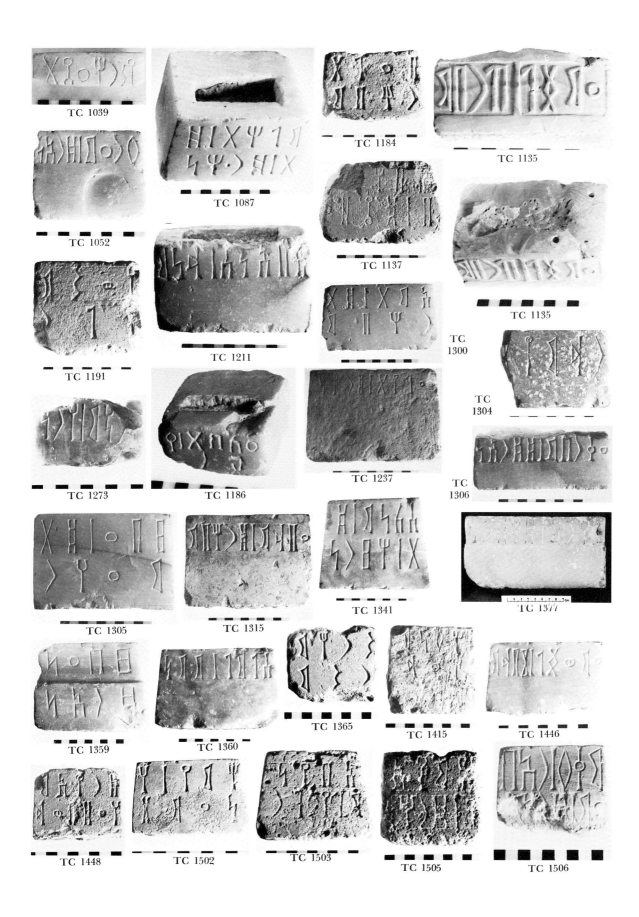

TC 1039

TC 1052

TC 1087

TC 1191

TC 1211

TC 1184

TC 1137

TC 1135

TC 1135

TC 1300

TC 1304

TC 1306

TC 1273

TC 1186

TC 1237

TC 1305

TC 1315

TC 1341

TC 1377

TC 1359

TC 1360

TC 1365

TC 1415

TC 1446

TC 1448

TC 1502

TC 1503

TC 1505

TC 1506

PLATE 79

TC 1520

TC 1527

TC 1527 (back)

TC 1528

TC 1538

TC 1599

TC 1539

TC 1533

TC 1590

TC 1599

TC 1540

TC 1610

TC 1611

TC 1612

TC 1618

TC 1622

TC 1624

TC 1650

TC 1650

TC 1727

TC 1651

TC 1652

TC 1665

TC 1666

TC 1702

TC 1711

TC 1725

TC 1726

TC 1726

TC 1749

TC 1742

TC 1758

PLATE 80

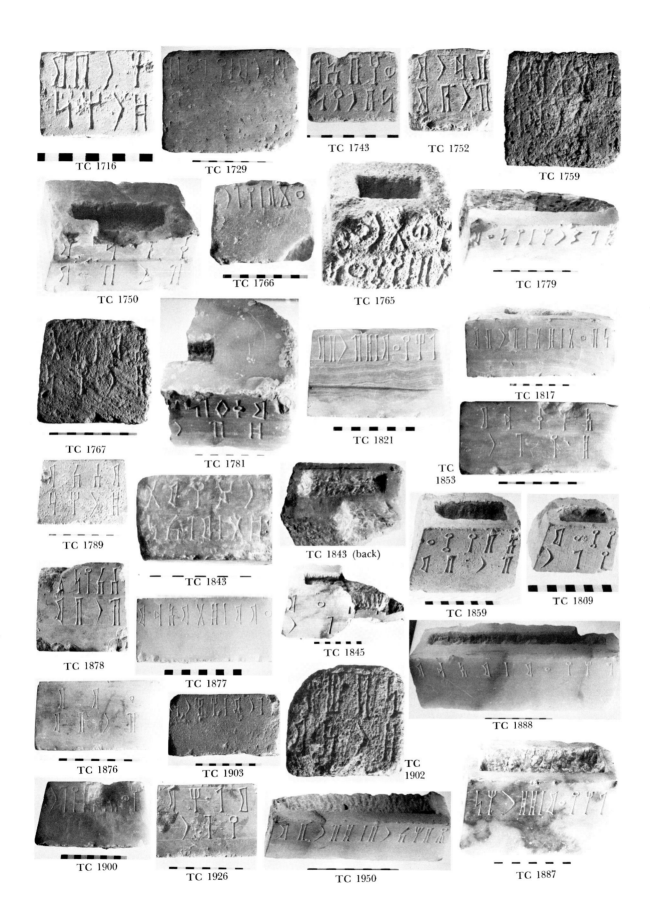

TC 1716

TC 1729

TC 1743

TC 1752

TC 1759

TC 1750

TC 1766

TC 1765

TC 1779

TC 1767

TC 1781

TC 1821

TC 1817

TC 1853

TC 1789

TC 1843 (back)

TC 1843

TC 1845

TC 1859

TC 1809

TC 1878

TC 1877

TC 1888

TC 1876

TC 1903

TC 1902

TC 1900

TC 1926

TC 1950

TC 1887

PLATE 81

TC 1927

TC 1994

TC 1995

TC 1996

TC 2047

TC 2044

TC 2052

TC 1997

TC 2066

TC 2048

TC 2088

TC 2084

TC 2089

TC 2091

TC 2085

TC 2109

TC 2116

TC 2167

TC 2159

TC 2211

TC 2162

TC 2168

TC 2163

TC 2212

TC 2278

TC 2537

TC 3001

TC 2277

TC 2274

TC 2536

TC 3002

TC 3003

PLATE 82

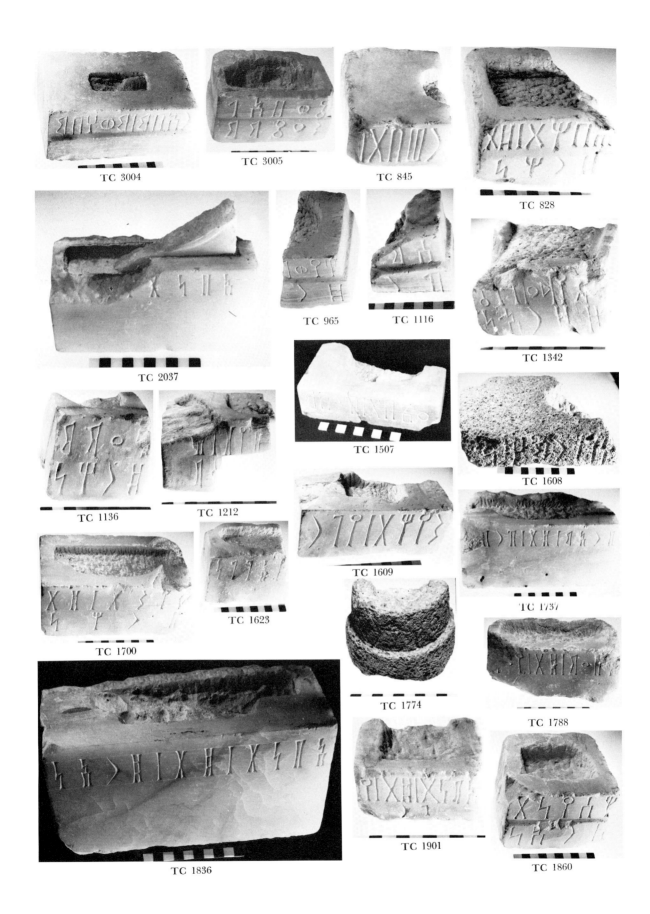

TC 3004

TC 3005

TC 845

TC 828

TC 2037

TC 965

TC 1116

TC 1342

TC 1507

TC 1608

TC 1136

TC 1212

TC 1609

TC 1737

TC 1700

TC 1623

TC 1774

TC 1788

TC 1836

TC 1901

TC 1860

PLATE 83

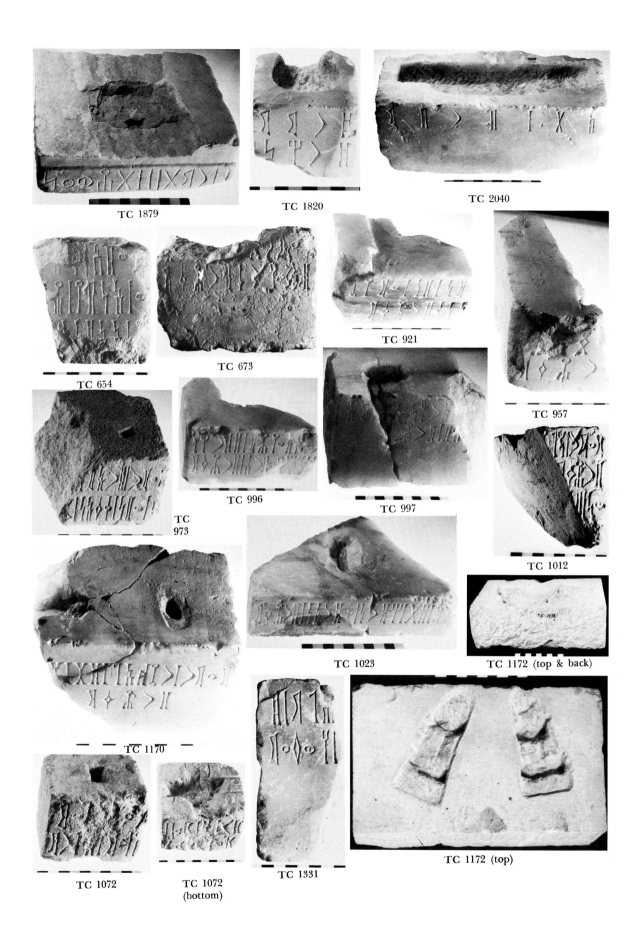

TC 1879

TC 1820

TC 2040

TC 654

TC 673

TC 921

TC 957

TC 973

TC 996

TC 997

TC 1012

TC 1170

TC 1023

TC 1172 (top & back)

TC 1072

TC 1072
(bottom)

TC 1331

TC 1172 (top)

PLATE 84

TC 1172

TC 1298

TC 1173

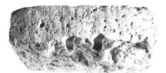

TC 1389

TC 1173 (top & back)

TC 1174 (back,
upside-down)

TC 1174

TC 1344

PLATE 85

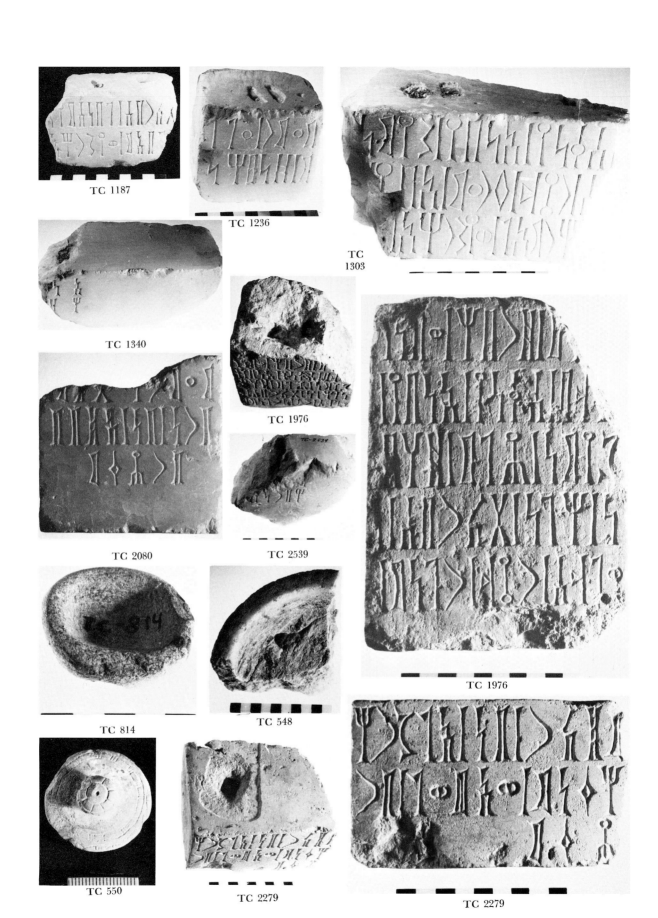

TC 1187

TC 1236

TC
1303

TC 1340

TC 1976

TC 2080

TC 2539

TC 1976

TC 814

TC 548

TC 550

TC 2279

TC 2279

PLATE 86

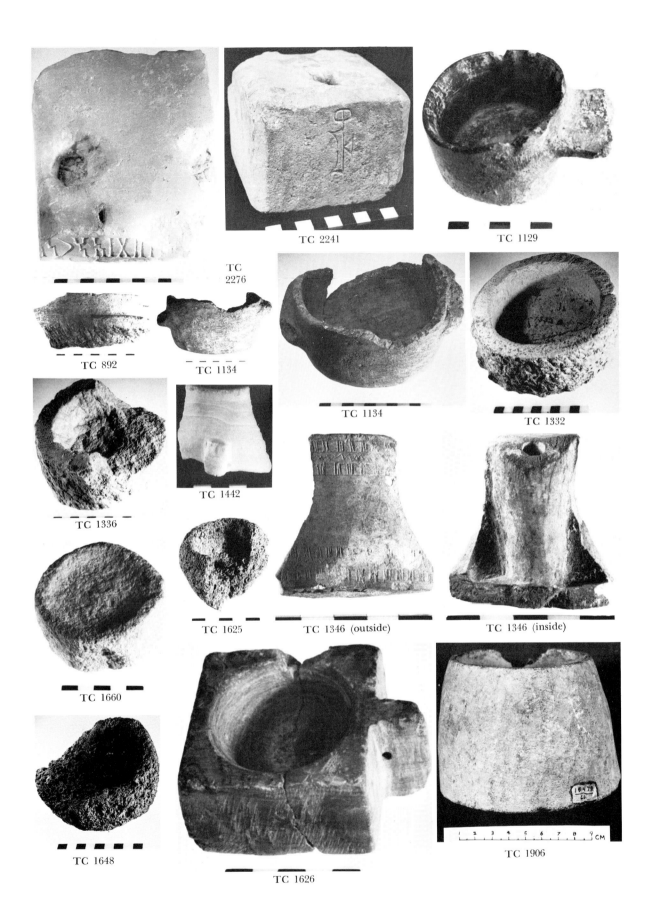

TC 2241

TC 1129

TC 2276

TC 892

TC 1134

TC 1134

TC 1332

TC 1336

TC 1442

TC 1625

TC 1346 (outside)

TC 1346 (inside)

TC 1660

TC 1648

TC 1626

TC 1906

Plate 87

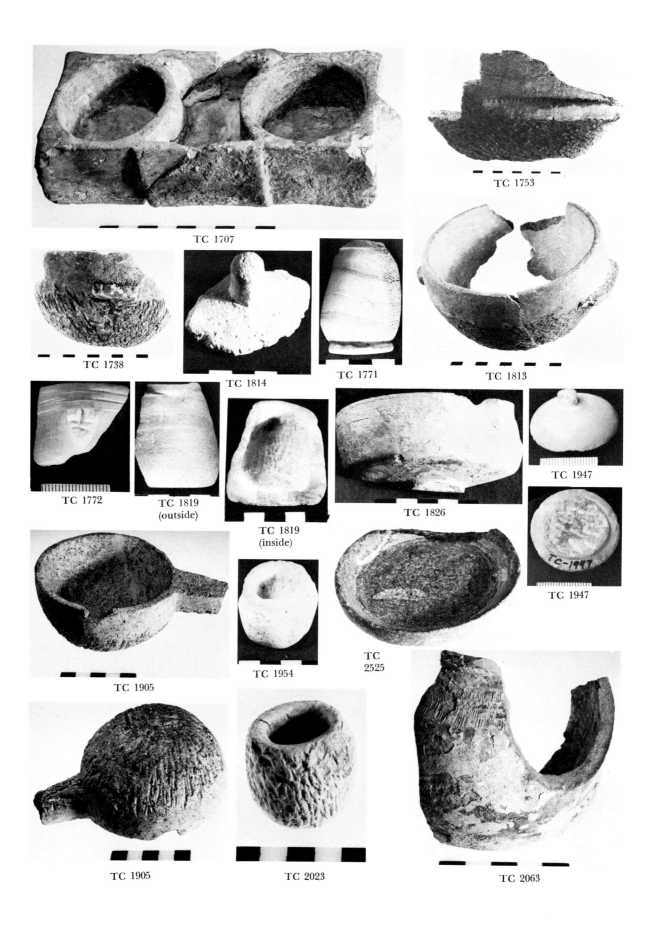

TC 1707

TC 1753

TC 1738

TC 1814

TC 1771

TC 1813

TC 1772

TC 1819
(outside)

TC 1819
(inside)

TC 1826

TC 1947

TC 1947

TC 1947

TC 1905

TC 1954

TC 2525

TC 1905

TC 2023

TC 2063

PLATE 88

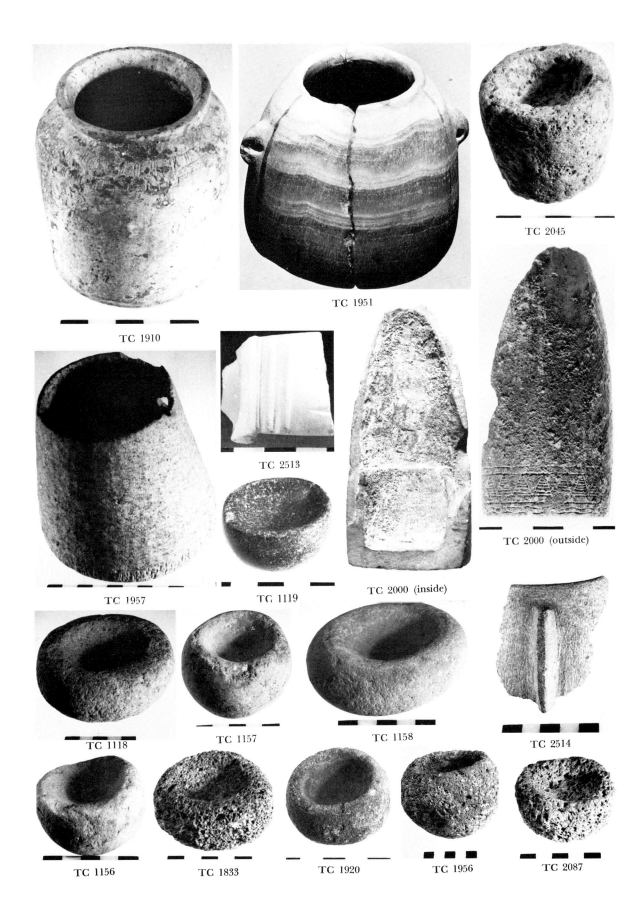

TC 1951

TC 2045

TC 1910

TC 2513

TC 2000 (outside)

TC 1957

TC 1119

TC 2000 (inside)

TC 1118

TC 1157

TC 1158

TC 2514

TC 1156

TC 1833

TC 1920

TC 1956

TC 2087

PLATE 89

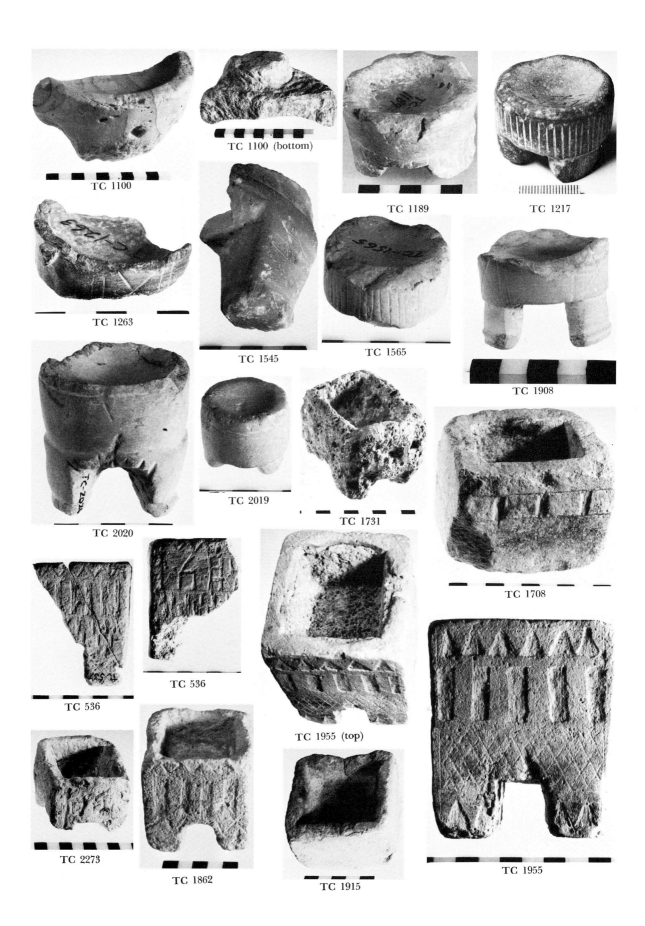

TC 1100 (bottom)

TC 1100

TC 1189

TC 1217

TC 1263

TC 1545

TC 1565

TC 1908

TC 2020

TC 2019

TC 1731

TC 1708

TC 536

TC 536

TC 536

TC 1955 (top)

TC 2273

TC 1862

TC 1915

TC 1955

PLATE 90

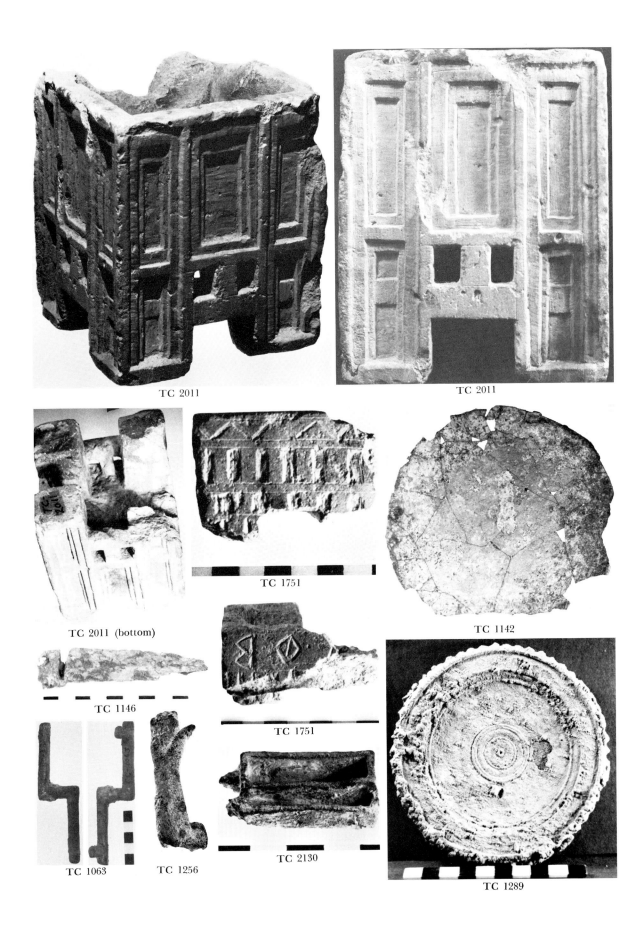

TC 2011

TC 2011

TC 2011 (bottom)

TC 1751

TC 1142

TC 1146

TC 1751

TC 1063

TC 1256

TC 2130

TC 1289

Plate 91

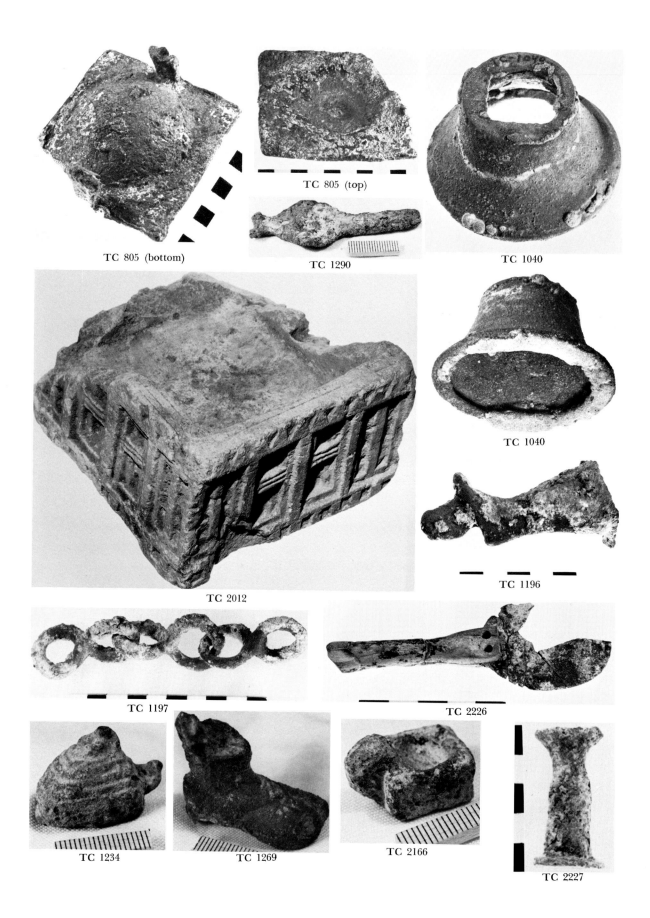

TC 805 (top)

TC 805 (bottom)

TC 1290

TC 1040

TC 1040

TC 1196

TC 2012

TC 1197

TC 2226

TC 1234

TC 1269

TC 2166

TC 2227

PLATE 92

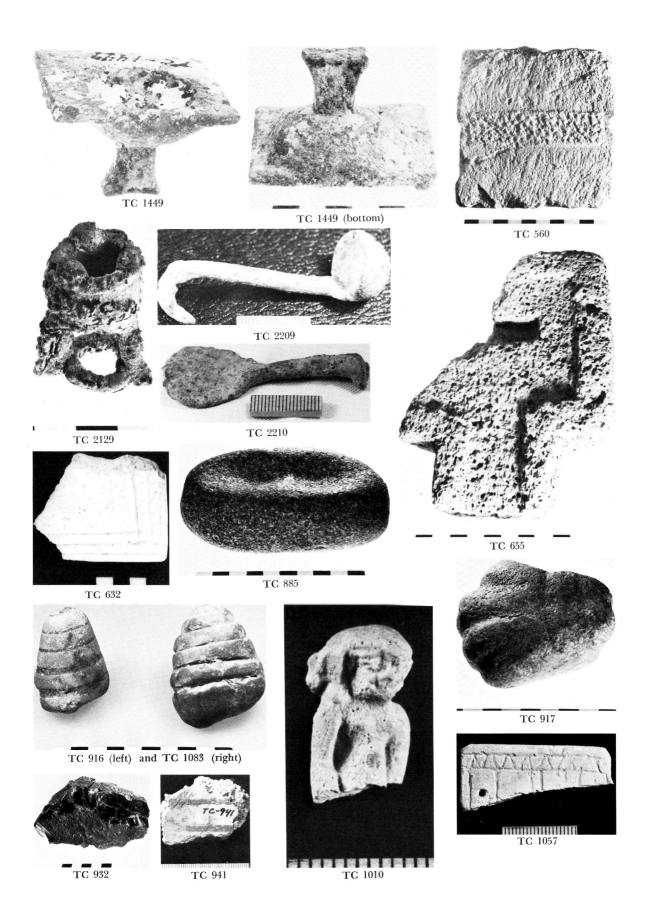

TC 1449

TC 1449 (bottom)

TC 560

TC 2209

TC 2210

TC 2129

TC 655

TC 632

TC 885

TC 917

TC 916 (left) and TC 1083 (right)

TC 932

TC 941

TC 1010

TC 1057

PLATE 93

TC 1002

TC 1068

TC 1086

TC 1770

TC 1548

TC 1278

TC 1583

TC 1916

TC 1870

TC 2213

TC 2245

TC 2213

TC 2527

TC 1934

TC 2001

TC 2024

TC 2280

TC 2532 (largest fragment)

TC 1190

TC 854

PLATE 94

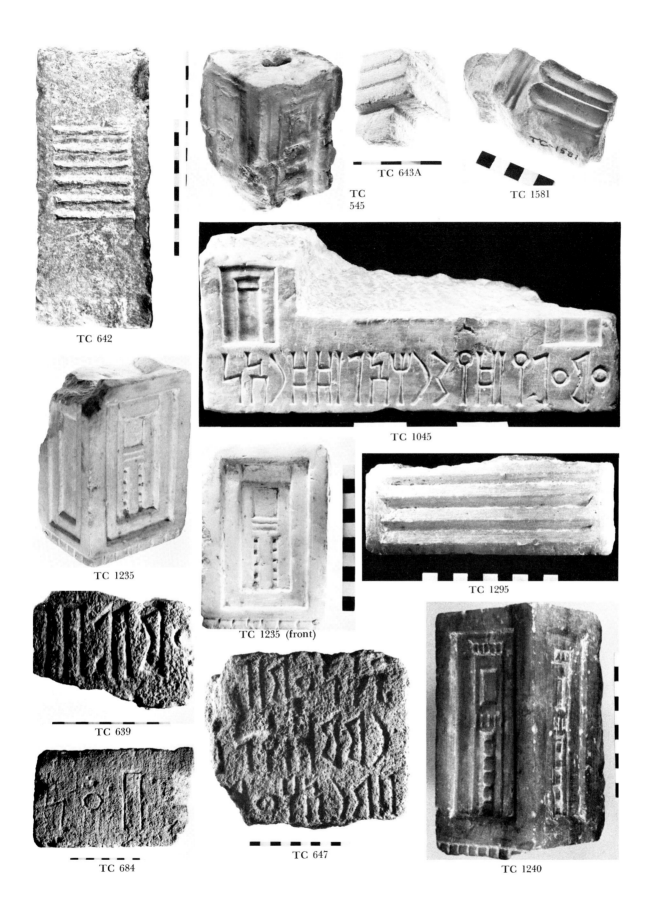

TC 642

TC 545

TC 643A

TC 1581

TC 1045

TC 1235

TC 1235 (front)

TC 1295

TC 639

TC 684

TC 647

TC 1240

PLATE 95

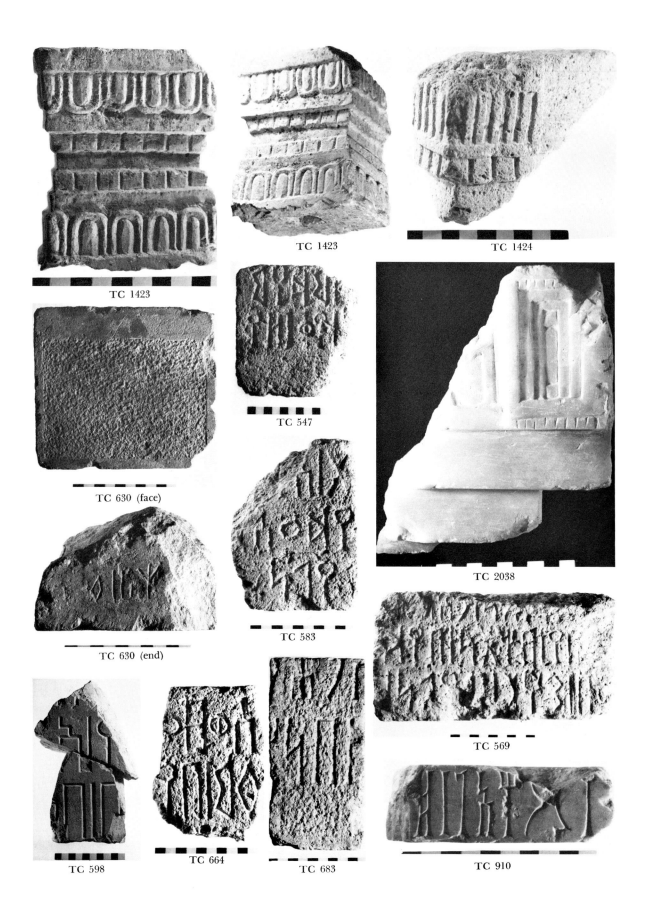

TC 1423

TC 1423

TC 1424

TC 630 (face)

TC 547

TC 2038

TC 630 (end)

TC 583

TC 569

TC 598

TC 664

TC 683

TC 910

PLATE 96

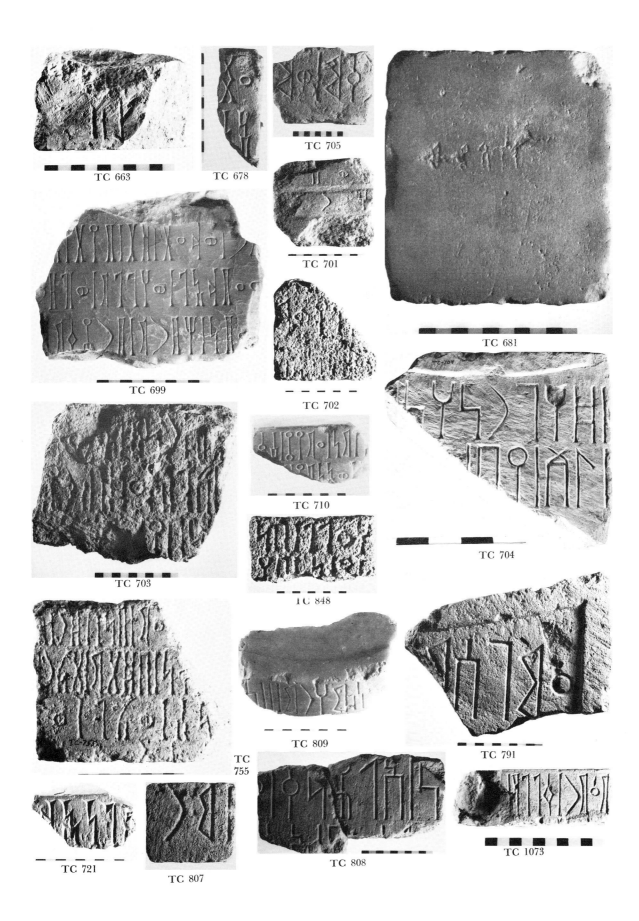

TC 663

TC 678

TC 705

TC 701

TC 681

TC 699

TC 702

TC 704

TC 710

TC 703

TC 848

TC 809

TC 791

TC 755

TC 721

TC 807

TC 808

TC 1073

PLATE 97

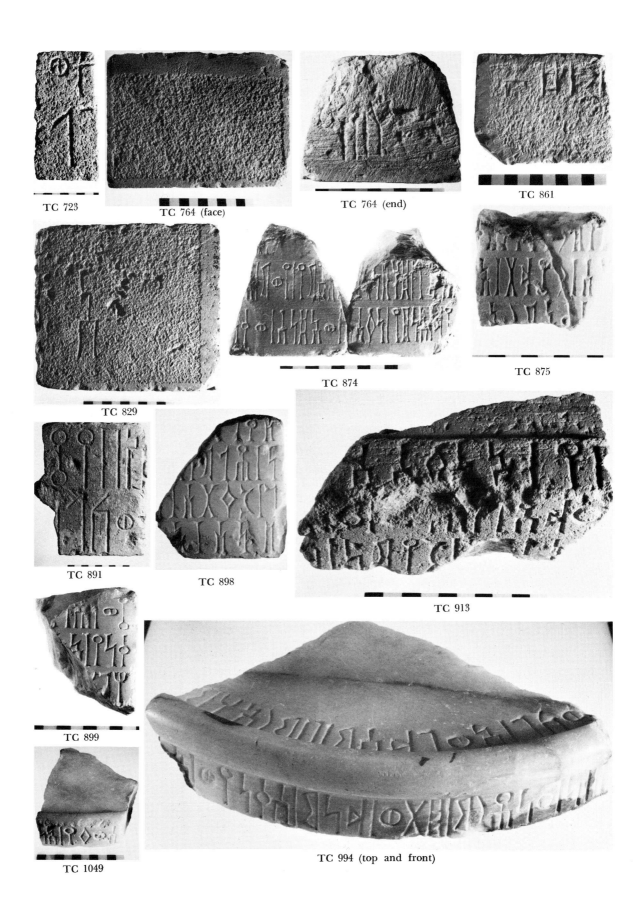

TC 723

TC 764 (face)

TC 764 (end)

TC 861

TC 829

TC 874

TC 875

TC 891

TC 898

TC 913

TC 899

TC 1049

TC 994 (top and front)

PLATE 98

TC 922

TC 924

TC 926

TC 929

TC 947

TC 956

TC 991

TC 994 (top)

TC 1014

TC 995

TC 1152

TC 1130

TC 1338

TC 1029

PLATE 99

TC 1001

TC 1028

TC 1069

TC 1015 (left)   TC 1015 (right)   TC 1048

TC 1201   TC 1239   TC 1339   TC 1154

PLATE 100

TC 1013

TC 1017

TC 1046

TC 1075

TC 1078

TC 1337

TC 1343

TC 1780

TC 1114

TC 1379

PLATE 101

TC 1131

TC 1155

TC 1176

TC 1334

TC 1748

TC 1227

TC 1388

TC 1314

TC 1262

TC 1345

PLATE 102

TC 1335

TC 2511

TC 1824

TC 1874 (bottom)

TC 2501

TC 1874 (interior)

TC 1874 (face)

TC 2508

PLATE 103

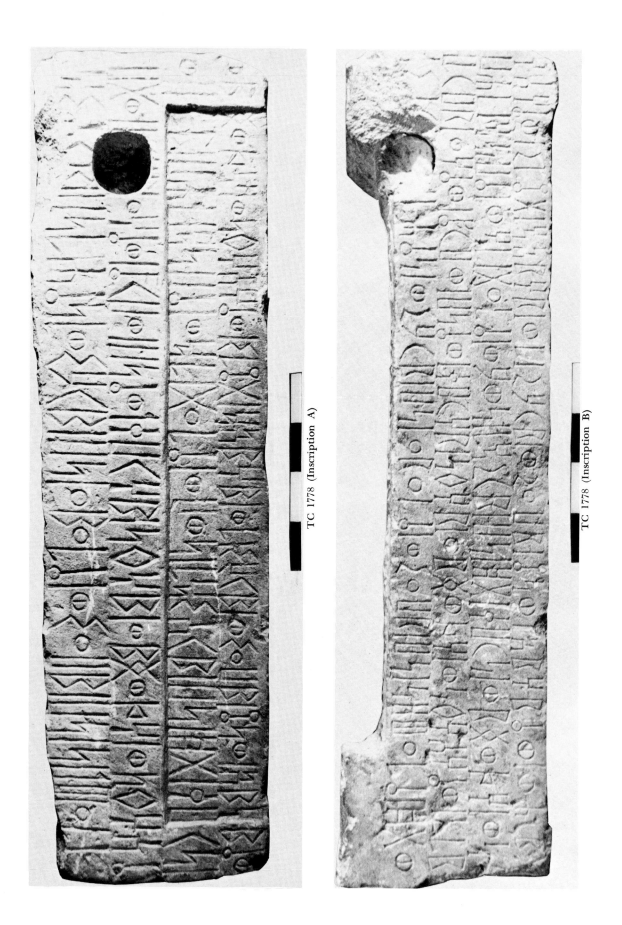

TC 1778 (Inscription A)

TC 1778 (Inscription B)

PLATE 104

TC 2114

TC 1395

TC 1396

TC 1620

TC 2160

TC 1825

TC 2529

TC 1238

PLATE 105

TC 1530 (front and top)

TC 1530 (bottom)

TC 1607 (front and top)

TC 1532

TC 1607 (front and bottom)

TC 1785 (front and top)

TC 1785 (front and bottom)

PLATE 106

TC 1613

TC 1613 (detail)

TC 1823

TC 1613 (detail)

TC 1881

TC 1881 (detail)

TC 1844

TC 1747 (front and bottom)

TC 1747 (front and top)

PLATE 107

Area A, Complex I, looking northwest over mud-
brick walls. The deep shaft is under the derrick.

View looking south along the east
side of the "temple courtyard"
(see Plan 1). The installation at
right center stands directly in front
of the "podium with column bases."
The mound of Timnaᶜ can be seen
in the background.

PLATE 108

"Podium with column bases" (across the center), looking east up the slope from the "temple courtyard" (see Plan 1). Near the foreground is the installation seen at the right center of Plate 108, below. Between this and the podium is a low wall of irregular stones. The large stones near the top of the picture belong to a massive wall attributed by the excavators to the earliest period of construction in the area.

"Podium with column bases" (see Plan 1), looking north. On the outer (west) end of each footing a square recess for the lower end of a column can be seen. A fragment of one column, containing a square mortise-and-tenon joint, was found.

PLATE 109

The "podium with column bases" (see Plan 1) and its foundation from the northwest. The squared limestone blocks are of the type termed marginally drafted, pecked masonry, though the details do not show up clearly in the photograph.

Details of the corner with pavement and drain some seven meters south of the "podium with column bases" (see Plan 1), looking south-south-west. This appears to have been part of a passageway running south from the front of the temple to which the podium belongs.

PLATE 110

Remains of structures uncovered to the north of the central temple in Complex III, looking east. The "drains" labeled on Plan 1 run from the right edge of the photograph to the termination of the wall at the left. The "fragmentary drain" is at a higher level behind the ashlar wall which enters the picture from the right edge. A bronze bowl with an ibex on the rim was found in the corner of two converging walls near the center of the photograph.

Pavement, drain and other structures immediately north of those shown in the photograph above, looking northeast. The wall end in the foreground at the right edge is the same as the one seen in the photograph above at the left edge. The corner of the wall built of massive stones in the background just to the right of center is marked by an "X" on Plan 1. The stone stairway shown in Plate 113, above, is in front of the high wall to the left of center.

Plate 111

The pavements, drains and other structures shown in the photographs on Plate 111 from the north. Rising up in the back are the ruins of the large temple, with the "podium with column bases" to the right.

Photograph adjoining the one above on the left, looking along the face of the wall to the east of the pavement area (the wall is also seen in Plate 111, below, at the right center). The three large stone steps leading up to the east are drawn on Plan 1.

PLATE 112

Broad stone stairway leading up from the south-southwest to the northeast corner of the pavement area, viewed from the north (see Plan 1). Arriving at the top of these steps, one would find himself near the bottom of the three steps seen in Plate 112, below. The wall to the east of this stairway, preserved to a considerable height, may be seen in Plate 111, below, just to the left of center. Ashy traces of a conflagration can be seen extending out on the wall in front of the second and third steps.

The heavy outer east-west wall on the north of Complex III, viewed along the north face from the northwest corner (see Plan 1, on which the hatching in the square inside the corner indicates a mud-brick fill). At the far end of this wall is the stairway shown in the photograph above. At the very top of the photograph in the center is the corner of a structure of massive masonry marked by an "X" on Plan 1 (also visible in the background of Plate 111, below).

PLATE 113

Detail of the construction of the wall shown in Plate 113, below, looking in from the north face at the mud-brick fill (indicated by hatching on Plan 1).

View up the central (east-west) passage of the burial chambers in Area B (see Plan 2). The photographer was standing on a wall of the group of crypts at the extreme left in Plan 2, and the corner of this structure appears in the lower left of the picture.

PLATE 114

Second crypt to the right of the entrance to the passage of Area B shown in Plate 114, below (see Plan 2), looking north down into it. Two slabs of stone of those which divided the chamber into three horizontal levels remain in place. Many slabs of this kind had already been removed when the site was excavated, perhaps in antiquity, and no undisturbed burials were discovered on the entire site.

View to the northwest over the series of eight crypts shown in the lower left corner of Plan 2. Walls belonging to the group of ten similar chambers to the west of the "retaining walls" (marked on Plan 2) can be seen behind, in the upper right part of the photograph.

PLATE 115

View to the north-northeast across the group of four crypts immediately to the east of those in the foreground of Plate 115, below. The high walls seen from the end in the background belong to the crypts just to the west of the room with the "altar" and the "alabaster cache" (see Plan 2).

Detail of southwest end of the first chamber, some 4.3 m. long, immediately to the west of the room with the "altar" and the "alabaster cache" (see Plan 2), showing the plastered interior which was peculiar to this tomb. The photograph includes the end (left) and the first stone of the west side (right) of the crypt. Slabs of stone forming the bottom of the upper level are shown in place. The photographer was looking almost directly to the west.

PLATE 116

View into the group of eight crypts immediately south of the room with the "alabaster cache" (see Plan 2), looking northeast. The south wall of the group runs across the lower right corner of the photograph, and the four chambers of the eastern half of the group fill the center (the horizontal slabs dividing the crypts into different levels have been omitted from the plan to avoid confusion). Behind are other burial chambers and the steep slope of the hill.

View looking northwest across the room with the "altar" and the "alabaster cache" (see Plan 2). In the lower left of the photograph is the north end of the group of crypts shown in the picture above. The cache of alabaster objects was in the southwest corner of the room which occupies the center of the photograph. In the opposite corner, visible behind and slightly to the right of a white stone slab, is a sacrificial altar of limestone with a grooved bull's head on the front to serve as a drain.

PLATE 117

Robert Shalkop with the cache of alabaster objects found in Room 1, Area B (see Plan 2 and Plate 117, below). The group of objects was discovered on May 18, 1951, the second day of excavation in Area B, beside the south wall of room 1 near the southwest corner. Another picture of the cache appears in *Qataban and Sheba*, p. 165, above (opp. p. 117, below, in the London edition).

Stone steps at the east end of the central passageway in Area B, looking east (see Plan 2, right center). The photographer was standing on the north wall of Room 1, immediately above the altar with the bull's head (cf. Plate 117, below).

PLATE 118

View of the series of eight crypts immediately to the east of the "retaining walls" (see Plan 2), looking west down the slope. The large slab across the third chamber on the left is not shown on the plan, and the two large stones at the far end of the central aisle are omitted also. Behind are the remains of the westernmost series of chambers.

In the foreground is the east central part of the series of eight crypts shown in the photograph above, looking east up the slope. In the center of the picture, above the top of the east wall of the group of crypts, is the upper part of the "arch" marked on Plan 2. The white, finely finished facing blocks can be seen higher up to the left. In the background is another group of eight burial chambers.

PLATE 119

In the foreground is the group of four burial chambers at the very top center of Plan 2, looking south-southeast. In the right background is the facing of carefully finished white stone seen also in Plate 119, below. In the upper left corner is part of a group of ten crypts.

Southeast part of the group of nine crypts on the east side of the wall with the "arch" (see Plan 2). On the side of the third partition, which rises much higher than the first two, are traces of a cremation (dark oval area) with sand above it; the word "cremation" is marked in this chamber on the plan. Some half a dozen such cremations were found on the site. The narrow walls shown across the ends of the first two chambers on the plan are quite low and do not appear in the photograph.

PLATE 120

Lay-Out of the Excavated Areas

Approximately two kilometers north of the ruins of ancient Timna' (Hajar Koḥlân), is a large outcropping of rock called Ḥeid Bin 'Aqîl by the people native to Wâdī Beiḥân. At the base of this rocky hill and on the scree-strewn slope of the southwest side lie the remains of the Timna' Cemetery.[1] During the first season (1950) of excavation in this cemetery, the only one known in the whole valley, A. M. Honeyman cleared selected tombs high up on the slope of the hill and others lower down.[2]

The work of the second campaign (1951), supervised by Robert L. Shalkop, was concentrated in two sectors. The first and largest sector begun during the second season, "Area A," was at the foot of the mound's west slope, where the staff had been attracted by the evidence of a large structure.[3] Work was carried out in this area continuously throughout the entire season, from February 19th until May 3rd. The plans of this sector, drawn by Robert L. Shalkop and Ellis Burcaw, were completed, originally in two parts (with Complex III separate from Complexes I and II), on May 11th and 12th. A second sector, designated "Area B," was located "about a hundred and fifty feet up on the slope of Haid bin Aqil."[4] Excavation in that area was limited to the period beginning with March 17th and ending with April 24th. No records giving the exact relationship of the two sectors to each other—or to the tombs cleared by Honeyman, apparently scattered in several areas—are available to this writer. We are indebted to Wendell Phillips for his statement that one of Honeyman's clearing operations came within "a few feet" of a cache of alabaster objects discovered the following season in Area B (see Plan 2, "alabaster cache").[5] This valuable bit of information explains also why TC 1626 from the second campaign and TC VI:5 from the first are each half of one stone object. These facts certainly suggest that objects in Group VI of the 1950 campaign came from tombs included in Area B during the following season.

The plans of Areas A and B drawn by the excavator with the assistance of Burcaw are reproduced below as Plans 1 and 2, following this brief appendix. In Area A, appearing on Plan 1, three sub-divisions were designated by the supervisor as Complexes I, II, and III. The massive structure of masonry and mud brick at the extreme west (on the left in the plan), near the center of which is a deep shaft of well-like proportions, comprises Complex I (see Plate 108, above).[6] The bracket on the plan indicates the extent of Complex I in general. The steps at the right end of the bracket belong to this complex, and then the dividing line jogs over to the west to run along the west face of the large stone wall with the two deep niches in it. This structure was interpreted at the time by W. F. Albright as a kind of mortuary temple, and there seems

[1] See *Archaeological Discoveries in South Arabia*, p. 10.
[2] Wendell Phillips, *Qataban and Sheba*, p. 110 (p. 112 in the London edition).
[3] *Ibid.*, p. 163 (p. 153 in the London ed.).
[4] *Ibid.*, p. 164.

[5] *Ibid.*, p. 167.
[6] Notations penciled in on a copy of Plan 1 at a later date, perhaps in March, 1954, as suggested by an accompanying letter, reverse the designations Complex I and Complex III. As the field catalogue clearly and repeatedly places the apsidal mud-brick walls and the shaft in Complex I, there is no doubt that the later notations are in error. *Qataban and Sheba*, p. 164, in agreement with this correction, indicates that the building with the deep shaft was first excavated and that clearing then proceeded up the slope. It would hardly be thought that the excavators would have numbered the first sector Complex III, proceeding backwards to II and I.

to be no reason to question this interpretation. At the time of clearing, the shaft was unique in South Arabia to the best of our knowledge. Although the shaft has the form of a well, the bottom of it, some 18.3 meters down,[7] was found to be still far above the modern underground water level.[8] A comparable temple-with-well complex was discovered by Frank P. Albright on November 17, 1952,[9] among the ruins of the ancient city of "Sumhuram"[10] on a hill overlooking the inlet known as Khôr Rûrî in the Dhofar Province of Oman.[11]

As can be seen from the registry of objects in Appendix II, a large number of objects were found in the shaft in the Timna' Cemetery mortuary temple during its clearing; but in the Sumhuram well, only a single object, a broken bull's-head offering table, was found (at a depth of 15 m.). The Sumhuram well was rectangular all of the way down (1.25 m. by 1.1 m. at the top, about 1 m. by 1 m. farther down), but the Timna' shaft was rectangular only in the upper part (about 6 m. or slightly more), and the lower part was smaller and round. Water was found in neither, though the soil taken from the Sumhuram shaft the last couple of meters was damp, and there were traces on the stone casing of various water levels (the question here, not solved, is whether this water was

salt water from the *khôr* or potable water from underground sources).

Complex II of Area A in the Timna' Cemetery was adjacent to Complex I on the east, starting up the slope. The dividing line between it and Complex III was unclear for part of the way. The line ran from the right end of the bracket marked "Complex II" on Plan 1 up along the west face of the large north-south wall for some distance, then jogged to the west about one meter to exclude the steps seen on the plan. At the north east-west wall, the line jogged some two meters to the west again, then north off the walls shown in the plan. Complex II was interpreted as a "second mausoleum, older than the first but without a deep hole in the ground." Inside the structure of Complex II, "a series of mud-brick benches which were probably designed to receive offerings to the dead" were found. "There were indications, too, that after this mausoleum had fallen into disuse, the spot had been occupied at three different times, very likely by people who used the foundations of the mausoleum on which to build a mud-brick dwellings."[12]

All of Area A shown in Plan 1 not included in Complexes I and II belongs to the designation Complex III, which thus covers by far the largest area. Major structures laid bare in Complex III are succinctly described by Wendell Phillips:

> A third mortuary building was then discovered up the slope from the second, with one of its walls actually adjoining that of the next one below. The masonry of this structure was even older than that of the others, and here [the workmen] uncovered a room with paving stones, its interior walls covered with plaster. The room even had cut-stone drains and a stairway—all dating back to the seventh or eighth century B.C.

The plan as it is shows that there was much more to Complex III than could be compressed into a single paragraph. A note on a copy of the plans, in the excavator's handwriting, tells us that "Major Complex [III][13] obviously is of many constructional stages, often too incoherent or fragmentary to relate to others." The remains that were found and recorded in this sector indicate a temple com-

---

[7] *Qataban and Sheba*, p. 167, gives its depth as 60 feet below the surface, and the lowest depth at which any objects in it were found, according to the field catalogue, was 60 feet. A notation "65'" on the copy of the plan mentioned in note 6 above appears to be incorrect.

[8] *Qataban and Sheba*, p. 167.

[9] The "well" is first mentioned in Frank P. Albright's faithfully kept field notebook under that date, and it presumably had not been uncovered or identified earlier during his excavation of the site.

[10] The inscriptions variously spell the name *SMHRM* or *SMRM*.

[11] Cf. Frank P. Albright, "The Himyaritic Temple at Khor Rory (Dhofar, Oman)," *Orientalia*, Vol. 22 (1953), pp. 284–87. At the time Albright wrote this brief report, the shaft had not been cleared to its full depth. On December 4th a depth of 15 m. was reached. Then work at Khôr Rûrî was interrupted until February 1st of 1953. The bottom of the well was reached on February 16th at a depth of 25.6 m. from the top of the casing. (It is hoped that a volume containing the final report on all of the archaeological work carried out in Dhofar by the American Foundation for the Study of Man will be published in about three years after the appearance of the present volume; this will include reports on the short seasons of 1958 and 1960, as well as the extensive work done in 1952–53 under the direction of Frank P. Albright.)

[12] *Qataban and Sheba*, p. 164.

[13] Corrected from "I"; see footnote 6, above.

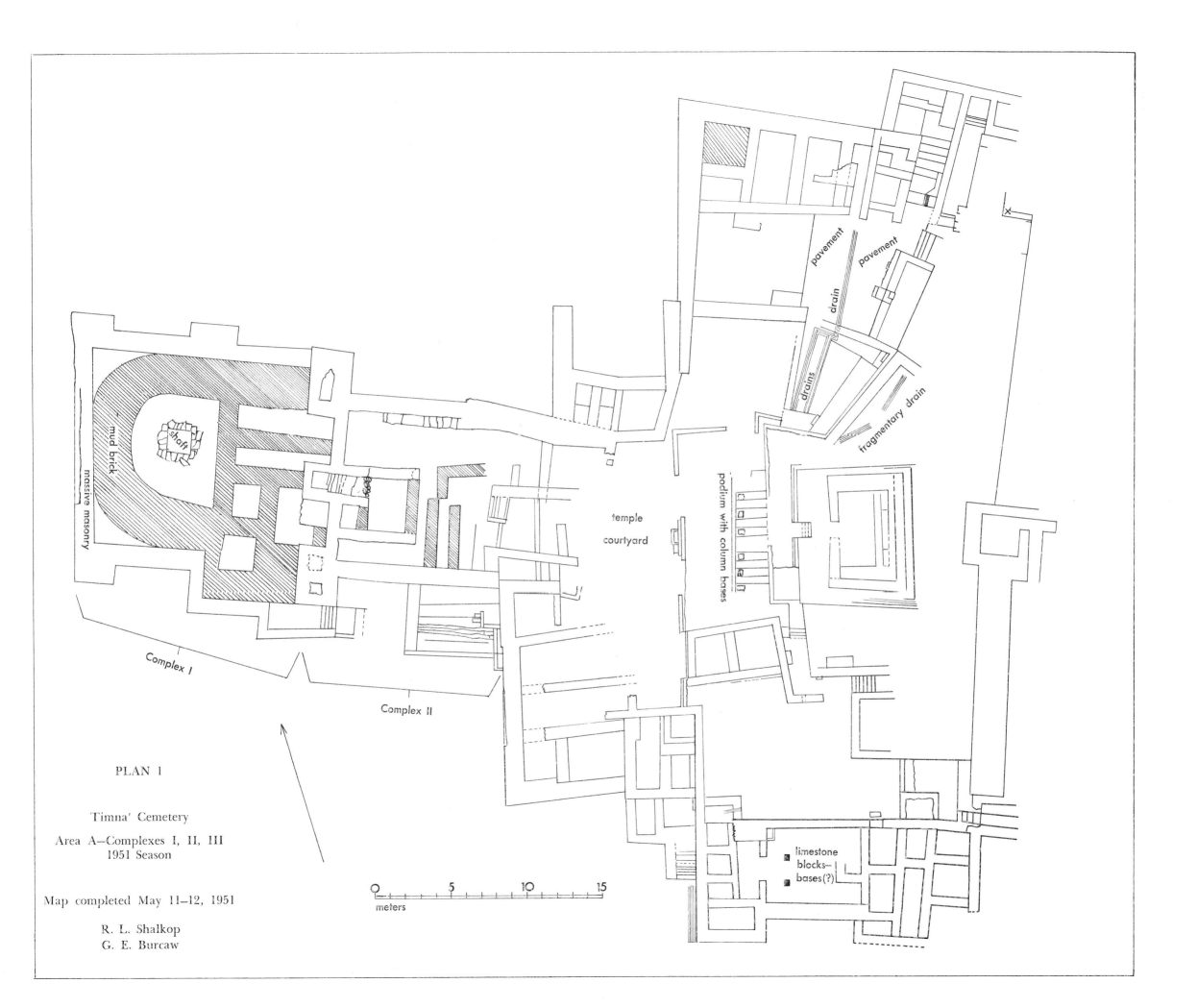

massive masonry

mud brick

shaft

Complex I

Complex II

pavement

pavement

drain

drains

fragmentary drain

temple

courtyard

podium with column bases

limestone
blocks—
bases(?)

PLAN 1

Timna' Cemetery

Area A—Complexes I, II, III
1951 Season

Map completed May 11–12, 1951

R. L. Shalkop
G. E. Burcaw

0   5   10   15

meters

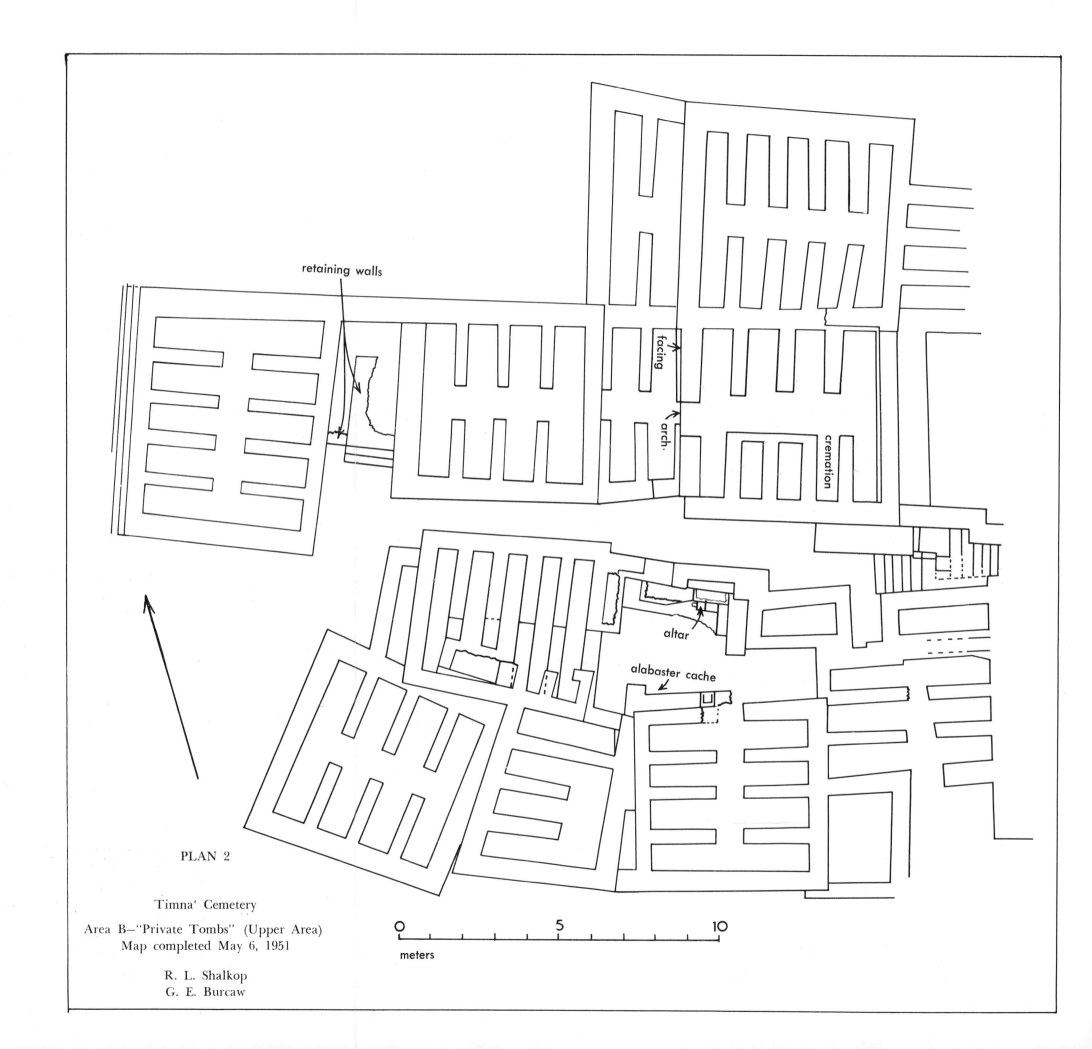

retaining walls

facing

arch.

cremation

altar

alabaster cache

PLAN 2

Timna' Cemetery

Area B—"Private Tombs" (Upper Area)
Map completed May 6, 1951

R. L. Shalkop
G. E. Burcaw

0   5   10

meters

plex of great magnificance, and it is regrettable that more was not preserved of it.[14] Various features of Complex III are illustrated by photographs in Plate 108, below, through Plate 114, above. The captions relate the photographs to the plan and to one another.

The lay-out of Area B, as shown in Plan 2, is considerably different from that of Area A. Here, rather than finding large structures with various related buildings, only series of crypts were found. Each crypt or chamber was about two meters long and something less than a meter wide. These were found to be arranged in groups,[15] most groups having either eight or ten crypts in them, half on one side of a central aisle and half on the other. These have been described as "multiple-roomed family tombs."[16] A fine collection of alabaster sculptured objects, two limestone objects (one inscribed), and an inscribed fragment of alabaster (TC 1517-1530) were found in the corner of an antechamber to one of these groups of crypts (see Plan 2, "Alabaster cache").[17] The photographs in Plate 114, below, through Plate 120 show some of the noteworthy constructions in Area B.

[14] In the field catalogue several sub-divisions for Complex III are given names such as "Upper Terrace," "Locus 1," "North Terrace," but no information as to exactly where these are is now available. (One notation suggests that the "Upper Terrace" was directly north of the "temple courtyard.") Including these terms in the registry (Appendix II) can, however, serve to show which objects belong together in area groupings.

[15] During excavation a number was assigned to each group, if the field catalogue is interpreted properly, but these were not marked on the plan when it was drawn after the close of the excavation. It is clear only that the "alabaster cache" was found in "Room 1." These numbers included in the registry below serve now to indicate which objects came from a single group of crypts or room.

[16] *Qataban and Sheba*, p. 164.

[17] *Ibid.*, p. 167.

Registry of Objects Recorded from the 1951 Season

The registry below lists all the items entered in the field catalogue during the second campaign of excavation in the cemetery at ancient Timna'. As far as practicable, this registry follows the exact arrangement of the field catalogue, including the placement of notes such as the one following item 992.

The Timna' Field Specimen Catalogue 1951" was maintained by Robert L. Shalkop, under whose direction the excavation in this area was conducted during the 1951 season. In the brief notes jotted down at the beginning of the catalogue, we are told that the code letters TC are used for the Timna' Cemetery and that numbers 501-1450 and 2501-2541 are from Area A, numbers 1501-2284 from Area B. (Numbering during the second season began with 501, and no numbers 1451-1500 or 2285-2500 were assigned.) One other notation precedes the catalogue: "'X' before or after cat. no. indicates specimen was discarded after cataloguing"; such entries are herein designated "discarded." From the sketches that sometimes accompany entries, it is clear that few of the discarded fragments were of any significance. For instance, many of the "inscribed fragments" have parts of only one or two letters.

Objects available for study, either physically or by suitable photograph, are described in the body of this volume, and the registry merely lists the number, the "locus" where found as given in the field catalogue, the date found, and a reference to the page where the description begins. Other objects, such as those discarded in the field, are described in the words given in the field catalogue or, less frequently, by standardized terminology. As the pottery is to be published at a later time, it is not described in this appendix. In all cases, the omission of locus or date indicates that it is the same as the last previouly mentioned locus or date.

501. Area A, Complex I, SE. quarter, sand fill. Small alabaster jar cap. 2.2 cm. dia. Feb. 19.
502. Pottery.
503. See p. 59.
504. See p. 17.
505. See p. 86.
506. See p. 21.
507,
508. Pottery.
509. Inscribed fragment. 8 by 5 by 4 cm. Coarse limestone. Discarded.
510. Complex I, area between apsidal mud-brick walls and central shaft. Rough rectangular stele with incised human face. 19 by 8 by 8 cm. Alabaster. Front and bottom are smooth, other face very rough. Discarded.
511–
514. Pottery.
515. See p. 100.
516,
517. Pottery.
518. Complex I, upper 15 feet of shaft. Flat, worked fragment. 17 by 13 cm. Alabaster. Feb. 20. Discarded.
519. Rectangular fragment. 10 by 7 cm. Alabaster. Possibly base of a statuette. Discarded.
520. Rough fragment. 9 by 10 cm. Alabaster. Possibly base of a statuette. Discarded.
521. Pottery.

522. Complex I, 15 to 20 feet down in shaft. Base of a statuette. 25 by 11 by 11 cm. Alabaster. Feb. 21. Discarded.
523. See p. 143.
524. Small inscribed fragment. 4.5 by 3 cm. Alabaster. Discarded.
525. See p. 132.
526. Rectangular fragment, inscribed. 11 by 7 cm. Limestone. Discarded.
527. Pottery.
528. See p. 129.
529. Complex I, SE. quarter, sand fill. Corner of large block. 17 by 14 cm. Limestone. Discarded.
530,
531. See p. 143.
532. Inscribed fragment. 14 by 7 cm. Limestone. Discarded.
533. Inscribed fragment. 9 by 9 by 7 cm. Limestone. Discarded.
534. Inscribed fragment. 13 by 11 by 7 cm. Limestone. Discarded.
535. See p. 59.
536. See p. 118.
537. Joins 536.
538. Inscribed fragment. 5 by 4 cm. Alabaster. Discarded.
539. Reportedly from cemetery; purchased. See p. 5.
540. See p. 10.
541,

542. Complex I, NE. quarter, sand fill. Pottery.
543. See p. 143.
544. Pottery.
545. See p. 137.
546. See p. 30.
547. Complex I, SW. quarter, outside walls. See p. 143.
548. See p. 100.
549. Joins 548.
550. Unknown locus. Feb. 22. See p. 100.
551. Fragment inscribed with single letter. 3 by 3 cm. Alabaster. Discarded.
552. Complex II, NE. quarter, inside walls. Pottery.
553. See p. 22.
554. See p. 121.
555. Cowrie shell. 2 by 1.5 cm.
556. Complex I, vertical shaft at 20 feet. See p. 59.
557–
559. Pottery.
560. Complex II, SE. quarter, inside walls. See p. 132.
561. Inscribed fragment. 13 by 11 cm. Limestone. Discarded.
562. See p. 100.
563. See p. 11.
564. Incised fragment. 3.5 by 2 cm. Alabaster. Discarded.
565. Area A in general. Pottery. Feb. 18–22.
566,
567. Complex II, NE. quarter, inside walls. Pottery. Feb. 24.

568. Complex I, shaft at 24 feet. Human head, female. 18 by 11 by 11 cm. Alabaster. Rough back; broken nose.
569. See p. 143.
570. See *JaPEHA*, pp. 216f., §378. Discarded.
571. Pottery.
572. Rim fragment. 4 by 4 cm. Steatite. Undecorated.
573,
574. Complex I, center, east of shaft. Pottery.
575. Inscribed fragment. 13 by 6 cm. Stone. Discarded.
576–
579. Pottery. Feb. 25.
580. Complex I, shaft at 38 feet. Base of altar. 24 by 20 by 8 cm. Limestone. Discarded.
581. Building block with pecked face. 15 by 13 by 11 cm. Limestone. Discarded.
582. Pottery.
583. Complex II, SE. quarter, outside walls. See p. 144.
584–
587. Pottery.
588. Fragment of copper or bronze. 4 by .5 cm. Discarded.
589. Unknown locus. Feb. 26. See p. 144.
590. Complex I, shaft at 30 feet. Pottery.
591. See p. 101.
592. Fragment. 16 by 4 cm. Steatite. Rough outer surface, smooth inside. Discarded.
593–
595. Complex II, east of niched stone wall. Pottery.
596. Decorated fragment (tips of ibex horns?). 11 by 7 cm. Limestone. Discarded.
597. Inscribed fragment. 12 by 9 cm. Limestone. Discarded.
598. Complex II, SE. quarter, outside walls. Feb. 27. See p. 144.
599,
600. Unknown locus. Pottery.
601. Complex II, east of niched stone wall. Inscribed fragment. 7 by 5 by 3 cm. Limestone. Feb. 28. Discarded.
602. Inscribed fragment. 5 by 4 cm. Alabaster. Discarded.
603. Complex I, shaft at 34 feet. Bull's horn. 4 by 3 cm. Alabaster. Discarded.
604,
605. Pottery.
606. Complex I, center, east of shaft. Pottery.
607,
608. See p. 132.
609. Fragment of maxilla with three molars from small

herbivorous mammal. 7 by 4 cm.
610. Decorated fragment. 4 by 3 by 2 cm. Discarded.
611. Decorated fragment. 11 by 6 cm. Limestone. Discarded.
612. Inscribed fragment. 16 by 10 cm. Limestone. March 1. Discarded.
613–
615. Pottery.
616,
617. Unknown locus. Pottery.
618–
620. Complex II, east of niched stone wall. Pottery.
621. See p. 11.
622. Fragment. 3 by 5 cm. Copper.
623. Spherical fragment. 1.5 cm. dia. Obsidian (?).
624. Vessel fragment. 14 by 7 cm. Steatite. Discarded.
625–
627. Pottery.
628. Complex I, shaft at 36 feet. Pottery.
629. See p. 11.
630. See p. 144.
631. See p. 11.
632. See p. 132.
633. See p. 36.
634. Pottery.
635. See p. 129.
636,
637. Complex I, center, east of shaft. Pottery.
638. Complex II, SE. quarter, outside walls. Pottery.
639. See p. 144.
640. Pierced fragment. 15 by 10 cm. Steatite. Discarded.
641. Complex I, shaft at 40 feet. Inscribed block. 27 by 9.5 cm. by 5.5 cm. Rough limestone. Discarded.
642. See p. 137.
643. Broken altar base. 20 by 12 by 9 cm. Limestone. Discarded.
643A. See p. 138.
644. Fragment of a statuette. 10 by 7.5 by 5.5 cm. Alabaster. Discarded.
645,
646. Pottery.
647. Complex II, east of niched stone wall. See p. 144.
648. See p. 22.
649–
651. Pottery.
652. Complex I, shaft at 42 feet. Three stones with four lines of inscription on each, forming a complete inscription. 32 by 27 by 17 cm.; 64 by 27 by 22 cm.; 45 by 27 by 21 cm. Limestone. March 4.
653. Unknown locus. See p. 59.

654. Complex II, SE. quarter, outside walls. See p. 93.
655. See p. 132.
656. Pottery.
657–
660. Complex I, center, east of shaft. Pottery.
661. Inscribed fragment. 5 by 4 cm. Alabaster. Discarded.
662. Fragment of horn from bull's head. 2.5 cm. by 2 cm. Alabaster.
663. Complex I, shaft at 42 feet. See p. 144.
664,
665. See p. 145.
666. Inscribed fragment. 19 by 16 by 7.5 cm. Limestone. Discarded.
667. Inscribed fragment. 8 by 6 cm. Limestone. Discarded.
668–
670. Pottery.
671. Complex II, east of niched stone wall. Pottery.
672. Inscribed block. 13 by 12 by 12 cm. Limestone. Discarded.
673. See p. 93.
674. See p. 59.
675. See p. 18.
676. See p. 145.
677. See p. 59.
678. See p. 145.
679. See p. 11.
680. Complex I, shaft at 44 feet. Inscribed fragment. 33 by 18 by 16 cm. Limestone. March 5. Discarded.
681. See p. 145.
682. Pottery.
683,
684. Complex I, east of niched stone wall. See p. 145.
685. See p. 44.
686. See p. 101.
686B. Fragments of 686. 9.5 by 4 cm. Discarded.
687. Ledge handle. 7 by 5 cm. Steatite. Discarded.
688. See p. 101.
689. Rim fragment. 7.5 by 3.5 cm. Steatite. Discarded.
690,
691. Pottery.
692. Complex I, center, east of shaft. March 6. See p. 131.
693. See p. 129.
694. See p. 101.
695. See p. 28.
696. See p. 36.
697. See p. 59.
698. See *JaPEHA*, pp. 209f., §367.
699. See p. 145.
700. See p. 146.
701. Unknown locus (purchased). March 1. See p. 146.
702,
703. Complex I, shaft at 46 feet. March 6. See p. 146.

704. Complex II, east of niched stone wall. March 8. See p. 146.
705. Complex I, shaft at 48 feet. See p. 147.
706. Inscribed fragment. 5.5 by 4.5 cm. Alabaster. Discarded.
707. See p. 147.
708. Fragment. 5 by 2 cm. Bronze.
709. See p. 22.
710. See p. 147.
711. See p. 101.
712. **Head of man. 22 by 12 by 12** cm. Alabaster. Groove for beard.
713. Unknown locus. Worked block. 13 by 12 by 5.5 cm. Limestone. Discarded.
714. See p. 44.
715. See p. 12.
716. See p. 60.
717–
720. Pottery.
721. Complex I, center, east of shaft. March 10. See p. 147.
722. Complex I, shaft at 50 feet. Pottery.
723. Complex II, east of niched stone wall. March 11. See p. 147.
724. See p. 60.
725. See p. 37.
726. See p. 22.
727. Complex I, shaft at 52 feet. See p. 60.
728. Inscribed fragment. 9 by 7 by 6 cm. Limestone. Discarded.
729–
732. Pottery.
733. See p. 37.
734. See p. 121.
735. Complex II, SE. quarter, outside walls. Inscribed block. 51 by 18 by 10 cm. Limestone. March 12.
736,
737. Pottery.
738. See p. 12.
739. Joins 738.
740. Bead. 2 by 1 cm. Glass.
741. Complex I, shaft at 52 feet. See p. 45.
742. Complex II, east of niched stone wall. See p. 121.
743. Inscribed fragment. 12 by 11 cm. Limestone. Discarded.
744. See p. 12.
745. Pottery.
746. Unknown locus. Building block. 19 by 18 by 6 cm. Limestone. Discarded.
747–
749. Complex II, SE. quarter, outside walls. Pottery. March 13.
750. See p. 101.
751,
752. Complex II, NE. quarter, outside walls. Pottery.

753. Decorated fragment. 11 by 4.5 cm. Limestone. Discarded.
754. Decorated fragment. 11 by 9 cm. Limestone. Discarded.
755,
756. See p. 147.
757–
760. Complex II, east of niched stone wall. Pottery.
761. See p. 12.
762. Inscribed fragment. 7 by 6 by 6 cm. Stone. Discarded.
763. Fragment of ibex head. 5.5 by 2.5 cm. Alabaster.
764. Complex I, shaft at 54 feet. See p. 148.
765. Unknown locus. March 14. See p. 12.
766. Complex II, SE. quarter, inside walls. See p. 60.
767. Inscribed fragment. 15 by 9 by 9 cm. Limestone. Discarded.
768. Fragment of ibex head. 14 by 8 by 5 cm. Limestone. Discarded.
769. Fragment of whetstone (?). 5.5 by 1.3 by .7 cm. Stone.
770–
775. Pottery.
776. Complex II, NE. quarter, outside walls. Inscribed fragment. 11 by 10 by 10 cm. Limestone. Discarded.
777,
778. Pottery.
779–
783. Outside Area A. Pottery. March 15.
784–
786. Complex III, SE. quarter, inside walls. See p. 60.
787. Statuette base. 8 by 8 by 5.5 cm. Weathered limestone. Discarded.
788. See p. 61.
789. Inscribed altar base. 11 by 10 by 6.5 cm. Limestone. Discarded.
790. Inscribed altar base. 11 by 10 by 6.5 cm. Limestone. Discarded.
791. See p. 148.
792. Bull's head. 10 by 7 by 5 cm. Stone.
793. See p. 148.
794. Bowl fragment. 15 by 9 cm. Rough steatite. Discarded.
795. Bowl fragment. 9 by 3.5 cm. Steatite. Discarded.
796. See p. 129.
797–
803. Pottery.
804. Inscribed fragment. 6.5 by 5 by 4.5 cm. Limestone. Discarded.
805. March 17. See p. 121.
806. See p. 6.
807–

809. See p. 148.
810. Joins 808.
811. Inscribed block. 10 by 7 by 4 cm. Limestone. Discarded.
812. See p. 61.
813. Decorated fragment. 9 by 8.5 by 8 cm. Alabaster. Discarded.
814. See p. 101.
815. Rim fragment. 8.5 by 5 cm. Steatite. Discarded.
816,
817. Pottery.
818. See p. 61.
819. See p. 12.
820. See p. 148.
821. See p. 101.
822. See p. 102.
823–
826. Pottery.
827. Unknown locus. Horse or camel figurine. 10 by 8 by 5 cm. Clay.
828. Complex I, shaft at 56 feet. See p. 87.
829. Complex III, SE. quarter, inside walls. March 18. See p. 149.
830. Architectural fragment. 15 by 15 by 13 cm. Limestone. Discarded.
831. See p. 18.
832. Inscribed fragment. 13 by 8 by 7 cm. Alabaster. Discarded.
833. Inscribed fragment. 8 by 6 by 6 cm. Alabaster. Discarded.
834. Inscribed fragment. 8 by 5.5 by 4.5 cm. Limestone. Discarded.
835. See p. 149.
836. Fragment with ibex horns in relief. 8.5 by 6.5 cm. Limestone. Discarded.
837–
841. Pottery.
842,
843. See p. 102.
844. Vessel fragment. 4 by 2 cm. Alabaster. Discarded.
845. Complex I, shaft at 56 feet. See p. 87.
846. See p. 129.
847. See p. 149.
848. Complex III, upper terrace. March 20. See p. 149.
849. Inscribed fragment. 5.5 by 5 cm. Alabaster. Discarded.
850. Inscribed fragment. 5.5 by 2 cm. Alabaster. Discarded.
851. Inscribed fragment. 7 by 6.5 cm. Limestone. Discarded.
852. See p. 30.
853. See p. 28.
854. See p. 138.
855. Pottery.
856. See p. 121.
857. March 21. See p. 61.

858. Inscribed base, possibly forged. 11.5 by 8 by 5.5 cm. Limestone. Discarded.
859. March 22. See p. 30.
860. Bull's head. 13 by 9 by 6.5 cm. Stone. Discarded.
861. See p. 149.
862. Inscribed fragment. 10 by 10 cm. Alabaster. Discarded.
863. See p. 149.
864. Fragment from base of vessel. 7 by 4 by 2.5 cm. Alabaster. Discarded.
865. March 24. See p. 133
866. Fragment from rim. 3 by 2.5 cm. Stone. Discarded.
867–
869. Pottery.
870. See p. 22.
871. Pottery.
872. See p. 37.
873. See p. 6.
874. See p. 149.
875–
877. See p. 150.
878. Inscribed fragment. 19 by 17 cm. Limestone.
879–
882. Outside Area A. Pottery.
883,
884. Complex I, shaft at 58 feet. Pottery. March 25.
885. See p. 133.
886. Complex III, upper terrace. Inscribed fragment. 7 by 5 cm. Limestone. Discarded.
887. See p. 150.
888. Inscribed fragment. 14 by 13 cm. Limestone. Discarded.
889. Fragment from bowl. 6 by 3 cm. Alabaster. Discarded.
890. Inscribed fragment. 6 by 4 cm. Alabaster. Discarded.
891. See p. 150.
892. See p. 102.
893. See p. 61.
894. See p. 121.
895. Pottery.
896. See p. 129.
897. Worked fragment with mortises on the top and part of an inscription on the front. 24 by 15 cm. Limestone. Discarded.
898,
899. See p. 150.
900. See p. 31.
901. Fragment from rim. 4 by 1 cm. Blue glass. March 26.
902. See p. 121.
903. Fragment. 4.5 by 4.5 cm. Bronze.
904–
906. See p. 102.
907. Fragment of human hand. 5 by 4.5 by 3.5 cm. Stone. Discarded.
908–
913. See p. 151.

914. Complex I, shaft at 60 feet. See p. 6.
915. Inscribed block. 60 by 34 by 32 cm. Limestone. Inscription not clear.
916,
917. Complex III, upper terrace. March 27. See p. 133.
918. See p. 32.
919. See p. 102.
920. See p. 18.
921. See p. 93.
922. See p. 152.
923. See p. 94.
924–
926. See p. 152.
927. Unknown locus. March 28. See p. 61.
928. See p. 62.
929. Complex III, upper terrace. See p. 152.
930. Joins 875.
931. Inscribed fragment. Limestone. Discarded.
932. See p. 133.
933. See p. 28.
934. Pottery.
935. See p. 103.
936–
938. Pottery.
939. April 2. See p. 153.
940. See p. 12.
941. See p. 133.
942. See p. 62.
943. April 3. See p. 153.
944. See p. 12.
945. Pottery.
946. See p. 103.
947. Complex III, north side. April 4. See p. 153.
948. Inscribed fragment. 25 by 16 by 10 cm. Limestone.
949. Three fragments containing five partial lines of an inscription. 10.5 by 10 by 7.5 cm.; 23 by 10 by 15 cm.; 17 by 15 by 12 cm. Stone. Discarded.
950. Inscribed fragment. 12 by 11 by 7 cm. Stone.
951. See p. 153.
952. See p. 121.
953. Fragment. 3 by 1.5 cm. Bronze. Discarded.
954. Pottery.
955. Complex III, south side. Inscribed fragment. 12 by 8.5 cm. Limestone. Discarded.
956. See p. 153.
957. See p. 94.
958. See p. 62.
959. See p. 103.
960. Pottery.
961. See p. 22.
962. Complex III, north side. April 5. See p. 32.
963. Ibex frieze. 45 by 31 by 18 cm. Limestone.
964. See p. 62.
965. See p. 87.

966,
967. Pottery.
968. Inscribed fragment. 24 by 20 cm. Limestone.
969. See *JaPEHA*, pp. 195–199, §350.
970. Inscribed fragment. 35.5 by 15 cm. Limestone.
971. Inscribed fragment. 37 by 13 cm. Limestone.
972. Inscribed fragment. 24.5 by 12.5 by 7.5 cm. Limestone.
973. See p. 94.
974. Pottery.
975. See p. 103.
976. See *Archaeological Discoveries in South Arabia*, p. 203.
977. Ring. 1.8 cm. dia. Iron (?).
978. Broken ring. Two fragments, 2 by .7 cm. each. Brass.
979. See p. 103.
980. Bead. 1.5 by .6 cm. dia. Amber glass.
981. Lid. 1.3 cm. dia. Stone.
982. Hoof. 2.5 by 1 cm. Bronze.
983. Human hand. 2 by 1 cm. Bronze.
984. Bead. .5 by 1 cm. dia. Shell.
985. Pottery.
986. Bull's head. 7 by 5 by 4 cm. Limestone.
987. Pottery.
988,
989. See p. 103.
990. See p. 45.
991,
992. See p. 153. Note: The addition, on April 4, 1951, of twenty men and sixty boys to the excavation crew at Timna' Cemetery, and, on April 8, 1951, of remaining workers from the discontinued South Gate and Temple I sites (producing a total of approximately 190 workers), requires the discontinuance of fully descriptive cataloguing until field and/or laboratory assistance is available. RLS
993. Two inscribed fragments. 17 by 15 cm.; 33 by 27 cm. Limestone.
994,
995. See p. 154.
996. See p. 94.
997. See p. 95.
998. Joins 997.
999. See p. 121.
1000. April 7. See p. 32.
1001. Fits fragments 993, which were not available for study. See p. 154.
1002. Complex III, south side. See p. 133.
1003. See p. 122.
1004–
1006. Pottery.
1007. Rim sherd. 1.3 by 1.1 cm. Blue glass.

1008,
1009. See p. 131.
1010. See p. 133.
1011. Complex III, north side. See p. 133.
1012. See p. 95.
1013,
1014. See p. 154.
1015. See p. 155.
1016. Joins 1023. Discarded.
1017,
1018. See p. 155.
1019. See p. 37.
1020,
1021. Pottery.
1022. Joins 874.
1023. See p. 95.
1024. Joins 1023.
1025. Inscribed fragment. 16 by 10 by 6.5 cm. Alabaster. Discarded.
1026. Joins 1015.
1027. Joins 1015.
1028. See p. 155.
1029. Complex III, south side. See p. 155.
1030. See p. 62.
1031. See p. 63.
1032. See p. 28.
1033. Joins 870.
1034. See p. 133.
1035–
1037. Pottery.
1038. Complex I, shaft at 65 feet. April 8. See p. 37.
1039. Complex III, upper terrace, north half. See p. 63.
1040. Locus 1. See p. 122.
1041. Container with ibex projecting from front. 14.5 by 11.5 cm. dia.; ibex measures 9.5 by 5 by 3 cm. (Aden Museum.)
1042. Complex III, upper terrace, north half. Slab with bull's head. 47 by 28 by 7.5 cm. Limestone.
1043. Inscribed fragment. 45 by 17 by 16 cm. Limestone. Parts of two lines are preserved.
1044. Inscribed fragment. 32.5 by 16.5 by 15 cm. Limestone. Parts of four lines preserved.
1045. See p. 138.
1046. See p. 156.
1047. See p. 33.
1048–
1051. Complex III, upper terrace, south half. See p. 156.
1052. See p. 63.
1053,
1054. See p. 104.
1055. See p. 133.
1056. Knob or lug. 2 by 3.5 cm. dia. Stone.
1057. See p. 133.
1058–
1062. Pottery.
1063. See p. 122.

1064. Rod in three pieces. 5.5, 8, and 2.7 by 6 cm. dia. Bronze.
1065,
1066. Pottery.
1067. Bead. 1.3 by 1 cm. Amber glass.
1068. Complex III, upper terrace, north half. See p. 134.
1069. See p. 156.
1070. Joins 1013.
1071. See p. 33.
1072. See p. 95.
1073. See p. 157.
1074. See p. 19.
1075,
1076. See p. 157.
1077. See p. 104.
1078. See p. 157.
1079–
1082. April 9. Pottery.
1083. See p. 134.
1084. See p. 122.
1085. Jar handle. 6 by 3.5 cm. Steatite.
1086. See p. 134.
1087. See p. 63.
1088–
1090. Complex III, south of terrace. Pottery.
1091. Complex III, south terrace. Ibex frieze. 58 by 32 by 24 cm. Limestone. Five ibex heads on one side, one on the end. April 10.
1092. Ibex frieze. 46 by 33 by 21 cm. Limestone. Six heads, as 1091.
1093. See p. 33.
1094. Ibex frieze. 35 by 24 by 24 cm. Limestone. Four heads; poor condition.
1095. See p. 33.
1096–
1099. Complex III, north terrace. Pottery.
1100. See p. 115.
1101,
1102. Pottery.
1103. See p. 104.
1104. See p. 134.
1105. Tube. 5.5 by 1.5 cm. Bronze.
1106. Foreleg of horse (?). 4 by 1 cm. Bronze.
1107. See p. 45.
1108. See p. 157.
1109. See *JaPEHA*, p. 213, §372.
1110. Complex III, south terrace. April 11. See *JaPEHA*, p. 213, §373.
1111–
1113. Pottery.
1114. See p. 157.
1115. See p. 87.
1116. See p. 88.
1117. See p. 23.
1118,
1119. See p. 114.
1120–
1128. Pottery.

1129. See p. 104.
1130,
1131. Complex III, north terrace. See p. 158.
1132. Complex III, south terrace. Pottery.
1133. Locus 2. Pottery.
1134. See p. 104.
1135. Complex III, north terrace. See p. 63.
1136. See p. 88.
1137. See p. 63.
1138–
1140. Pottery.
1141,
1142. Complex III, south terrace. April 12. See p. 122.
1143. Male head. 9 by 5 by 4.5 cm. Bronze. Shoulder-length hair; moustache; circlet on head.
1144,
1145. See p. 34.
1146. See p. 122.
1147–
1151. Pottery.
1152. See p. 158.
1153. Fragment with a forged inscription. 13 by 10.5 cm. Limestone.
1154,
1155. See p. 158.
1156,
1157. See p. 114.
1158. Complex III, north terrace. See p. 114.
1159–
1164. Pottery.
1165. Joins 553.
1166. See *JaPEHA*, pp. 180f., §339.
1167. Complex III, south terrace. Pottery. April 14.
1168. See *JaPEHA*, p. 218, §380.
1169. Inscribed statuette base. 19.5 by 14 by 14 cm. Stone. April 15.
1170. See p. 96.
1171. See *JaPEHA*, pp. 181ff., §340.
1172–
1174. See p. 96.
1175. See *JaPEHA*, pp. 184f., §342.
1176. See p. 158.
1177. See p. 37.
1178–
1182. Pottery.
1183. See p. 122.
1184. See p. 64.
1185. See p. 158.
1186. See p. 64.
1187. See p. 97.
1188. See p. 34.
1189. See p. 115.
1190. See p. 139.
1191. Complex III, north terrace. See p. 64.
1192. Inscribed block. 17 by 11 by 6 cm. Limestone.
1193. See p. 64.
1194,
1195. Pottery.

1196. See p. 122.
1197. See p. 123.
1198. Cone. 1.5 cm. dia. Stone.
1199. Complex III, south terrace. Inscribed fragment. 8 by 7 by 6 cm. Limestone. April 16. Discarded.
1200. Inscribed fragment. 10 by 11 by 3 cm. Limestone. Discarded.
1201. See p. 159.
1202–
1205. Pottery.
1206. See p. 104.
1207–
1210. See p. 123.
1211. April 17. See p. 64.
1212. See p. 88.
1213. See p. 45.
1214. Inscription. 8.5 by 6.5 by 3.5 cm. Alabaster. Discarded.
1215. See p. 34.
1216. See p. 38.
1217. See p. 115.
1218. See p. 123.
1219,
1220. Pottery.
1221–
1224. Complex III, north terrace. Pottery.
1225. See p. 159.
1226. Inscription. 9 by 9 by 5 cm. Limestone. Discarded.
1227. See p. 159.
1228. Inscription. 8 by 6 by 3 cm. Alabaster. Discarded.
1229. Inscription. 9 by 6 by 8 cm. Alabaster. Discarded.
1230. See p. 6.
1231. Animal figurine. 4.5 by 1.5 cm. Stone.
1232–
1234. See p. 123.
1235. Complex III, south terrace. See p. 139.
1236. See p. 97.
1237. See p. 64.
1238. See p. 168.
1239. See p. 159.
1240. See p. 139.
1241,
1242. See p. 105.
1243. Pottery.
1244–
1246. See p. 105.
1247. Pottery. See *JaPEHA*, p. 218, §381.
1248–
1255. Pottery.
1256–
1259. See p. 124.
1260. Fragment. 2 by 1.5 cm. Bronze.
1261. Complex III, north terrace. 17 by 9 by 5 cm. Limestone. Joins 993 and 1001.
1262. April 18. See p. 159.
1263. See p. 116.
1264–

1268. Pottery.
1269. See p. 124.
1270. Complex III, south terrace. Inscribed base. 25 by 25 by 9 cm. Limestone.
1271. Inscription. 7.5 by 5 by 4 cm. Limestone. Discarded.
1272. Inscription. 12 by 10 by 4 cm. Limestone. Discarded.
1273. See p. 64.
1274. Inscription. 9 by 5.5 by 5 cm. Alabaster. Discarded.
1275. Inscription. 10 by 7 by 6 cm. Alabaster. Discarded.
1276. See p. 20.
1277. See p. 38.
1278. See p. 134.
1279. See p. 105.
1280. See p. 134.
1281–
1288. Pottery.
1289. See p. 124.
1290–
1293. See p. 125.
1294. April 19. See p. 23.
1295. See p. 140.
1296. See p. 35.
1297. See p. 159.
1298. See p. 97.
1299. See p. 160.
1300 See p. 65.
1301,
1302. Locus 3. April 21. See p. 38.
1303. See p. 97.
1304–
1306. See p. 65.
1307. See p. 23.
1308. Hand. 4.5 by 4 by 2.5 cm. Alabaster. Discarded.
1309–
1312. See p. 38.
1313. Joins 1296.
1314. See p. 160.
1315. See p. 65.
1316. See p. 6.
1317. See p. 12.
1318. See p. 105.
1319–
1325. Locus 4. Pottery.
1326. See p. 130.
1327,
1328. See p. 39.
1329. See p. 6.
1330. Inscription. 8.5 by 7 by 4 cm. Alabaster. Discarded.
1331. See p. 98.
1332. See p. 105.
1333. Locus 3. See p. 45.
1334,
1335. See p. 160.
1336. See p. 105.
1337–
1339. Locus 4. See p. 161.
1340. See p. 98.
1341. See p. 65.
1342. See p. 88.
1343. See p. 161.
1344. See p. 98.
1345. See p. 161.
1346. See p. 106.

1347. Complex III, south terrace. See p. 130.
1348,
1349. See p. 125.
1350. Hand. 3.5 by 2 cm. Bronze.
1351. See p. 135.
1352. See p. 131.
1353. See p. 125.
1354,
1355. Locus 4. April 22. See p. 66.
1356,
1357. See p. 162.
1358. See p. 23.
1359,
1360. See p. 66.
1361. See p. 6.
1362. Hand. 4 by 4 by 3.5 cm. Alabaster. Discarded.
1363. Inscription. 4 by 5 by 1.5 cm. Alabaster.
1364. See p. 46.
1365. See p. 66.
1366. See p. 19.
1367. Weathered face. 12 by 10 by 6 cm. Limestone. Discarded.
1368. See p. 130.
1369–
1373. Pottery.
1374. Complex I, SE. quarter, outside walls. April 23. see p. 66.
1375. See p. 162.
1376,
1377. See p. 67.
1378. See p. 46.
1379. See p. 162.
1380. See p. 39.
1381. See p. 7.
1382–
1386. Pottery.
1387. April 24. See p. 67.
1388. See p. 162.
1389. See p. 98.
1390. See p. 39.
1391–
1393. Pottery.
1394. Complex III, north terrace. April 25. See p. 39.
1395,
1396. See p. 162.
1397–
1400. Pottery.
1401. See p. 39.
1402. Complex I, SE. quarter, outside walls. See p. 162.
1403. Inscription. 5 by 5 by 4 cm. Limestone. Discarded.
1404. Fragment of stone vessel. 9 by 7 by 2 cm. Steatite. Discarded.
1405. Worked fragments. 3 by 3 by 1 cm. Alabaster. Discarded.
1406. See p. 7.
1407. Inscription. 4.5 by 4 by 2.5 cm. Alabaster.
1408–
1411. Pottery.
1412. Complex III, north terrace. Inscription. 14 by 9 by 5 cm. Stone. April 26. Discarded.

1413. Inscription. 10 by 7 by 6.5 cm. Stone. Discarded.
1414. Inscribed base. 8 by 6 by 4 cm. Stone. Discarded.
1415. See p. 67.
1416. Inscription. 3.5 by 3 by 2 cm. Alabaster.
1417. See p. 106.
1418. Fragment of vessel. 6 by 4 cm. Stone. Discarded.
1419–
1422. Pottery.
1423,
1424. See p. 141.
1425. Worked piece. 13 by 8 by 4 cm. Stone. Discarded.
1426. Complex III, north of terrace. Inscription. 26 by 7 by 5 cm. Stone. Discarded.
1427. Two fragments of an inscription. 6 by 4 by 3 cm.; 9 by 8 by 6 cm. Alabaster. Discarded.
1428. Inscription. 6 by 5 by 4 cm. Alabaster.
1429. Bull's horn. 5 by 2 cm. Alabaster. Discarded.
1430. Hand. 6 by 4 by 2.5 cm. Alabaster. Discarded.
1431. Pottery.
1432. Complex III, south terrace. Sacrificial table. 41 by 31 by 7 cm. Limestone.
1433. Complex III, east terrace. Inscription. 10.5 by 10 by 5 cm. Limestone. April 28. Discarded.
1434–
1439. Pottery.
1440,
1441. Pottery. April 29.
1442. See p. 106.
1443. Fragment of rim. 4 by 3 cm. Alabaster.
1444. See p. 106.
1445. See p. 35.
1446. See p. 67.
1447. See p. 162.
1448. See p. 67.
1449. See p. 125.
1450. See p. 135. Note: Area A is continued under catalogue numbers 2501–2541.
1501. Area B, Room 1. May 17. See *JaPEHA*, p. 214, §374.
1502,
1503. See p. 67.
1504–
1506. See p. 68.
1507. See p. 88.
1508. See p. 163.
1509. Inscribed fragment. 11 by 7 by 6 cm. Limestone. Discarded.
1510. Inscribed fragment. 6 by 3 cm. Limestone. Discarded.
1511. Inscribed fragment. 4 by 3.5 cm. Alabaster. Discarded.
1512. Plaque with bull's head. 12 by 9 by 5 cm. Alabaster.
1513. Votive plaque, plain. 13 by

8.5 by 4 cm. Alabaster. Discarded.
1514–
1516. Pottery.
1517. Room 1, Cache 1. Female head with long hair; the nose is broken and the left eye is missing. 9 by 13 by 9 cm. Alabaster. March 18.
1518. See p. 13.
1519. See p. 40.
1520. See p. 68.
1521. See p. 54.
1522,
1523. See p. 46.
1524,
1525. See p. 55.
1526. Plain votive plaque. 14 by 8.5 by 3 cm. Alabaster.
1527. See p. 68.
1528. See p. 69.
1529. Altar. 45 by 20 by 13 cm. Rough limestone.
1530. See p. 168.
1531. Room 1. Altar. 36 by 15 by 6 cm. Limestone.
1532. See p. 169.
1533. See p. 69.
1534. See *JaPEHA*, pp. 96f., §218.
1535,
1536. See p. 56.
1537. Inscribed base. 10 by 7 by 5 cm. Limestone. Faint characters. Discarded.
1538–
1540. See p. 69.
1541. See p. 47.
1542. See p. 13.
1543. See p. 7.
1544. See p. 17.
1545. See p. 116.
1546. See p. 13.
1547. Bull's horn. 3 by 1.5 cm. Alabaster. Discarded.
1548. See p. 135.
1549–
1553. Pottery.
(1554 and 1555 are omitted in the field catalogue.)
1556. March 19. See p. 7.
1557. See p. 23.
1558. Fragment of votive plaque. 7 by 6 by 3 cm. Alabaster. Discarded.
1559. See p. 10.
1560–
1564. Pottery.
1565. See p. 116.
1566. See p. 14.
1567. See p. 24.
1568,
1569. See p. 56.
1570. Plain votive plaque. 20 by 14 by 5 cm. Alabaster. Discarded.
1571. See *JaPEHA*, pp. 105f., §232.
1572. See p. 57.
1573. See p. 47.
1574. See p. 17.
1575. Pottery.

1576. Inscribed fragment. 6 by 5 cm. Alabaster. Discarded.
1577. Inscribed fragment. 9 by 7 by 5 cm. Alabaster. Discarded.
1578. See p. 163.
1579. Inscribed fragment. 15 by 9 by 7 cm. Limestone. Discarded.
1580. Inscribed fragment. 13 by 12 by 6 cm. Limestone. Discarded.
1581. See p. 141.
1582. See p. 10.
1583,
1584. March 20. See p. 135.
1585,
1586. See p. 131.
1587. See p. 14.
1588,
1589. See p. 7.
1590. See p. 69.
1591. Inscribed fragment. 12 by 9 cm. Limestone. Discarded.
1592,
1593. Pottery.
1594–
1598. Pottery. March 21.
1599. See p. 70.
1600. Room 1, below cache floor level. Decorated fragment. 2.5 by 2.5 cm. Limestone.
1601. Pottery.
1602. See p. 40.
1603. See p. 7.
1604. See p. 19.
1605. See p. 40.
1606. Inscribed fragment. 6 by 6 cm. Limestone. Discarded.
1607. See p. 169.
1608,
1609. Set p. 89.
1610–
1612. See p. 70.
1613. Locus 2 (Area B). March 22. See p. 169.
1614. Pottery.
1615,
1616. See p. 47.
1617. See p. 57.
1618. See p. 70.
1619. See p. 24.
1620. See p. 163.
1621. See p. 48.
1622. See p. 71.
1623. See p. 89.
1624. See p. 71.
1625,
1626. See p. 106.
1627–
1631. Pottery.
1632–
1634. Pottery. March 24.
1635. Fragment from base of a dish. 5 by 4 cm. Alabaster. Discarded.
1636. See p. 125.
1637. See p. 40.
1638. See p. 19.
1639. See p. 24.
1640. See p. 57.

1641. See p. 48.
1642. See p. 35.
1643. Inscribed fragment. 7 by 5.5 by 5 cm. Limestone. Discarded.
1644. See p. 163.
1645. See p. 19.
1646,
1647. Pottery.
1648. See p. 106.
1649. See p. 163.
1650–
1652. March 25. See p. 71.
1653. Uninscribed stele base. 11 by 8 by 6 cm. Alabaster. Discarded.
1654. See p. 57.
1655–
1659. Pottery.
1660. See p. 107.
1661. Two fragments joining 1619. March 26.
1662–
1664. See p. 24.
1665. See p. 71.
1666. See p. 72.
1667. See p. 57.
1668. See p. 17.
1669. Pottery.
1670. See p. 107.
1671–
1677. Pottery.
1678. Locus 3. See p. 48.
1679–
1682. Pottery.
1683. See p. 135.
1684. See p. 131.
1685. See p. 135.
1686. Locus 4. See p. 41.
1687–
1689. Pottery.
1690. See p. 72.
1691. See p. 48.
1692. See p. 17.
1693. See p. 131.
1694–
1699. Pottery. March 27.
1700. See p. 89.
1701. Locus 5. See p. 89.
1702. See p. 72.
1703,
1704. Pottery.
1705,
1706. Locus 6. Pottery.
1707. See p. 107.
1708. See p. 118.
1709. See p. 19.
1710. See p. 7.
1711. March 28. See p. 72.
1712–
1715. Pottery.
1716. See p. 72.
1717–
1720. Pottery.
1721. See p. 114.
1722. Joins 1619.
1723,
1724. Locus 7. Pottery.
1725,
1726. See p. 72.
1727. See p. 73.

1728. See p. 48.
1729. Locus 8. March 29. See p. 73.
1730. See p. 163.
1731. See p. 118.
1732–
1735. Pottery.
1736. Locus 9. April 1. See p. 49.
1737. See p. 90.
1738. See p. 107.
1739–
1741. Locus 7. Pottery.
1742,
1743. See p. 73.
1744. See p. 19.
1745. See p. 35.
1746. See p. 125.
1747. See p. 170.
1748. April 2. See p. 163.
1749,
1750. See p. 73.
1751. See p. 119.
1752. See p. 74.
1753. Locus 9. See p. 107.
1754,
1755. Pottery.
1756. See p. 107.
1757–
1759. See p. 74.
1760. Locus 11. April 3. See *JaPEHA*, p. 75, §185.
1761–
1763. Pottery.
1764,
1765 Locus 10. See p. 74.
1766. April 4. See p. 74.
1767. See p. 75.
1768. See p. 49.
1769. Pottery.
1770. See p. 135.
1771. Locus 12. See p. 107.
1772. See p. 108.
1773. See p. 49.
1774. See p. 90.
1775. Pottery.
1776. April 5. See p. 24.
1777. See p. 14.
1778. See p. 164.
1779. See p. 75.
1780. See p. 165.
1781. See p. 75.
1782,
1783. Locus 10. See p. 75. (Note identical to the one following item 992 occurs here.)
1784. Inscribed fragment. 21 by 16 by 9 cm. Alabaster.
1785. See p. 170.
1786. Pottery.
1787. Locus 12. See p. 49.
1788. See p. 90.
1789. Locus 11. See p. 75.
1790. See p. 76.
1791–
1794. Pottery.
1795. See p. 8.
1796–
1801. Locus 12. Pottery.
1802. See p. 108.
1803. April 7. Joins 1777.
1804,

1805. Locus 11. See p. 41.
1806. See p. 108.
1807–
1810. Pottery.
1811,
1812. Locus 14. Pottery.
1813,
1814. See p. 108.
1815. See p. 76.
1816. Locus 13. See p. 14.
1817. See p. 76.
1818. See p. 14.
1819. See p. 109.
1820. Locus 12. See p. 90.
1821. See p. 76.
1822. See p. 18.
1823. See p. 170.
1824,
1825. See p. 165.
1826. See p. 109.
1827–
1832. Locus 11. Pottery. April 8.
1833. See p. 114.
1834. Pottery.
1835. See p. 50.
1836. Locus 12. See p. 90.
1837. Locus 13. See *Archaeological Discoveries in South Arabia,* p. 202.
1838–
1841. Pottery.
1842. See p. 50.
1843. See p. 76.
1844. See p. 171.
1845. Locus 12. See p. 77.
1846,
1847. See p. 25.
1848,
1849. Pottery.
1850. Locus 13. Fragment from rim of vessel. 6.5 by 3.5 cm. Alabaster. April 9.
1851,
1852. See p. 26.
1853. See p. 77.
1854,
1855. Pottery.
1856–
1858. Locus 11. Pottery.
1859. See p. 77.
1860. Locus 12. See p. 91.
1861. Inscribed fragment. 13 by 10 by 10 cm. Limestone.
1862. See p. 119.
1863,
1864. Pottery.
1865,
1866. Locus 14. Pottery.
1867. See p. 109.
1868. See p. 58.
1869. Locus 11. See p. 77.
1870. See p. 135.
1871. See p. 50.
1872,
1873. Locus 13. See p. 50.
1874. See p. 165.
1875. Pottery.
1876–
1878. Locus 14. See p. 77.
1879. Locus 13. See p. 91.
1880. See p. 41.

1881. See p. 171
1882. Locus 13-1. April 10. See p. 8.
1883. Female head. 21.5 by 12 by 9 cm. Alabaster. Eyes intact; nose chipped.
1884. See p. 9.
1885. See p. 14. Note: 1882–1885 constitute a group of objects found *in situ*.
1886–
1888. Locus 13. See p. 78.
1889. See p. 42.
1890. Locus 11. See p. 15.
1891. See p. 125.
1892–
1899. Pottery.
1900. Locus 15. See p. 78.
1901. See p. 91.
1902,
1903. See p. 78.
1904. Joins 1813.
1905,
1906. Locus 0-2. See p. 109.
1907. See p. 58.
1908. See p. 116.
1909,
1910. See p. 110.
1911. Pottery.
1912–
1914. Locus 0-1. Pottery.
1915. See p. 119.
1916. See p. 135.
1917. See p. 58.
1918. See p. 126.
1919. Locus 0. See p. 51.
1920. See p. 114.
1921,
1922. Locus 13. Pottery.
1923. Locus 12. Pottery.
1924. See p. 110.
1925. See p. 51.
1926–
1928. Locus 13. See p. 79.
1929. Pottery.
1930–
1933. See p. 126.
1934. See p. 135.
1935–
1940. See p. 131.
1941. Pottery.
1942–
1945. Locus 16. Pottery. April 11.
1946,
1947. See p. 110.
1948. See p. 51.
1949. Locus 13-2. Joins 1507.
1950. See p. 79.
1951. See p. 110.
1952. See p. 111.
1953. Pottery.
1954. See p. 111.
1955. Locus 0-5. See p. 119.
1956. See p. 114.
1957. See p. 111.
1958–
1963. Pottery.
1964–
1974. Locus 15. Pottery.
1975. Locus 16. April 12. See p. 8.
1976. See p. 98.

1977–
1980. Locus 0-5. Pottery.
1981. See p. 15.
1982. Locus 13. See p. 8.
1983. See p. 165.
1984–
1989. Pottery.
1990. See p. 15.
1991,
1992. Locus 16. Pottery.
1993. See p. 166.
1994,
1995. See p. 79.
1996. See p. 80.
1997. Locus 15. See p. 80.
1998. See p. 10.
1999. See p. 8.
2000. See p. 111.
2001. See p. 135.
2002–
2006. Pottery.
2007. Locus 16. Pottery.
2008. See p. 18.
2009. See p. 51.
2010. See p. 52.
2011. See p. 120.
2012. April 14. See p. 120.
2013. See p. 8.
2014. See p. 80.
2015–
2017. Pottery.
2018. See p. 42.
2019. See p. 116.
2020. See p. 117.
2021,
2022. Pottery.
2023. See p. 112.
2024. See p. 135.
2025–
2028. Pottery.
2029–
2035. Locus 13. Pottery.
2036. See p. 126.
2037. Locus 16. April 15. See p. 86.
2038. See p. 142.
2039. See p. 19.
2040. See p. 91.
2041. See p. 8.
2042. Pottery.
2043. Locus 18. April 16. See p. 9.
2044. See p. 80.
2045. See p. 112.
2046–
2048. Locus 21. April 17. See p. 80.
2049. Fragment of statuette. 9 by 8 by 3 cm. Alabaster.
2050. Pottery.
2051. Locus 19. See *JaPEHA*, p. 106, §233.
2052. Locus 20. See p. 81.
2053. See p. 10.
2054–
2059. Pottery.
2060–
2062. Locus 21. Pottery.
2063. See p. 112.
2064. See p. 15.
2065. See p. 114.
2066. Unknown locus. April 18. See p. 81.

2067–
2069. Pottery.
2070–
2075. Locus 4. Pottery.
2076. See p. 42.
2077. Inscription. 14 by 12 by 8 cm. Limestone.
2078. Locus 20. See p. 52.
2079. See p. 42.
2080. See p. 99.
2081. Inscription in raised characters. 15 by 7 by 6 cm. Alabaster. Discarded.
2082. See p. 52.
2083. Inscribed base. 12 by 8 by 6 cm. Limestone. Discarded.
2084,
2085. See p. 81.
2086. Pottery.
2087. Locus 4. See p. 114.
2088,
2089. See p. 81.
2090. See p. 52.
2091. See p. 82.
2092,
2093. Pottery.
2094–
2107. Locus 18. Pottery.
2108. See p. 26.
2109. See p. 82.
2110–
2113. See p. 126.
2114. April 19. See p. 166.
2115. Inscription. 22 by 19 by 15 cm. Limestone. Two faces are inscribed.
2116. See p. 82.
2117–
2119. Pottery.
2120. See p. 166.
2121–
2127. Pottery.
2128. See p. 130.
2129. See p. 126.
2130–
2132. See p. 127.
2133–
2140. Locus 4. Pottery.
2141–
2158. Locus 18. Pottery.
2159. Locus 20. See p. 82.
2160. See p. 166.
2161,
2162. See p. 82.
2163. See p. 83.
2164,
2165. Pottery.
2166. See p. 127.
2167,
2168. Locus 4. See p. 83.
2169. Inscribed base. 9.5 by 7 by 5.5 cm. Alabaster. Discarded.
2170. See p. 58.
2171. See p. 83.
2172. See p. 127.
2173. See p. 26.
2174–
2181. Pottery.
2182. Locus 4-2. See p. 42.
2183. See p. 53.

2184. Locus 4. April 21. See p. 9.
2185–
2188. Pottery.
2189. Locus 18. Joins 2064.
2190–
2207. Pottery.
2208,
2209. See p. 127.
2210. See p. 128.
2211. See p. 83.
2212. See p. 84.
2213. See p. 136.
2214–
2217. Pottery.
2218. Locus 0-6. See p. 43.
2219. Locus 18. See p. 136.
2220. Dice. 1.5 by 1.5 by 1.5 cm. Plaster.
2221. See p. 112.
2222. See p. 136.
2223. Ring. 2.2 cm. dia. Bronze.
2224,
2225. See p. 131.
2226,
2227. April 22. See p. 128.
2228–
2238. Pottery.
2239. Locus 21. Pottery.
2240. See p. 53.
2241. See p. 99.
2242. See p. 84.
2243. See p. 112.
2244. See p. 43.
2245. See p. 136.
2246. Hand. 5.5 by 5 by 1.5 cm. Alabaster.
2247–
2250. Pottery.
2251–
2257. Locus 4. Pottery.
2258. Ring. 3 cm. dia. by 2 cm. Glass.
2259. See p. 9.

2260. Ring. 2.5 by .5 cm. Clay.
2261. Ring. 2 by 1 cm. Shell.
2262. Fragment of vessel. 3.5 by 1.5 cm. Glass.
2263. Fragment of vessel. 3 by 2 cm. Glass.
2264. Twelve beads. .4 to .1 cm. dia. Stone and glass.
2265–
2267. Locus 23. Pottery. April 23.
2268. Locus 22. Rim sherd. 5 by 3 cm.
2269. Pottery.
2270. See p. 9.
2271,
2272. See p. 112.
2273. See p. 120.
2274. See p. 84.
2275. Pottery.
2276. April 24. See p. 99.
2277,
2278. See p. 84.
2279. See p. 99.
2280. See p. 136.
2281–
2284. Pottery.

2501. Complex III, south. April 29. See p. 166.
2502. Complex III, north. See *JaPEHA,* p. 194, §349.
2503. Complex III, east. Inscription. 14 by 10 by 6 cm. Limestone.
2504. Plaque. 15 by 9 by 8 cm. Alabaster. Discarded.
2505. See p. 43.
2506. Broken plaque with one ear of bull's head preserved. 24 by 15 by 45 cm. Discarded.
2507. April 30. See p. 9.
2508. See p. 167.
2509. Joins 598.

2510,
2511. May 1. See p. 167.
2512. Broken plaque for bull's head. 13 by 10 by 6 cm. Alabaster. Discarded.
2513–
2516. See p. 113.
2517,
2518. Pottery.
2519. Inscribed sherd. 8 by 6 cm. Discarded.
2520–
2523. Pottery.
2524. See *Archaeological Discoveries in South Arabia,* p. 206.
2525. See p. 113.
2526. See p. 128.
2527. See p. 136.
2528. Pottery.
2529. See p. 167.
2530. See p. 26.
2531. See p. 15.
2532. May 2. See p. 136.
2533. See p. 15.
2534. See p. 29.
2535. Two parts of an inscription in relief. 10.5 by 9 by 4 cm.; 18 by 20 by 8 cm. Alabaster.
2536,
2537. See p. 84.
2538. Inscribed base. 18 by 18 by 5 cm. Limestone. May 3. Discarded.
2539. See p. 99.
2540,
2541. Pottery.

Unnumbered objects assigned new numbers:
3000. See p. 9.
3001–
3005. See p. 85.

INDEX

FIELD STAFF

AMERICAN FOUNDATION ARABIAN EXPEDITIONS
I & II (BEIHÂN); III (YEMEN); IV (DHOFÂR)

WENDELL PHILLIPS	Leader I-II-III-IV
PROF. W. F. ALBRIGHT	Chief Archaeologist I-II
DR. FRANK P. ALBRIGHT	Chief Archaeologist III-IV
WILLIAM B. TERRY	Field Director—Director of Photography I
GLADYS TERRY	Business Manager I
EILEEN SALAMA	Arabist—Secretary II-III-IV
CHARLES MCCOLLUM	Chief of Motor Transport I—Field Director II—Administrative Director III-IV
GEORGE FARRIER	Motor Transport Specialist I Administrative Assistant II-III—Field Director IV
ROBERT CARMEAN	Motor Transport Specialist II—Field Director III
RICHARD BUSSEY	Business Manager III-IV
DR. ALBERT JAMME	Epigrapher I-II-III-IV
PROF. ALEXANDER HONEYMAN	Archaeologist-Epigrapher I
DR. FRISO HEYBROEK	Geologist I
DR. RICHARD LEB. BOWEN	Engineer Archaeologist I
JAMES SWAUGER	Archaeologist II
DONALD DRAGOO	Archaeologist II
ELLIS BURCAW	Archaeologist II
ROBERT SHALKOP	Archaeologist II
GUS VAN BEEK	Archaeologist II
RALF ANDREWS	Archaeologist III-IV
JAMES RUBRIGHT	Archaeologist III-IV
KENNETH BROWN	Assistant Archaeologist I
JOHN SIMPSON	Assistant Archaeologist II
HARRY SCARFF	Architect III-IV
DR. LOUIS KRAUSE	Physician I
DR. JAMES MCNINCH	Surgeon I
DR. VALLENTIN DE MIGNARD	Surgeon II
CMDR. C. H. GILLILAND	Physician III-IV
GIRAIR PALAMOUDIAN	Surveyor-Draftsman II
OCTAVE ROMAINE	Photographer I
WALLACE WADE	Director of Photography II
CHESTER STEVENS	Photographer II Director of Photography III-IV

SUBSTANTIAL CONTRIBUTORS

AMERICAN FOUNDATION FOR THE STUDY OF MAN
GOVERNMENTAL and ACADEMIC ORGANIZATIONS

AMERICAN GEOGRAPHICAL SOCIETY	UNITED STATES NAVY
CARNEGIE MUSEUM	TRINITY CHURCH (N. Y.)
LEON FALK TRUST	UNIVERSITY OF ALEXANDRIA
HOWARD HEINZ ENDOWMENT	UNIVERSITY OF CALIFORNIA
HUMANITIES FUND, INC.	THE JOHNS HOPKINS UNIVERSITY
LIBRARY OF CONGRESS	UNIVERSITY OF LOUVAIN
A. W. MELLON EDUCATIONAL & CHARITABLE TRUST	UNIVERSITY OF REDLANDS
SARAH MELLON SCAIFE FOUNDATION	ST. ANDREWS UNIVERSITY

187

CORPORATIONS AND COMPANIES

AMERICAN ANODE COMPANY
AMERICAN TRUST COMPANY
BARBER-GREENE COMPANY
BORDEN COMPANY
BRUSH DEVELOPMENT COMPANY
CHRYSLER CORPORATION
CALIFORNIA TEXAS OIL CO. LTD.
CITIES SERVICE OIL COMPANY
COCA-COLA CORPORATION
COLGATE-PALMOLIVE-PEET
    COMPANY
COLT'S MANUFACTURING
    COMPANY
EASTMAN KODAK COMPANY
FAIRBANKS MORSE & COMPANY
GENERAL FOODS CORPORATION
GOODYEAR TIRE AND RUBBER
    COMPANY
GRAFLEX, INC.

GRAY MANUFACTURING COMPANY
GRIFFIN & HOWE, INC.
GULF OIL CORPORATION
HALLICRAFTERS COMPANY
H. J. HEINZ COMPANY
GEO. A. HORMEL & COMPANY
INTERNATIONAL BUSINESS
    MACHINES CORP.
INTERNATIONAL GENERAL
    ELECTRIC CO.
ISTHMIAN STEAMSHIP COMPANY
R. G. LeTOURNEAU, INC.
LINK RADIO CORPORATION
LYMAN GUN SIGHT CORPORATION
MARINE TRANSPORT LINE, INC.
MARLIN FIREARMS COMPANY
OLIN INDUSTRIES, INC.
PAN AMERICAN WORLD AIRWAYS
PLYMOUTH OIL COMPANY

REMINGTON RAND, INC.
RICHFIELD OIL CORPORATION
ROYAL TYPEWRITER
    COMPANY, INC.
ASSOCIATED OIL COMPANIES IN
    THE ROYAL DUTCH SHELL
    GROUP
SOCONY-VACUUM OIL COMPANY
SQUARE D COMPANY
E. R. SQUIBB & SONS
STOKELY-VAN CAMP, INC.
THE TEXAS COMPANY
UNITED STATES STEEL
    CORPORATION
V-M CORPORATION
WILLYS OVERLAND MOTORS, INC.
ZENITH RADIO CORPORATION

INDIVIDUALS

PAUL G. BENEDUM
HELEN W. BUCKNER
WALKER G. BUCKNER
S. BAYARD COLGATE
W. W. CROCKER
DR. GILBERT DARLINGTON
WALTER E. DITMARS (deceased)
SIDNEY EHRMAN
CLARENCE FRANCIS

E. ROLAND HARRIMAN
H. J. HEINZ II
SAMUEL S. HIMMELL
LESTER W. HINK
COL. CHARLES F. H. JOHNSON
DR. HARRY KATZ
H. H. THE AGA KHAN (deceased)
GEORGE D. LOCKHART
JAMES LOCHEAD

J. K. MOFFITT
LENORD MUDGE
JOHN I. MOORE
H. H. PHILLIPS
WENDELL PHILLIPS
SAMUEL F. PRYOR
JAMES C. REA
ALAN AND SARAH SCAIFE
JOHN B. TREVOR

BOARD OF DIRECTORS
AMERICAN FOUNDATION FOR THE STUDY OF MAN

PAUL C. AIKEN
    Lawyer, and former
    Assistant Postmaster General

WILLIAM F. ALBRIGHT
    Chairman Emeritus, Oriental Seminary
    Johns Hopkins University

S. BAYARD COLGATE (1952-1963)
    Board Chairman, Colgate-Palmolive-Peet Co.

WALTER E. DITMARS (1952-1962)
    President, Gray Manufacturing Co.

T. A. McINERNY
    Pres. T. A. McInerny, Inc., Washington, D.C.

JAMES K. MOFFITT (1949-1955)
    Chairman Trustees,
    Crocker 1st Nat. Bank, S. F.

CHARLES J. NAGER
    Member, Eagan and Nager Law Firm

CHESTER W. NIMITZ (1949-1952)
    Fleet Admiral, U. S. N.
    Regent, Univ. of California

WENDELL PHILLIPS
    President

SAMUEL F. PRYOR
    Vice President, Pan American World Airways

WILLIAM B. TERRY
    Vice President

GLADYS W. TERRY
    Secretary

LOWELL THOMAS
    Author, and CBS Commentator